512 One-Story Home Plans

CONTENTS

page **04**

page **06**

RESOURCES

Instructions for ordering and an explanation of what will be included in your package.

Any plan in this book can be customized to fit your precise requirements with our simple and cost-effective modification services. Also see page 32 for additional information.

Obtain a construction cost estimate for your dream home based on your zip code.

page **13**

page **20**

SAVE up to $600 on your plans.
**Call us at 1-800-235-5700 to find out how,
or visit our website www.familyhomeplans.com**

Design, Build and Decorate
Your New Home on Your Kitchen Table

Don't let the frustration of complicated home design software get between you and your dream. Visualize and test your ideas using our proven design systems.

HOME QUICK PLANNER

Design and Decorate Your New Home

Go ahead! Knock down walls and move cabinets, bathroom fixtures, furniture, windows and doors—even whole rooms. 700 pre-cut, reusable peel-and-stick furniture, fixture and architectural symbols. Includes 1/4-in. scale Floor Plan Grid, stairs, outlets, switches, lights, plus design ideas.

Regularly $22.95   Special Offer: $19.95

3-D HOME KIT

"Build" Your New Home

Construct a three-dimensional scale model home of up to 3,000 square feet. (For larger homes, order an extra kit.) A complete assortment of cardboard building materials—from brick, stone, clapboards, roofing and decking to windows, doors, skylights, stairs, bathroom fixtures, kitchen cabinets and more. Includes Floor Plan Grid, interior walls, special Scaled Ruler and Roof Slope Calculator, professional design notes and complete model building instructions.

Regularly $33.95   Special Offer: $29.95

the Garlinghouse company

Helping to build dreams since 1907

To order, call
1-800-235-5700

Monday - Friday 8 a.m. - 8 p.m. Eastern Time

512 One-Story Home Plans

GARLINGHOUSE, LLC

Editorial Director	Steve Culpepper
Art Director	Christopher Berrien
Managing Editor	Debra Cochran
Art Production Manager	Debra Novitch
Associate Editor	Gia C. Manalio
Art & Production Staff	Gregg Davis
	Cindy King
	Andy Russell
Exec. Director of Operations	Wade Schmelter
Senior Accountant	Angela West
Director of Home Plan Sales	Sue Lavigne
Architectural Plan Reviewer	Jeanne Devins
Accounts Receivable/Payable	Monika Jackson
Telesales Team	Juliana Blamire
	Randolph Hollingsworth
	Renee Johnson
	Barbara Neal
	Carol Patenaude
	Robert Rogala
	Alice Sonski
Fulfillment Supervisor	Audrey Sutton
Fulfillment Support	Javier Gonzalez

Publisher
Jerry Stoeckigt

Advertising Sales
1-800-279-7361

Newsstand Distributor
Curtis Circulation Company
730 River Road, New Milford, New Jersey 07646
Phone: 201-634-7400 Fax: 201-634-7499

For Plan Orders in Canada
The Garlinghouse Company
102 Ellis Street, Penticton, BC V2A 4L5
1-800-361-7526

For Designer's Submission Information,
e-mail us at dcochran@aimmedia.com

512 ONE-STORY HOME PLANS
Library of Congress: 2003114356
ISBN: 1-893536-11-4

ACTIVE INTEREST MEDIA

Efrem Zimbalist III	CHAIRMAN & CEO
Andrew W. Clurman	GROUP PUBLISHER AND COO
Robert M. Cohn	SR. VICE PRESIDENT
William T. Berry	CHIEF FINANCIAL OFFICER
Patricia B. Fox	VP CIRCULATION, PRODUCTION & OPERATIONS
Sarah M. Hill	VP MARKETING & PROMOTION

above Set between nearly identical gables and below matching dormers, the porch is accentuated by woodwork and a bay window.

Design 99692

Price Code	A
Total Finished	1,595 sq. ft.
Main Finished	1,595 sq. ft.
Dimensions	59'x47'
Foundation	Basement
	Crawlspace
Bedrooms	3
Full Baths	2

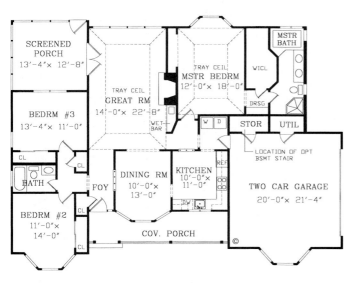

MAIN FLOOR

A Lovely Balance

Windows define this home, from its bay windows to its walls of windows. Unlike many of today's home designs, this floor plan does not combine the living areas into one big open space. Instead, each one is separate, created for a specific purpose. Immediately to the right of the foyer is the dining room, with direct access to the kitchen. Straight back is the great-room, featuring a tray ceiling and fireplace. A wetbar, just steps from the kitchen, is inside the great-room. The split-bedroom design offers privacy for everyone, with the master suite located in the right wing and the secondary bedrooms in the left. The master bedroom has a decorative ceiling and bay window. The walk-in closet, dressing area, and five-piece bath add convenience to beauty. One of the secondary bedrooms has a bay window looking out to the front yard while the other has two large windows that overlook the rear screen porch. Storage, from closet space to a storage room at the rear of the garage, completes the design. This home is designed with basement and crawlspace foundation options.

Please note: The photographed home may have been modified to suit homeowner preferences. If you order plans, have a builder or design professional check them against the photographs to confirm construction details.

Walk-Out Lower Level

above Sloping and hipped rooflines, a gable, a turret, and a rounded dormer give this home an air of regality, while its mix of brick and stone siding lends an earthy, organic touch.

The 2,961-square-foot main level of this elegant plan provides all the spaces needed for daily living. A two-sided fireplace creates an immediate warm welcome into the V-shape foyer. To the right, the impressive master suite, with its own octagonal sitting room, shares a wing with a graceful, octagonal, secluded library. To the left are the common areas, both formal and informal. Here the counter-lined kitchen easily serves both the dining room and the breakfast area. Fireplaces warm the great-room and the hearth room, casting their glow under decorative ceilings. A laundry room and three-car garage provide utilitarian elements to the floor.

The 2,416-square-foot walk-out lower level is a home within itself, designed for entertainment. Here there are rooms that cater to every pleasure from the exercise room to the media room, the gathering room featuring a bar adjacent to the wine cellar, and a billiards room leading out to the patio. On both levels, four baths are convenient to all areas. In addition, storage space abounds. Decks and porches provide outdoor living space and bays of windows bring a part of the outdoors in. This home is designed with a basement foundation.

below Nestled in the turret, under a 13-foot ceiling, the library exudes elegance, providing a setting that any lover of literature would relish.

left This home is all about detail and the great-room illustrates this with exquisite style. Whether it is the bay of windows, arched entrance, or decorative ceiling, every inch of this room captures attention.

below A wide entry to the hearth room promotes a sense of privacy in the breakfast area, while allowing it to bask in the glow of the fireplace.

Please note: The photographed home may have been modified to suit homeowner preferences. If you order plans, have a builder or design professional check them against the photographs to confirm construction details.

Design 50063

Price Code	L
Total Finished	5,377 sq. ft.
Main Finished	2,961 sq. ft.
Lower Finished	2,416 sq. ft.
Basement Unfinished	271 sq. ft.
Garage Unfinished	758 sq. ft.
Dimensions	89' x 59'2"
Foundation	Basement
Bedrooms	3
Full Baths	2
Half Baths	2

LOWER FLOOR

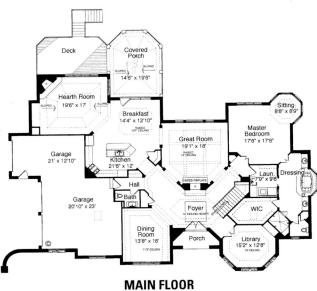

MAIN FLOOR

Courtyard Charisma

Craftsman style blends with Mediterranean chic in this eclectic design, which was intended to create private outdoor living spaces. Rather than the traditional backyard deck, porch, or patio, this design creates a charming courtyard that captures the feel of a warm-weather home while remaining suitable for all sorts of climates. The floor plan is set up for informal entertaining, with spaces defined by changes in floor treatments and ceiling heights, as opposed to walls. The kitchen sits in the bend of an L, anchoring the family room and breakfast room. The breakfast room opens to the courtyard patio, and the master suite and the other two bedrooms all open to the outdoors. This home is designed with a crawlspace foundation.

above This home wraps around one side of the courtyard while the rest of the large, useful space is enclosed by the high stucco wall.

below On warm and sunny mornings, you may take a few steps out of the breakfast area to enjoy your coffee in the midst of the charming courtyard.

Design 32119

Price Code	H
Total Finished	3,028 sq. ft.
Main Finished	3,028 sq. ft.
Garage Unfinished	672 sq. ft.
Porch Unfinished	756 sq. ft.
Dimensions	86'x92'
Foundation	Crawlspace
Bedrooms	3
Full Baths	2
Half Baths	1

Please note: The photographed home may have been modified to suit homeowner preferences. If you order plans, have a builder or design professional check them against the photographs to confirm construction details.

above The dining room opens to the living room, providing a formal and sophisticated space for entertaining.

left An unusually shaped island with prep sink and range separates the kitchen from the casual breakfast nook. Whether you choose to dine at the table or at the island, you are sure to experience a pleasing meal.

below left With the doors closed, the family room sports a homey atmosphere. When opened to the porch, the doors create a more spacious environment.

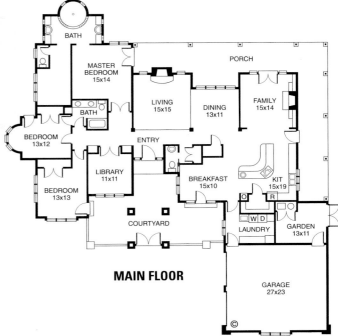

MAIN FLOOR

above The covered porch and the combination of brick and lap siding form an appealing facade.

Ranch Style

Stylish features overlay the sensible layout of this cost-efficient design to create a ranch-style home that's anything but typical. The entry offers a clear view through the family room to a bank of windows that showcases the backyard. A triangular notch in the ceiling above an arched window accents this wall of light. The dining room also has a view through the family room. Nearby, the efficient kitchen, which includes a center island, opens to the breakfast room, which features a sliding glass door to the rear deck. A three-sided fireplace links the kitchen, family room, and breakfast area. On the opposite side of the home, all three bedrooms create a private retreat. The two secondary bedrooms overlook the front yard and share a full hall bath. The master suite includes a walk-in closet, a full bath with dual vanity, and a sliding glass door to its own rear deck. This home is designed with a combination basement and crawlspace foundation.

Please note: The photographed home may have been modified to suit homeowner preferences. If you order plans, have a builder or design professional check them against the photographs to confirm construction details.

MAIN FLOOR

Design 19299

Price Code	C
Total Finished	1,980 sq. ft.
Main Finished	1,980 sq. ft.
Garage Unfinished	484 sq. ft.
Dimensions	64'8"×55'
Foundation	Combo Basement/Crawl
Bedrooms	3
Full Baths	2
Half Baths	1

PHOTOGRAPHY: H.W. MILLER

above & below From the front and rear of this home, its simplistic design hosts a variety of detail that hints at its well-designed interior.

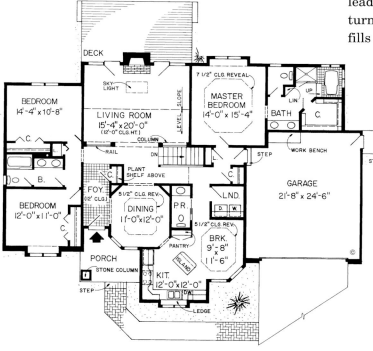

MAIN FLOOR

Deceptively Detailed

A long, tiled entry inside the foyer ushers guests into the formal dining room, but keeps the rest of the spaces out of the public eye. The living room, marked by a columned rail, lies straight ahead, embellished by a sloped ceiling, skylight, and fireplace. In the front of the home, the dining room leads to the efficient, counter-lined kitchen, which in turn opens to the breakfast nook. The master suite fills the space behind with its walk-in closet and five-piece bath. The two secondary bedrooms share the left wing with their own bath. A laundry room, closets, and a garage with workbench, round out the plan. This home is designed with a basement foundation.

Please note: The photographed home may have been modified to suit homeowner preferences. If you order plans, have a builder or design professional check them against the photographs to confirm construction details.

Design 20099

Price Code	D
Total Finished	2,020 sq. ft.
First Finished	2,020 sq. ft.
Basement Unfinished	2,020 sq. ft.
Garage Unfinished	534 sq. ft.
Deck Unfinished	252 sq. ft.
Dimensions	68' x 46'
Foundation	Basement
Bedrooms	3
Full Baths	2
Half Baths	1

above A sloping stone wall, pair of gables, arched covered porch, and turret use the beauty and contrast of geometry to provide this home with curb appeal.

Luxurious Details

Once inside this home, the appeal finds form in raised, decorative ceilings and bays of windows. The vast great-room forms the hub of the plan, open to the kitchen with serving bar, and formal dining area. The master suite fills the left wing and is designed to impress with an octagonal window-lined sitting area and five-piece bath with walk-in closet. The secondary bedrooms share a bath in the right wing; the front with its window seat would be a nice place for a library.

The lower level encompasses 1,911 square feet that can be finished to expand the living space. This extra room would be ideal for a bedroom, exercise room, kitchen, and bathroom with sauna. A large, open space is perfect for a recreation room. This home is designed with a basement foundation.

Please note: The photographed home may have been modified to suit homeowner preferences. If you order plans, you may wish to have a builder or design professional check them against the photographs to confirm construction details.

Design 92688

Price Code	D
Total Finished	2,041 sq. ft.
Main Finished	2,041 sq. ft.
Lower Unfinished	1,911 sq. ft.
Garage Unfinished	547 sq. ft.
Deck Unfinished	180 sq. ft.
Porch Unfinished	70 sq. ft.
Dimensions	67'6"x63'6"
Foundation	Basement
Bedrooms	3
Full Baths	2

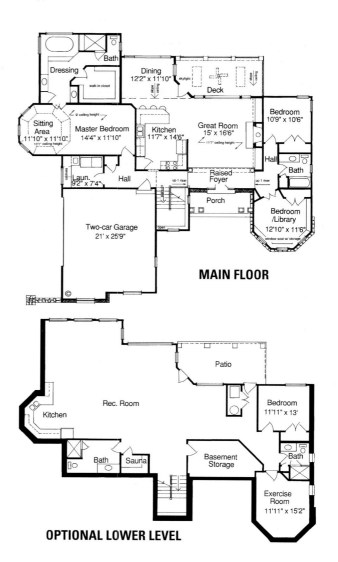

MAIN FLOOR

OPTIONAL LOWER LEVEL

above A sure attention grabber, the soaring Palladian window presents a spectacular contrast to the simplicity of this home's facade.

Privacy for All

Design 20054

Price Code	A
Total Finished	1,461 sq. ft.
Main Finished	1,461 sq. ft.
Basement Unfinished	1,458 sq. ft.
Garage Unfinished	528 sq. ft.
Dimensions	58'×40'
Foundation	Basement
Bedrooms	3
Full Baths	2

Inside this home, each room enjoys its own distinct space, allowing privacy for any activity. The entry is the picture of efficiency with a tiled floor and coat closet. To the left, the living room features a sloped ceiling and an angled fireplace. The front porch spans the length of the living room, allowing just the right amount of light into the tall windows. The dining room and breakfast area are down a short hall, both with easy access to the counter-lined kitchen. A deck wraps from the two-car garage to the dining room, offering an ideal place to dine during the warmer seasons. In the left wing are the bedrooms, one of which could be easily converted into a private den. This home is designed with a basement foundation.

Please note: The photographed home may have been modified to suit homeowner preferences. If you order plans, have a builder or design professional check them against the photographs to confirm construction details.

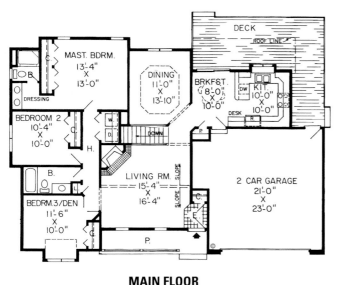

MAIN FLOOR

above The garage's unusual angle and bay window storage alcove add to the curb appeal of this home.

Private Master Suite

Everything about this home draws attention. Right away, visitors are ushered into the elongated great-room, topped by a high, decorative ceiling. Also centrally located are the efficient kitchen and dining area. To the right of the plan, two secondary bedrooms share a full hall bath. The master suite, with its impressive vaulted bath and walk-in closet, fills the left rear of the home. Throughout, well-planned details abound, such as built-ins and a soundproof wall separating the master bedroom from the public areas. Covered porches in both front and back provide outdoor living space. This home is designed with basement, slab, and crawlspace foundation options.

Please note: The photographed home may have been modified to suit homeowner preferences. If you order plans, have a builder or design professional check them against the photographs to confirm construction details.

Design 99694

Price Code	B
Total Finished	1,709 sq. ft.
Main Finished	1,709 sq. ft.
Garage Unfinished	448 sq. ft.
Porch Unfinished	323 sq. ft.
Dimensions	70'x60'
Foundation	Basement
	Crawlspace
	Slab
Bedrooms	3
Full Baths	2
Half Baths	1

COV. PORCH
30'-5"x 8'-0"

FRENCH DR

BUILT IN

DINING RM
14'-0"x 10'-0"

SNACK BAR

KITCHEN
14'-8"x 9'-4"

10' HIGH
STEPPED CLG

GREAT RM
14'-0"x 22'-8"

CL

BEDRM #2
10'-0"x 12'-8"

T.V.

TRAY CEIL

MSTR BEDRM
12'-0"x 18'-4"

SOUNDPROOF WALL

FOYER

BUILT IN

CL

BATH

WICL

VAULTED CEIL.

DRSG AREA

MSTR BATH

LOCATION OF OPT'L BSMT STAIR

STOR

UTIL

CL

PANT

LAV

COV. PORCH

BEDRM #3
12'-4"x 12'-0"

TWO CAR GARAGE
20'-0"x 21'-0"

LAUN RM
W D

MAIN FLOOR

above This home presents a cozy and classic facade outside, but inside it's filled with all the modern amenities and details today's families require.

Design 24651

Price Code	C
Total Finished	1,821 sq. ft.
Main Finished	1,821 sq. ft.
Basement Unfinished	742 sq. ft.
Garage Unfinished	1,075 sq. ft.
Dimensions	56' x 42'
Foundation	Basement
Bedrooms	3
Full Baths	2

MAIN FLOOR

Modern Classic

A traditional front porch shelters guests as they approach the entry, which opens onto a wide-open space containing the living room and dining room. The large living room is visually separated into two distinct areas, each defined by different ceiling heights. A fireplace and built-ins enhance the space. Steps away from the dining room, the U-shape kitchen is open to the breakfast area, where a walk-in pantry and laundry room add to its usefulness. Secondary bedrooms fill the left wing of the 1,821-square-foot home, with a skylit full bath between them. On the right side of the design is the master suite. A tray ceiling crowns the bedroom; a vaulted ceiling caps its five-piece bath, which features a whirlpool tub. In the rear, a deck provides additional room for extending living space in warmer months. The garage is placed discretely beneath the home. This home is designed with a basement foundation.

Please note: The photographed home may have been modified to suit homeowner preferences. If you order plans, have a builder or design professional check them against the photographs to confirm construction details.

PHOTOGRAPHY: JOHN EHRENCLOU

Built to Please

above Friendly gables, a trio of charming dormers, and an inviting front porch give this home the rich rustic character that we know and love as "country."

below In the family room, lovely quarter-round accent windows top the rear windows, which flank the classic brick hearth. The French doors to the right lead out onto the rear deck.

Dormers, gables, and a covered porch give this home classic appeal. Inside, this is a dream home—one that is all about convenience. Gorgeous volume ceilings add scale and detail to the master bedroom, dining room, family room, and breakfast nook. The literature lover will adore the immediate entry into the library from the foyer. Roomy walk-in closets flank the passageway from the master bedroom to the master bath, and a built-in desk, generous counter space, and central cooking island make an efficient kitchen. The secondary bedrooms share a private left wing with a hall bath and nearby laundry. On the upper level, 1,681 square feet of bonus space offers plenty of room for future expansion. This home is designed with a basement foundation.

Design 98904

Price Code	F
Total Finished	2,614 sq. ft.
Main Finished	2,614 sq. ft.
Bonus Unfinished	1,681 sq. ft.
Basement Unfinished	2,563 sq. ft.
Garage Unfinished	596 sq. ft.
Deck Unfinished	635 sq. ft.
Porch Unfinished	200 sq. ft.
Dimensions	70'10"x78'9"
Foundation	Basement
Bedrooms	3
Full Baths	2
Half Baths	1

Please note: The photographed home may have been modified to suit homeowner preferences. If you order plans, have a builder or design professional check them against the photographs to confirm construction details.

above Simple yet elegant columns define the entry to the formal dining room. A bay window, one of three in this light-filled plan, looks out over the rear deck to the backyard beyond.

left In this version of the plan, the homeowner has modified the spacious master bedroom to replace the bay window with a set of French doors, providing direct access to the rear deck

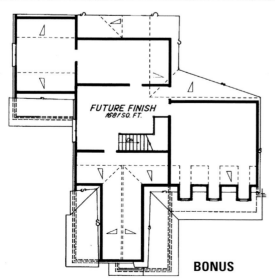

BONUS

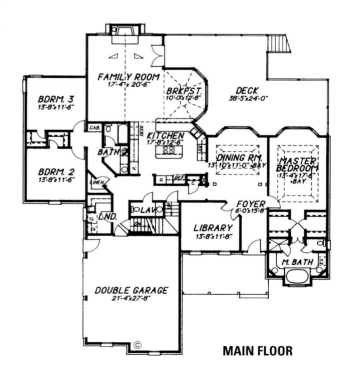

MAIN FLOOR

above Lap siding gables contrast nicely with this home's brick facing and tall, block windows.

Efficient Living

A long tiled foyer set inside a recessed entry promotes privacy in this home's design. Straight ahead in the rear of the home lies the great-room, set under a cathedral ceiling and warmed by a fireplace. To the right, a hutch and raised ceiling create a formal atmosphere in the dining room. Immediately accessible is the kitchen, surrounded by counters including a bar that juts into the window-lined breakfast room. A built-in desk and pantry add to the room's efficiency. A wetbar benefits all common areas.

The left side of the design houses all three bedrooms, each with generous closet space. A full hall bath accommodates the secondary bedrooms as well as the common areas. The master suite features its own skylit five-piece bath with whirlpool tub. Its closet is almost a room in itself.

A full garage connects to the main living space through a utility area featuring a laundry room and large closet. This home is designed with a basement foundation. Alternate foundation options available at an additional charge. Please call 1-800-235-5700 for more information.

Design 94986

Price Code	B
Total Finished	1,604 sq. ft.
Main Finished	1,604 sq. ft.
Bonus Unfinished	409 sq. ft.
Garage Unfinished	466 sq. ft.
Dimensions	48'8"x48'
Foundation	Basement
Bedrooms	3
Full Baths	2

Please note: The photographed home may have been modified to suit homeowner preferences. If you order plans, have a builder or design professional check them against the photographs to confirm construction details.

MAIN FLOOR

above Charming details such as the entry gable, porch, and bay window combine to create a welcoming facade.

below This homeowner modified the plan so that the garage opens to the side.

OPTIONAL CRAWLSPACE/SLAB FOUNDATION

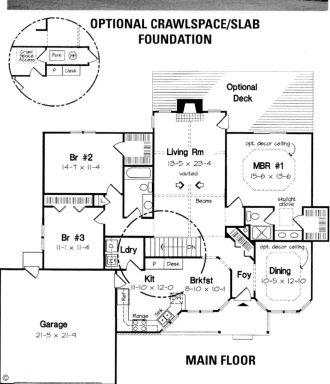

MAIN FLOOR

Details and Options

The covered porch provides shelter for the entry. Inside, a foyer separates the dining room from the breakfast area and the kitchen. Placing the kitchen/breakfast area and dining room up front means the living room and bedrooms are at the rear of the home, where it's naturally quieter and more private. A full bath is located between the living room and two bedrooms. The master suite has the entire right rear corner of the house. The master bathroom features a large walk-in closet, double vanity, and separate water closet. For those who enjoy outdoor living, an optional deck is offered, accessible through sliding glass doors off the master bedroom. This home is designed with basement, slab, and crawlspace foundation options.

Please note: The photographed home may have been modified to suit homeowner preferences. If you order plans, have a builder or design professional check them against the photographs to confirm construction details.

Design 34029

Price Code	B
Total Finished	1,686 sq. ft.
Main Finished	1,686 sq. ft.
Basement Unfinished	1,676 sq. ft.
Garage Unfinished	484 sq. ft.
Dimensions	61'x54'
Foundation	Basement
	Crawlspace
	Slab
Bedrooms	3
Full Baths	1
3/4 Baths	1

Elegance Throughout

above A double-pillared arched porch creates a stunning contrast to a trio of gables, giving this home classic curb appeal.

An elegant porch leads directly into the foyer, designed with guests in mind. Immediately to the right, columns mark the boundaries of the formal dining room. The space opens into the vast great-room whose 11-foot ceiling makes it seem even larger than its actual dimensions. This space is ideal for formal and casual gatherings. Steps away, the breakfast room, with bay window nook, blends into the counter-lined kitchen, rounding out the common areas. A large laundry room, with closet and hanging space, and garage increase the efficiency of the plan. In the opposite wing, the three bedrooms are designed for maximum privacy. The master suite fills the rear, with its bedroom alcove, walk-in closet, and five-piece bath. The other rooms enjoy ample closet space and proximity to a full hall bath. A rear deck and porch allow outdoor living. This home is designed with a basement foundation.

below The dining room exudes elegance, as seen in its pillared entry and its magnificently detailed ceiling.

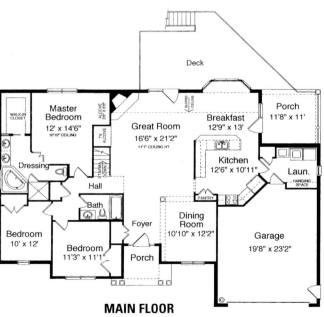

MAIN FLOOR

Master Bedroom 12' x 14'6" 10'10" CEILING

WALK-IN CLOSET

Dressing

Bedroom 10' x 12'

Bedroom 11'3" x 11'1"

Hall

Bath

Foyer

Porch

Deck

Great Room 16'6" x 21'2" 11'1" CEILING HT

Breakfast 12'9" x 13'

Porch 11'8" x 11'

Kitchen 12'6" x 10'11"

PANTRY

Laun.

HANGING SPACE

Dining Room 10'10" x 12'2"

Garage 19'8" x 23'2"

above A change in the floor and the walls differentiates the great-room and breakfast area, however, the open design allows both to share in the walls of windows and angled fireplace.

Design 50032

Price Code	C
Total Finished	1,860 sq. ft.
Main Finished	1,860 sq. ft.
Basement Unfinished	1,860 sq. ft.
Porch Unfinished	69 sq. ft.
Dimensions	64'2"x44'2"
Foundation	Basement
Bedrooms	3
Full Baths	2

Please note: The photographed home may have been modified to suit homeowner preferences. If you order plans, have a builder or design professional check them against the photographs to confirm construction details.

PHOTOGRAPHY: BOB GREENSPAN, BOB GREENSPAN PHOTOGRAPHY

above   This home's wide-ranging layout inside its sturdy brick exterior promises convenience and comfort.

A Family Favorite

below   The living room, with its wall of windows and one of the home's fireplaces, creates an elegant atmosphere for entertaining.

Plenty of room, with specific spaces created for specific uses, helps the owners of this home accommodate all the daily activities within four basic living zones. Thoughtfully planned to allow separation between functions, the zones include space for entertaining, family gathering, activity/work, and private retreats. The activity room, located between the kitchen and garage, is a multipurpose space that's packed with storage and countertop area, and was designed to serve as a coat room, laundry, home office, or hobby room. Just inside the front door is the loosely organized entertaining zone, which includes the living room and dining room. The hearth room, breakfast area, and kitchen comprise the family gathering area. On the opposite side of the home is the private bedroom area, which includes a roomy master bedroom that's big enough to include a sitting area, and two secondary bedrooms. This home is designed with a basement foundation.

above The activity room, out of the way at the front of the home yet connected to the family spaces, is perfect for homework and crafts.

below The hearth room features a distinctive fireplace flanked by built-ins.

above Abundant windows in the breakfast area bring natural light into the open family spaces at the rear of the home.

below An angled island adds serving space to the long runs of counter space elsewhere in the kitchen.

MAIN FLOOR

Design 32319

Price Code	J
Total Finished	3,600 sq. ft.
Main Finished	3,600 sq. ft.
Basement Unfinished	3,600 sq. ft.
Garage Unfinished	828 sq. ft.
Dimensions	109'2" x 55'10"
Foundation	Basement
Bedrooms	3
Full Baths	2
Half Baths	1
3/4 Baths	1

Please note: The photographed home may have been modified to suit homeowner preferences. If you order plans, have a builder or design professional check them against the photographs to confirm construction details.

above A soaring gable set between two others adds an elegant touch to the recessed entry.

Choose Your Bedrooms

A tiled foyer leads past a closet and a gallery into the home's common areas. In the great-room, a fireplace flanked by windows overlooking the porch casts its glow under a raised ceiling. To the right, built-in bookshelves embellish the short hall to the master suite. The suite features a private five-piece bath with whirlpool tub and walk-in closet. A bump-out window bay lights up the bedroom. To the left are the breakfast room, with bay window, and kitchen. The two are separated only by a snack bar. Toward the front of the design, two bedrooms share a full hall bath. The front bedroom is illuminated by transom windows, while the other features a built-in bookshelf and could be easily converted into a den. A laundry room and extra space in the garage add utilitarian elements to the plan. This home is designed with basement, slab, and crawlspace foundation options. Alternate foundation options available at an additional charge. Please call 1-800-235-5700 for more information.

Please note: The photographed home may have been modified to suit homeowner preferences. If you order plans, have a builder or design professional check them against the photographs to confirm construction details.

Design 68038

Price Code	A
Total Finished	1,478 sq. ft.
Main Finished	1,478 sq. ft.
Basement Unfinished	1,478 sq. ft.
Garage Unfinished	482 sq. ft.
Dimensions	42'x55'8"
Foundation	Basement
	Crawlspace
	Slab
Bedrooms	3
Full Baths	2

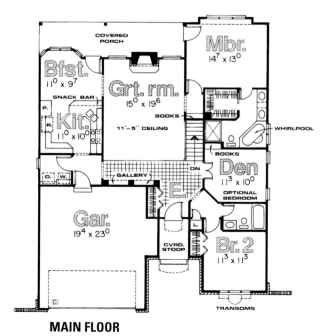

MAIN FLOOR

above If it is true what they say about the eyes being the windows to the soul, then surely this home's tall, keystoned sets of windows provide a glimpse of the beauty found within.

Please note: The photographed home may have been modified to suit homeowner preferences. If you order plans, have a builder or design professional check them against the photographs to confirm construction details.

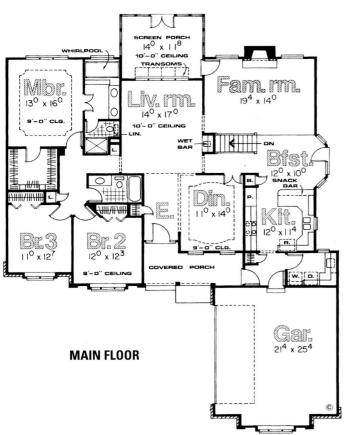

MAIN FLOOR

Perfect for Entertaining

Once inside the long foyer, guests are immediately ushered into the formal dining room or straight ahead to the living room, which is ideal for entertaining with its wetbar and access to the screen porch. Nearby, the family room is perfect for more casual gatherings, with its cozy fireplace and proximity to the breakfast area. Windows line the breakfast nook, which is separated from the kitchen by only a snack bar. The kitchen is almost completely surrounded by counters, a pantry enhancing its efficiency. The three bedrooms are privately located in the left wing. This home is designed with basement, slab, and crawlspace foundation options. Alternate foundation options available at an additional charge. Please call 1-800-235-5700 for more information.

Design 68036

Price Code	D
Total Finished	2,120 sq. ft.
Main Finished	2,120 sq. ft.
Garage Unfinished	548 sq. ft.
Dimensions	58'×68'
Foundation	Basement
	Crawlspace
	Slab
Bedrooms	3
Full Baths	2

PHOTOGRAPHY: CHRIS A. LITTLE

Single-Level Luxury

above Graceful gables accent the front entry, which is accompanied by a small, elegant porch. To the right is a discrete three-car garage.

below The long living room at the center of the home serves as an elegant axis from which the public, private, and utility spaces of this well-planned design radiate.

At over 2,200 square feet, this home offers single-level luxury that's complete in every respect. With its elegant window details, large kitchen with attached breakfast area, three bedrooms, and three-car garage, this traditionally designed home is magnificently designed for maximum livability and practical function.

The bedrooms are set apart from the common areas, creating a strong definition of private and public. The living room, kitchen, and breakfast nook blend into each other, promoting a family-friendly atmosphere. And while closets abound through both areas, a large utility room allows for even more storage space. This home is designed with a crawlspace foundation.

Please note: The photographed home may have been modified to suit homeowner preferences. If you order plans, have a builder or design professional check them against the photographs to confirm construction details.

above The rear of the home offers ample space for outdoor living with its covered porch (perfect for screening) and long deck.

above A sun-filled corner of the kitchen is given over to the breakfast nook. The angled breakfast bar provides extra work space.

below Looking back from the living room, we see the formal dining room. Decorative columns and pilasters separate the spaces.

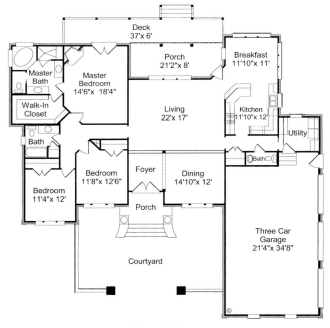

MAIN FLOOR

Design 94676

Price Code	D
Total Finished	2,201 sq. ft.
Main Finished	2,201 sq. ft.
Garage Unfinished	853 sq. ft.
Deck Unfinished	222 sq. ft.
Porch Unfinished	240 sq. ft.
Dimensions	71'10"x 66'10"
Foundation	Crawlspace
Bedrooms	3
Full Baths	2
Half Baths	1

PHOTOGRAPHY: BOB GREENSPAN, BOB GREENSPAN PHOTOGRAPHY

above White trimmed windows and gables accentuate the home's dark, rustic siding.

Wall of Light

The 3,148-square-foot main floor of this home is defined by large open spaces. The front door opens to a large entry that leads straight to the dining room, backed by a window-lined gallery; down stairs to the lower level; or to the left and the rest of the common areas. The master suite fills the right wing, accessible via the gallery. In the rear, a screen porch extends living space outdoors. A portion of the lower level is finished, allowing room for the secondary bedrooms and entertainment areas. A vast storage/mechanical room rounds out the floor. This home is designed with a basement foundation.

Please note: The photographed home may have been modified to suit homeowner preferences. If you order plans, have a builder or design professional check them against the photographs to confirm construction details.

below Light cabinetry, a raised ceiling, and a large bay of windows add brilliance and scale to the kitchen.

top left Every corner of the living room is filled with elegant efficiency from its wall of windows and built-in cabinetry, to the fireplace that it shares with the breakfast room.

top right A transom, tall windows, and French doors illuminate the gallery, allowing natural light to radiate through to the formal dining room.

left A large, arched set of windows draws light into the kitchen, providing a cheery, well-lit area in which to cook or dine.

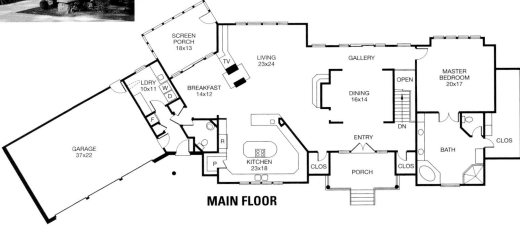

MAIN FLOOR

SCREEN PORCH 18x13

LDRY 10x11

BREAKFAST 14x12

LIVING 23x24

GALLERY

DINING 16x14

OPEN

MASTER BEDROOM 20x17

GARAGE 37x22

KITCHEN 23x18

ENTRY

DN

CLOS

PORCH

CLOS

BATH

CLOS

LOWER FLOOR

EXERCISE 12x18

BILLIARDS 16x19

UP

RECREATION 22x20

TV

STORAGE/MECH

BAR

BEDROOM 12x13

BAT

CLOS

BEDROOM 12x13

CLOS

CLOS

CLOS

Design 32421

Price Code	L
Total Finished	4,643 sq. ft.
Main Finished	3,148 sq. ft.
Lower Finished	1,495 sq. ft.
Basement Unfinished	1,653 sq. ft.
Garage Unfinished	828 sq. ft.
Porch Unfinished	206 sq. ft.
Dimensions	133'8"x 59'8"
Foundation	Basement
Bedrooms	3
Full Baths	3
Half Baths	1

Picture-Perfect Efficiency

above A gable topping an arched entry is the focal point of this home's facade, while white-trimmed, multi-paned windows and brick facing provide additional timeless appeal.

Design 99434

Price Code	C
Total Finished	1,850 sq. ft.
Main Finished	1,850 sq. ft.
Garage Unfinished	487 sq. ft.
Dimensions	62'x48'
Foundation	Basement
Bedrooms	3
Full Baths	2

Please note: The photographed home may have been modified to suit homeowner preferences. If you order plans, have a builder or design professional check them against the photographs to confirm construction details.

The 1,850-square-foot interior of this home emanates efficiency. Windows and plenty of transoms light up the rooms. A fireplace serves as an additional heat source in the great-room. A hutch and a wetbar serve the formal dining area, with the kitchen only steps away. U-shape counters and a work island enhance the kitchen. Its built-in desk is also useful. A full bath is conveniently located near all rooms, while the master suite has its own private bath. Tile covers the heavy-traffic areas, including the bathrooms. In the right wing, a secondary bedroom allows for an optional door placement and an easy conversion into a den. All three of the bedrooms are secluded in that wing, promoting privacy away from the common areas. Behind the spacious garage, a large, counter-lined laundry room and generous closet add additional convenience to the plan. This home is designed with a basement foundation. Alternative foundation options available at an additional charge. Please call 1-800-235-5700 for more information.

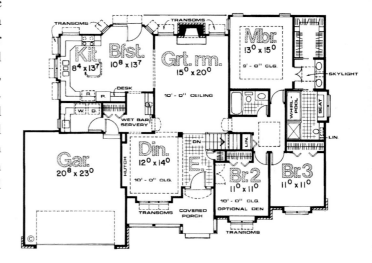

MAIN FLOOR

above The smaller gable topping the entry complements the large, gabled garage.

Country Home

Design 68187

Price Code	E
Total Finished	2,144 sq. ft.
Main Finished	2,144 sq. ft.
Garage Unfinished	504 sq. ft.
Porch Unfinished	341 sq. ft.
Dimensions	67' x 52'
Foundation	Slab
Bedrooms	4
Full Baths	2

Please note: The photographed home may have been modified to suit homeowner preferences. If you order plans, have a builder or design professional check them against the photographs to confirm construction details.

Traditional shapes and forms dominate the design of this home, from the front porch with fan window transom and sidelites to the cheery gables that face the street. Inside the foyer, arched openings left and right lead to the dining room and study. A vaulted ceiling tops the large living room, which has a broad fireplace. Centering the shared spaces is the kitchen, which is open to the living room and the sizable breakfast nook, all of which wrap around a small rear porch. The master suite is contained in the right wing of the home. Three secondary bedrooms, each with a large closet, fill the left rear corner. This home is designed with a slab foundation. Alternative foundation options available at an additional charge. Please call 1-800-235-5700 for more information.

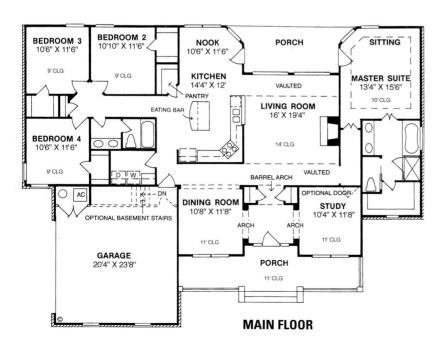

MAIN FLOOR

above This home's discrete side-load garage doesn't attract attention away from the appealing bay windows flanking the entry.

Elegant Charm

Architectural details abound throughout this 2,860-square-foot home, adding charm and beauty to this practical design. The entry leads into the impressive great-room, which is open to the dining room and separated from the atrium by columns and lowered soffits. To the right, the master suite, with its room-size closet and luxurious bath, fills an entire wing. A secondary bedroom and a den, which can easily be converted into another bedroom, occupy the opposite wing. Windows, skylights, and tall ceilings abound, creating an open and airy atmosphere throughout the home. The large garage offers enough space to accommodate two vehicles or to set up a storage area. This home is designed with a slab foundation.

Design 24661

Price Code	G
Total Finished	2,860 sq. ft.
Main Finished	2,860 sq. ft.
Garage Unfinished	558 sq. ft.
Dimensions	80'×56'8"
Foundation	Slab
Bedrooms	3
Full Baths	2

Please note: The photographed home may have been modified to suit homeowner preferences. If you order plans, have a builder or design professional check them against the photographs to confirm construction details.

Br 2
15-2 x 19-9

Den/ Br 3
13-11 x 20-3

Wet Bar

Skylights

Atrium
35-0 x 11-1

Mstr. Br
14-4 x 16-10
Trey Clg.

Serving

Soffit

Soffit

Skylights

Brkfst.
10-1 x 13-5

Kitchen
13-0 x 13-5

Island

Pantry

Shelves

Furn

Great Rm
19-0 x 23-4
Flat Clg. @ 14'-0"

Linen

Whirlpool

Garage
21-5 x 24-9

Dining Rm
14-1 x 11-0

9'-0" Clg.

9'-0" Clg.

MAIN FLOOR

above An octagonal bay, wide porch, and brick and clapboard facing give this traditional design extra style.

Design 34043

Price Code	B
Total Finished	1,583 sq. ft.
Main Finished	1,583 sq. ft.
Basement Unfinished	1,573 sq. ft.
Garage Unfinished	484 sq. ft.
Dimensions	70'x46'
Foundation	Basement
	Crawlspace
	Slab
Bedrooms	3
Full Baths	2

Country Home

This convenient plan is perfect for the modern family with a taste for classic design. Traditional Victorian touches in this three-bedroom home include a romantic front porch and an intriguing breakfast bay just off the kitchen. The arrangement of the kitchen between the breakfast and formal dining rooms makes for comfort and efficiency, while the wide-open living room, which opens out to the deck, rounds out the common areas.

In the private wing, the master suite enjoys a skylit, five-piece compartmentalized bath, while two secondary bedrooms boast ample closet space. This home is designed with basement, slab, and crawlspace foundation options.

Please note: The photographed home may have been modified to suit homeowner preferences. If you order plans, have a builder or design professional check them against the photographs to confirm construction details.

MAIN FLOOR

OPTIONAL SLAB/CRAWLSPACE FOUNDATION

Quick and Easy Customizing
Make Changes to Your Home Plan in 4 Easy Steps

Here's an **affordable** and **efficient** way to make **custom changes** to your home plan.

1 Select the house plan that most closely meets your needs. Purchase of a reproducible master (vellum) is necessary to make changes to a plan.

2 Call 800-235-5700 to place your order. Tell the sales representative you're interested in customizing a plan. A $50 refundable consultation fee will be charged. Then you'll need to complete a customization checklist indicating all the changes you wish to make to your plan, attaching sketches if necessary. If you proceed with the custom changes, the $50 will be credited to the total amount charged.

3 Fax the completed customization checklist to our design consultant at 1-866-477-5173 or e-mail blarochelle@drummonddesigns.com. Within 24 to 48* business hours you will be provided with a written cost estimate to modify your plan. Our design consultant will contact you by phone if you wish to discuss any of your changes in greater detail.

4 Once you approve the estimate, a 75% retainer fee is collected and customization work gets underway. Preliminary drawings can usually be completed within 5 to10* business days. Following approval of these preliminary drawings, your design changes are completed within 5 to 10* business days. Your remaining 25% balance due is collected prior to shipment of your completed drawings. You will be shipped five sets of revised blueprints, or a reproducible master.

BEFORE

AFTER

Sample Modification Pricing Guide

CATEGORIES	AVERAGE COST
Adding or removing living space (square footage)	Quote required
Adding or removing a garage	$400—$680
Garage: Front entry to side load or vice versa	Starting at $300
Adding a screened porch	$280—$600
Adding a bonus room in the attic	$450—$780
Changing full basement to crawlspace or vice versa	Starting at $220
Changing full basement to slab or vice versa	Starting at $260
Changing exterior building material	Starting at $200
Changing roof lines	$360—$630
Adjusting ceiling height	$280—$500
Adding, moving, or removing an exterior opening	$55 per opening
Adding or removing a fireplace	$90—$200
Modifying a non-bearing wall or room	$55 per room
Changing exterior walls from 2"x4" to 2"x6"	Starting at $200
Redesigning a bathroom or a kitchen	$120—$280
Reverse plan right reading	Quote required
Adapting plans for local building code requirements	Quote required
Engineering stamping only	Quote required
Any other engineering services	Quote required
Adjust plan for handicapped accessibility	Quote required
Interactive Illustrations (choices of exterior materials)	Quote required
Metric conversion of home plan	$400

Note: Prices are subject to change according to plan size and style. Please remember that figures shown are average costs. Your quote may be higher or lower depending upon your specific requirements.

Design 20002

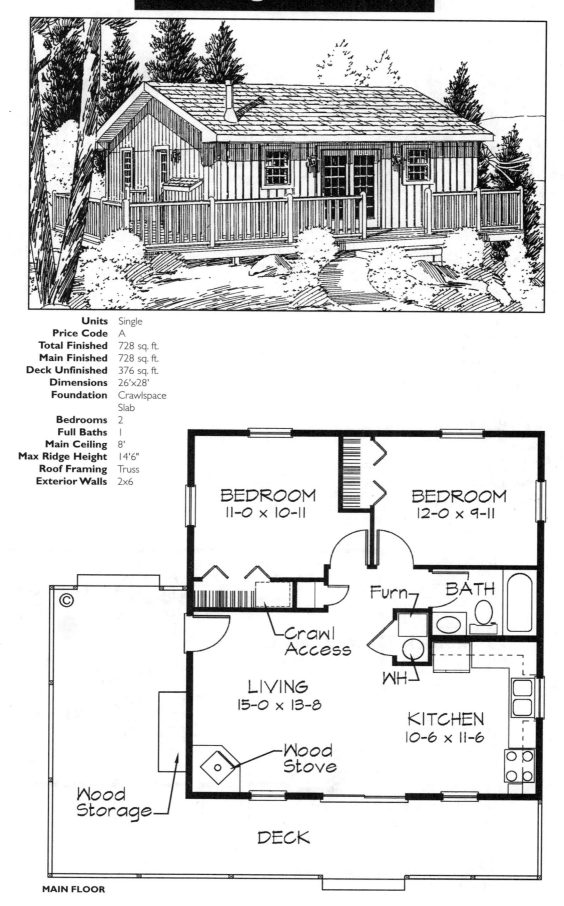

Units	Single
Price Code	A
Total Finished	728 sq. ft.
Main Finished	728 sq. ft.
Deck Unfinished	376 sq. ft.
Dimensions	26'x28'
Foundation	Crawlspace
	Slab
Bedrooms	2
Full Baths	1
Main Ceiling	8'
Max Ridge Height	14'6"
Roof Framing	Truss
Exterior Walls	2x6

BEDROOM
11-0 x 10-11

BEDROOM
12-0 x 9-11

Furn

BATH

Crawl
Access

WH

LIVING
15-0 x 13-8

KITCHEN
10-6 x 11-6

Wood
Stove

Wood
Storage

DECK

MAIN FLOOR

Design 94307

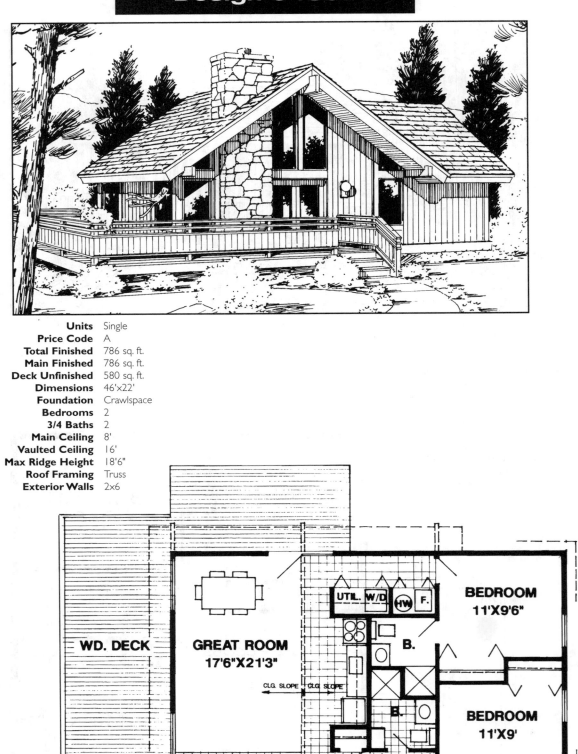

Units	Single
Price Code	A
Total Finished	786 sq. ft.
Main Finished	786 sq. ft.
Deck Unfinished	580 sq. ft.
Dimensions	46'x22'
Foundation	Crawlspace
Bedrooms	2
3/4 Baths	2
Main Ceiling	8'
Vaulted Ceiling	16'
Max Ridge Height	18'6"
Roof Framing	Truss
Exterior Walls	2x6

WD. DECK

GREAT ROOM
17'6"X21'3"

CLG. SLOPE   CLG. SLOPE

UTIL. W/D   HW   F.

B.

B.

BEDROOM
11'X9'6"

BEDROOM
11'X9'

©

MAIN FLOOR

Design 65136

Units	Duplex
Price Code	A
Total Finished	834 sq. ft.
Main Finished	834 sq. ft.
Garage Unfinished	208 sq. ft.
Dimensions	48'x44'
Foundation	Basement
Bedrooms	2
Full Baths	1
Main Ceiling	8'
Max Ridge Height	20'5"
Exterior Walls	2x6

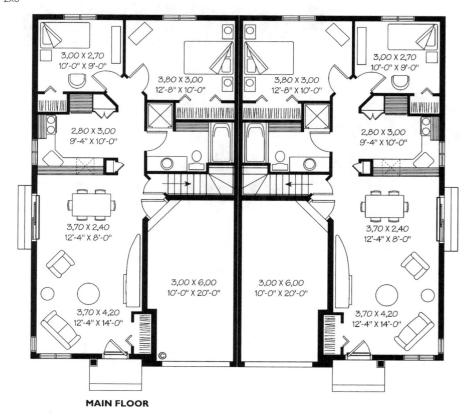

MAIN FLOOR

Design 65263

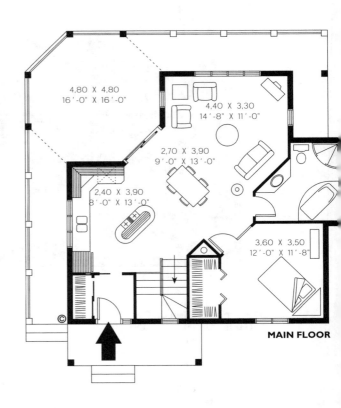

Units	Single
Price Code	A
Total Finished	840 sq. ft.
Main Finished	840 sq. ft.
Porch Unfinished	466 sq. ft.
Dimensions	33'x31'
Foundation	Basement
Bedrooms	1
Full Baths	1
Main Ceiling	8'
Max Ridge Height	22'11"
Roof Framing	Truss
Exterior Walls	2x6

4,80 X 4,80
16'-0" X 16'-0"

4,40 X 3,30
14'-8" X 11'-0"

2,70 X 3,90
9'-0" X 13'-0"

2,40 X 3,90
8'-0" X 13'-0"

3,60 X 3,50
12'-0" X 11'-8"

MAIN FLOOR

Design 94126

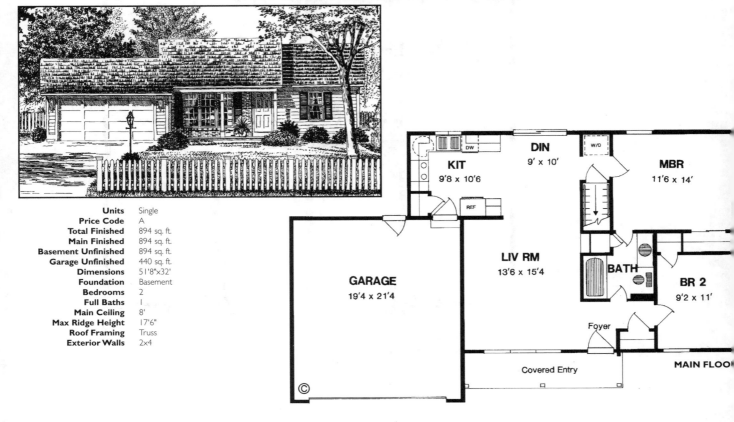

Units	Single
Price Code	A
Total Finished	894 sq. ft.
Main Finished	894 sq. ft.
Basement Unfinished	894 sq. ft.
Garage Unfinished	440 sq. ft.
Dimensions	51'8"x32'
Foundation	Basement
Bedrooms	2
Full Baths	1
Main Ceiling	8'
Max Ridge Height	17'6"
Roof Framing	Truss
Exterior Walls	2x4

DW

KIT
9'8 x 10'6

DIN
9' x 10'

W/D

MBR
11'6 x 14'

REF

LIV RM
13'6 x 15'4

BATH

BR 2
9'2 x 11'

GARAGE
19'4 x 21'4

Foyer

Covered Entry

MAIN FLOO

Design 90433

Units	Single
Price Code	A
Total Finished	928 sq. ft.
Main Finished	928 sq. ft.
Porch Unfinished	230 sq. ft.
Dimensions	32'x29'
Foundation	Crawlspace
	Slab
Bedrooms	2
Full Baths	1
Half Baths	1
Roof Framing	Stick

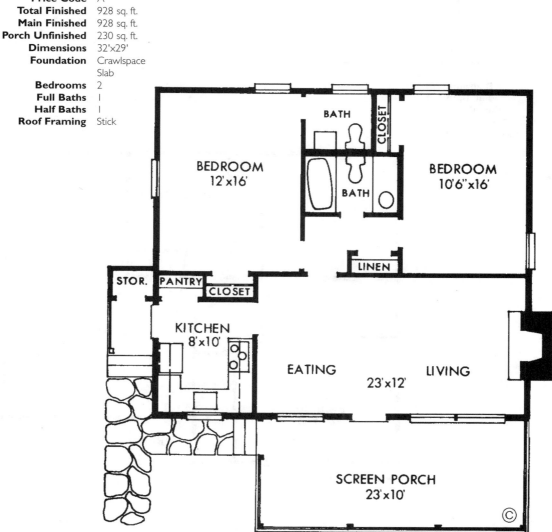

MAIN FLOOR

Units	Single
Price Code	A
Total Finished	930 sq. ft.
Main Finished	930 sq. ft.
Porch Unfinished	102 sq. ft.
Dimensions	35'x28'6"
Foundation	Crawlspace
	Slab
Bedrooms	3
Full Baths	1
Main Ceiling	8'
Roof Framing	Stick
Exterior Walls	2x4

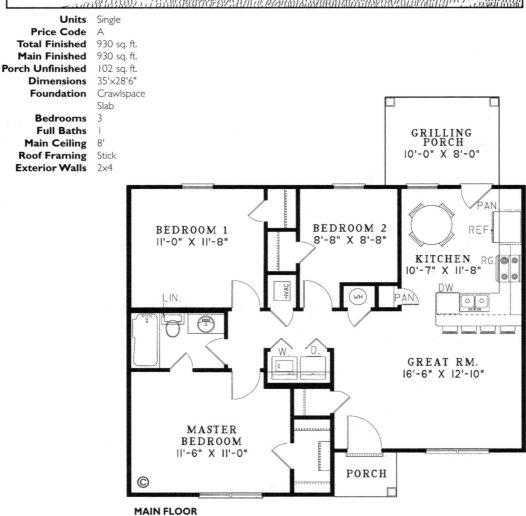

MAIN FLOOR

Design 51004

Units	Single
Price Code	A
Total Finished	936 sq. ft.
Main Finished	936 sq. ft.
Basement Unfinished	936 sq. ft.
Porch Unfinished	42 sq. ft.
Dimensions	32'x34'8"
Foundation	Basement
Bedrooms	2
Full Baths	1
Main Ceiling	8'
Max Ridge Height	19'
Roof Framing	Truss
Exterior Walls	2x4

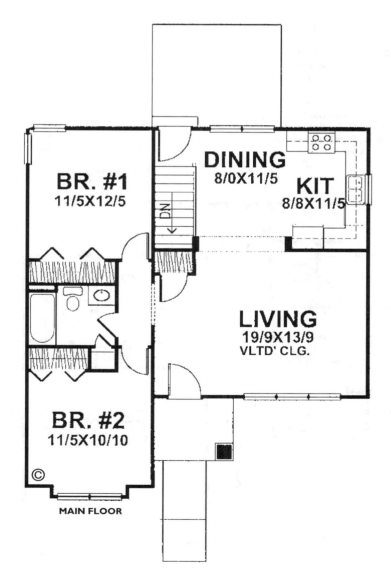

BR. #1
11/5X12/5

DINING
8/0X11/5

KIT
8/8X11/5

LIVING
19/9X13/9
VLTD' CLG.

BR. #2
11/5X10/10

MAIN FLOOR

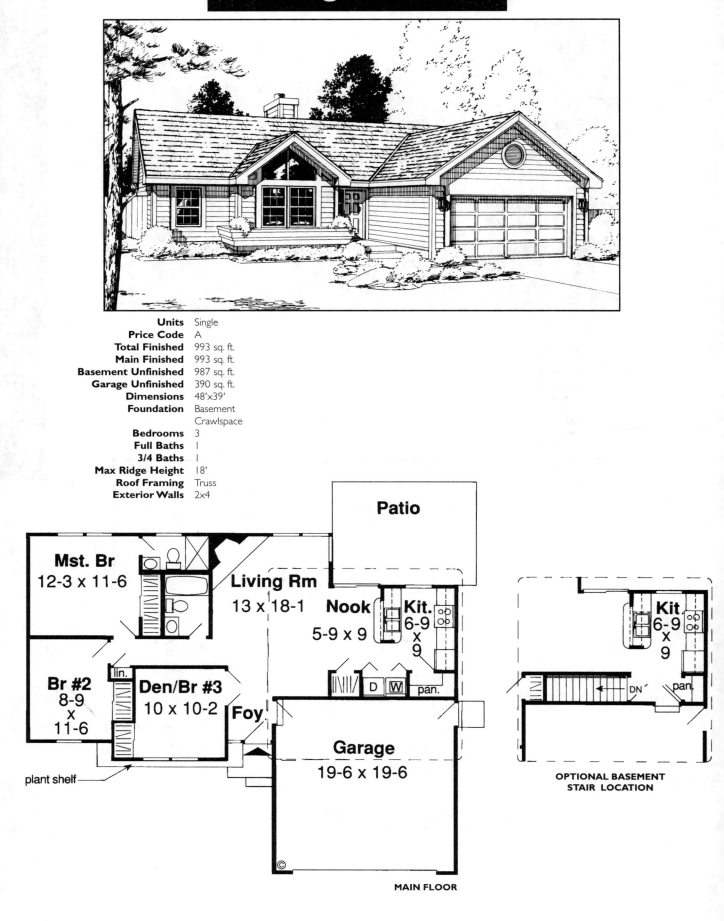

Units	Single
Price Code	A
Total Finished	993 sq. ft.
Main Finished	993 sq. ft.
Basement Unfinished	987 sq. ft.
Garage Unfinished	390 sq. ft.
Dimensions	48'x39'
Foundation	Basement
	Crawlspace
Bedrooms	3
Full Baths	1
3/4 Baths	1
Max Ridge Height	18'
Roof Framing	Truss
Exterior Walls	2x4

Patio

Mst. Br
12-3 x 11-6

Living Rm
13 x 18-1

Nook
5-9 x 9

Kit.
6-9 x 9

Br #2
8-9 x 11-6

lin.

Den/Br #3
10 x 10-2

Foy

D W pan.

plant shelf

Garage
19-6 x 19-6

MAIN FLOOR

Kit
6-9 x 9

DN pan.

OPTIONAL BASEMENT STAIR LOCATION

Design 92426

Units	Single
Price Code	A
Total Finished	997 sq. ft.
Main Finished	997 sq. ft.
Dimensions	49'6"x33'6"
Foundation	Crawlspace
Bedrooms	3
Full Baths	2
Max Ridge Height	16'
Roof Framing	Stick
Exterior Walls	2x4

Design 65056

Units	Single
Price Code	A
Total Finished	1,019 sq. ft.
Main Finished	1,019 sq. ft.
Dimensions	32'x37'
Foundation	Basement
Bedrooms	2
Full Baths	1

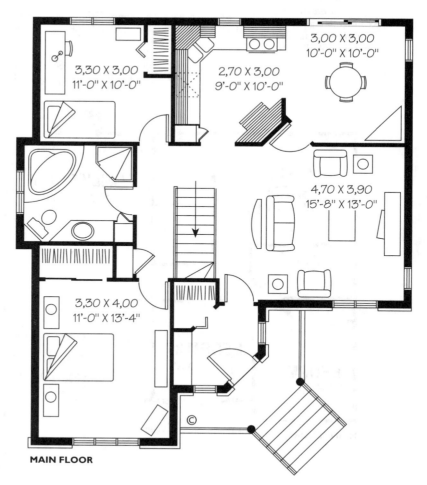

3,30 X 3,00
11'-0" X 10'-0"

2,70 X 3,00
9'-0" X 10'-0"

3,00 X 3,00
10'-0" X 10'-0"

4,70 X 3,90
15'-8" X 13'-0"

3,30 X 4,00
11'-0" X 13'-4"

MAIN FLOOR

To order blueprints, call **800-235-5700** or visit us on the web, **familyhomeplans.com**

Design 82102

Units	Single
Price Code	A
Total Finished	1,023 sq. ft.
Main Finished	1,023 sq. ft.
Garage Unfinished	471 sq. ft.
Porch Unfinished	94 sq. ft.
Dimensions	45'x47'
Foundation	Basement
	Crawlspace
	Slab
Bedrooms	3
Full Baths	2
Main Ceiling	8'
Max Ridge Height	15'6"
Roof Framing	Stick
Exterior Walls	2x4, 2x6

MAIN FLOOR

Design 98469

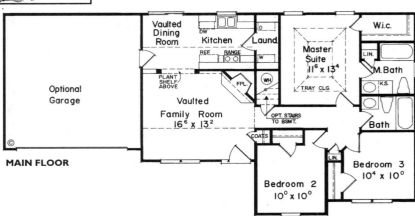

Units	Single
Price Code	A
Total Finished	1,042 sq. ft.
Main Finished	1,042 sq. ft.
Basement Unfinished	1,042 sq. ft.
Garage Unfinished	400 sq. ft.
Dimensions	60'x30'
Foundation	Basement
	Crawlspace
Bedrooms	3
Full Baths	2
Main Ceiling	9'
Max Ridge Height	22'
Roof Framing	Stick
Exterior Walls	2x4

MAIN FLOOR

Units	Single
Price Code	A
Total Finished	1,052 sq. ft.
Main Finished	1,052 sq. ft.
Basement Unfinished	1,052 sq. ft.
Dimensions	32'8"x36'
Foundation	Basement
Bedrooms	2
Full Baths	1
Main Ceiling	8'
Max Ridge Height	18'1"
Roof Framing	Truss
Exterior Walls	2x6

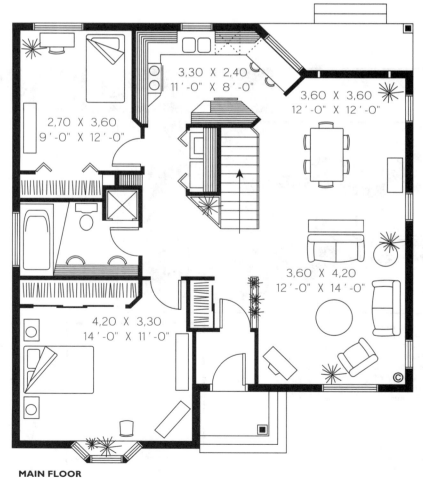

3,30 X 2,40
11'-0" X 8'-0"

3,60 X 3,60
12'-0" X 12'-0"

2,70 X 3,60
9'-0" X 12'-0"

3,60 X 4,20
12'-0" X 14'-0"

4,20 X 3,30
14'-0" X 11'-0"

MAIN FLOOR

Design 55022

Units	Single
Price Code	A
Total Finished	1,064 sq. ft.
Main Finished	1,064 sq. ft.
Deck Unfinished	405 sq. ft.
Dimensions	38'x34'
Foundation	Basement
Bedrooms	2
Full Baths	1
Main Ceiling	8'
Max Ridge Height	21'

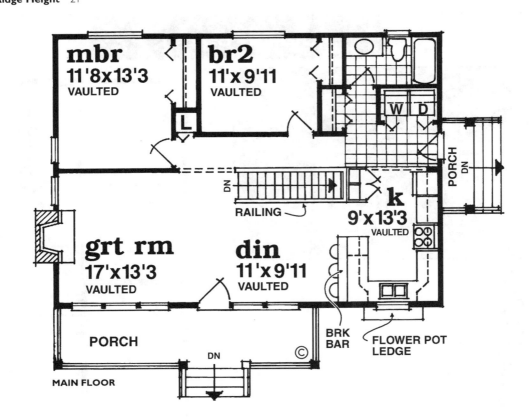

Design 65329

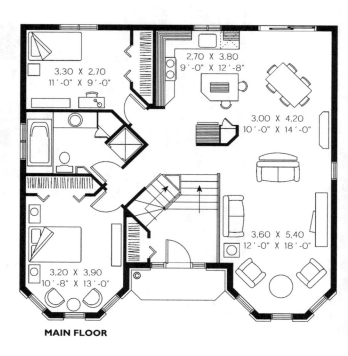

Units	Single
Price Code	A
Total Finished	1,065 sq. ft.
Main Finished	1,065 sq. ft.
Basement Unfinished	1,065 sq. ft.
Dimensions	34'x33'8"
Foundation	Basement
Bedrooms	2
Full Baths	1
Main Ceiling	8'
Max Ridge Height	24'
Roof Framing	Truss
Exterior Walls	2x6

3.30 X 2.70
11'-0" X 9'-0"

2.70 X 3.80
9'-0" X 12'-8"

3.00 X 4.20
10'-0" X 14'-0"

3.60 X 5.40
12'-0" X 18'-0"

3.20 X 3.90
10'-8" X 13'-0"

MAIN FLOOR

Design 65241

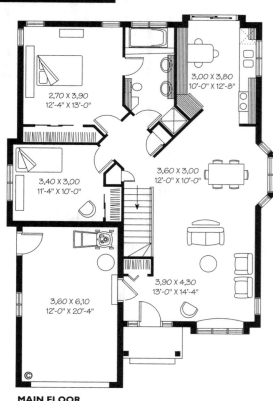

Units	Single
Price Code	A
Total Finished	1,068 sq. ft.
Main Finished	1,068 sq. ft.
Basement Unfinished	1,068 sq. ft.
Garage Unfinished	245 sq. ft.
Dimensions	30'8"x48'
Foundation	Basement
Bedrooms	2
Full Baths	1
Main Ceiling	8'
Max Ridge Height	22'1"
Roof Framing	Truss
Exterior Walls	2x6

2.70 X 3.90
12'-4" X 13'-0"

3.00 X 3.80
10'-0" X 12'-8"

3.40 X 3.00
11'-4" X 10'-0"

3.60 X 3.00
12'-0" X 10'-0"

3.60 X 6.10
12'-0" X 20'-4"

3.90 X 4.30
13'-0" X 14'-4"

MAIN FLOOR

Design 52013

Units	Single
Price Code	A
Total Finished	1,085 sq. ft.
Main Finished	1,085 sq. ft.
Basement Unfinished	1,105 sq. ft.
Dimensions	48'x36'
Foundation	Basement
	Crawlspace
Bedrooms	3
Full Baths	2
Main Ceiling	9'
Max Ridge Height	21'
Roof Framing	Stick
Exterior Walls	2x4

CAD FILES AVAILABLE
For more information call
800-235-5700

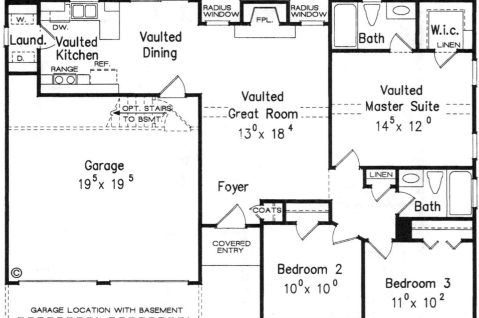

Laund.

Vaulted Kitchen

Vaulted Dining

RADIUS WINDOW   FPL.   RADIUS WINDOW

Bath

W.i.c.   LINEN

Vaulted Master Suite
14^5 x 12^0

OPT. STAIRS TO BSMT.

Vaulted Great Room
13^0 x 18^4

LINEN

Bath

Garage
19^5 x 19^5

Foyer

COATS

COVERED ENTRY

Bedroom 2
10^0 x 10^0

Bedroom 3
11^0 x 10^2

GARAGE LOCATION WITH BASEMENT

MAIN FLOOR

Design 65093

Units	Single
Price Code	A
Total Finished	1,087 sq. ft.
Main Finished	1,087 sq. ft.
Dimensions	46'x40'4"
Foundation	Basement
Bedrooms	2
Full Baths	1

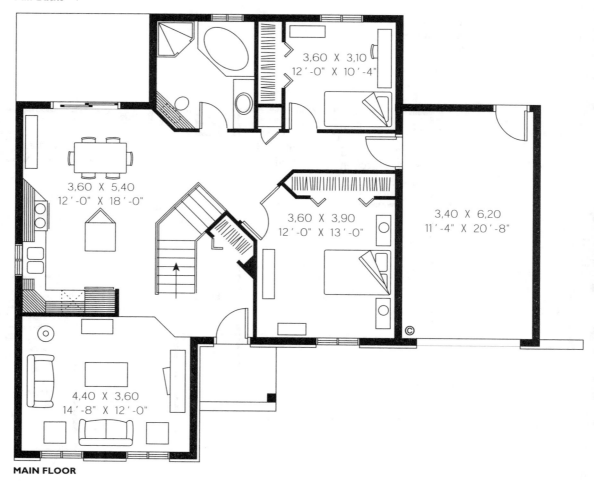

3,60 X 3,10
12'-0" X 10'-4"

3,60 X 5,40
12'-0" X 18'-0"

3,60 X 3,90
12'-0" X 13'-0"

3,40 X 6,20
11'-4" X 20'-8"

4,40 X 3,60
14'-8" X 12'-0"

MAIN FLOOR

Design 99690

PHOTOGRAPHY: MARK ENGLUND

Units	Single
Price Code	A
Total Finished	1,097 sq. ft.
Main Finished	1,097 sq. ft.
Garage Unfinished	461 sq. ft.
Dimensions	56'x35'
Foundation	Basement
	Crawlspace
	Slab
Bedrooms	3
Full Baths	1
3/4 Baths	1
Max Ridge Height	20'1"
Roof Framing	Stick
Exterior Walls	2x4

OPTIONAL BASEMENT STAIR LOCATION

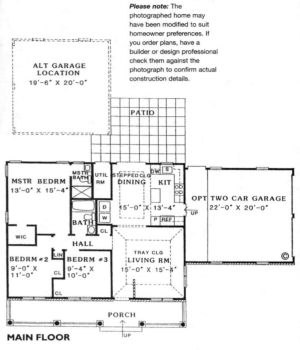

Please note: The photographed home may have been modified to suit homeowner preferences. If you order plans, have a builder or design professional check them against the photograph to confirm actual construction details.

MAIN FLOOR

Design 98468

Units	Single
Price Code	A
Total Finished	1,104 sq. ft.
Main Finished	1,104 sq. ft.
Basement Unfinished	1,104 sq. ft.
Garage Unfinished	400 sq. ft.
Dimensions	46'6"x41'
Foundation	Basement
	Crawlspace
	Slab
Bedrooms	3
Full Baths	2
Main Ceiling	9'
Max Ridge Height	21'
Roof Framing	Stick
Exterior Walls	2x4

MAIN FLOOR

GARAGE LOCATION W/BASEMENT

Units	Single
Price Code	A
Total Finished	1,112 sq. ft.
Main Finished	1,112 sq. ft.
Garage Unfinished	563 sq. ft.
Dimensions	64'x33'
Foundation	Crawlspace
	Slab
Bedrooms	3
Full Baths	2
Main Ceiling	8'-9'
Max Ridge Height	21'6"
Roof Framing	Stick
Exterior Walls	2x4

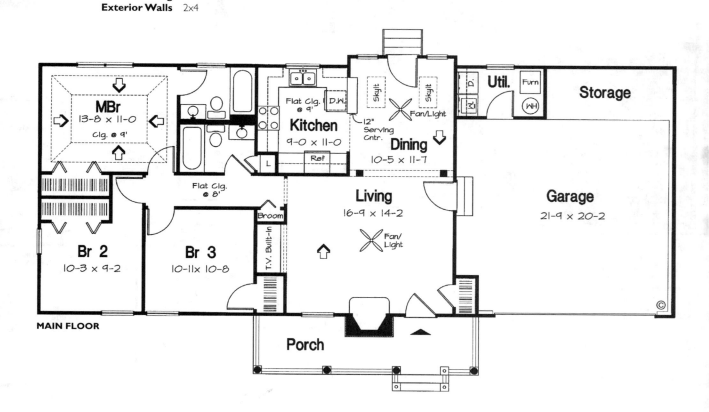

MAIN FLOOR

Design 63137

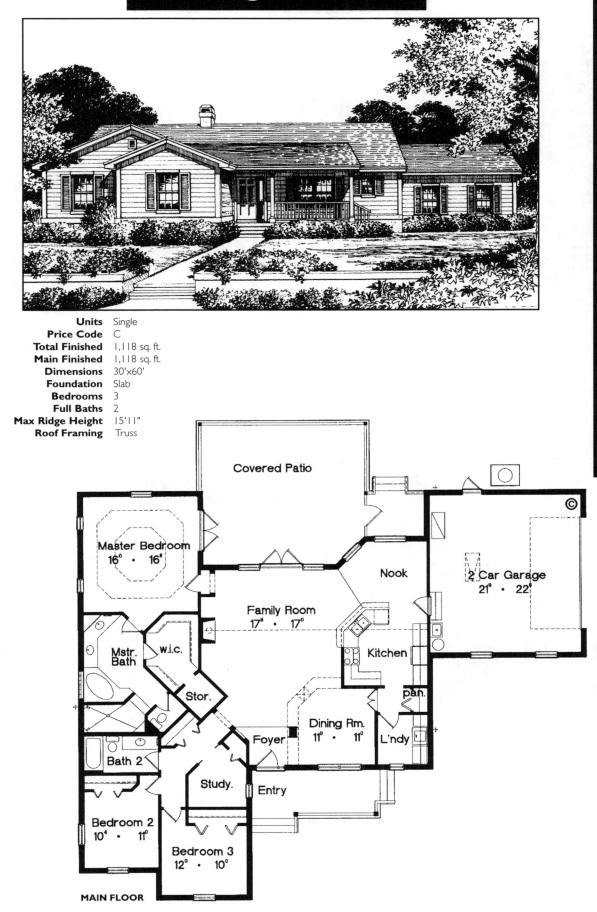

Units	Single
Price Code	C
Total Finished	1,118 sq. ft.
Main Finished	1,118 sq. ft.
Dimensions	30'x60'
Foundation	Slab
Bedrooms	3
Full Baths	2
Max Ridge Height	15'11"
Roof Framing	Truss

Covered Patio

Master Bedroom
16⁰ · 16⁸

2 Car Garage
21⁰ · 22⁰

Nook

Family Room
17⁸ · 17⁰

Kitchen

Mstr. Bath

w.i.c.

Stor.

pan.

Dining Rm.
11⁰ · 11⁰

L'ndy

Foyer

Bath 2

Study.

Entry

Bedroom 2
10⁴ · 11⁰

Bedroom 3
12⁰ · 10⁰

MAIN FLOOR

Design 96538

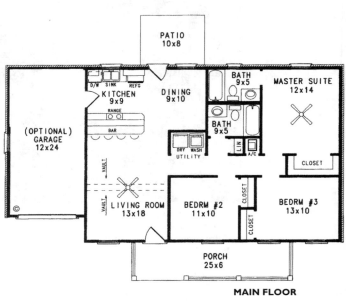

Units	Single
Price Code	A
Total Finished	1,120 sq. ft.
Main Finished	1,120 sq. ft.
Garage Unfinished	288 sq. ft.
Porch Unfinished	150 sq. ft.
Dimensions	52'x34'
Foundation	Slab
Bedrooms	3
Full Baths	2
Main Ceiling	8'
Max Ridge Height	19'
Roof Framing	Stick
Exterior Walls	2x4

PATIO 10x8

KITCHEN 9x9 — D/W SINK REFG — RANGE — BAR

(OPTIONAL) GARAGE 12x24

DINING 9x10

BATH 9x5

MASTER SUITE 12x14

BATH 9x5

DRY WASH UTILITY LIN A/C

CLOSET

LIVING ROOM 13x18

BEDRM #2 11x10

CLOSET

CLOSET

BEDRM #3 13x10

PORCH 25x6

MAIN FLOOR

Design 52062

CAD FILES AVAILABLE For more information call 800-235-5700

Units	Single
Price Code	A
Total Finished	1,124 sq. ft.
Main Finished	1,124 sq. ft.
Basement Unfinished	652 sq. ft.
Garage Unfinished	458 sq. ft.
Dimensions	43'4"x31'6"
Foundation	Basement
Bedrooms	3
Full Baths	2
Roof Framing	Stick

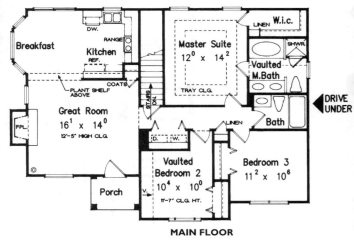

Breakfast

Kitchen REF.

DW. RANGE

LINEN W.i.c.

Master Suite 12⁰ x 14²

SHWR

Vaulted M.Bath

PLANT SHELF ABOVE

COATS

TRAY CLG.

DRIVE UNDER

Great Room 16¹ x 14⁰ 12'-5" HIGH CLG.

FPL.

STAIRS DN.

LINEN

Bath

D. W.

Vaulted Bedroom 2 10⁴ x 10⁰ 1'-7" CLG. HT.

Bedroom 3 11² x 10⁶

Porch

MAIN FLOOR

Design 65401

Units	Single
Price Code	A
Total Finished	1,109 sq. ft.
Main Finished	1,109 sq. ft.
Basement Unfinished	1,109 sq. ft.
Deck Unfinished	35 sq. ft.
Porch Unfinished	24 sq. ft.
Dimensions	32'8"x37'
Foundation	Basement
Bedrooms	2
Full Baths	1
Main Ceiling	8'
Max Ridge Height	23'4"
Roof Framing	Truss
Exterior Walls	2×6

12'-0"x 9'-0"
3,60 x 2,70

12'-0"x 10'-8"
3,60 x 3,20

11'-0"x 10'-0"
3,30 x 3,00

13'-0"x 12'-0"
3,90 x 3,60

12'-0"x 12'-0"
3,60 x 3,60

MAIN FLOOR

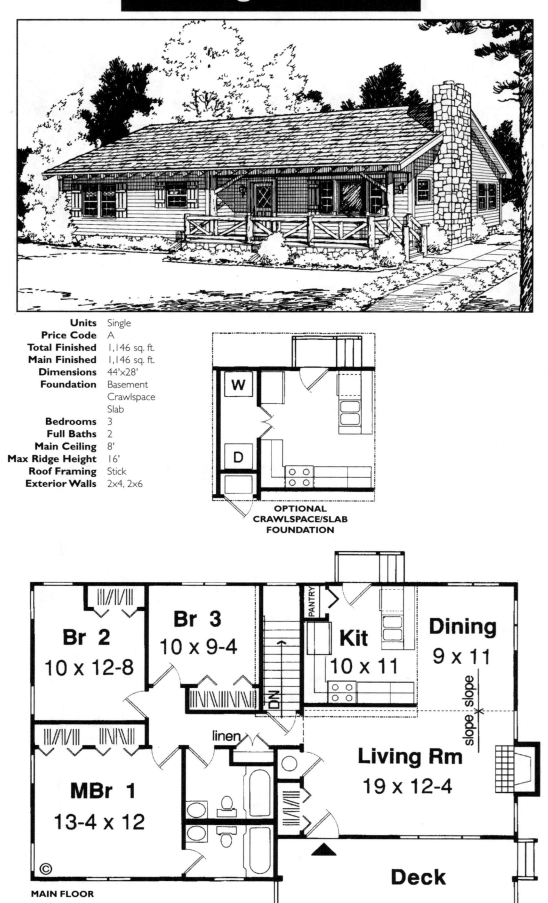

Units	Single
Price Code	A
Total Finished	1,146 sq. ft.
Main Finished	1,146 sq. ft.
Dimensions	44'x28'
Foundation	Basement
	Crawlspace
	Slab
Bedrooms	3
Full Baths	2
Main Ceiling	8'
Max Ridge Height	16'
Roof Framing	Stick
Exterior Walls	2x4, 2x6

W

D

**OPTIONAL
CRAWLSPACE/SLAB
FOUNDATION**

Br 2
10 x 12-8

Br 3
10 x 9-4

PANTRY

Kit
10 x 11

Dining
9 x 11

DN

slope slope

MBr 1
13-4 x 12

linen

Living Rm
19 x 12-4

Deck

MAIN FLOOR

Design 65395

Units	Single
Price Code	A
Total Finished	1,147 sq. ft.
Main Finished	1,147 sq. ft.
Dimensions	44'x30'
Foundation	Basement
Bedrooms	3
Full Baths	1
Main Ceiling	8'
Max Ridge Height	21'8"
Roof Framing	Truss
Exterior Walls	2x6

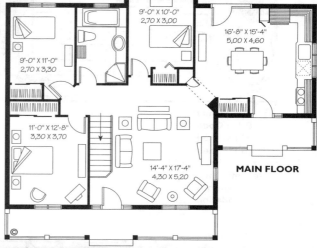

MAIN FLOOR

Design 97296

Units	Single
Price Code	A
Total Finished	1,166 sq. ft.
Main Finished	1,166 sq. ft.
Basement Unfinished	1,166 sq. ft.
Dimensions	43'4"x34'
Foundation	Basement
Bedrooms	3
Full Baths	2
Max Ridge Height	22'3"
Roof Framing	Stick
Exterior Walls	2x4

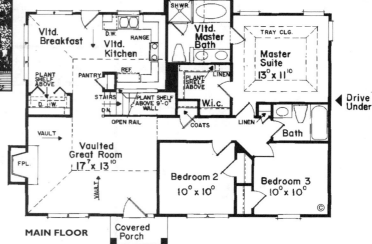

MAIN FLOOR

Units	Single
Price Code	A
Total Finished	1,169 sq. ft.
Main Finished	1,169 sq. ft.
Basement Unfinished	1,194 sq. ft.
Garage Unfinished	400 sq. ft.
Dimensions	40'x49'6"
Foundation	Basement
	Crawlspace
	Slab
Bedrooms	3
Full Baths	2
Main Ceiling	9'
Max Ridge Height	21'
Roof Framing	Stick
Exterior Walls	2x4

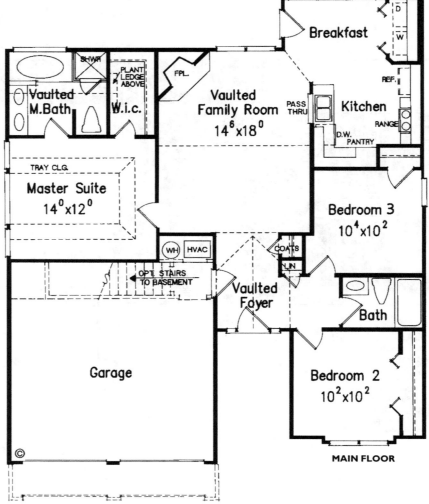

MAIN FLOOR

Design 82040

Units	Single
Price Code	A
Total Finished	1,172 sq. ft.
Main Finished	1,172 sq. ft.
Garage Unfinished	213 sq. ft.
Porch Unfinished	127 sq. ft.
Dimensions	37'x53'
Foundation	Crawlspace
	Slab
Bedrooms	2
Full Baths	2
Main Ceiling	9'
Roof Framing	Stick
Exterior Walls	2x4

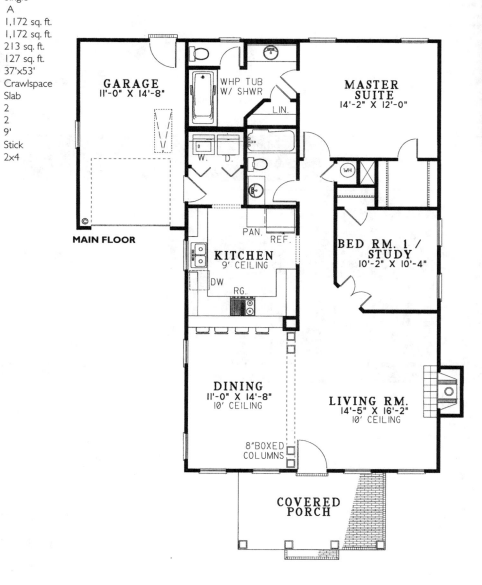

MAIN FLOOR

GARAGE
11'-0" X 14'-8"

WHP TUB
W/ SHWR

LIN.

W.   D.

MASTER
SUITE
14'-2" X 12'-0"

WH

PAN.   REF.

KITCHEN
9' CEILING

DW

RG.

BED RM. 1 /
STUDY
10'-2" X 10'-4"

DINING
11'-0" X 14'-8"
10' CEILING

LIVING RM.
14'-5" X 16'-2"
10' CEILING

8" BOXED
COLUMNS

COVERED
PORCH

Design 65075

Units	Single
Price Code	A
Total Finished	1,176 sq. ft.
Main Finished	1,176 sq. ft.
Basement Unfinished	1,176 sq. ft.
Garage Unfinished	401 sq. ft.
Porch Unfinished	110 sq. ft.
Dimensions	58'x28'
Foundation	Basement
Bedrooms	3
Full Baths	1
Max Ridge Height	18'10"
Roof Framing	Truss
Exterior Walls	2x6

MAIN FLOOR

4,50 X 7,90
15'-0"X 26'-4"

4,50 X 3,60
15'-0"X 12'-0"

4,60 X 3,60
15'-0"X 12'-0"

2,70 X 3,70
9'-0"X 12'-4"

3,60 X 3.10
12'-0"X 10'-4"

3,60 X 3,70
12'-0"X 12'-4"

Design 65064

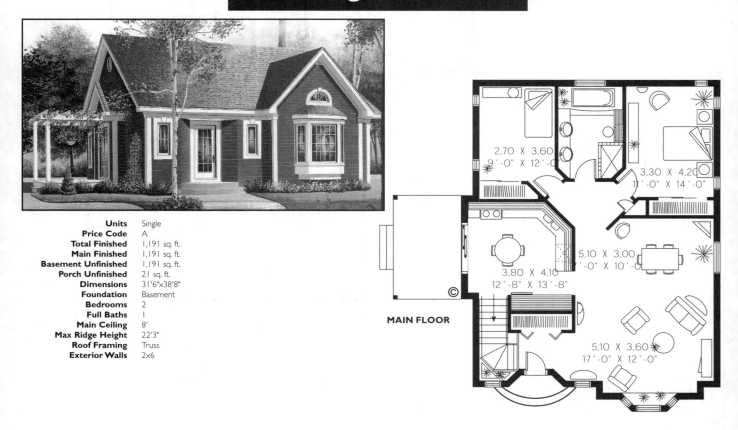

Units	Single
Price Code	A
Total Finished	1,191 sq. ft.
Main Finished	1,191 sq. ft.
Basement Unfinished	1,191 sq. ft.
Porch Unfinished	21 sq. ft.
Dimensions	31'6"x38'8"
Foundation	Basement
Bedrooms	2
Full Baths	1
Main Ceiling	8'
Max Ridge Height	22'3"
Roof Framing	Truss
Exterior Walls	2x6

MAIN FLOOR

2,70 X 3,60
9'-0" X 12'-0"

3,30 X 4,20
11'-0" X 14'-0"

3,80 X 4,10
12'-8" X 13'-8"

5,10 X 3,00
1'-0" X 10'-0"

5,10 X 3,60
17'-0" X 12'-0"

Design 92430

Units	Single
Price Code	A
Total Finished	1,197 sq. ft.
Main Finished	1,197 sq. ft.
Garage Unfinished	380 sq. ft.
Porch Unfinished	76 sq. ft.
Dimensions	52'x42'
Foundation	Crawlspace
	Slab
Bedrooms	3
Full Baths	2
Main Ceiling	8'
Vaulted Ceiling	12'
Max Ridge Height	17'8"
Roof Framing	Truss
Exterior Walls	2x4

OPTIONAL BAY

MASTER BEDROOM
14x12

VAULT

VAULT

FAMILY ROOM
14x18

DINING
10x9

PLANT SHELF

BEDROOM 3
12x11

BEDROOM 2
12x11

MAIN FLOOR

GARAGE
19x20

Units	Single
Price Code	A
Total Finished	1,199 sq. ft.
Main Finished	1,199 sq. ft.
Garage Unfinished	484 sq. ft.
Porch Unfinished	34 sq. ft.
Dimensions	44'2"x42'6¾"
Foundation	Slab
Bedrooms	3
Full Baths	2
Main Ceiling	8'
Vaulted Ceiling	11'
Max Ridge Height	18'
Roof Framing	Stick
Exterior Walls	2x4

MAIN FLOOR

Design 32323

PHOTOGRAPHY: ED GOHLICH

Units	Single
Price Code	A
Total Finished	1,200 sq. ft.
Main Finished	1,200 sq. ft.
Porch Unfinished	200 sq. ft.
Dimensions	51'4"x34'
Foundation	Crawlspace
Bedrooms	2
Full Baths	2
Main Ceiling	8'
Vaulted Ceiling	12'4"
Max Ridge Height	16'4"
Roof Framing	Stick
Exterior Walls	2x4

Please note: The photographed home may have been modified to suit homeowner preferences. If you order plans, have a builder or design professional check them against the photograph to confirm actual construction details.

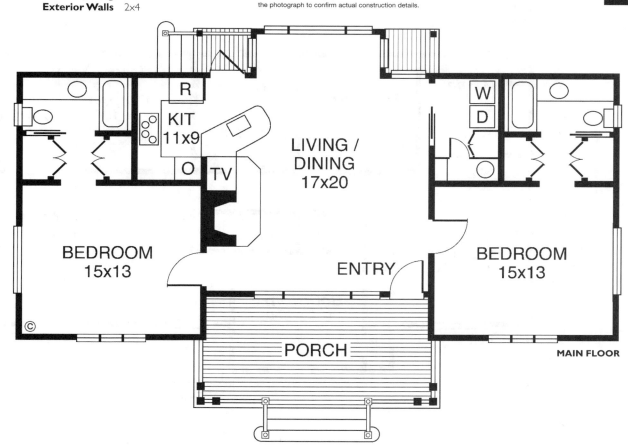

MAIN FLOOR

Units	Single
Price Code	A
Total Finished	1,208 sq. ft.
Main Finished	1,208 sq. ft.
Basement Unfinished	728 sq. ft.
Garage Unfinished	480 sq. ft.
Deck Unfinished	100 sq. ft.
Porch Unfinished	40 sq. ft.
Dimensions	48'×29'
Foundation	Basement
Bedrooms	3
Full Baths	2
Max Ridge Height	17'10"
Roof Framing	Truss
Exterior Walls	2×4

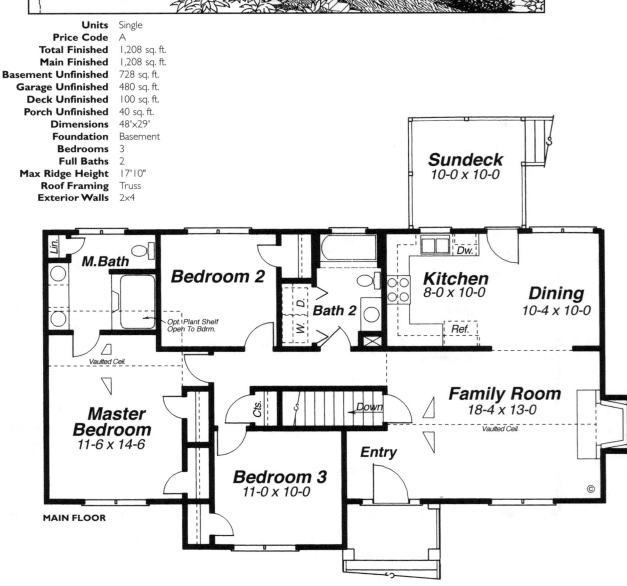

Sundeck
10-0 x 10-0

M.Bath

Bedroom 2

Opt. Plant Shelf Open To Bdrm.

Bath 2

W. D.

Kitchen
8-0 x 10-0

Dw.

Dining
10-4 x 10-0

Ref.

Vaulted Ceil.

Master Bedroom
11-6 x 14-6

Cts.

Down

Family Room
18-4 x 13-0

Vaulted Ceil.

Entry

Bedroom 3
11-0 x 10-0

MAIN FLOOR

Design 98925

Units	Single
Price Code	A
Total Finished	1,208 sq. ft.
Main Finished	1,208 sq. ft.
Basement Unfinished	760 sq. ft.
Garage Unfinished	448 sq. ft.
Deck Unfinished	100 sq. ft.
Porch Unfinished	40 sq. ft.
Dimensions	50'4"x29'
Foundation	Basement
Bedrooms	3
Full Baths	2
Max Ridge Height	25'
Roof Framing	Truss
Exterior Walls	2x4

Sundeck 10-0 x 10-0

M.Bath

Bedroom 2

Kitchen 8-0 x 10-0

Dining 10-4 x 10-0

OPT.PLANT SHELF OPEN TO BDRM

Bath 2

W. D.

Ref.

Dw.

Master Bedroom 11-6 x 14-6

Cts.

Down

Family Room 18-4 x 13-0

Bedroom 3 11-0 x 10-0

Entry

MAIN FLOOR

Design 98954

Units	Single
Price Code	A
Total Finished	1,208 sq. ft.
Main Finished	1,208 sq. ft.
Garage Unfinished	448 sq. ft.
Deck Unfinished	100 sq. ft.
Porch Unfinished	40 sq. ft.
Dimensions	48'x29'
Foundation	Basement
Bedrooms	3
Full Baths	2
Main Ceiling	8'
Max Ridge Height	17'
Roof Framing	Stick
Exterior Walls	2x6

Sundeck 10-0 x 10-0

M.Bath

Bedroom 2

Kitchen 8-0 x 10-0

Dining 10-4 x 10-0

OPT.PLANT SHELF OPEN TO BDRM

Bath 2

W. D.

Ref.

Dw.

Master Bedroom 11-6 x 14-6

Cts.

Down

Family Room 18-4 x 13-0

Bedroom 3 11-0 x 10-0

Entry

MAIN FLOOR

Design 60045

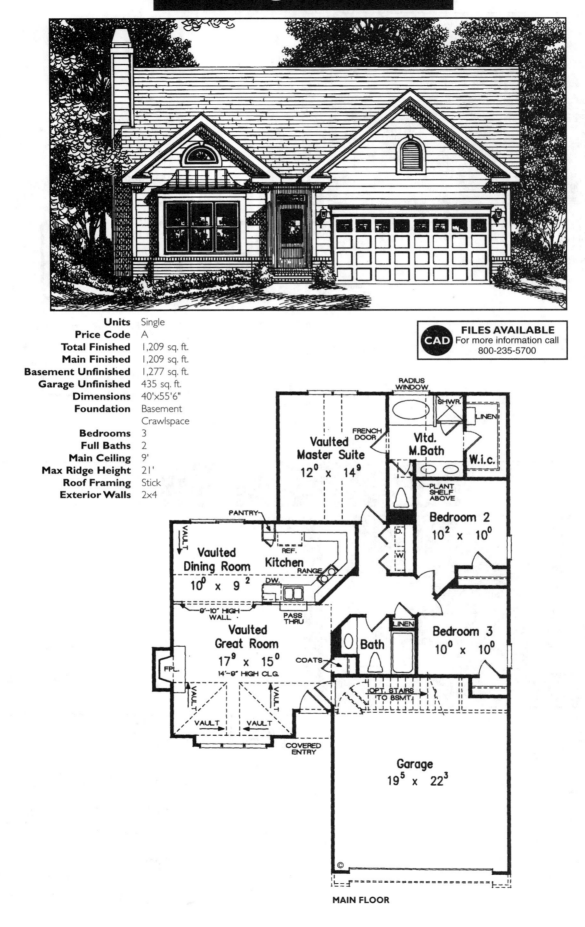

Units	Single
Price Code	A
Total Finished	1,209 sq. ft.
Main Finished	1,209 sq. ft.
Basement Unfinished	1,277 sq. ft.
Garage Unfinished	435 sq. ft.
Dimensions	40'x55'6"
Foundation	Basement
	Crawlspace
Bedrooms	3
Full Baths	2
Main Ceiling	9'
Max Ridge Height	21'
Roof Framing	Stick
Exterior Walls	2x4

CAD **FILES AVAILABLE**
For more information call
800-235-5700

MAIN FLOOR

RADIUS WINDOW

Vaulted Master Suite
12⁰ x 14⁹

FRENCH DOOR

SHWR.

Vltd. M.Bath

LINEN

W.i.c.

PLANT SHELF ABOVE

Bedroom 2
10² x 10⁰

PANTRY

REF.

Vaulted Dining Room
10⁰ x 9²

Kitchen

RANGE

DW.

PASS THRU

9'-10" HIGH WALL

VAULT

Vaulted Great Room
17⁹ x 15⁰
14'-9" HIGH CLG.

FPL.

VAULT

VAULT

VAULT

VAULT

COVERED ENTRY

LINEN

Bath

COATS

Bedroom 3
10⁰ x 10⁰

OPT. STAIRS TO BSMT.

Garage
19⁵ x 22³

Design 82101

Units	Single
Price Code	A
Total Finished	1,210 sq. ft.
Main Finished	1,210 sq. ft.
Garage Unfinished	435 sq. ft.
Porch Unfinished	178 sq. ft.
Dimensions	49'2"×50'2"
Foundation	Basement
	crawlspace
	slab
Bedrooms	3
Full Baths	1
3/4 Baths	1
Main Ceiling	8'
Max Ridge Height	17'6"
Exterior Walls	2x4, 2x6

MAIN FLOOR

Design 60026

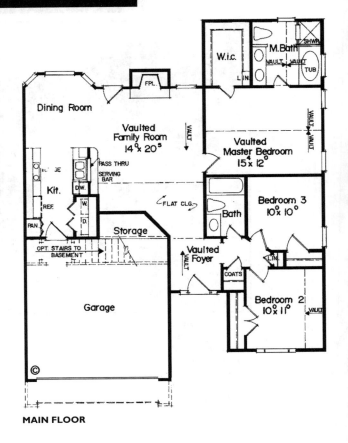

Units	Single
Price Code	A
Total Finished	1,215 sq. ft.
Main Finished	1,215 sq. ft.
Basement Unfinished	1,268 sq. ft.
Garage Unfinished	390 sq. ft.
Dimensions	40'x49'
Foundation	Basement
	Crawlspace
	Slab
Bedrooms	3
Full Baths	2
Main Ceiling	8'
Max Ridge Height	19'6"
Roof Framing	Stick
Exterior Walls	2x4

MAIN FLOOR

Design 90682

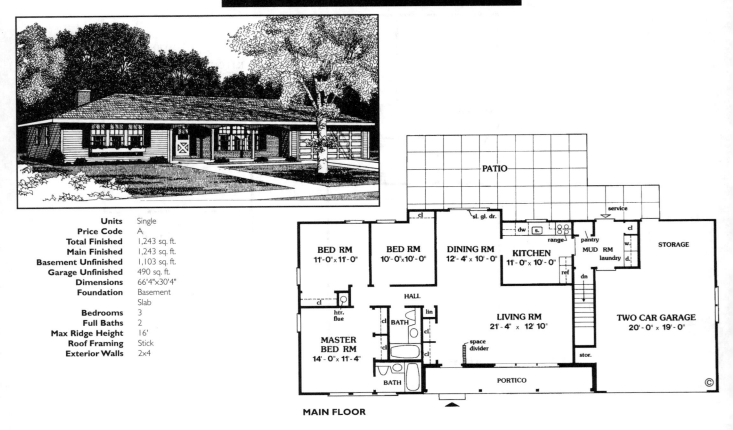

Units	Single
Price Code	A
Total Finished	1,243 sq. ft.
Main Finished	1,243 sq. ft.
Basement Unfinished	1,103 sq. ft.
Garage Unfinished	490 sq. ft.
Dimensions	66'4"x30'4"
Foundation	Basement
	Slab
Bedrooms	3
Full Baths	2
Max Ridge Height	16'
Roof Framing	Stick
Exterior Walls	2x4

MAIN FLOOR

Design 96519

Units	Single
Price Code	A
Total Finished	1,243 sq. ft.
Main Finished	1,243 sq. ft.
Garage Unfinished	523 sq. ft.
Dimensions	52'x41'
Foundation	Crawlspace
	Slab
Bedrooms	3
Full Baths	2
Main Ceiling	8'
Vaulted Ceiling	10'
Max Ridge Height	17'
Roof Framing	Stick
Exterior Walls	2x4

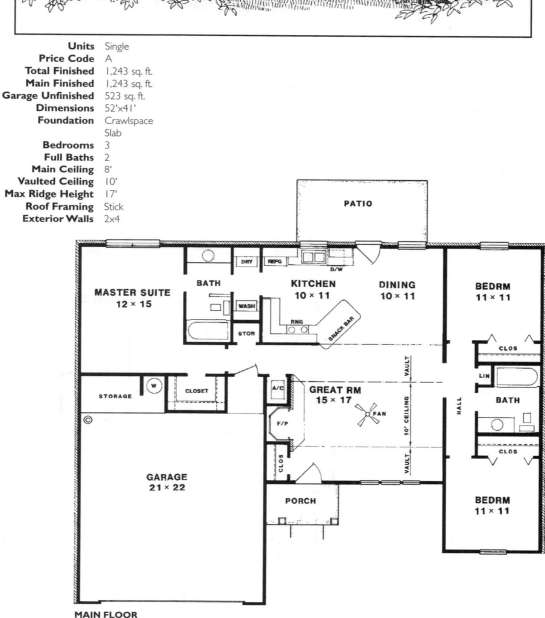

MAIN FLOOR

Design 96511

Units	Single
Price Code	A
Total Finished	1,247 sq. ft.
Main Finished	1,247 sq. ft.
Garage Unfinished	512 sq. ft.
Dimensions	43'x60'
Foundation	Crawlspace Slab
Bedrooms	3
Full Baths	2
Main Ceiling	8'
Max Ridge Height	19'
Roof Framing	Stick
Exterior Walls	2x4

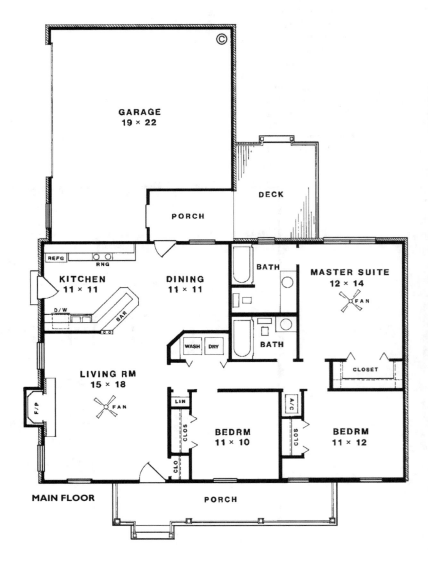

Design 51020

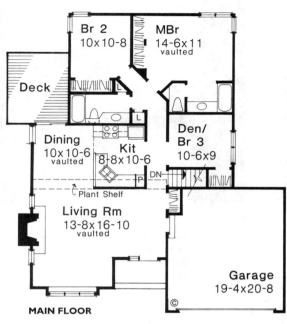

Units	Single
Price Code	A
Total Finished	1,252 sq. ft.
Main Finished	1,252 sq. ft.
Basement Unfinished	1,252 sq. ft.
Garage Unfinished	420 sq. ft.
Deck Unfinished	120 sq. ft.
Dimensions	44'8"x50'8"
Foundation	Basement
Bedrooms	3
Full Baths	2
Main Ceiling	8'
Max Ridge Height	21'6"
Roof Framing	Truss
Exterior Walls	2x4

Br 2 10x10-8

MBr 14-6x11 vaulted

Deck

Dining 10x10-6 vaulted

Kit 8-8x10-6

Den/ Br 3 10-6x9

Plant Shelf

Living Rm 13-8x16-10 vaulted

Garage 19-4x20-8

MAIN FLOOR

Design 92559

Units	Single
Price Code	A
Total Finished	1,265 sq. ft.
Main Finished	1,265 sq. ft.
Garage Unfinished	523 sq. ft.
Dimensions	64'10"x38'5"
Foundation	Crawlspace
	Slab
Bedrooms	3
Full Baths	2
Max Ridge Height	20'
Roof Framing	Stick
Exterior Walls	2x4

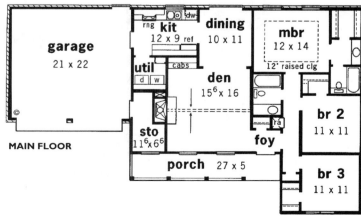

garage 21 x 22

kit 12 x 9

dining 10 x 11

mbr 12 x 14 12' raised clg

util

den 15⁶ x 16

sto 11⁶x6⁶

foy

br 2 11 x 11

br 3 11 x 11

porch 27 x 5

MAIN FLOOR

To order blueprints, call **800-235-5700** or visit us on the web, **familyhomeplans.com**   **69**

Units	Single
Price Code	A
Total Finished	1,266 sq. ft.
Main Finished	1,266 sq. ft.
Basement Unfinished	1,280 sq. ft.
Garage Unfinished	480 sq. ft.
Dimensions	40'x51'10"
Foundation	Basement
	Crawlspace
Bedrooms	3
Full Baths	2
Main Ceiling	8'
Max Ridge Height	23'
Roof Framing	Stick
Exterior Walls	2x4

CAD FILES AVAILABLE
For more information call
800-235-5700

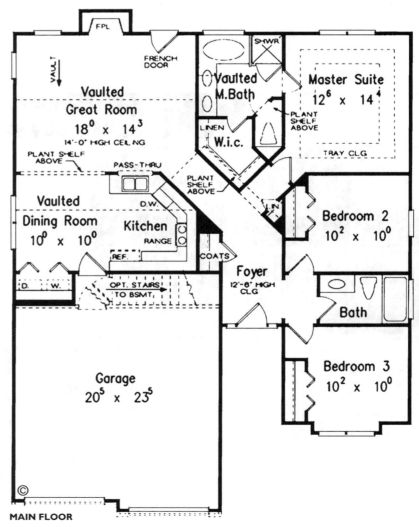

MAIN FLOOR

Design 34353

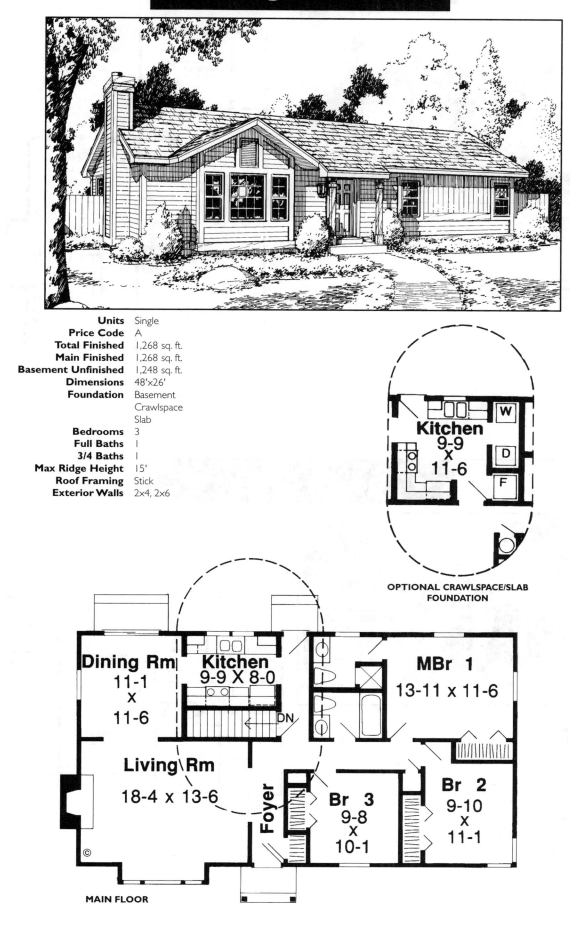

Units	Single
Price Code	A
Total Finished	1,268 sq. ft.
Main Finished	1,268 sq. ft.
Basement Unfinished	1,248 sq. ft.
Dimensions	48'x26'
Foundation	Basement
	Crawlspace
	Slab
Bedrooms	3
Full Baths	1
3/4 Baths	1
Max Ridge Height	15'
Roof Framing	Stick
Exterior Walls	2x4, 2x6

Kitchen
9-9
X
11-6
W
D
F

OPTIONAL CRAWLSPACE/SLAB FOUNDATION

Dining Rm
11-1
x
11-6

Kitchen
9-9 X 8-0

DN

MBr 1
13-11 x 11-6

Living Rm
18-4 x 13-6

Foyer

Br 3
9-8
x
10-1

Br 2
9-10
x
11-1

MAIN FLOOR

Design 91553

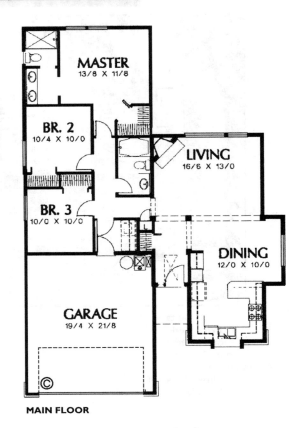

MAIN FLOOR

Units	Single
Price Code	A
Total Finished	1,271 sq. ft.
Main Finished	1,271 sq. ft.
Garage Unfinished	440 sq. ft.
Dimensions	40'x58'
Foundation	Crawlspace
Bedrooms	3
Full Baths	1
3/4 Baths	1
Max Ridge Height	19'6"
Roof Framing	Truss
Exterior Walls	2x6

Design 97620

MAIN FLOOR

Units	Single
Price Code	A
Total Finished	1,271 sq. ft.
Main Finished	1,271 sq. ft.
Basement Unfinished	1,292 sq. ft.
Garage Unfinished	400 sq. ft.
Dimensions	56'6"x33'10"
Foundation	Basement Crawlspace
Bedrooms	3
Full Baths	2
Main Ceiling	9'
Max Ridge Height	23'6"
Roof Framing	Stick
Exterior Walls	2x4

Design 65073

Units	Single
Price Code	A
Total Finished	1,272 sq. ft.
Main Finished	1,272 sq. ft.
Garage Unfinished	274 sq. ft.
Dimensions	42'x42'
Foundation	Basement
Bedrooms	3
Full Baths	1

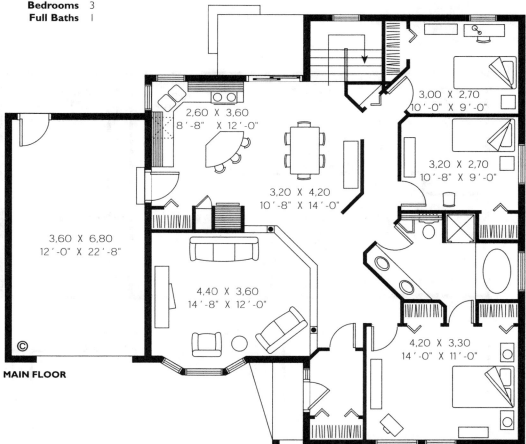

3,00 X 2,70
10'-0" X 9'-0"

3,20 X 2,70
10'-8" X 9'-0"

2,60 X 3,60
8'-8" X 12'-0"

3,20 X 4,20
10'-8" X 14'-0"

3,60 X 6,80
12'-0" X 22'-8"

4,40 X 3,60
14'-8" X 12'-0"

4,20 X 3,30
14'-0" X 11'-0"

MAIN FLOOR

Design 98747

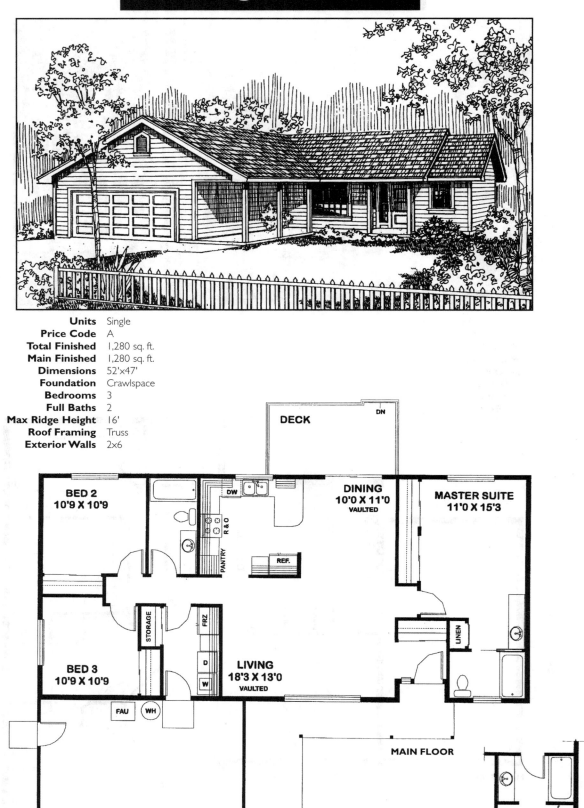

Units	Single
Price Code	A
Total Finished	1,280 sq. ft.
Main Finished	1,280 sq. ft.
Dimensions	52'x47'
Foundation	Crawlspace
Bedrooms	3
Full Baths	2
Max Ridge Height	16'
Roof Framing	Truss
Exterior Walls	2x6

DECK

DN

BED 2
10'9 X 10'9

DW

DINING
10'0 X 11'0
VAULTED

MASTER SUITE
11'0 X 15'3

PANTRY

R & O

REF.

STORAGE

FRZ

LINEN

BED 3
10'9 X 10'9

D

W

LIVING
18'3 X 13'0
VAULTED

FAU

WH

MAIN FLOOR

OPTIONAL
MASTER BATH

LINEN

GARAGE
21'3 X 21'9

To order blueprints, call **800-235-5700** or visit us on the web, **familyhomeplans.com**

Design 82042

Units	Single
Price Code	A
Total Finished	1,281 sq. ft.
Main Finished	1,281 sq. ft.
Dimensions	44'x54'8"
Foundation	Crawlspace
	Slab
Bedrooms	3
Full Baths	2
Main Ceiling	9'
Roof Framing	Stick
Exterior Walls	2x4

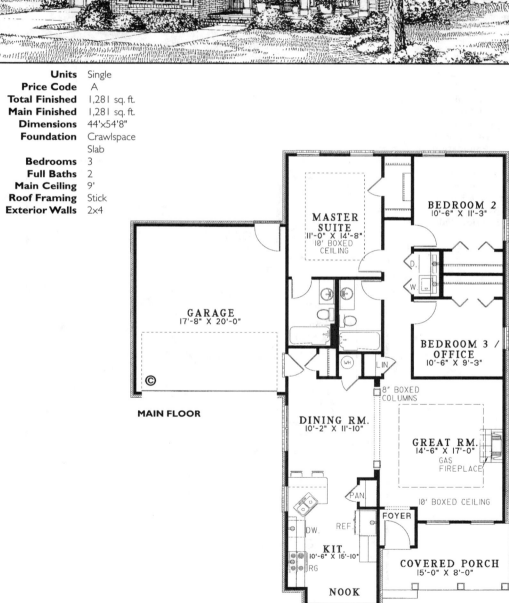

MAIN FLOOR

GARAGE
17'-8" X 20'-0"

MASTER SUITE
11'-0" X 14'-8"
10' BOXED CEILING

BEDROOM 2
10'-6" X 11'-3"

BEDROOM 3 / OFFICE
10'-6" X 9'-3"

8" BOXED COLUMNS

DINING RM.
10'-2" X 11'-10"

GREAT RM.
14'-6" X 17'-0"
GAS FIREPLACE
10' BOXED CEILING

FOYER

KIT.
10'-6" X 15'-10"

NOOK

COVERED PORCH
15'-0" X 8'-0"

Design 93021

Units	Single
Price Code	A
Total Finished	1,282 sq. ft.
Main Finished	1,282 sq. ft.
Garage Unfinished	501 sq. ft.
Dimensions	48'10"x52'6"
Foundation	Crawlspace
	Slab
Bedrooms	3
Full Baths	2
Max Ridge Height	20'
Roof Framing	Stick
Exterior Walls	2x4

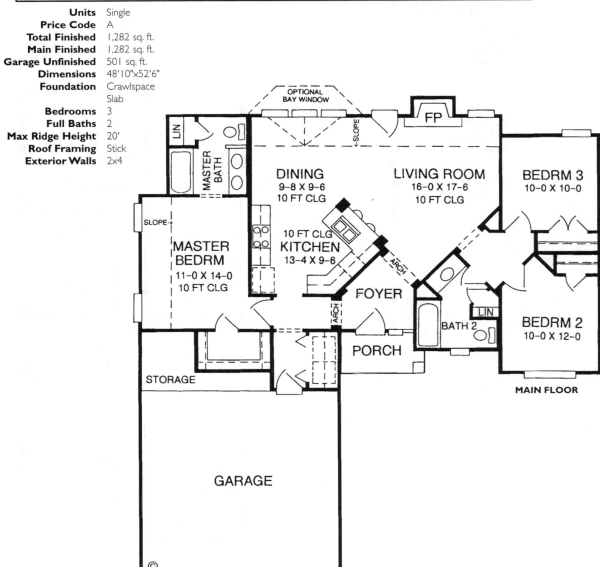

OPTIONAL BAY WINDOW

FP

LIN

MASTER BATH

DINING
9-8 X 9-6
10 FT CLG

LIVING ROOM
16-0 X 17-6
10 FT CLG

BEDRM 3
10-0 X 10-0

SLOPE

MASTER BEDRM
11-0 X 14-0
10 FT CLG

10 FT CLG
KITCHEN
13-4 X 9-6

ARCH

FOYER

ARCH

LIN

BATH 2

BEDRM 2
10-0 X 12-0

STORAGE

PORCH

MAIN FLOOR

GARAGE

Design 63140

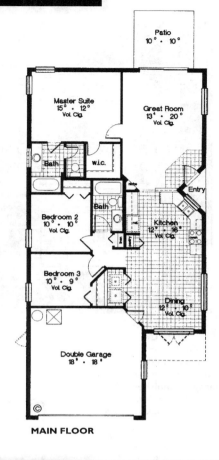

Units	Single
Price Code	A
Total Finished	1,284 sq. ft.
Main Finished	1,284 sq. ft.
Garage Unfinished	375 sq. ft.
Dimensions	30'x60'10"
Foundation	Slab
Bedrooms	3
Full Baths	2
Main Ceiling	8'
Max Ridge Height	15'11"
Roof Framing	Truss

Patio
10° · 10°

Master Suite
15° · 12°
Vol. Clg.

Great Room
13⁴ · 20°
Vol. Clg.

Bath

w.i.c.

Entry

Bedroom 2
10° · 10°
Vol. Clg.

Bath

Kitchen
12° · 16°
Vol. Clg.

Bedroom 3
10° · 9°
Vol. Clg.

Dining
12° · 10°
Vol. Clg.

Double Garage
18° · 18°

MAIN FLOOR

Design 91832

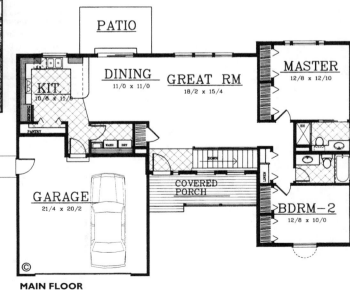

Units	Single
Price Code	A
Total Finished	1,288 sq. ft.
Main Finished	1,288 sq. ft.
Basement Unfinished	1,288 sq. ft.
Garage Unfinished	478 sq. ft.
Dimensions	56'x40'
Foundation	Basement
	Crawlspace
	Slab
Bedrooms	2
Full Baths	1
3/4 Baths	1
Main Ceiling	9'
Max Ridge Height	18'8"
Roof Framing	Truss
Exterior Walls	2x6

PATIO

KIT.
10/8 x 11/8

DINING
11/0 x 11/0

GREAT RM
18/2 x 15/4

MASTER
12/8 x 12/10

PANTRY

WASH DRY

GARAGE
21/4 x 20/2

COVERED PORCH

DOWN

BDRM-2
12/8 x 10/0

MAIN FLOOR

Design 97653

Units	Single
Price Code	A
Total Finished	1,290 sq. ft.
Main Finished	1,290 sq. ft.
Basement Unfinished	1,306 sq. ft.
Garage Unfinished	441 sq. ft.
Dimensions	46'x53'4"
Foundation	Basement
	Crawlspace
	Slab
Bedrooms	3
Full Baths	2
Main Ceiling	8'
Max Ridge Height	22'
Roof Framing	Stick
Exterior Walls	2x4

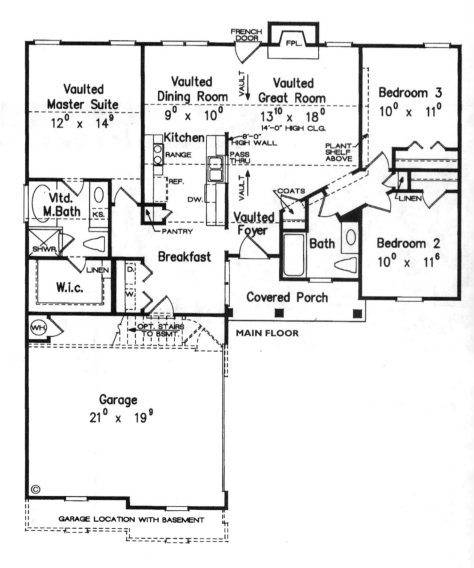

Design 93222

Units	Single
Price Code	A
Total Finished	1,292 sq. ft.
Main Finished	1,276 sq. ft.
Lower Finished	16 sq. ft.
Basement Unfinished	392 sq. ft.
Garage Unfinished	728 sq. ft.
Dimensions	48'x38'
Foundation	Basement
Bedrooms	3
Full Baths	2
Main Ceiling	8'
Max Ridge Height	16'
Roof Framing	Stick
Exterior Walls	2x4

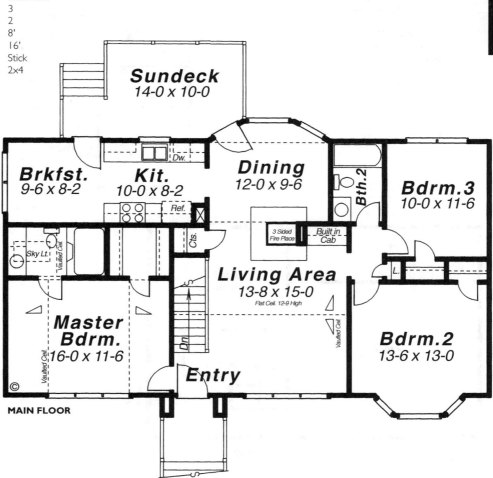

Sundeck
14-0 x 10-0

Brkfst.
9-6 x 8-2

Kit.
10-0 x 8-2

Dw.

Ref.

Dining
12-0 x 9-6

Bth.2

Bdrm.3
10-0 x 11-6

Sky Lt.

Vaulted Ceil.

Cts.

3 Sided Fire Place

Built in Cab

L.

Living Area
13-8 x 15-0
Flat Ceil. 12-9 High

Vaulted Ceil.

Master Bdrm.
16-0 x 11-6

Vaulted Ceil.

Dn

Bdrm.2
13-6 x 13-0

Entry

MAIN FLOOR

Units	Single
Price Code	A
Total Finished	1,293 sq. ft.
Main Finished	1,209 sq. ft.
Lower Finished	84 sq. ft.
Basement Unfinished	495 sq. ft.
Garage Unfinished	660 sq. ft.
Dimensions	42'x31'
Foundation	Basement
Bedrooms	3
Full Baths	2
Main Ceiling	8'
Second Ceiling	8'
Max Ridge Height	31'
Roof Framing	Stick
Exterior Walls	2x4

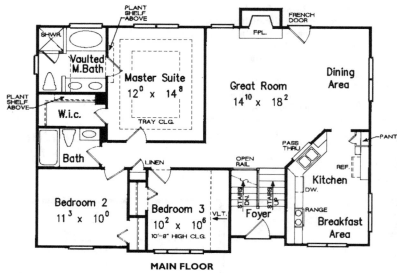

MAIN FLOOR

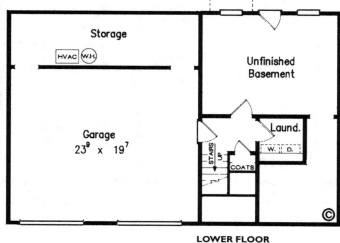

LOWER FLOOR

Design 92523

Units	Single
Price Code	A
Total Finished	1,293 sq. ft.
Main Finished	1,293 sq. ft.
Garage Unfinished	433 sq. ft.
Porch Unfinished	76 sq. ft.
Dimensions	51'10"x40'4"
Foundation	Slab
Bedrooms	3
Full Baths	2
Max Ridge Height	22'
Roof Framing	Stick
Exterior Walls	2×4

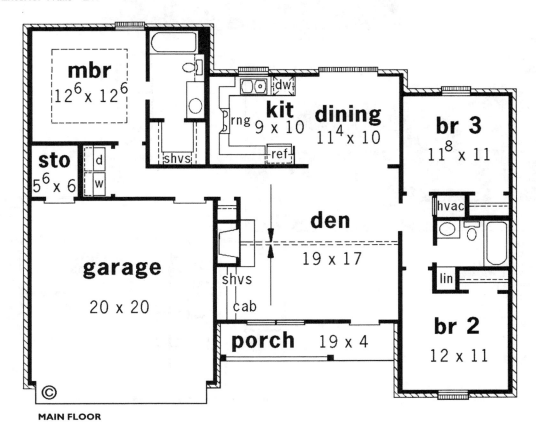

MAIN FLOOR

Design 92431

**OPTIONAL
MASTER BATH**

Units	Single
Price Code	A
Total Finished	1,296 sq. ft.
Main Finished	1,296 sq. ft.
Basement Unfinished	1,336 sq. ft.
Garage Unfinished	380 sq. ft.
Dimensions	46'x42'
Foundation	Basement
	Crawlspace
	Slab
Bedrooms	3
Full Baths	2
Main Ceiling	8'
Vaulted Ceiling	12'
Max Ridge Height	17'6"
Roof Framing	Truss
Exterior Walls	2x4

OPTIONAL BAY

BEDROOM 2
11x11

FAMILY ROOM
16x20

DINING

KITCHEN
10x10

VLT.

BEDROOM 3
11x10

W D

12' CEILING

WH

MASTER BEDROOM
12x14

VLT.

GARAGE
19x20

©

MAIN FLOOR

Design 55017

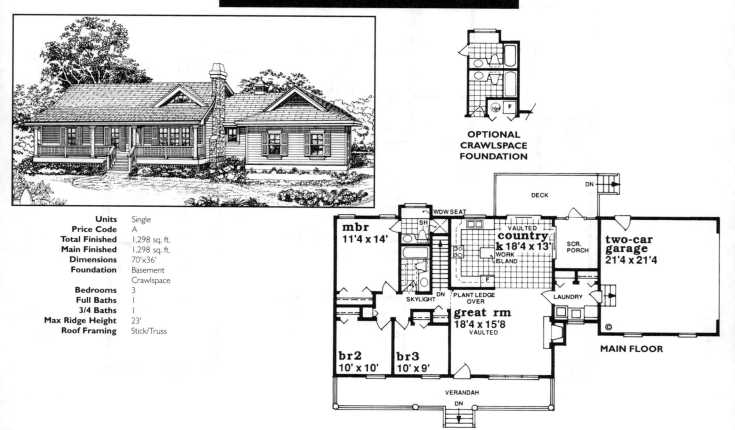

**OPTIONAL
CRAWLSPACE
FOUNDATION**

Units	Single
Price Code	A
Total Finished	1,298 sq. ft.
Main Finished	1,298 sq. ft.
Dimensions	70'x36'
Foundation	Basement
	Crawlspace
Bedrooms	3
Full Baths	1
3/4 Baths	1
Max Ridge Height	23'
Roof Framing	Stick/Truss

DN

DECK

WDW SEAT

mbr
11'4 x 14'

SH

country k 18'4 x 13'
WORK ISLAND

VAULTED

SCR. PORCH

two-car garage
21'4 x 21'4

DN

SKYLIGHT

PLANT LEDGE OVER

F

LAUNDRY

great rm
18'4 x 15'8
VAULTED

©

br2
10' x 10'

br3
10' x 9'

MAIN FLOOR

VERANDAH

DN

To order blueprints, call **800-235-5700** or visit us on the web, **familyhomeplans.com**

Design 52015

Units	Single
Price Code	A
Total Finished	1,304 sq. ft.
Main Finished	1,304 sq. ft.
Basement Unfinished	1,326 sq. ft.
Garage Unfinished	458 sq. ft.
Dimensions	50'x41'
Foundation	Basement
	Crawlspace
Bedrooms	3
Full Baths	2
Main Ceiling	8'
Max Ridge Height	23'6'
Roof Framing	Stick
Exterior Walls	2x4

CAD FILES AVAILABLE For more information call 800-235-5700

OPTIONAL BASEMENT STAIR LOCATION

Kitchen
RANGE
REF. DW.
PANTRY
Dining Room 10⁰x 11⁵
D. W.
STAIRS TO BSMT.
Garage 20⁰x 19⁹

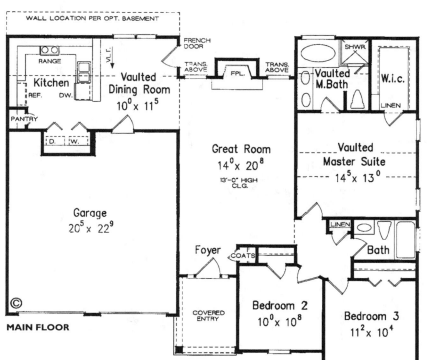

WALL LOCATION PER OPT. BASEMENT

RANGE
Kitchen
REF. DW.
PANTRY
D. W.

FRENCH DOOR
TRANS. ABOVE
FPL.
TRANS. ABOVE

Vaulted Dining Room 10⁰x 11⁵

Great Room 14⁰x 20⁸
13'-0" HIGH CLG.

SHWR.
Vaulted M.Bath
W.I.C.
LINEN

Vaulted Master Suite 14⁵x 13⁰

Garage 20⁵x 22⁹

LINEN
Bath

Foyer
COATS
COVERED ENTRY

Bedroom 2 10⁰x 10⁸

Bedroom 3 11²x 10⁴

MAIN FLOOR

Units	Single
Price Code	A
Total Finished	1,305 sq. ft.
Main Finished	1,305 sq. ft.
Garage Unfinished	418 sq. ft.
Dimensions	50'x50'
Foundation	Basement
	Crawlspace
	Slab
Bedrooms	3
Full Baths	1
Main Ceiling	8'
Max Ridge Height	23'4"
Roof Framing	Stick
Exterior Walls	2x4, 2x6

* Alternate foundation options available at an additional charge.
Please call 1-800-235-5700 for more information.

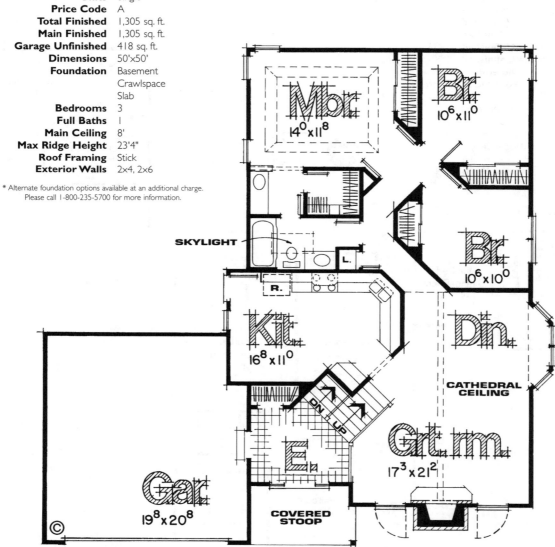

MAIN FLOOR

Design 20161

PHOTOGRAPHY: JOHN EHRENCLOU

Units	Single
Price Code	A
Total Finished	1,307 sq. ft.
Main Finished	1,307 sq. ft.
Basement Unfinished	1,298 sq. ft.
Garage Unfinished	462 sq. ft.
Dimensions	50'x40'
Foundation	Basement
	Crawlspace
	Slab
Bedrooms	3
Full Baths	2
Main Ceiling	8'
Max Ridge Height	19'
Roof Framing	Stick
Exterior Walls	2x6

**OPTIONAL
CRAWLSPACE/SLAB
FOUNDATION**

Please note: The photographed home may have been modified to suit homeowner preferences. If you order plans, have a builder or design professional check them against the photograph to confirm actual construction details.

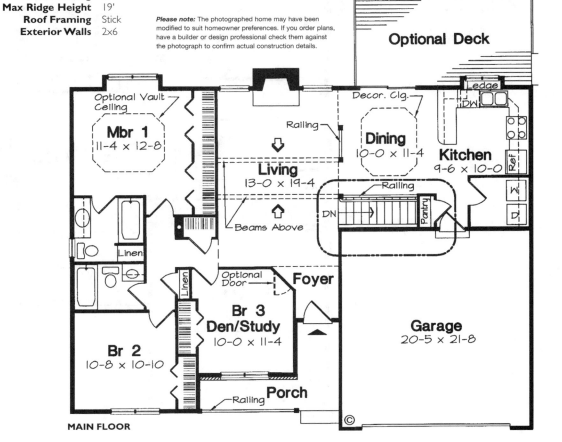

MAIN FLOOR

Design 68096

Units	Single
Price Code	A
Total Finished	1,311 sq. ft.
Main Finished	1,311 sq. ft.
Garage Unfinished	439 sq. ft.
Deck Unfinished	112 sq. ft.
Dimensions	34'8"x58'4"
Foundation	Crawlspace
	Slab
Bedrooms	3
Full Baths	2
Main Ceiling	9'
Max Ridge Height	22'6"
Exterior Walls	2x4

* Alternate foundation options available at an additional charge.
Please call 1-800-235-5700 for more information.

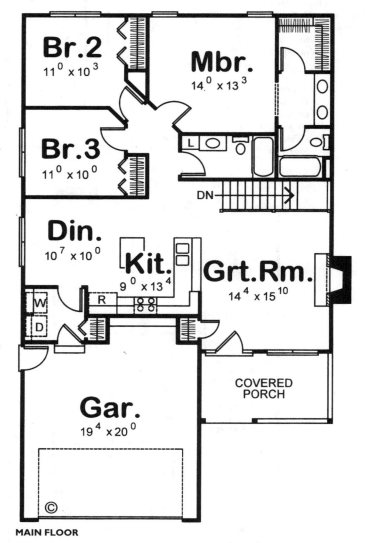

MAIN FLOOR

Design 24700

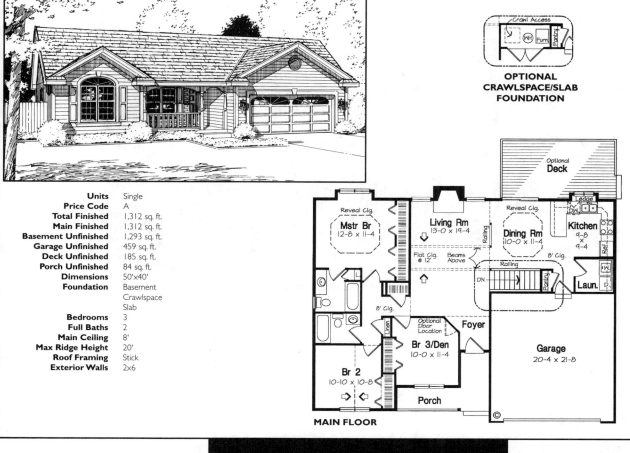

OPTIONAL CRAWLSPACE/SLAB FOUNDATION

Units	Single
Price Code	A
Total Finished	1,312 sq. ft.
Main Finished	1,312 sq. ft.
Basement Unfinished	1,293 sq. ft.
Garage Unfinished	459 sq. ft.
Deck Unfinished	185 sq. ft.
Porch Unfinished	84 sq. ft.
Dimensions	50'x40'
Foundation	Basement
	Crawlspace
	Slab
Bedrooms	3
Full Baths	2
Main Ceiling	8'
Max Ridge Height	20'
Roof Framing	Stick
Exterior Walls	2x6

MAIN FLOOR

Design 97731

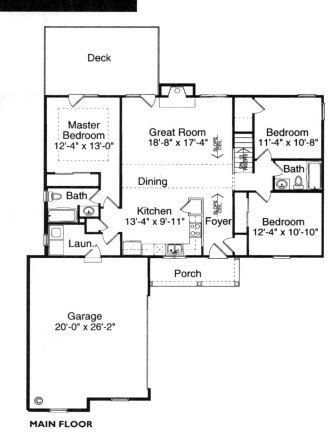

Units	Single
Price Code	A
Total Finished	1,315 sq. ft.
Main Finished	1,315 sq. ft.
Basement Unfinished	1,315 sq. ft.
Garage Unfinished	488 sq. ft.
Porch Unfinished	75 sq. ft.
Dimensions	50'x54'8"
Foundation	Basement
Bedrooms	3
Full Baths	2
Main Ceiling	8'
Max Ridge Height	18'
Roof Framing	Truss
Exterior Walls	2x4

MAIN FLOOR

Units	Single
Price Code	A
Total Finished	1,322 sq. ft.
Main Finished	1,322 sq. ft.
Garage Unfinished	528 sq. ft.
Dimensions	44'6"x58'2"
Foundation	Crawlspace
	Slab
Bedrooms	3
Full Baths	1
3/4 Baths	1
Main Ceiling	8'-10'
Max Ridge Height	19'4"
Roof Framing	Stick
Exterior Walls	2x4

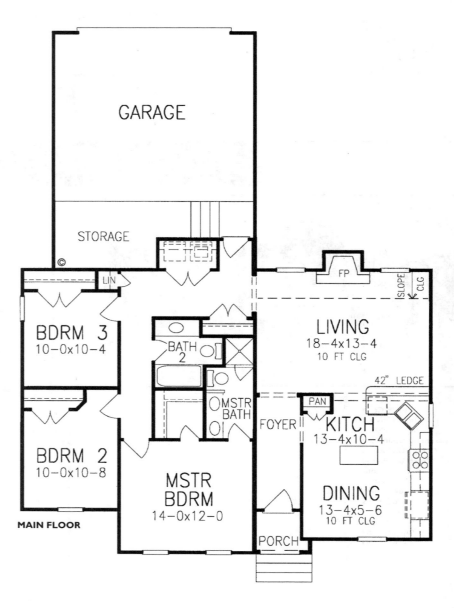

GARAGE

STORAGE

LIN

BDRM 3
10-0x10-4

BATH 2

LIVING
18-4x13-4
10 FT CLG

FP

SLOPE CLG

42" LEDGE

MSTR BATH

PAN

FOYER

KITCH
13-4x10-4

BDRM 2
10-0x10-8

MSTR BDRM
14-0x12-0

DINING
13-4x5-6
10 FT CLG

PORCH

MAIN FLOOR

Design 93072

Units	Single
Price Code	A
Total Finished	1,322 sq. ft.
Main Finished	1,322 sq. ft.
Garage Unfinished	528 sq. ft.
Porch Unfinished	72 sq. ft.
Dimensions	44'6"x58'2"
Foundation	Crawlspace
	Slab
Bedrooms	3
Full Baths	1
3/4 Baths	1
Main Ceiling	8'-10'
Max Ridge Height	19'8"
Roof Framing	Stick
Exterior Walls	2x4

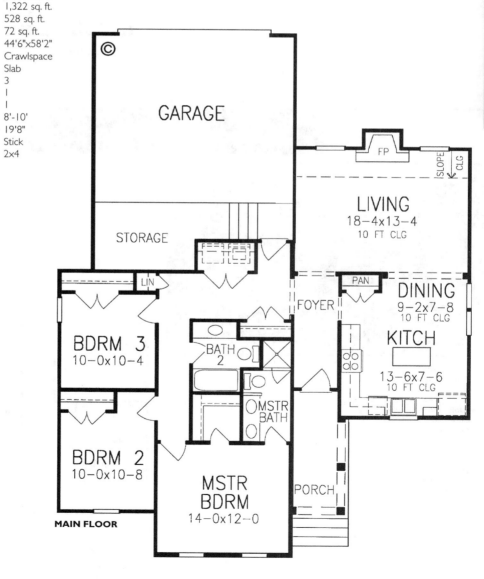

MAIN FLOOR

Design 65152

Units	Single
Price Code	A
Total Finished	1,328 sq. ft.
Main Finished	1,328 sq. ft.
Porch Unfinished	172 sq. ft.
Dimensions	46'8"x34'
Foundation	Basement
Bedrooms	3
Full Baths	1
Main Ceiling	8'
Max Ridge Height	29'
Roof Framing	Truss
Exterior Walls	2x6

MAIN FLOOR

Design 93453

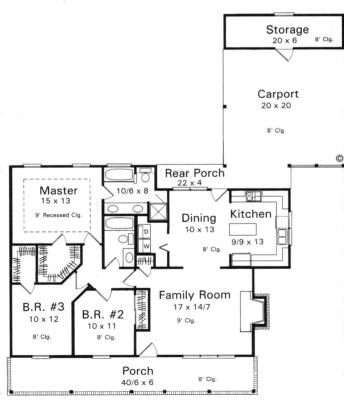

Units	Single
Price Code	A
Total Finished	1,333 sq. ft.
Main Finished	1,333 sq. ft.
Garage Unfinished	520 sq. ft.
Dimensions	55'6"x64'3"
Foundation	Crawlspace Slab
Bedrooms	3
Full Baths	2
Main Ceiling	8'
Max Ridge Height	19'5"
Roof Framing	Stick
Exterior Walls	2x4

MAIN FLOOR

Design 65096

Units	Single
Price Code	A
Total Finished	1,336 sq. ft.
Main Finished	1,336 sq. ft.
Garage Unfinished	325 sq. ft.
Deck Unfinished	40 sq. ft.
Porch Unfinished	100 sq. ft.
Dimensions	58'x36'
Foundation	Basement
Bedrooms	3
Full Baths	1
Main Ceiling	8'
Max Ridge Height	26'10"
Roof Framing	Truss
Exterior Walls	2×6

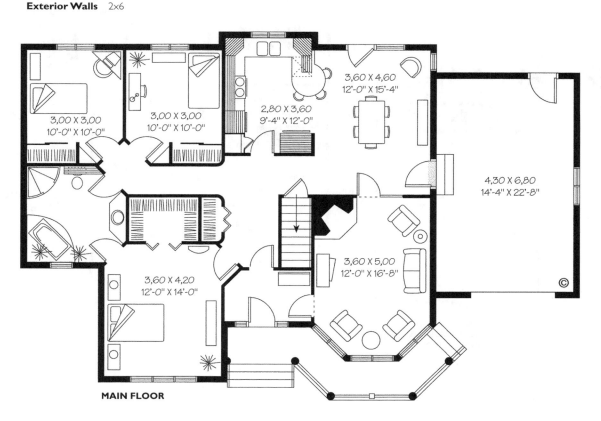

3,00 X 3,00
10'-0" X 10'-0"

3,00 X 3,00
10'-0" X 10'-0"

2,80 X 3,60
9'-4" X 12'-0"

3,60 X 4,60
12'-0" X 15'-4"

4,30 X 6,80
14'-4" X 22'-8"

3,60 X 4,20
12'-0" X 14'-0"

3,60 X 5,00
12'-0" X 16'-8"

MAIN FLOOR

Design 52024

Units	Single
Price Code	A
Total Finished	1,338 sq. ft.
Main Finished	1,338 sq. ft.
Basement Unfinished	1,360 sq. ft.
Dimensions	49'x48'
Foundation	Basement Crawlspace
Bedrooms	3
Full Baths	2
Main Ceiling	8'
Max Ridge Height	19'6"
Roof Framing	Stick
Exterior Walls	2x4

CAD **FILES AVAILABLE**
For more information call
800-235-5700

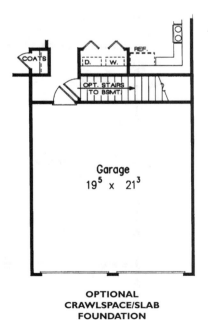

**OPTIONAL
CRAWLSPACE/SLAB
FOUNDATION**

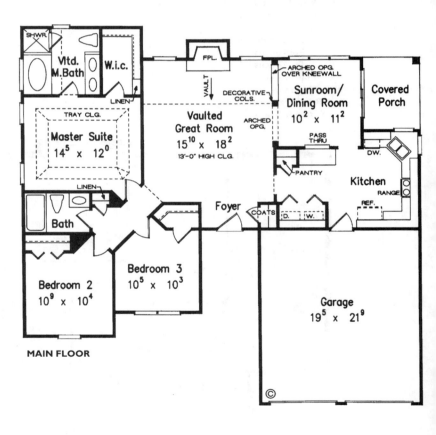

MAIN FLOOR

Design 52177

BONUS

Opt. Bonus Room 13⁵ x 19¹⁰

Units	Single
Price Code	A
Total Finished	1,342 sq. ft.
Main Finished	1,342 sq. ft.
Bonus Unfinished	350 sq. ft.
Basement Unfinished	1,340 sq. ft.
Garage Unfinished	459 sq. ft.
Dimensions	52'6"x39'10"
Foundation	Basement
	Crawlspace
	Slab
Bedrooms	3
Full Baths	2
Main Ceiling	9'
Second Ceiling	8'
Max Ridge Height	22'6"
Roof Framing	Stick
Exterior Walls	2x4

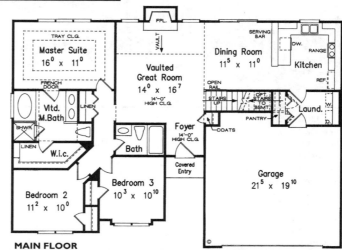

MAIN FLOOR

Design 62022

Units	Single
Price Code	A
Total Finished	1,342 sq. ft.
Main Finished	1,342 sq. ft.
Garage Unfinished	400 sq. ft.
Dimensions	32'8"x64'10"
Foundation	Crawlspace
	Slab
Bedrooms	3
Full Baths	2
Main Ceiling	9'
Roof Framing	Stick
Exterior Walls	2x4

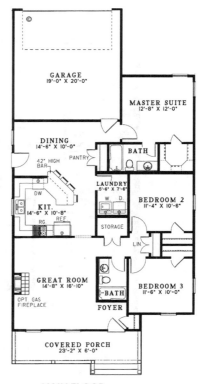

MAIN FLOOR

Units	Single
Price Code	A
Total Finished	1,342 sq. ft.
Main Finished	1,342 sq. ft.
Basement Unfinished	1,342 sq. ft.
Garage Unfinished	416 sq. ft.
Dimensions	57'x45'
Foundation	Basement
Bedrooms	3
Full Baths	2
Main Ceiling	9'
Max Ridge Height	23'5"
Roof Framing	Truss
Exterior Walls	2x6

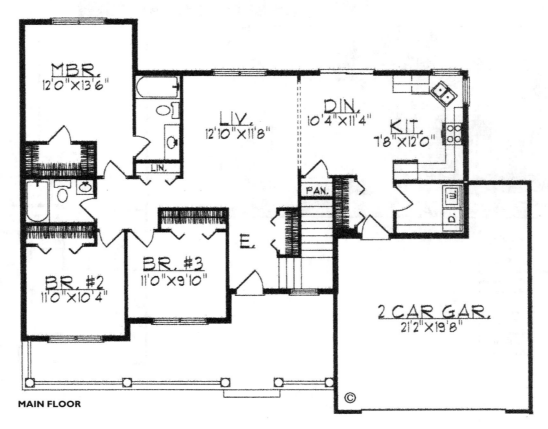

MAIN FLOOR

To order blueprints, call **800-235-5700** or visit us on the web, **familyhomeplans.com**

Design 98912

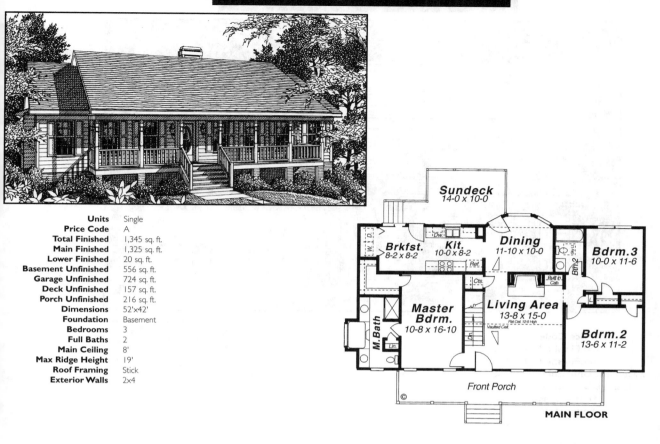

Units	Single
Price Code	A
Total Finished	1,345 sq. ft.
Main Finished	1,325 sq. ft.
Lower Finished	20 sq. ft.
Basement Unfinished	556 sq. ft.
Garage Unfinished	724 sq. ft.
Deck Unfinished	157 sq. ft.
Porch Unfinished	216 sq. ft.
Dimensions	52'x42'
Foundation	Basement
Bedrooms	3
Full Baths	2
Main Ceiling	8'
Max Ridge Height	19'
Roof Framing	Stick
Exterior Walls	2x4

Sundeck 14-0 x 10-0

Brkfst. 8-2 x 8-2

Kit. 10-0 x 8-2

Dining 11-10 x 10-0

Bdrm.3 10-0 x 11-6

Master Bdrm. 10-8 x 16-10

Living Area 13-8 x 15-0

Bdrm.2 13-6 x 11-2

M.Bath

Front Porch

MAIN FLOOR

Design 98434

Units	Single
Price Code	A
Total Finished	1,346 sq. ft.
Main Finished	1,346 sq. ft.
Basement Unfinished	1,358 sq. ft.
Garage Unfinished	395 sq. ft.
Dimensions	39'x51'
Foundation	Basement
	Crawlspace
	Slab
Bedrooms	3
Full Baths	2
Max Ridge Height	21'6"
Roof Framing	Stick
Exterior Walls	2x4

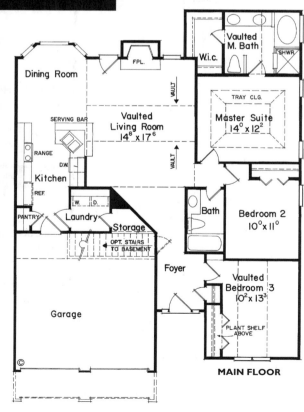

Dining Room

Vaulted M. Bath

Wi.c.

FPL.

Vaulted Living Room 14⁸ x 17⁶

TRAY CLG.

Master Suite 14⁰ x 12²

SERVING BAR

RANGE

DW

Kitchen

REF.

PANTRY

Laundry

Storage

OPT. STAIRS TO BASEMENT

Bath

Bedroom 2 10⁰ x 11⁰

Foyer

Garage

Vaulted Bedroom 3 10² x 13³

PLANT SHELF ABOVE

MAIN FLOOR

Design 97272

Units	Single
Price Code	A
Total Finished	1,354 sq. ft.
Main Finished	1,354 sq. ft.
Basement Unfinished	1,390 sq. ft.
Garage Unfinished	434 sq. ft.
Dimensions	47'x46'
Foundation	Basement
	Crawlspace
Bedrooms	3
Full Baths	2
Main Ceiling	9'
Max Ridge Height	24'9"
Roof Framing	Stick
Exterior Walls	2x4

CAD **FILES AVAILABLE**
For more information call
800-235-5700

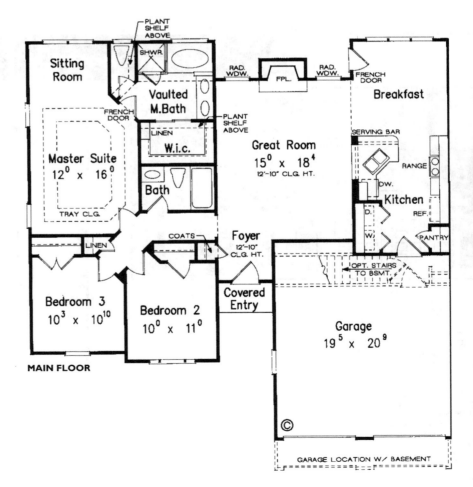

MAIN FLOOR

Design 20156

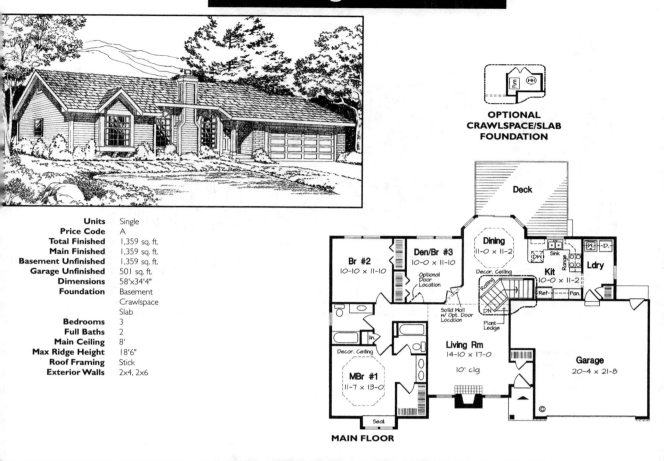

OPTIONAL CRAWLSPACE/SLAB FOUNDATION

Units	Single
Price Code	A
Total Finished	1,359 sq. ft.
Main Finished	1,359 sq. ft.
Basement Unfinished	1,359 sq. ft.
Garage Unfinished	501 sq. ft.
Dimensions	58'x34'4"
Foundation	Basement
	Crawlspace
	Slab
Bedrooms	3
Full Baths	2
Main Ceiling	8'
Max Ridge Height	18'6"
Roof Framing	Stick
Exterior Walls	2x4, 2x6

Deck

Br #2 10-10 x 11-10

Den/Br #3 10-0 x 11-10

Optional Door Location

Dining 11-0 x 11-2

Kit 10-0 x 11-2

Ldry

Decor. Ceiling

Solid Wall w/ Opt. Door Location

Plant Ledge

Living Rm 14-10 x 17-0 10' clg

Decor. Ceiling

MBr #1 11-7 x 13-0

Garage 20-4 x 21-8

Seat

MAIN FLOOR

Design 94982

Units	Single
Price Code	A
Total Finished	1,360 sq. ft.
Main Finished	1,360 sq. ft.
Garage Unfinished	544 sq. ft.
Dimensions	52'x46'
Foundation	Basement
Bedrooms	3
Full Baths	2
Max Ridge Height	18'
Roof Framing	Stick
Exterior Walls	2x4

* Alternate foundation options available at an additional charge. Please call 1-800-235-5700 for more information.

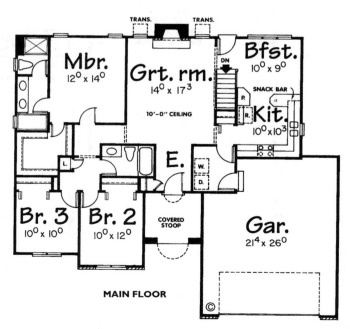

TRANS.   TRANS.

Mbr. 12⁰ x 14⁰

Grt. rm. 14⁰ x 17³
10'-0" CEILING

Bfst. 10⁰ x 9⁰

SNACK BAR

Kit. 10⁰ x 10³

E.

Br. 3 10⁰ x 10⁰

Br. 2 10⁰ x 12⁰

COVERED STOOP

Gar. 21⁴ x 26⁰

MAIN FLOOR

Units	Single
Price Code	A
Total Finished	1,363 sq. ft.
Main Finished	1,363 sq. ft.
Garage Unfinished	434 sq. ft.
Porch Unfinished	85 sq. ft.
Dimensions	56'10"x45'10"
Foundation	Crawlspace
	Slab
Bedrooms	3
Full Baths	2
Max Ridge Height	21'
Roof Framing	Stick
Exterior Walls	2x4

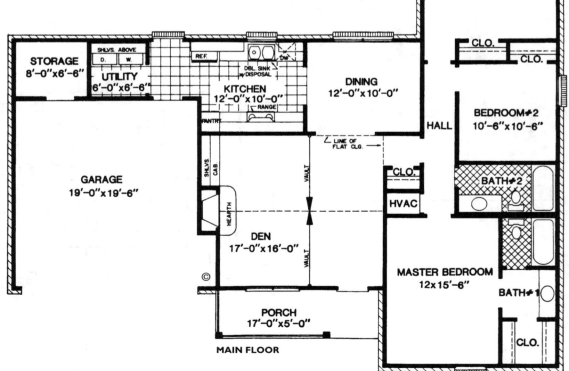

MAIN FLOOR

Design 94688

Units	Single
Price Code	A
Total Finished	1,363 sq. ft.
Main Finished	1,363 sq. ft.
Porch Unfinished	276 sq. ft.
Dimensions	30'x60'
Foundation	Slab
Bedrooms	3
Full Baths	2
Main Ceiling	9'
Max Ridge Height	25'9"
Roof Framing	Stick
Exterior Walls	2x4

Patio 16'x 6'

Master Bath

Porch 16'x 6'

Master Bedroom 13'4"x 13'

Future Storage

Future Carport 12'x 20'

Living 15'8"x 14'

Walk-In Closet

Bedroom 11'x 9'11"

Kitchen 11'x 11'

Bath

Dining 11'x 12'

Foyer

Bedroom 11'x 10'

Porch 30'x 6'

MAIN FLOOR

Design 98985

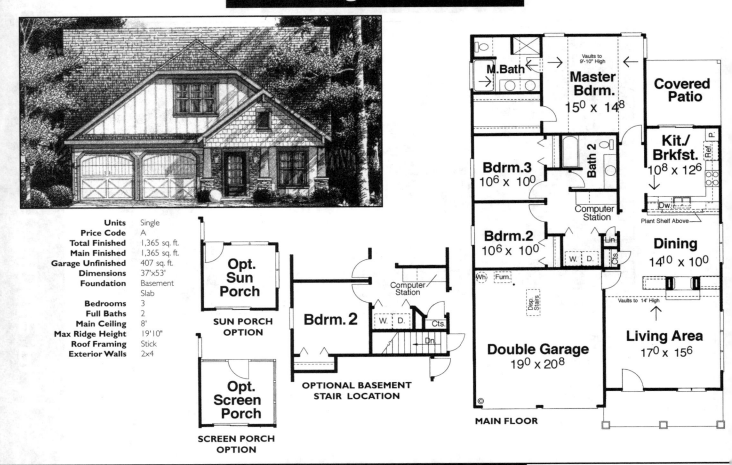

Units	Single
Price Code	A
Total Finished	1,365 sq. ft.
Main Finished	1,365 sq. ft.
Garage Unfinished	407 sq. ft.
Dimensions	37'x53'
Foundation	Basement
	Slab
Bedrooms	3
Full Baths	2
Main Ceiling	8'
Max Ridge Height	19'10"
Roof Framing	Stick
Exterior Walls	2x4

Opt. Sun Porch

SUN PORCH OPTION

Opt. Screen Porch

SCREEN PORCH OPTION

Bdrm. 2

OPTIONAL BASEMENT STAIR LOCATION

Computer Station

M.Bath

Master Bdrm.
15^0 x 14^8

Covered Patio

Bdrm.3
10^6 x 10^0

Bath 2

Kit./Brkfst.
10^8 x 12^6

Computer Station

Bdrm.2
10^6 x 10^0

Dining
14^{10} x 10^0

Vaults to 9'-10" High

Plant Shelf Above

Double Garage
19^0 x 20^8

Living Area
17^0 x 15^6

Vaults to 14' High

Disp. Stairs

Wh   Furn.

MAIN FLOOR

Design 99639

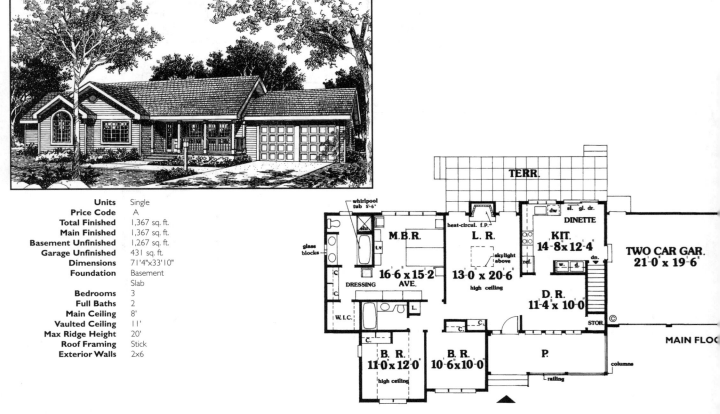

Units	Single
Price Code	A
Total Finished	1,367 sq. ft.
Main Finished	1,367 sq. ft.
Basement Unfinished	1,267 sq. ft.
Garage Unfinished	431 sq. ft.
Dimensions	71'4"x33'10"
Foundation	Basement
	Slab
Bedrooms	3
Full Baths	2
Main Ceiling	8'
Vaulted Ceiling	11'
Max Ridge Height	20'
Roof Framing	Stick
Exterior Walls	2x6

TERR.

whirlpool tub 5'-6"

glass blocks

M.B.R.
16-6 x 15-2

DRESSING AVE.

W.I.C.

heat-circul. f.p.

L.R.
13-0 x 20-6
high ceiling

skylight above

DINETTE

KIT.
14-8x12-4

dw   sl. gl. dr.

ref.

TWO CAR GAR.
21-0 x 19-6

D.R.
11-4 x 10-0

STOR.

B.R.
11-0 x 12-0
high ceiling

B.R.
10-6 x 10-0

P.

columns

railing

MAIN FLOO

Design 98411

Units	Single
Price Code	A
Total Finished	1,373 sq. ft.
Main Finished	1,373 sq. ft.
Basement Unfinished	1,386 sq. ft.
Dimensions	50'4"x45'
Foundation	Basement
	Crawlspace
Bedrooms	3
Full Baths	2
Main Ceiling	9'
Max Ridge Height	23'6"
Roof Framing	Stick
Exterior Walls	2x4, 2x6

CAD FILES AVAILABLE
For more information call
800-235-5700

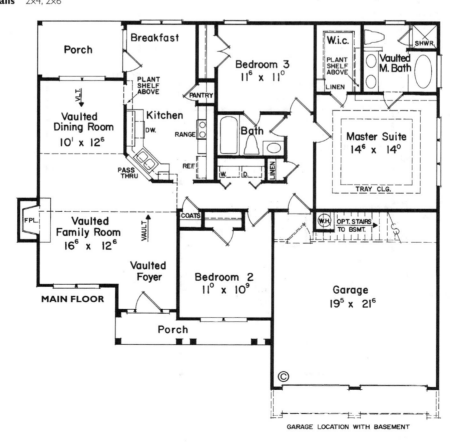

Units	Single
Price Code	A
Total Finished	1,377 sq. ft.
Main Finished	1,377 sq. ft.
Bonus Unfinished	349 sq. ft.
Porch Unfinished	588 sq. ft.
Dimensions	44'x51'
Foundation	Crawlspace
	Slab
Bedrooms	3
Full Baths	1
Main Ceiling	9'
Second Ceiling	8'
Roof Framing	Truss
Exterior Walls	2x4

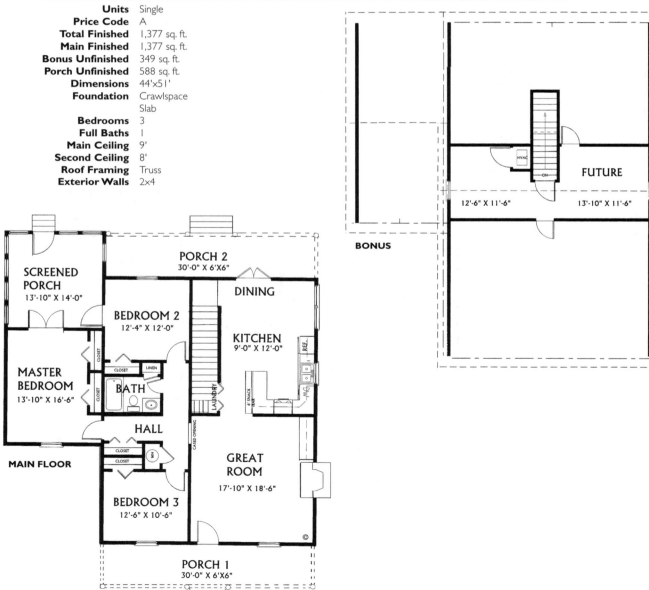

BONUS

FUTURE

12'-6" X 11'-6"   13'-10" X 11'-6"

MAIN FLOOR

SCREENED PORCH
13'-10" X 14'-0"

MASTER BEDROOM
13'-10" X 16'-6"

BEDROOM 2
12'-4" X 12'-0"

CLOSET CLOSET LINEN

BATH

HALL

CLOSET
CLOSET WH

BEDROOM 3
12'-6" X 10'-6"

PORCH 2
30'-0" X 6'X6"

DINING

KITCHEN
9'-0" X 12'-0"

REF.

6' SNACK BAR

LAUNDRY

CASED OPENING

GREAT ROOM
17'-10" X 18'-6"

PORCH 1
30'-0" X 6'X6"

Design 82003

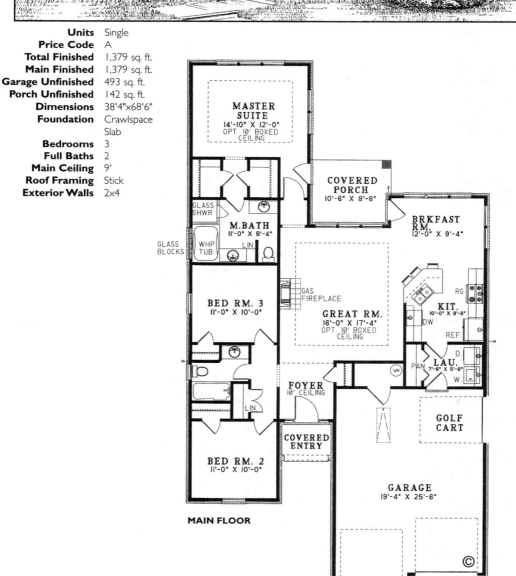

Units	Single
Price Code	A
Total Finished	1,379 sq. ft.
Main Finished	1,379 sq. ft.
Garage Unfinished	493 sq. ft.
Porch Unfinished	142 sq. ft.
Dimensions	38'4"x68'6"
Foundation	Crawlspace Slab
Bedrooms	3
Full Baths	2
Main Ceiling	9'
Roof Framing	Stick
Exterior Walls	2x4

MASTER SUITE
14'-10" X 12'-0"
OPT. 10' BOXED CEILING

COVERED PORCH
10'-6" X 8'-8"

BRKFAST RM.
12'-0" X 9'-4"

GLASS SHWR

M.BATH
11'-0" X 8'-4"

GLASS BLOCKS

WHP TUB

LIN

GAS FIREPLACE

KIT.
10'-0" X 9'-6"

RG

REF.

BED RM. 3
11'-0" X 10'-0"

GREAT RM.
16'-0" X 17'-4"
OPT. 10' BOXED CEILING

DW

PAN

LAU.
7'-6" X 5'-6"

D

W

WH

LIN

FOYER
10' CEILING

GOLF CART

COVERED ENTRY

BED RM. 2
11'-0" X 10'-0"

GARAGE
19'-4" X 25'-6"

MAIN FLOOR

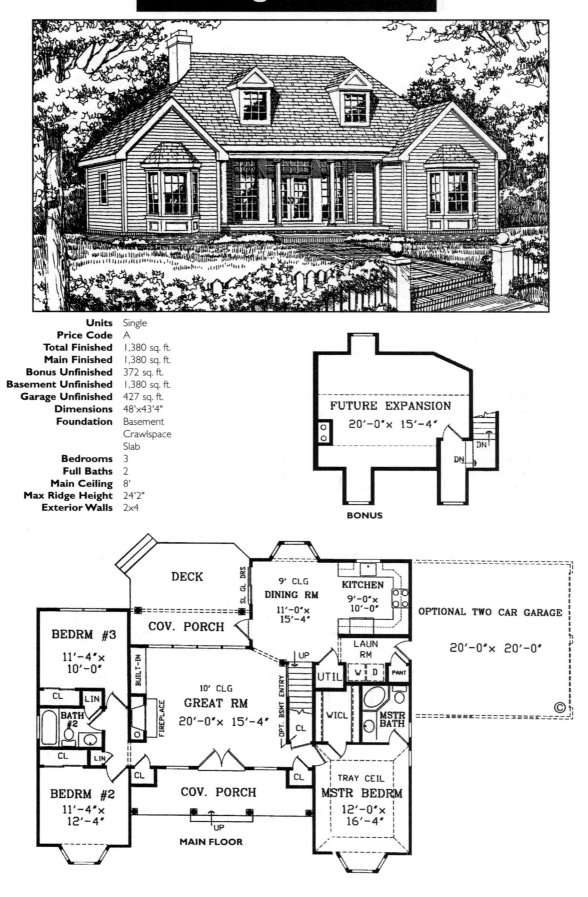

Units	Single
Price Code	A
Total Finished	1,380 sq. ft.
Main Finished	1,380 sq. ft.
Bonus Unfinished	372 sq. ft.
Basement Unfinished	1,380 sq. ft.
Garage Unfinished	427 sq. ft.
Dimensions	48'x43'4"
Foundation	Basement
	Crawlspace
	Slab
Bedrooms	3
Full Baths	2
Main Ceiling	8'
Max Ridge Height	24'2"
Exterior Walls	2x4

FUTURE EXPANSION
20'-0" x 15'-4"

DN

DN

BONUS

DECK

SL. GL. DRS.

9' CLG
DINING RM
11'-0" x
15'-4"

KITCHEN
9'-0" x
10'-0"

OPTIONAL TWO CAR GARAGE
20'-0" x 20'-0"

©

COV. PORCH

BEDRM #3
11'-4" x
10'-0"

BUILT-IN

10' CLG
GREAT RM
20'-0" x 15'-4"

FIREPLACE

UP

OPT. BSMT ENTRY

LAUN
RM

UTIL

W D

PANT

CL

WICL

MSTR
BATH

CL

LIN

BATH
#2

CL

LIN

BEDRM #2
11'-4" x
12'-4"

CL

COV. PORCH

UP

CL

TRAY CEIL
MSTR BEDRM
12'-0" x
16'-4"

MAIN FLOOR

Design 92425

DECK 13'-10" x 9'-7"

DINING 10'-0" x 12'-0" 9' CEILING

36" FIREPLACE WITH TV NICHE ABOVE

9' CEILING

MASTER BDRM 16'-0" x 12'-0"

HERS HIS LINEN

FAMILY ROOM 14'-0" x 18'-0" 12' CEILING

KITCH 10'-0" x 15'-0"

PANTRY

BEDRM 2 11'-0" x 12'-8" 9' CEILING

BEDRM 3 11'-0" x 12'-0" 9' CEILING

9' CEILING

PORCH

OPTIONAL BASEMENT STAIR LOCATION

MAIN FLOOR

GARAGE 19'-8" x 20'-0"

Units	Single
Price Code	A
Total Finished	1,381 sq. ft.
Main Finished	1,381 sq. ft.
Dimensions	50'x50'4"
Foundation	Basement
	Slab
Bedrooms	3
Full Baths	2
Main Ceiling	9'
Vaulted Ceiling	12'
Max Ridge Height	18'8"
Roof Framing	Truss
Exterior Walls	2x4

Design 96924

PHOTOGRAPHY: COURTESY OF THE DESIGNER

Please note: The photographed home may have been modified to suit homeowner preferences. If you order plans, have a builder or design professional check them against the photograph to confirm actual construction details.

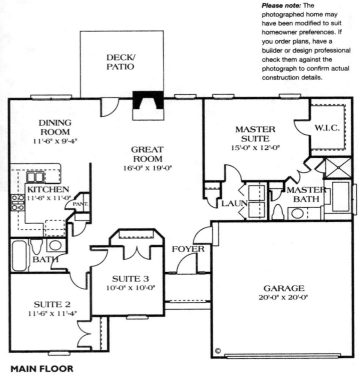

DECK/ PATIO

DINING ROOM 11'-6" x 9'-4"

GREAT ROOM 16'-0" x 19'-0"

MASTER SUITE 15'-0" x 12'-0"

W.I.C.

KITCHEN 11'-6" x 11'-0"

PANT.

LAUN

MASTER BATH

FOYER

BATH

SUITE 3 10'-0" x 10'-0"

GARAGE 20'-0" x 20'-0"

SUITE 2 11'-6" x 11'-4"

MAIN FLOOR

Units	Single
Price Code	A
Total Finished	1,383 sq. ft.
Main Finished	1,383 sq. ft.
Basement Unfinished	1,460 sq. ft.
Garage Unfinished	416 sq. ft.
Deck Unfinished	120 sq. ft.
Porch Unfinished	29 sq. ft.
Dimensions	50'x40'
Foundation	Basement
	Crawlspace
	Slab
Bedrooms	3
Full Baths	2
Main Ceiling	9'
Max Ridge Height	20'6"
Roof Framing	Truss
Exterior Walls	2x4

Units	Single
Price Code	A
Total Finished	1,385 sq. ft.
Main Finished	1,385 sq. ft.
Garage Unfinished	658 sq. ft.
Dimensions	53'x29'8"
Foundation	Basement
Bedrooms	3
Full Baths	1
3/4 Baths	1
Max Ridge Height	15'8"
Roof Framing	Stick
Exterior Walls	2x4

* Alternate foundation options available at an additional charge.
Please call 1-800-235-5700 for more information.

MAIN FLOOR

LOWER FLOOR

Units	Single
Price Code	A
Total Finished	1,387 sq. ft.
Main Finished	1,387 sq. ft.
Dimensions	43'x63'10"
Foundation	Slab
Bedrooms	2
Full Baths	2

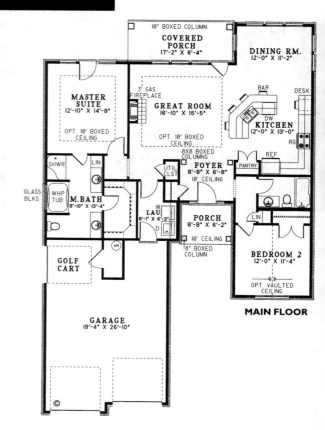

MAIN FLOOR

Design 65165

Units	Single
Price Code	A
Total Finished	1,387 sq. ft.
Main Finished	1,387 sq. ft.
Porch Unfinished	126 sq. ft.
Dimensions	44'8"x34'
Foundation	Basement
Bedrooms	2
Full Baths	1
Main Ceiling	8'
Max Ridge Height	44'8"
Roof Framing	Truss
Exterior Walls	2x6

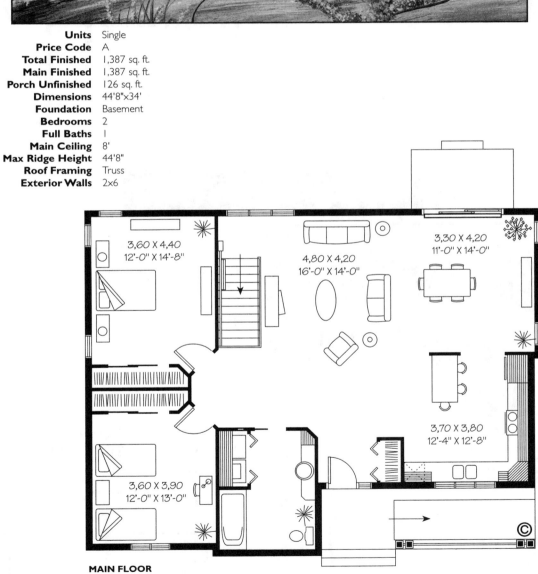

3,60 X 4,40
12'-0" X 14'-8"

4,80 X 4,20
16'-0" X 14'-0"

3,30 X 4,20
11'-0" X 14'-0"

3,70 X 3,80
12'-4" X 12'-8"

3,60 X 3,90
12'-0" X 13'-0"

MAIN FLOOR

Units	Single
Price Code	A
Total Finished	1,388 sq. ft.
Main Finished	1,388 sq. ft.
Garage Unfinished	400 sq. ft.
Dimensions	48'x46'
Foundation	Crawlspace
	Slab
Bedrooms	3
Full Baths	2
Main Ceiling	8'
Max Ridge Height	18'
Roof Framing	Truss
Exterior Walls	2x4

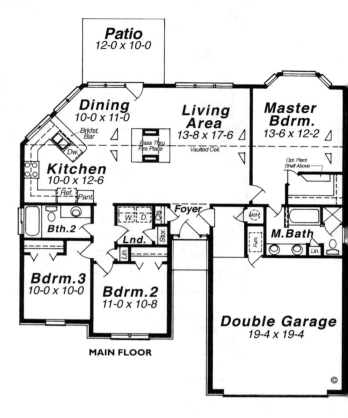

Patio 12-0 x 10-0

Dining 10-0 x 11-0

Living Area 13-8 x 17-6 Vaulted Ceil.

Master Bdrm. 13-6 x 12-2

Brkfst. Bar

Pass Thru Fire Place

Opt. Plant Shelf Above

Kitchen 10-0 x 12-6

Ref. Pant

Foyer

M. Bath

Bth.2

W. D.

Lnd.

Stor.

Fum

Lin.

Bdrm.3 10-0 x 10-0

Bdrm.2 11-0 x 10-8

Double Garage 19-4 x 19-4

MAIN FLOOR

Units	Single
Price Code	A
Total Finished	1,390 sq. ft.
Main Finished	1,390 sq. ft.
Garage Unfinished	590 sq. ft.
Porch Unfinished	66 sq. ft.
Dimensions	67'4"x32'10"
Foundation	Crawlspace
	Slab
Bedrooms	3
Full Baths	2
Main Ceiling	9'
Max Ridge Height	22'6"
Roof Framing	Stick
Exterior Walls	2x4

sto 4 x 8⁶   **sto** 4 x 8⁶

w   d   ref   dw

util 7 x 7

kit 10 x 11⁶

dining 12 x 11

br 2 12 x 11

garage 22 x 22

rng

lin

ledge

mbr 13 x 15

den 16 x 17

br 3 12 x 11

porch 4 x 16

MAIN FLOOR

Design 34054

Units	Single
Price Code	A
Total Finished	1,400 sq. ft.
Main Finished	1,400 sq. ft.
Basement Unfinished	1,400 sq. ft.
Garage Unfinished	528 sq. ft.
Dimensions	50'x28'
Foundation	Basement
	Crawlspace
	Slab
Bedrooms	3
Full Baths	2
Main Ceiling	8'
Max Ridge Height	17'
Roof Framing	Stick
Exterior Walls	2x4, 2x6

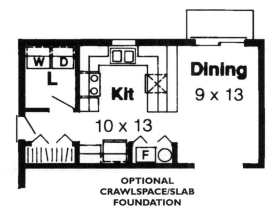

OPTIONAL CRAWLSPACE/SLAB FOUNDATION

W D
L
Kit
10 x 13
Dining 9 x 13
F

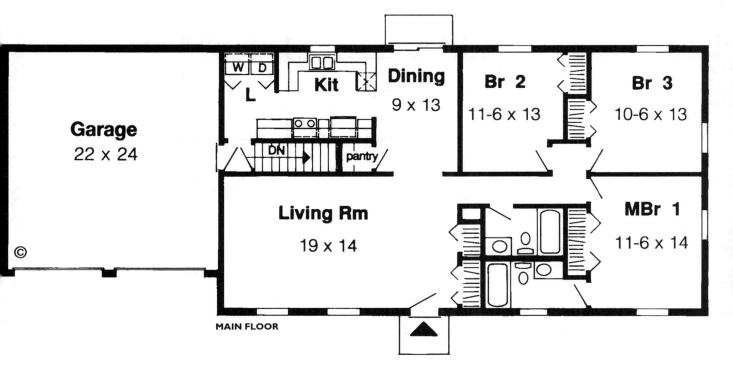

MAIN FLOOR

Garage 22 x 24

W D
L
Kit
Dining 9 x 13
Br 2 11-6 x 13
Br 3 10-6 x 13

DN
pantry

Living Rm 19 x 14

MBr 1 11-6 x 14

Design 62024

Units	Single
Price Code	A
Total Finished	1,401 sq. ft.
Main Finished	1,401 sq. ft.
Garage Unfinished	488 sq. ft.
Porch Unfinished	314 sq. ft.
Dimensions	39'x70'6"
Foundation	Crawlspace
	Slab
Bedrooms	3
Full Baths	2
Main Ceiling	9'
Roof Framing	Stick
Exterior Walls	2x6

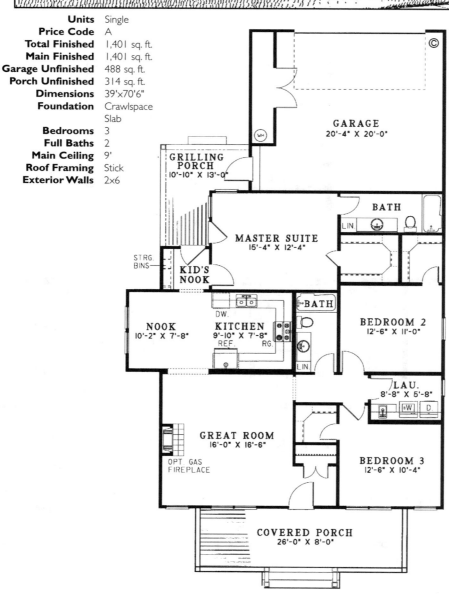

GARAGE
20'-4" X 20'-0"

GRILLING PORCH
10'-10" X 13'-0"

BATH

MASTER SUITE
15'-4" X 12'-4"

STRG. BINS

KID'S NOOK

NOOK
10'-2" X 7'-8"

KITCHEN
9'-10" X 7'-8"

DW. REF. RG.

BATH

LIN.

BEDROOM 2
12'-6" X 11'-0"

LAU.
8'-8" X 5'-8"

W D

GREAT ROOM
16'-0" X 16'-6"

OPT. GAS FIREPLACE

BEDROOM 3
12'-6" X 10'-4"

COVERED PORCH
26'-0" X 8'-0"

MAIN FLOOR

To order blueprints, call **800-235-5700** or visit us on the web, **familyhomeplans.com**

Design 94690

Units	Single
Price Code	A
Total Finished	1,401 sq. ft.
Main Finished	1,401 sq. ft.
Porch Unfinished	137 sq. ft.
Dimensions	30'x59'10"
Foundation	Slab
Bedrooms	3
Full Baths	2
Main Ceiling	9'
Max Ridge Height	20'6"
Roof Framing	Stick
Exterior Walls	2x4

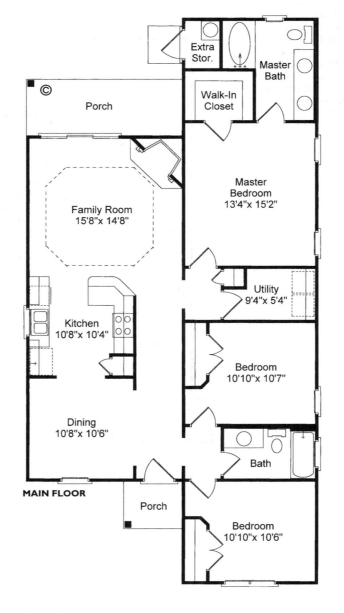

Extra Stor.

Master Bath

Porch

Walk-In Closet

Master Bedroom
13'4"x 15'2"

Family Room
15'8"x 14'8"

Utility
9'4"x 5'4"

Kitchen
10'8"x 10'4"

Bedroom
10'10"x 10'7"

Dining
10'8"x 10'6"

MAIN FLOOR

Bath

Porch

Bedroom
10'10"x 10'6"

Units	Single
Price Code	A
Total Finished	1,404 sq. ft.
Main Finished	1,404 sq. ft.
Dimensions	62'x48'2"
Foundation	Slab
Bedrooms	3
Full Baths	2
Max Ridge Height	20'7"

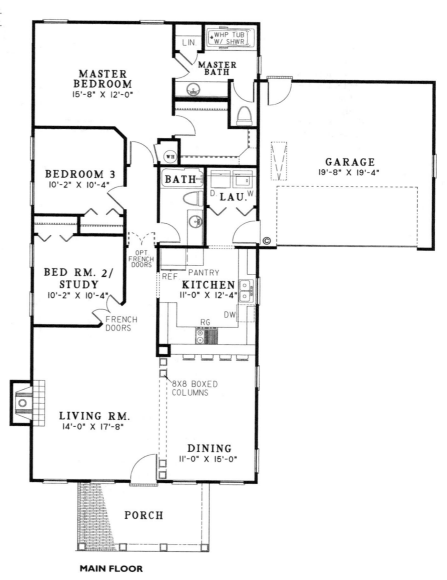

MAIN FLOOR

Design 94689

Units	Single
Price Code	A
Total Finished	1,405 sq. ft.
Main Finished	1,405 sq. ft.
Dimensions	42'x51'
Foundation	Slab
Bedrooms	3
Full Baths	2
Main Ceiling	8'
Max Ridge Height	19'4"
Roof Framing	Stick
Exterior Walls	2x4

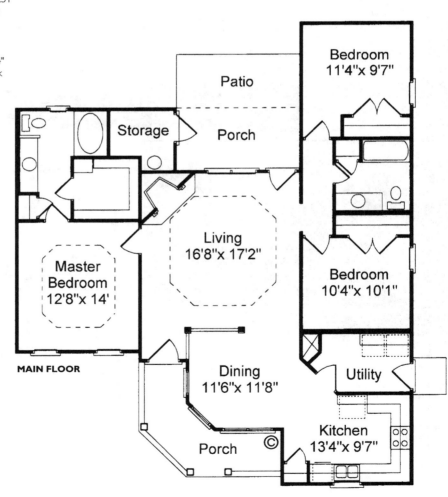

Storage

Patio

Porch

Bedroom
11'4"x 9'7"

Living
16'8"x 17'2"

Master
Bedroom
12'8"x 14'

Bedroom
10'4"x 10'1"

MAIN FLOOR

Dining
11'6"x 11'8"

Utility

Porch

Kitchen
13'4"x 9'7"

Design 99928

Units	Single
Price Code	A
Total Finished	1,407 sq. ft.
Main Finished	1,407 sq. ft.
Basement Unfinished	1,286 sq. ft.
Garage Unfinished	457 sq. ft.
Porch Unfinished	108 sq. ft.
Dimensions	64'x39'4"
Foundation	Basement
Bedrooms	3
Full Baths	2
Main Ceiling	9'
Vaulted Ceiling	11'6"
Max Ridge Height	21'6"
Roof Framing	Truss
Exterior Walls	2x6

Design 91807

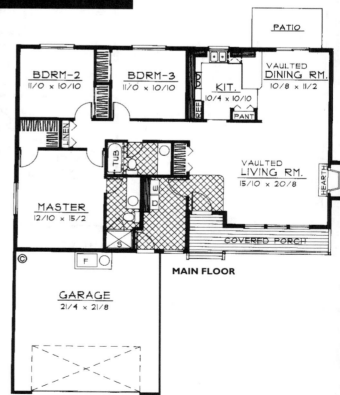

Units	Single
Price Code	A
Total Finished	1,410 sq. ft.
Main Finished	1,410 sq. ft.
Garage Unfinished	484 sq. ft.
Dimensions	47'x54'
Foundation	Crawlspace
	Slab
Bedrooms	3
Full Baths	1
3/4 Baths	1
Max Ridge Height	18'
Exterior Walls	2x6

Design 90990

Units	Single
Price Code	A
Total Finished	1,423 sq. ft.
Main Finished	1,423 sq. ft.
Basement Unfinished	1,423 sq. ft.
Garage Unfinished	399 sq. ft.
Dimensions	54'x49'
Foundation	Basement
Bedrooms	3
Full Baths	1
3/4 Baths	1
Exterior Walls	2x6

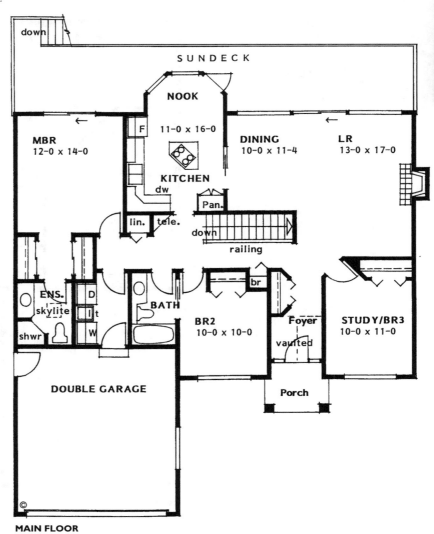

MAIN FLOOR

Design 65155

Units	Single
Price Code	A
Total Finished	1,426 sq. ft.
Main Finished	1,426 sq. ft.
Basement Unfinished	1,426 sq. ft.
Garage Unfinished	440 sq. ft.
Dimensions	42'x56'
Foundation	Basement
Bedrooms	3
Full Baths	2
Main Ceiling	8'
Max Ridge Height	21'5"
Roof Framing	Truss
Exterior Walls	2x4

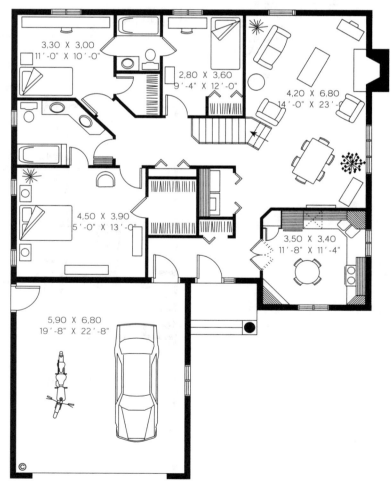

MAIN FLOOR

To order blueprints, call **800-235-5700** or visit us on the web, **familyhomeplans.com**

Design 55019

Units	Single
Price Code	A
Total Finished	1,428 sq. ft.
Main Finished	1,428 sq. ft.
Garage Unfinished	528 sq. ft.
Dimensions	68'x38'
Foundation	Basement
Bedrooms	3
Full Baths	2
Main Ceiling	8'
Max Ridge Height	20'
Roof Framing	Truss

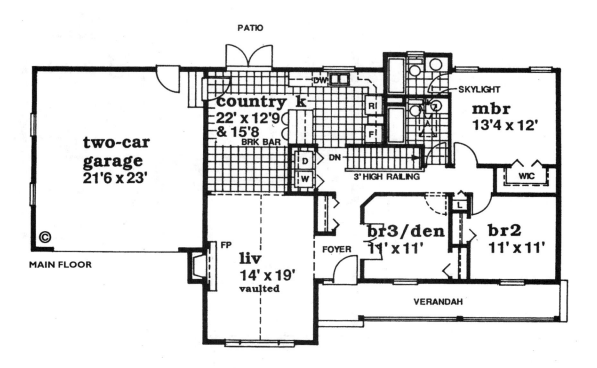

PATIO

two-car garage
21'6 x 23'

country k
22' x 12'9
& 15'8

BRK BAR

DW

SKYLIGHT

mbr
13'4 x 12'

RI

F

D

W

DN

3' HIGH RAILING

WIC

MAIN FLOOR

FP

liv
14' x 19'
vaulted

FOYER

br3/den
11' x 11'

L

br2
11' x 11'

VERANDAH

Units	Single
Price Code	A
Total Finished	1,431 sq. ft.
Main Finished	1,431 sq. ft.
Garage Unfinished	410 sq. ft.
Deck Unfinished	110 sq. ft.
Dimensions	44'x57'1"
Foundation	Slab
Bedrooms	3
Full Baths	2
Max Ridge Height	23'2"
Roof Framing	Stick
Exterior Walls	2x4

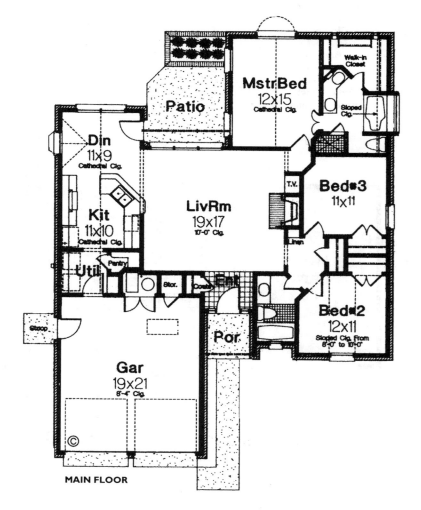

MAIN FLOOR

Design 97274

FILES AVAILABLE
For more information call
800-235-5700

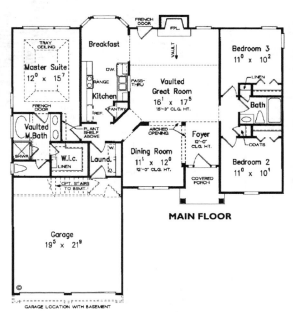

MAIN FLOOR

GARAGE LOCATION WITH BASEMENT

Units	Single
Price Code	A
Total Finished	1,432 sq. ft.
Main Finished	1,432 sq. ft.
Basement Unfinished	1,454 sq. ft.
Garage Unfinished	440 sq. ft.
Dimensions	49'x52'4"
Foundation	Basement
	Crawlspace
Bedrooms	3
Full Baths	2
Max Ridge Height	24'2"
Roof Framing	Stick
Exterior Walls	2x4

Design 96802

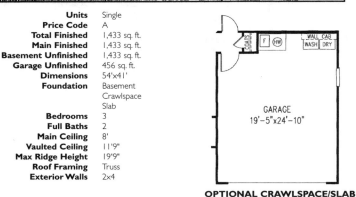

OPTIONAL CRAWLSPACE/SLAB
FOUNDATION

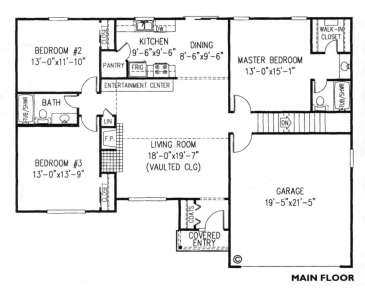

MAIN FLOOR

Units	Single
Price Code	A
Total Finished	1,433 sq. ft.
Main Finished	1,433 sq. ft.
Basement Unfinished	1,433 sq. ft.
Garage Unfinished	456 sq. ft.
Dimensions	54'x41'
Foundation	Basement
	Crawlspace
	Slab
Bedrooms	3
Full Baths	2
Main Ceiling	8'
Vaulted Ceiling	11'9"
Max Ridge Height	19'9"
Roof Framing	Truss
Exterior Walls	2x4

Units	Single
Price Code	A
Total Finished	1,433 sq. ft.
Main Finished	1,433 sq. ft.
Garage Unfinished	504 sq. ft.
Dimensions	50'x58'
Foundation	Basement
Bedrooms	3
Full Baths	2
Main Ceiling	8'
Max Ridge Height	19'4"
Roof Framing	Stick
Exterior Walls	2x4

* Alternate foundation options available at an additional charge.
Please call 1-800-235-5700 for more information.

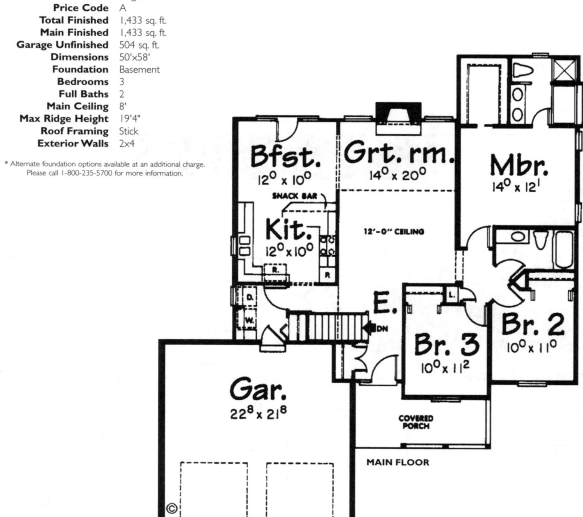

Bfst. 12⁰ x 10⁰

Grt. rm. 14⁰ x 20⁰

Mbr. 14⁰ x 12¹

SNACK BAR

Kit. 12⁰ x 10⁰

12'-0" CEILING

E.

Br. 3 10⁰ x 11²

Br. 2 10⁰ x 11⁰

Gar. 22⁸ x 21⁸

COVERED PORCH

MAIN FLOOR

Design 96509

Units	Single
Price Code	A
Total Finished	1,438 sq. ft.
Main Finished	1,438 sq. ft.
Garage Unfinished	486 sq. ft.
Deck Unfinished	282 sq. ft.
Porch Unfinished	126 sq. ft.
Dimensions	54'x57'
Foundation	Crawlspace
	Slab
Bedrooms	3
Full Baths	2
Max Ridge Height	19'
Roof Framing	Stick
Exterior Walls	2x4

GARAGE 22 × 22

DECK

DINING 12 × 11

KITCHEN 12 × 10

BATH

MASTER SUITE 13 × 15

PANTRY

REFG

BATH

GREAT RM 17 × 18

WASH DRY

SHELVES

STOR

CLOSET

BEDRM 14 × 11

BEDRM 11 × 13

FOYER

PORCH

MAIN FLOOR

Design 97660

Units	Single
Price Code	A
Total Finished	1,441 sq. ft.
Main Finished	1,441 sq. ft.
Basement Unfinished	1,441 sq. ft.
Dimensions	50'x50'4"
Foundation	Basement
	Crawlspace
Bedrooms	3
Full Baths	2
Main Ceiling	9'
Max Ridge Height	22'4"
Roof Framing	Stick
Exterior Walls	2x4

FPL.

Vaulted Dining Room 11⁰ x 10⁰

Vaulted Master Suite 12⁰ x 15⁰

VAULT

FRENCH DOOR

SHWR

Vltd. M.Bath

PASS THRU

PASS THRU

RANGE

DW.

Vaulted Great Room 17⁶ x 22⁰
18'-0" HIGH CLG.

W.i.c.

LINEN

Kitchen

REF.

COATS

W. D.

Bath

LINEN

Breakfast

PLANT SHELF ABOVE

Vaulted Foyer

PANTRY

OPT. STAIRS TO BSMT.

Storage

Vaulted Bedroom 2 10⁰ x 10⁴

Bedroom 3 10⁴ x 10⁰

Garage 20⁸ x 21⁸

MAIN FLOOR

Design 62025

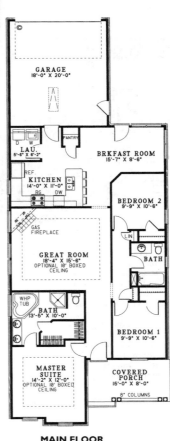

Units	Single
Price Code	A
Total Finished	1,442 sq. ft.
Main Finished	1,442 sq. ft.
Garage Unfinished	417 sq. ft.
Porch Unfinished	172 sq. ft.
Dimensions	34'8"x71'
Foundation	Crawlspace
	Slab
Bedrooms	3
Full Baths	2
Main Ceiling	9'
Exterior Walls	2x4

GARAGE
19'-0" X 19'-8"

LAU.
5'-8" X 8'-2"

BATH

GRILLING
PORCH
6'-6" X 10'-0"

PANTRY

MASTER SUITE
13'-4" X 11'-5"

DINING
14'-4" X 11'-0"

42" H.
BAR

OPT GAS
FIREPLACE

PANTRY

GREAT ROOM
23'-8" X 13'-0"

REF.

KIT.
10'-0" X 11'-2"

RG.

DW

LIN

BATH

LIN

FOYER
13'-4" X 4'-6"

BEDROOM 2
10'-0" X 9'-6"

BEDROOM 3
10'-0" X 10'-8"

COVERED
PORCH
13'-4" X 8'-0"

MAIN FLOOR

Design 62027

Units	Single
Price Code	A
Total Finished	1,449 sq. ft.
Main Finished	1,449 sq. ft.
Garage Unfinished	360 sq. ft.
Porch Unfinished	148 sq. ft.
Dimensions	29'2"x76'10"
Foundation	Crawlspace
	Slab
Bedrooms	3
Full Baths	2
Main Ceiling	9'
Exterior Walls	2x4

GARAGE
18'-0" X 20'-0"

PANTRY

LAU.
5'-6" X 8'-2"

BRKFAST ROOM
15'-7" X 8'-6"

REF.

KITCHEN
14'-0" X 11'-0"

RG.

DW

BEDROOM 2
9'-9" X 10'-6"

LIN

BATH

GAS
FIREPLACE

GREAT ROOM
18'-4" X 15'-6"
OPTIONAL 10' BOXED
CEILING

WHP
TUB

BATH
13'-5" X 10'-0"

PANTRY

BEDROOM 1
9'-9" X 10'-6"

MASTER
SUITE
14'-2" X 12'-0"
OPTIONAL 10' BOXED
CEILING

COVERED
PORCH
15'-0" X 8'-0"

8" COLUMNS

MAIN FLOOR

Design 24718

Units	Single
Price Code	A
Total Finished	1,452 sq. ft.
Main Finished	1,452 sq. ft.
Garage Unfinished	584 sq. ft.
Deck Unfinished	158 sq. ft.
Porch Unfinished	89 sq. ft.
Dimensions	67'x47'
Foundation	Crawlspace
	Slab
Bedrooms	3
Full Baths	2
Main Ceiling	8'
Max Ridge Height	21'
Roof Framing	Stick
Exterior Walls	2x4

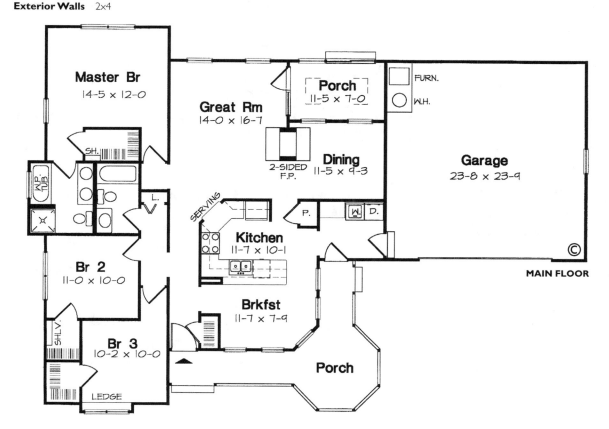

MAIN FLOOR

Units	Single
Price Code	A
Total Finished	1,454 sq. ft.
Main Finished	1,454 sq. ft.
Dimensions	67'x34'10"
Foundation	Basement
	Crawlspace
	Slab
Bedrooms	3
Full Baths	2
Max Ridge Height	16'2"
Roof Framing	Stick
Exterior Walls	2x4

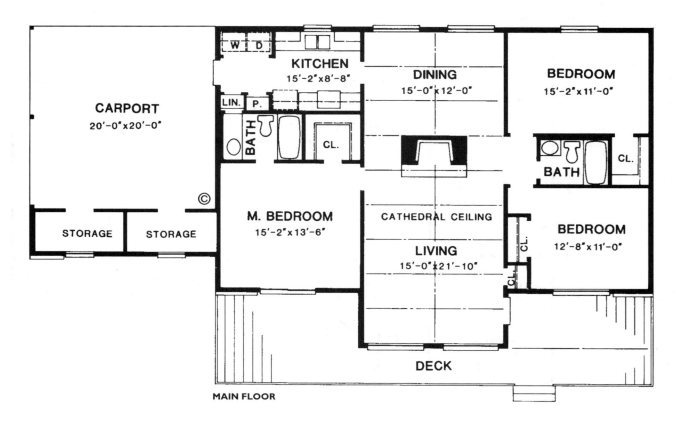

MAIN FLOOR

Design 20164

PHOTOGRAPHY: GAUTHIER ROOFING AND SIDING

Units	Single
Price Code	A
Total Finished	1,456 sq. ft.
Main Finished	1,456 sq. ft.
Basement Unfinished	1,448 sq. ft.
Garage Unfinished	452 sq. ft.
Dimensions	50'x45'4"
Foundation	Basement
	Crawlspace
	Slab
Bedrooms	3
Full Baths	2
Main Ceiling	8'
Max Ridge Height	19'
Roof Framing	Stick
Exterior Walls	2x6

Please note: The photographed home may have been modified to suit homeowner preferences. If you order plans, have a builder or design professional check them against the photograph to confirm actual construction details.

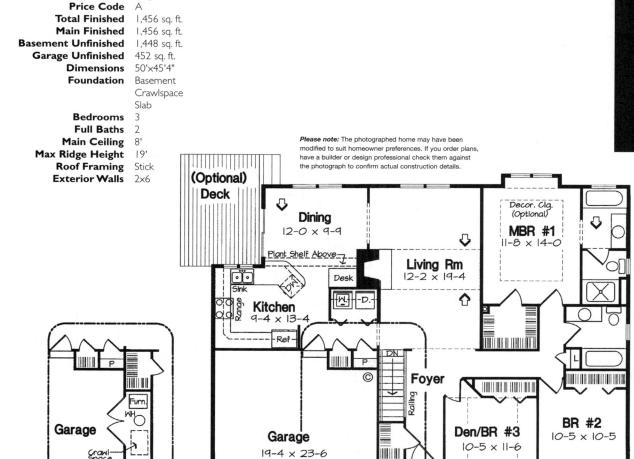

OPTIONAL CRAWLSPACE/SLAB FOUNDATION

MAIN FLOOR

Units	Single
Price Code	A
Total Finished	1,459 sq. ft.
Main Finished	1,459 sq. ft.
Basement Unfinished	1,466 sq. ft.
Garage Unfinished	390 sq. ft.
Dimensions	51'x53'4"
Foundation	Basement
	Crawlspace
Bedrooms	3
Full Baths	2
Main Ceiling	9'
Max Ridge Height	24'
Roof Framing	Stick
Exterior Walls	2x4

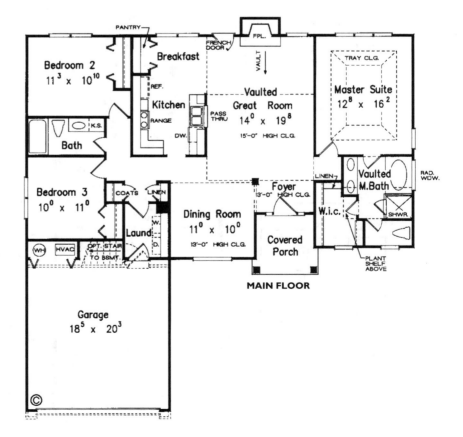

MAIN FLOOR

Design 97137

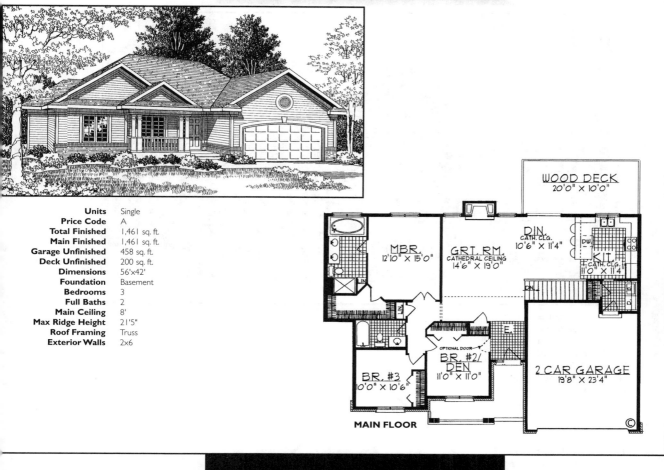

Units	Single
Price Code	A
Total Finished	1,461 sq. ft.
Main Finished	1,461 sq. ft.
Garage Unfinished	458 sq. ft.
Deck Unfinished	200 sq. ft.
Dimensions	56'x42'
Foundation	Basement
Bedrooms	3
Full Baths	2
Main Ceiling	8'
Max Ridge Height	21'5"
Roof Framing	Truss
Exterior Walls	2x6

WOOD DECK 20'0" X 10'0"

MBR. 12'10" X 15'0"

GRT. RM. CATHEDRAL CEILING 14'6" X 19'0"

DIN. CATH. CLG. 10'6" X 11'4"

KIT. CATH. CLG. 11'0" X 11'4

BR. #3 10'0" X 10'6"

BR. #2/ DEN 11'0" X 11'0"

OPTIONAL DOOR

2 CAR GARAGE 19'8" X 23'4"

MAIN FLOOR

Design 93165

Units	Single
Price Code	A
Total Finished	1,472 sq. ft.
Main Finished	1,472 sq. ft.
Basement Unfinished	1,472 sq. ft.
Garage Unfinished	424 sq. ft.
Dimensions	48'x56'4"
Foundation	Basement
Bedrooms	3
Full Baths	2
Max Ridge Height	19'8"
Roof Framing	Stick
Exterior Walls	2x6

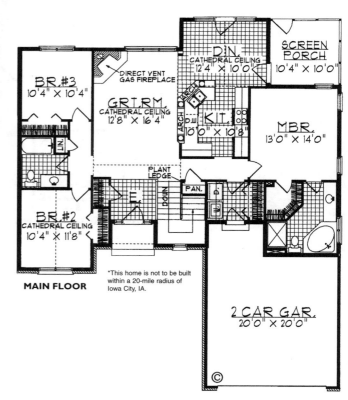

BR. #3 10'4" X 10'4"

DIRECT VENT GAS FIREPLACE

DIN. CATHEDRAL CEILING 12'4" X 10'0"

SCREEN PORCH 10'4" X 10'0"

GRT. RM. CATHEDRAL CEILING 12'8" X 16'4"

KIT. 10'0" X 10'8"

MBR. 13'0" X 14'0"

BR. #2 CATHEDRAL CEILING 10'4" X 11'8"

PLANT LEDGE

DOWN

PAN.

MAIN FLOOR

*This home is not to be built within a 20-mile radius of Iowa City, IA.

2 CAR GAR. 20'0" X 20'0"

Units	Single
Price Code	A
Total Finished	1,475 sq. ft.
Main Finished	1,475 sq. ft.
Garage Unfinished	455 sq. ft.
Porch Unfinished	234 sq. ft.
Dimensions	43'x43'
Foundation	Crawlspace
	Slab
Bedrooms	3
Full Baths	2
Max Ridge Height	24'
Roof Framing	Stick
Exterior Walls	2x4

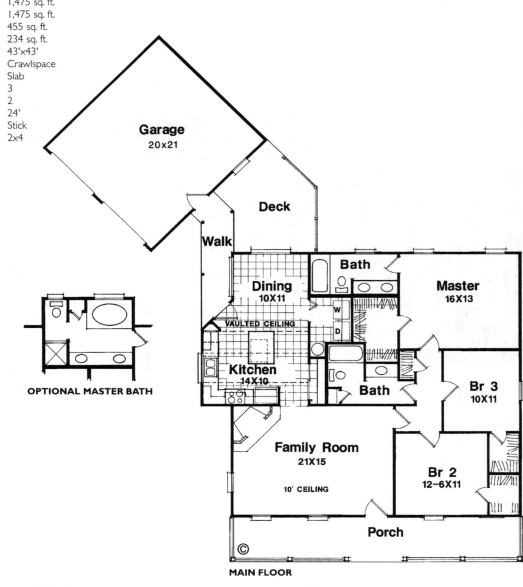

OPTIONAL MASTER BATH

Garage 20x21

Deck

Walk

Dining 10X11

VAULTED CEILING

Bath

Master 16X13

Kitchen 14X10

Bath

Br 3 10X11

Family Room 21X15

10' CEILING

Br 2 12-6X11

Porch

MAIN FLOOR

Design 90689

Units	Single
Price Code	A
Total Finished	1,476 sq. ft.
Main Finished	1,476 sq. ft.
Basement Unfinished	1,361 sq. ft.
Garage Unfinished	548 sq. ft.
Dimensions	75'9"x34'6"
Foundation	Basement
	Slab
Bedrooms	3
Full Baths	2
Max Ridge Height	19'
Roof Framing	Stick
Exterior Walls	2x6

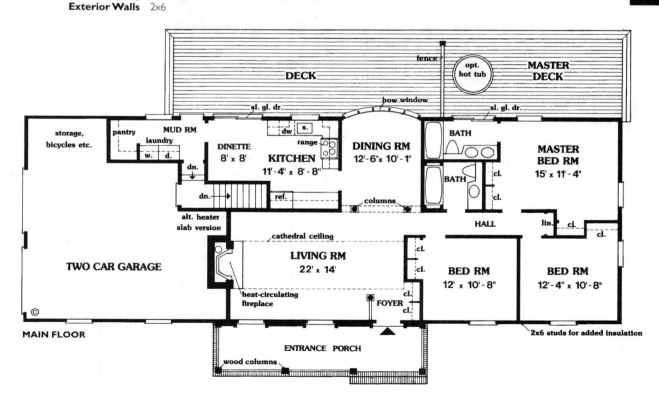

MAIN FLOOR

Design 94828

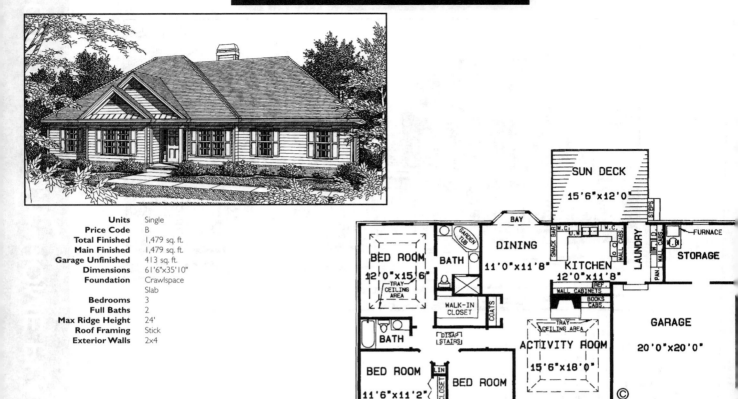

Units	Single
Price Code	B
Total Finished	1,479 sq. ft.
Main Finished	1,479 sq. ft.
Garage Unfinished	413 sq. ft.
Dimensions	61'6"x35'10"
Foundation	Crawlspace
	Slab
Bedrooms	3
Full Baths	2
Max Ridge Height	24'
Roof Framing	Stick
Exterior Walls	2x4

SUN DECK 15'6"x12'0"

BAY

DINING 11'0"x11'8"

BED ROOM 12'0"x15'6" TRAY CEILING AREA

BATH

W.C. W.C.

SNACK BAR

KITCHEN 12'0"x11'8"

WALL CABS.

LAUNDRY

FURNACE

STORAGE

WALL CABINETS

BOOKS CABS.

WALK-IN CLOSET

COATS

BATH

DISAP. STAIRS

BED ROOM 11'6"x11'2"

LIN CLOSET CLOSET

BED ROOM 10'6"x14'0"

TRAY CEILING AREA

ACTIVITY ROOM 15'6"x18'0"

GARAGE 20'0"x20'0"

STOOP

STEP

ALCOVE

WOOD COLUMN

BRICK WATERTABLE

MAIN FLOOR

Design 61032

Units	Single
Price Code	A
Total Finished	1,485 sq. ft.
Main Finished	1,485 sq. ft.
Dimensions	51'6"x49'
Foundation	Crawlspace
	Slab
Bedrooms	3
Full Baths	2

DINING ROOM 11'-0" X 9'-4"

ATRIUM DOOR

WHP TUB W/ SHWR

M.BATH 15'-8" X 10'-8"

LIN

BREAKFAST ROOM 10'-0" X 7'-8"

OPEN BAR

GAS FIREPLACE

KITCHEN 15'-2" X 10'-8"

REF

D.W.

GREAT ROOM 9' BOXED CEILING 13'-6" X 19'-8"

MASTER SUITE 9' BOXED CEILING 15'-8" X 12'-0"

BATH

PAN

HVAC

WH

BEDROOM 2 10'-2" X 10'-8"

LIN

BEDROOM 3 10'-0" X 10'-8"

FOYER 6'-8" X 7'-0"

GARAGE 20'-10" X 20'-0"

MAIN FLOOR

PORCH 9' CEIL 16'-5" X 5'-0"

Design 82026

1,001-1,500 sq. ft. HOME PLANS

Units	Single
Price Code	A
Total Finished	1,485 sq. ft.
Main Finished	1,485 sq. ft.
Garage Unfinished	415 sq. ft.
Porch Unfinished	180 sq. ft.
Dimensions	51'6"x49'10"
Foundation	Crawlspace
	Slab
Bedrooms	3
Full Baths	2
Main Ceiling	9'
Roof Framing	Stick
Exterior Walls	2x4

MAIN FLOOR

Units	Single
Price Code	A
Total Finished	1,485 sq. ft.
Main Finished	1,485 sq. ft.
Garage Unfinished	701 sq. ft.
Dimensions	51'6"x63'
Foundation	Crawlspace
Bedrooms	3
Full Baths	2
Max Ridge Height	22'
Roof Framing	Stick/Truss
Exterior Walls	2x6

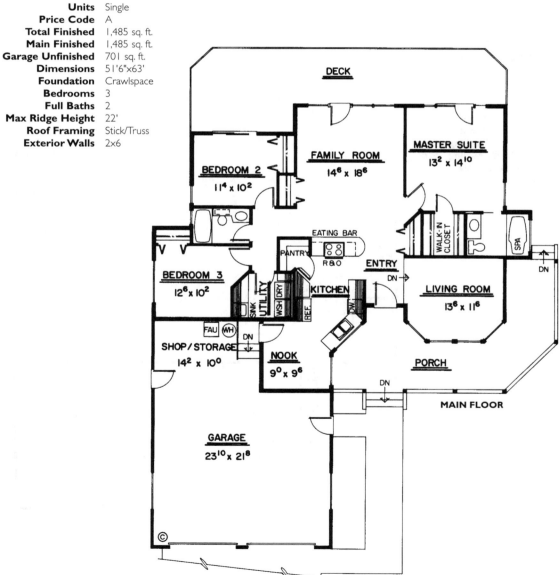

Design 34154

Units	Single
Price Code	A
Total Finished	1,486 sq. ft.
Main Finished	1,486 sq. ft.
Garage Unfinished	462 sq. ft.
Dimensions	56'x48'
Foundation	Basement
	Crawlspace
	Slab
Bedrooms	3
Full Baths	2
Main Ceiling	8'
Max Ridge Height	18'
Roof Framing	Stick
Exterior Walls	2x4, 2x6

OPTIONAL CRAWLSPACE/SLAB FOUNDATION

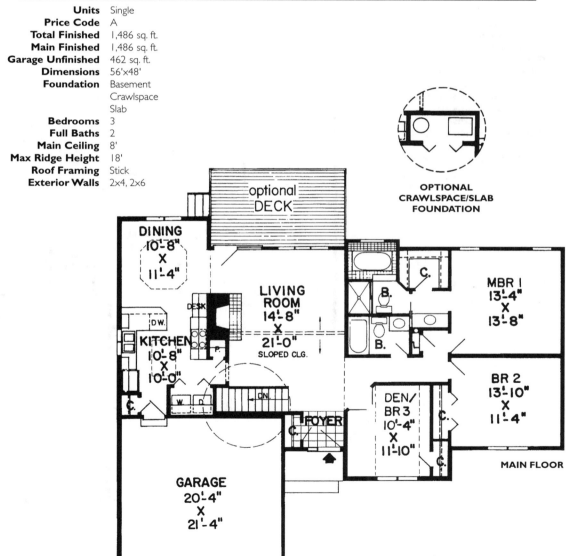

DINING
10'-8"
X
11'-4"

optional
DECK

LIVING
ROOM
14'-8"
X
21'-0"
SLOPED CLG.

DESK

MBR 1
13'-4"
X
13'-8"

B.

B.

C.

KITCHEN
10'-8"
X
10'-0"

DW.

W D

DN

FOYER

DEN/
BR 3
10'-4"
X
11'-10"

BR 2
13'-10"
X
11'-4"

C.

C.

C.

C.

GARAGE
20'-4"
X
21'-4"

MAIN FLOOR

Units	Single
Price Code	F
Total Finished	1,487 sq. ft.
Main Finished	1,487 sq. ft.
Garage Unfinished	567 sq. ft.
Porch Unfinished	104 sq. ft.
Dimensions	52'x65'6"
Foundation	Crawlspace
Bedrooms	3
Full Baths	2
Max Ridge Height	22'2"
Exterior Walls	2x6
Roof Framing	Stick/Truss

** Alternate foundation options available at an additional charge.
Please call 1-800-235-5700 for more information.*

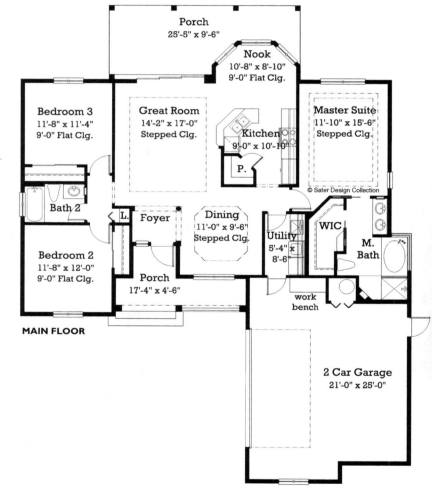

MAIN FLOOR

Design 64182

Units	Single
Price Code	F
Total Finished	1,487 sq. ft.
Main Finished	1,487 sq. ft.
Garage Unfinished	567 sq. ft.
Porch Unfinished	99 sq. ft.
Dimensions	52'6"x66'
Foundation	Crawlspace
Bedrooms	3
Full Baths	2
Max Ridge Height	24'2"
Roof Framing	Stick/Truss
Exterior Walls	2x6

* Alternate foundation options available at an additional charge.
Please call 1-800-235-5700 for more information.

MAIN FLOOR

Porch 25'-5" x 9'-6"
Nook 10'-8" x 8'-10" 9'-0" Flat Clg.
Bedroom 3 11'-8" x 11'-4" 9'-0" Flat Clg.
Great Room 14'-2" x 17'-0" Stepped Clg.
Kitchen 9'-0" x 10'-10"
Master Suite 11'-10" x 15'-8" Stepped Clg.
Bath 2
Foyer
Dining 11'-0" x 9'-6" Stepped Clg.
Utility 5'-4" x 8'-6"
WIC
M. Bath
Bedroom 2 11'-8" x 12'-0" 9'-0" Flat Clg.
Porch 16'-4" x 4'-6"
work bench
2 Car Garage 21'-0" x 25'-0"
© Sater Design Collection

Design 64183

Units	Single
Price Code	F
Total Finished	1,487 sq. ft.
Main Finished	1,487 sq. ft.
Garage Unfinished	567 sq. ft.
Porch Unfinished	99 sq. ft.
Dimensions	52'6"x66'
Foundation	Crawlspace
Bedrooms	3
Full Baths	2
Max Ridge Height	24'2"
Exterior Walls	2x6

* Alternate foundation options available at an additional charge.
Please call 1-800-235-5700 for more information.

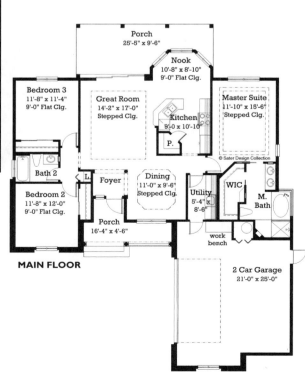

MAIN FLOOR

Porch 25'-5" x 9'-6"
Nook 10'-8" x 8'-10" 9'-0" Flat Clg.
Bedroom 3 11'-8" x 11'-4" 9'-0" Flat Clg.
Great Room 14'-2" x 17'-0" Stepped Clg.
Kitchen 9'-0 x 10'-10"
Master Suite 11'-10" x 15'-6" Stepped Clg.
Bath 2
Foyer
Dining 11'-0" x 9'-6" Stepped Clg.
Utility 5'-4" x 8'-6"
WIC
M. Bath
Bedroom 2 11'-8" x 12'-0" 9'-0" Flat Clg.
Porch 16'-4" x 4'-6"
work bench
2 Car Garage 21'-0" x 25'-0"
© Sater Design Collection

Units	Single
Price Code	A
Total Finished	1,490 sq. ft.
Main Finished	1,490 sq. ft.
Garage Unfinished	386 sq. ft.
Porch Unfinished	20 sq. ft.
Dimensions	31'6"x72'10"
Foundation	Crawlspace
	Slab
Bedrooms	3
Full Baths	2
Main Ceiling	9'
Exterior Walls	2x4

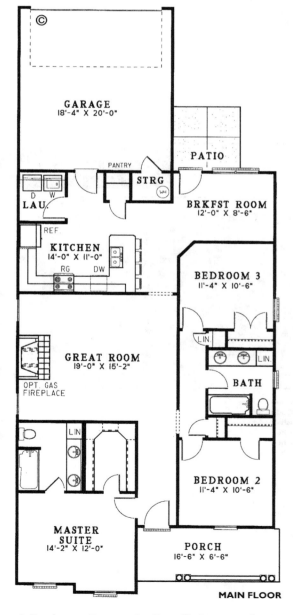

MAIN FLOOR

Design 97382

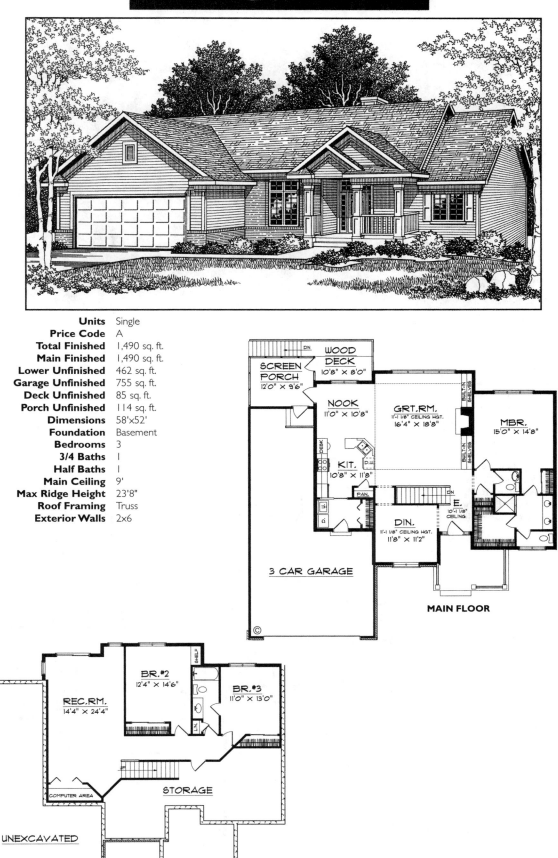

Units	Single
Price Code	A
Total Finished	1,490 sq. ft.
Main Finished	1,490 sq. ft.
Lower Unfinished	462 sq. ft.
Garage Unfinished	755 sq. ft.
Deck Unfinished	85 sq. ft.
Porch Unfinished	114 sq. ft.
Dimensions	58'x52'
Foundation	Basement
Bedrooms	3
3/4 Baths	1
Half Baths	1
Main Ceiling	9'
Max Ridge Height	23'8"
Roof Framing	Truss
Exterior Walls	2x6

MAIN FLOOR

SCREEN PORCH 12'0" × 9'6"

WOOD DECK 10'8" × 8'0"

NOOK 11'0" × 10'8"

GRT. RM. 11'-1 1/8" CEILING HGT. 16'4" × 18'8"

MBR. 15'0" × 14'8"

KIT. 10'8" × 11'8"

DIN. 11'-1 1/8" CEILING HGT. 11'8" × 11'2"

3 CAR GARAGE

LOWER FLOOR

REC. RM. 14'4" × 24'4"

BR. #2 12'4" × 14'6"

BR. #3 11'0" × 13'0"

COMPUTER AREA

STORAGE

UNEXCAVATED

PHOTOGRAPHY: JOHN EHRENCLOU

Units	Single
Price Code	A
Total Finished	1,492 sq. ft.
Main Finished	1,492 sq. ft.
Basement Unfinished	1,486 sq. ft.
Garage Unfinished	462 sq. ft.
Dimensions	56'x48'
Foundation	Basement
	Crawlspace
	Slab
Bedrooms	3
Full Baths	2
Main Ceiling	8'
Vaulted Ceiling	13'
Max Ridge Height	19'
Roof Framing	Stick
Exterior Walls	2x4, 2x6

Please note: The photographed home may have been modified to suit homeowner preferences. If you order plans, have a builder or design professional check them against the photograph to confirm actual construction details.

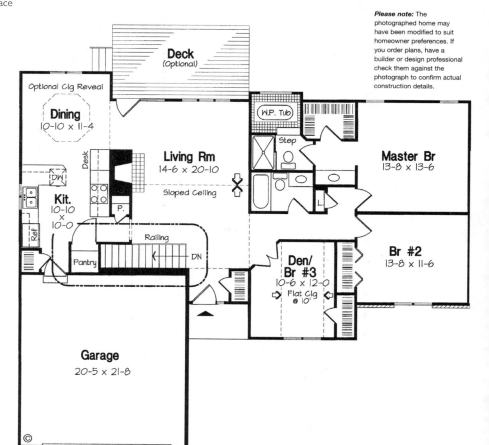

OPTIONAL CRAWLSPACE/SLAB FOUNDATION

MAIN FLOOR

Design 99106

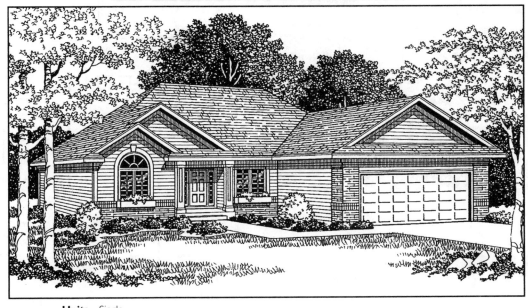

Units	Single
Price Code	A
Total Finished	1,495 sq. ft.
Main Finished	1,495 sq. ft.
Basement Unfinished	1,495 sq. ft.
Dimensions	48'x58'8"
Foundation	Basement
Bedrooms	3
Full Baths	2
Max Ridge Height	20'6"
Roof Framing	Truss
Exterior Walls	2x4

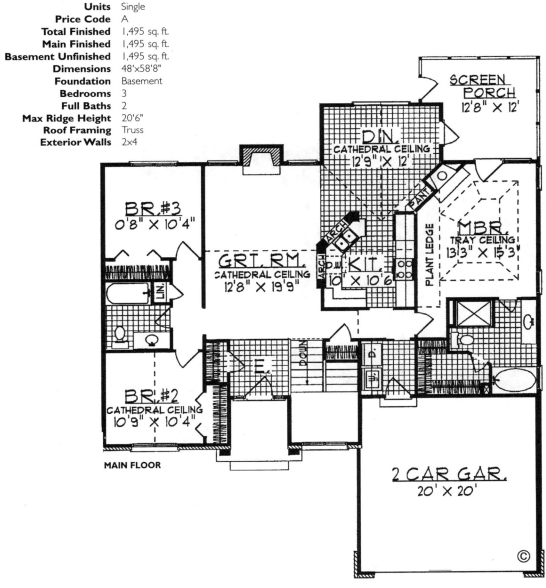

SCREEN PORCH
12'8" X 12'

DIN.
CATHEDRAL CEILING
12'9" X 12'

MBR
TRAY CEILING
13'3" X 15'3"

PLANT LEDGE

BR. #3
0'8" X 10'4"

GRT. RM.
CATHEDRAL CEILING
12'8" X 19'9"

KIT.
X 10'6"

ARCH

BR. #2
CATHEDRAL CEILING
10'9" X 10'4"

MAIN FLOOR

2 CAR GAR.
20' X 20'

CAD FILES AVAILABLE
For more information call
800-235-5700

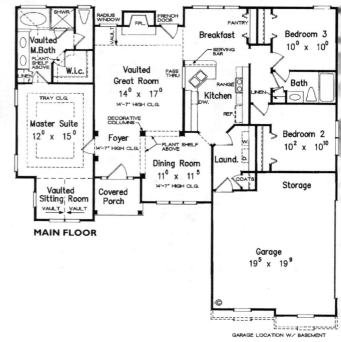

MAIN FLOOR

Units	Single
Price Code	B
Total Finished	1,502 sq. ft.
Main Finished	1,502 sq. ft.
Basement Unfinished	1,555 sq. ft.
Garage Unfinished	448 sq. ft.
Dimensions	51'x50'6"
Foundation	Basement
	Crawlspace
Bedrooms	3
Full Baths	2
Max Ridge Height	24'9"
Roof Framing	Stick
Exterior Walls	2x4

**OPTIONAL BASEMENT
STAIR LOCATION**

GARAGE LOCATION W/ BASEMENT

MAIN FLOOR

Units	Single
Price Code	B
Total Finished	1,503 sq. ft.
Main Finished	1,503 sq. ft.
Basement Unfinished	1,503 sq. ft.
Garage Unfinished	427 sq. ft.
Porch Unfinished	35 sq. ft.
Dimensions	59'8"x44'4"
Foundation	Basement
Bedrooms	3
Full Baths	1
Main Ceiling	8'
Max Ridge Height	21'2"
Roof Framing	Truss
Exterior Walls	2x6

Design 61009

Units	Single
Price Code	B
Total Finished	1,504 sq. ft.
Main Finished	1,504 sq. ft.
Dimensions	39'6"x72'5"
Foundation	Slab
Bedrooms	3
Full Baths	2

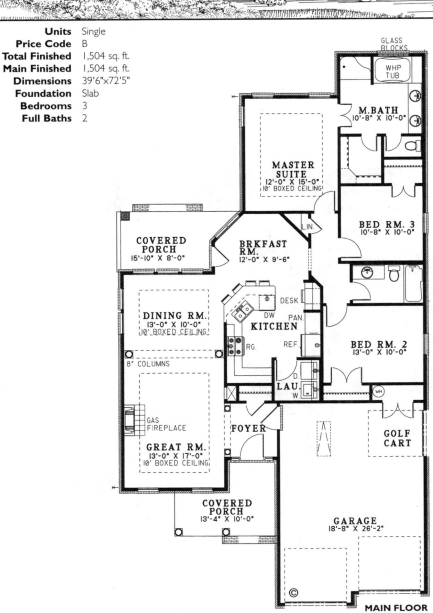

MAIN FLOOR

Units	Single
Price Code	B
Total Finished	1,504 sq. ft.
Main Finished	1,504 sq. ft.
Garage Unfinished	424 sq. ft.
Dimensions	59'8"x44'4"
Foundation	Basement
Bedrooms	3
Full Baths	1

4,70 X 3,30
15'-8" X 11'-0"

3,20 X 3,70
10'-8" X 12'-4"

3,00 X 3,00
10'-0" X 10'-0"

3,60 X 4,80
12'-0" X 16'-0"

6,20 X 6,10
20'-8" X 20'-4"

3,30 X 3,70
10'-0" X 12'-4"

3,90 X 5,20
13'-0" X 17'-4"

MAIN FLOOR

Units	Single
Price Code	B
Total Finished	1,506 sq. ft.
Main Finished	1,506 sq. ft.
Garage Unfinished	405 sq. ft.
Dimensions	40'x52'4"
Foundation	Basement Crawlspace
Bedrooms	3
Full Baths	2
Main Ceiling	9'
Max Ridge Height	25'4"
Roof Framing	Stick
Exterior Walls	2x4

CAD FILES AVAILABLE For more information call 800-235-5700

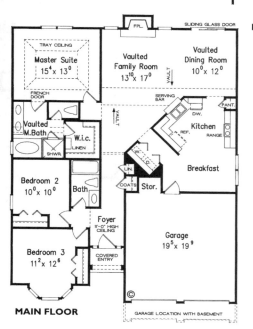

Breakfast

Garage
19⁵ x 19⁹

OPTIONAL BASEMENT STAIR LOCATION

TRAY CEILING

Master Suite
15⁴ x 13⁰

Vaulted Family Room
13¹⁰ x 17⁰

Vaulted Dining Room
10⁰ x 12⁰

Vaulted M.Bath

W.i.c.

Kitchen

Bedroom 2
10⁰ x 10⁰

Bath

Breakfast

Stor.

Bedroom 3
11² x 12⁶

Foyer
11'-0" HIGH CEILING

Garage
19⁵ x 19⁹

COVERED ENTRY

GARAGE LOCATION WITH BASEMENT

MAIN FLOOR

Design 99936

Units	Single
Price Code	B
Total Finished	1,506 sq. ft.
Main Finished	1,506 sq. ft.
Basement Unfinished	1,506 sq. ft.
Garage Unfinished	440 sq. ft.
Deck Unfinished	198 sq. ft.
Porch Unfinished	295 sq. ft.
Dimensions	48'x58'
Foundation	Basement
Bedrooms	3
Full Baths	2
Max Ridge Height	25'
Roof Framing	Truss
Exterior Walls	2×6

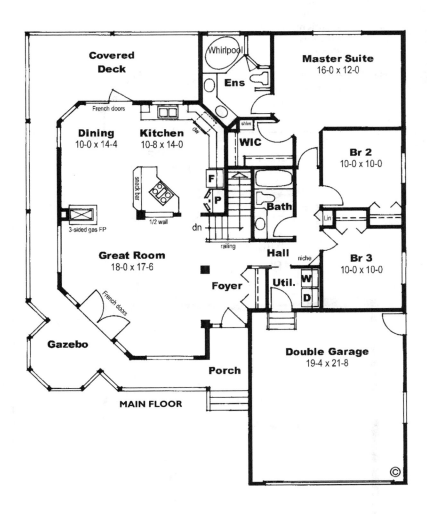

Covered Deck

Whirlpool

Master Suite
16-0 x 12-0

Ens

French doors

Dining
10-0 x 14-4

Kitchen
10-8 x 14-0

WIC

shlvs

Br 2
10-0 x 10-0

snack bar

F

1/2 wall

P

Bath

Lin

3-sided gas FP

dn

railing

Great Room
18-0 x 17-6

Hall

niche

Br 3
10-0 x 10-0

French doors

Foyer

Util.

W
D

Gazebo

Double Garage
19-4 x 21-8

Porch

MAIN FLOOR

Units	Single
Price Code	B
Total Finished	1,508 sq. ft.
Main Finished	1,508 sq. ft.
Basement Unfinished	1,439 sq. ft.
Garage Unfinished	440 sq. ft.
Dimensions	60'x47'
Foundation	Basement
Bedrooms	3
Full Baths	2
Main Ceiling	8'
Max Ridge Height	21'9"
Roof Framing	Truss
Exterior Walls	2x4

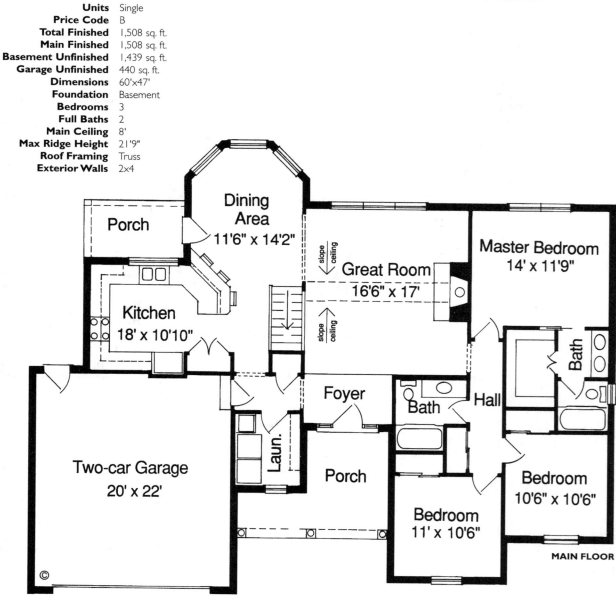

Porch

Dining Area
11'6" x 14'2"

Kitchen
18' x 10'10"

Great Room
16'6" x 17'
slope ceiling

Master Bedroom
14' x 11'9"

Bath

Foyer

Laun.

Bath

Hall

Two-car Garage
20' x 22'

Porch

Bedroom
11' x 10'6"

Bedroom
10'6" x 10'6"

MAIN FLOOR

Design 94691

Units	Single
Price Code	B
Total Finished	1,510 sq. ft.
Main Finished	1,510 sq. ft.
Porch Unfinished	132 sq. ft.
Dimensions	38'x58'6"
Foundation	Slab
Bedrooms	3
Full Baths	2
Main Ceiling	9'
Max Ridge Height	21'4"
Roof Framing	Stick
Exterior Walls	2x4

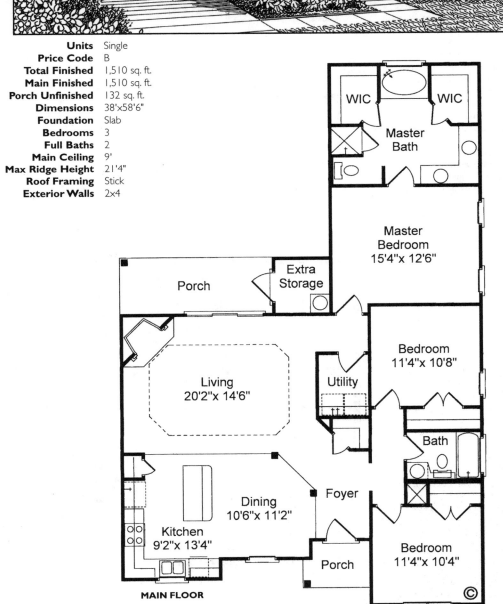

MAIN FLOOR

WIC · WIC · Master Bath · Master Bedroom 15'4"x 12'6" · Porch · Extra Storage · Living 20'2"x 14'6" · Bedroom 11'4"x 10'8" · Utility · Dining 10'6"x 11'2" · Foyer · Bath · Kitchen 9'2"x 13'4" · Porch · Bedroom 11'4"x 10'4"

Units	Single
Price Code	B
Total Finished	1,515 sq. ft.
Main Finished	1,515 sq. ft.
Garage Unfinished	528 sq. ft.
Porch Unfinished	225 sq. ft.
Dimensions	51'x60'
Foundation	Crawlspace
	Slab
Bedrooms	3
Full Baths	2
Max Ridge Height	35'
Roof Framing	Stick
Exterior Walls	2x4

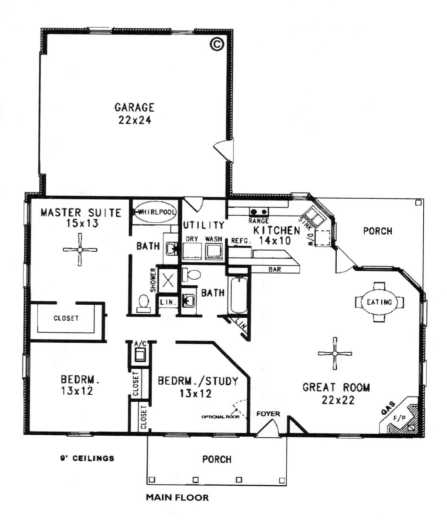

MAIN FLOOR

Design 64203

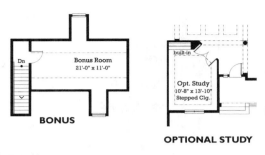

BONUS

Bonus Room
21'-0" x 11'-0"

Dn

OPTIONAL STUDY

built-in

Opt. Study
10'-8" x 13'-10"
Stepped Clg.

Units	Single
Price Code	G
Total Finished	1,526 sq. ft.
Main Finished	1,526 sq. ft.
Bonus Unfinished	336 sq. ft.
Dimensions	65'x54'6"
Foundation	Crawlspace
Bedrooms	3
Full Baths	2
Roof Framing	Stick/Truss
Exterior Walls	2x6

* Alternate foundation options available at an additional charge.
Please call 1-800-235-5700 for more information.

Master Bedroom
13'-0" x 14'-4"
Tray Ceiling

Porch
24'-0" x 9'-0"

Dn

workbench

Garage
21'-0" x 22'-0"

fireplace

Whirlpool

M. Bath

WIC

built-in entertainment center

Kitchen
9'-0" x 11'-0"

Stor.

Up

Dn

Utility

Great Room
14'-0" x 17'-6"
Coffered Ceiling

© Sater Design Collection

art niche

Dining
12'-10" x 12'-8"
Stepped Clg.

Cl

Cl

Foyer

Bath

Bedroom 2
10'-8" x 13'-2"

Porch
27'-6" x 6'-0"

Cl

MAIN FLOOR

Bedroom 1
11'-0" x 11'-11"

Design 64377

BONUS

Bonus Room
21'-0" x 11'-0"

Dn

Units	Single
Price Code	G
Total Finished	1,526 sq. ft.
Main Finished	1,526 sq. ft.
Bonus Unfinished	336 sq. ft.
Garage Unfinished	579 sq. ft.
Porch Unfinished	226 sq. ft.
Dimensions	64'x54'
Foundation	Crawlspace
Bedrooms	3
Full Baths	2
Max Ridge Height	24'6"
Roof Framing	Stick/Truss
Exterior Walls	2x6

* Alternate foundation options available at an additional charge.
Please call 1-800-235-5700 for more information.

OPTIONAL STUDY

built-in

Opt. Study
10'-8" x 13'-10"
Stepped Clg.

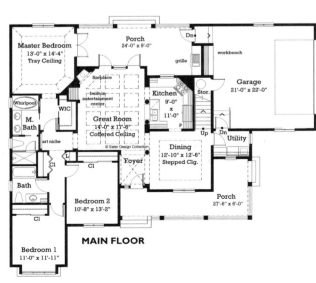

Master Bedroom
13'-0" x 14'-4"
Tray Ceiling

Porch
24'-0" x 9'-0"

Dn

grille

workbench

Garage
21'-0" x 22'-0"

fireplace

built-in entertainment center

Whirlpool

M. Bath

WIC

Kitchen
9'-0" x 11'-0"

Stor.

Up

Dn

Utility

Great Room
14'-0" x 17'-6"
Coffered Ceiling

© Sater Design Collection

art niche

Cl

Cl

Foyer

Dining
12'-10" x 12'-8"
Stepped Clg.

Bath

Bedroom 2
10'-8" x 13'-2"

Porch
27'-6" x 6'-0"

Cl

MAIN FLOOR

Bedroom 1
11'-0" x 11'-11"

Design 99610

Units	Single
Price Code	B
Total Finished	1,528 sq. ft.
Main Finished	1,528 sq. ft.
Basement Unfinished	1,367 sq. ft.
Garage Unfinished	494 sq. ft.
Dimensions	77'x26'8"
Foundation	Basement
	Slab
Bedrooms	3
Full Baths	2
Main Ceiling	8'
Max Ridge Height	21'
Roof Framing	Stick
Exterior Walls	2x6

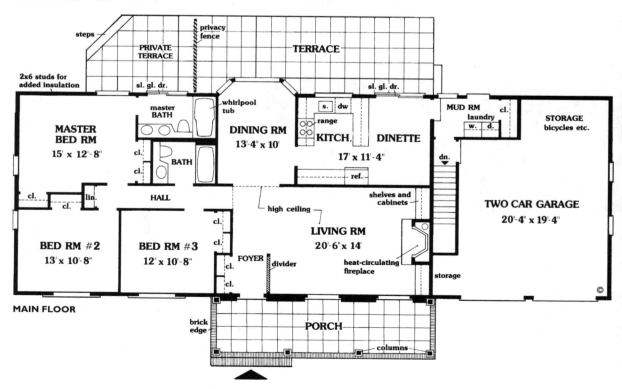

Design 98522

Units	Single
Price Code	B
Total Finished	1,528 sq. ft.
Main Finished	1,528 sq. ft.
Garage Unfinished	440 sq. ft.
Deck Unfinished	160 sq. ft.
Porch Unfinished	24 sq. ft.
Dimensions	40'x60'8"
Foundation	Slab
Bedrooms	3
Full Baths	2
Main Ceiling	8'10"
Max Ridge Height	23'6"
Roof Framing	Stick
Exterior Walls	2x4

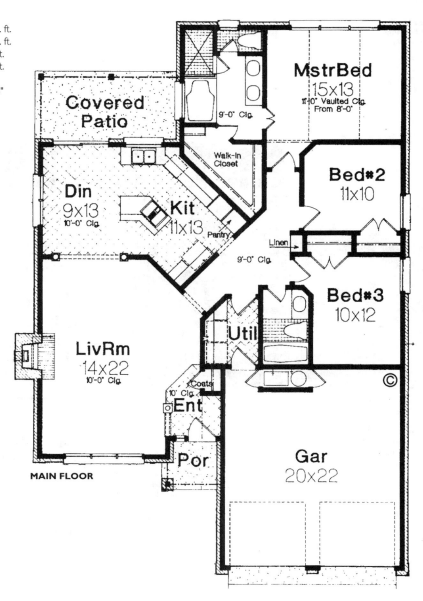

Covered Patio

MstrBed
15x13
11'0" Vaulted Clg.
From 8'-0"

9'-0" Clg.

Walk-In Closet

Din
9x13
10'-0" Clg.

Kit
11x13

Pantry

Bed#2
11x10

Linen

9'-0" Clg.

Bed#3
10x12

LivRm
14x22
10'-0" Clg.

Util

Coats

Ent
10' Clg.

Por

Gar
20x22

MAIN FLOOR

Design 98496

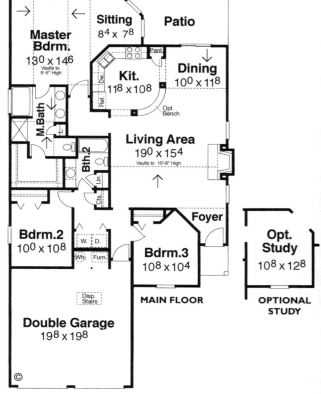

Units	Single
Price Code	B
Total Finished	1,531 sq. ft.
Main Finished	1,531 sq. ft.
Basement Unfinished	1,527 sq. ft.
Garage Unfinished	441 sq. ft.
Dimensions	50'x56'
Foundation	Crawlspace
	Slab
Bedrooms	3
Full Baths	2
Main Ceiling	8'
Max Ridge Height	21'
Roof Framing	Stick
Exterior Walls	2x4

MAIN FLOOR

Patio

Dining Room
12⁰ x 10³

Family Room
15⁵ x 18⁰
(HIGH CLG.)

Vaulted M. Bath

Master Suite
13⁵ x 14⁹

TRAY CLG.

FRENCH DOOR

SERVING BAR

Breakfast
10² x 9⁸

Kitchen

REF.

D.W.

SLOPED CLG.

FPL.

TUB

SHWR.

W.I.C.

PLANT SHELF

VAULT

VAULT

LINEN

Bath

K.S.

Laundry

RANGE

PANTRY

W.H

HVAC

COATS

Foyer

Storage

Bedroom 2
11⁰ x 11³

Bedroom 3
11⁰ x 11⁰

Garage

Design 98982

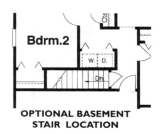

Units	Single
Price Code	B
Total Finished	1,532 sq. ft.
Main Finished	1,532 sq. ft.
Garage Unfinished	428 sq. ft.
Dimensions	38'x66'
Foundation	Basement
	Slab
Bedrooms	3
Full Baths	2
Main Ceiling	8'
Max Ridge Height	22'2"
Roof Framing	Stick
Exterior Walls	2x4

Master Bdrm.
13⁰ x 14⁶
Vaults to 9'-5" High

Sitting
8⁴ x 7⁸

Patio

Kit.
11⁸ x 10⁸

Dining
10⁰ x 11⁸

Pant.

Ref.

Dw.

Opt. Bench

M.Bath

Living Area
19⁰ x 15⁴
Vaults to 10'-8" High

Bth.2

Lin.

Cts.

Bdrm.2
10⁰ x 10⁸

W. D.

Whl

Furn.

Foyer

Bdrm.3
10⁸ x 10⁴

Opt. Study
10⁸ x 12⁸

Disp. Stairs

Double Garage
19⁸ x 19⁸

MAIN FLOOR

OPTIONAL STUDY

Bdrm.2

Cts.

W. D.

Dn.

OPTIONAL BASEMENT STAIR LOCATION

Design 99167

Units	Single
Price Code	B
Total Finished	1,537 sq. ft.
Main Finished	1,537 sq. ft.
Basement Unfinished	1,537 sq. ft.
Dimensions	52'x50'
Foundation	Basement
Bedrooms	3
Full Baths	2
Max Ridge Height	26'4"
Roof Framing	Truss
Exterior Walls	2x6

MBR.
13'0" X 14'6"

LIV.
VAULTED CEILING
14'0" X 18'0"

DIN.
13'6" X 11'0"

PAN.

KIT.
13'6" X 12'0"

DW

E.
VAULTED
CEILING

DN.

LIN.

LIN.

STO.
4'8" X 10'8"

BR. #2
11'0" X 11'6"

BR. #3
10'-1 1/8" CEILING
11'8" X 10'6"

2 CAR GAR.
19'8" X 19'2"

MAIN FLOOR

Units	Single
Price Code	B
Total Finished	1,539 sq. ft.
Main Finished	1,539 sq. ft.
Basement Unfinished	1,530 sq. ft.
Garage Unfinished	460 sq. ft.
Deck Unfinished	160 sq. ft.
Porch Unfinished	182 sq. ft.
Dimensions	50'x45'4"
Foundation	Basement
	Crawlspace
	Slab
Bedrooms	3
Full Baths	2
Main Ceiling	8'
Max Ridge Height	21'
Roof Framing	Stick
Exterior Walls	2x6

Deck

Dining
17-3 x 9-9

Breakfast Bar

Shelves

Flat Clg.
@ 11'-0"

MBr 1
11-8 x 14-0

W.P.

Decor Clg.

Desk

Flue

Kitchen
13-5 x 9-8

Range

DW

Ref

W   D

Living Rm
12-2 x 19-4

Pantry

DN

Flat Clg.
@ 8'-0" TYP

Hall

Linen

Railing

Foy

Garage
19-5 x 23-6

Den/Br 3
10-5 x 11-6

Br 2
10-6 x 12-3

Porch

MAIN FLOOR

Design 93161

Units	Single
Price Code	B
Total Finished	1,540 sq. ft.
Main Finished	1,540 sq. ft.
Basement Unfinished	1,540 sq. ft.
Dimensions	60'4"x46'
Foundation	Basement
Bedrooms	3
Full Baths	2
Main Ceiling	8'
Vaulted Ceiling	12'6"
Max Ridge Height	21'4"
Roof Framing	Stick
Exterior Walls	2x6

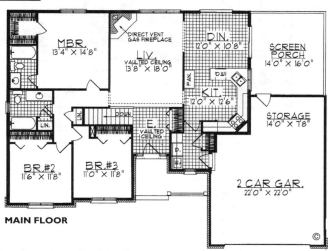

MAIN FLOOR

Design 98460

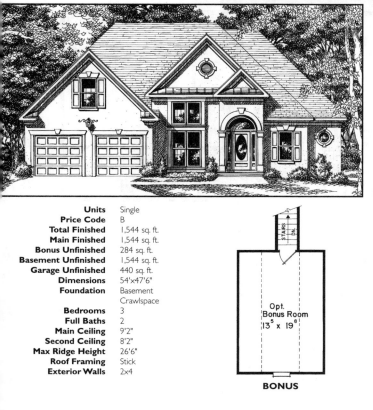

Units	Single
Price Code	B
Total Finished	1,544 sq. ft.
Main Finished	1,544 sq. ft.
Bonus Unfinished	284 sq. ft.
Basement Unfinished	1,544 sq. ft.
Garage Unfinished	440 sq. ft.
Dimensions	54'x47'6"
Foundation	Basement
	Crawlspace
Bedrooms	3
Full Baths	2
Main Ceiling	9'2"
Second Ceiling	8'2"
Max Ridge Height	26'6"
Roof Framing	Stick
Exterior Walls	2x4

CAD FILES AVAILABLE For more information call 800-235-5700

OPTIONAL BASEMENT STAIR LOCATION

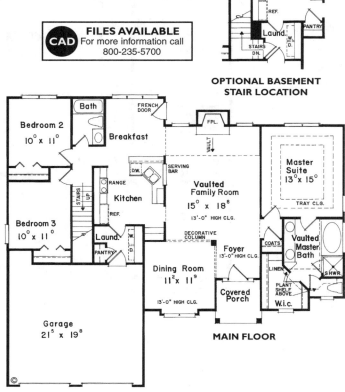

Opt. Bonus Room 13⁵ x 19⁸

BONUS

MAIN FLOOR

Design 94116

Units	Single
Price Code	B
Total Finished	1,546 sq. ft.
Main Finished	1,546 sq. ft.
Basement Unfinished	1,530 sq. ft.
Garage Unfinished	440 sq. ft.
Dimensions	60'x43'
Foundation	Basement
Bedrooms	3
Full Baths	1
3/4 Baths	1
Main Ceiling	9'2"
Max Ridge Height	23'
Roof Framing	Truss
Exterior Walls	2x4

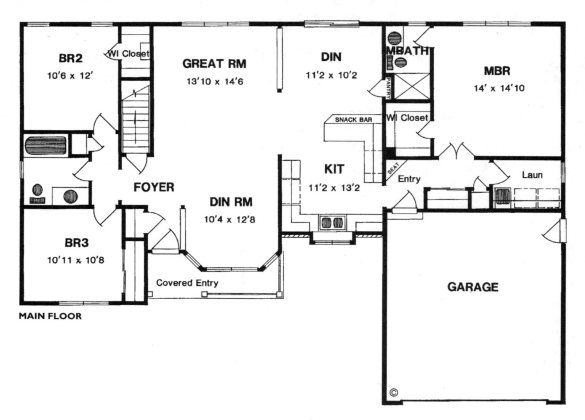

MAIN FLOOR

Design 93455

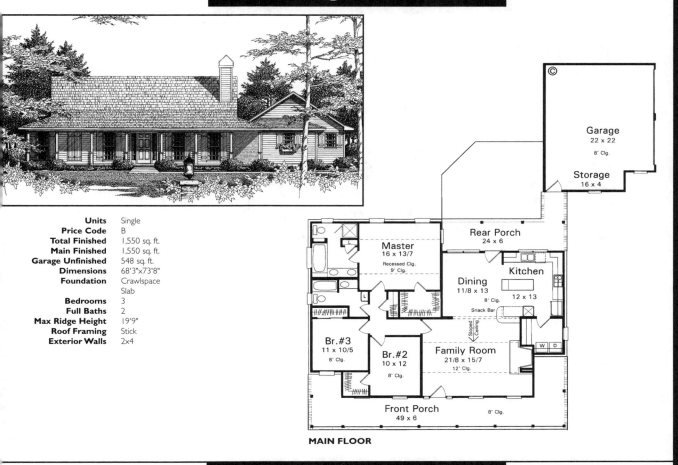

Units	Single
Price Code	B
Total Finished	1,550 sq. ft.
Main Finished	1,550 sq. ft.
Garage Unfinished	548 sq. ft.
Dimensions	68'3"x73'8"
Foundation	Crawlspace
	Slab
Bedrooms	3
Full Baths	2
Max Ridge Height	19'9"
Roof Framing	Stick
Exterior Walls	2x4

Garage 22 x 22 — 8' Clg.

Storage 16 x 4

Rear Porch 24 x 6

Master 16 x 13/7 — Recessed Clg. 9' Clg.

Kitchen 12 x 13

Dining 11/8 x 13 — 8' Clg.

Snack Bar

Sloped Ceiling

Br. #3 11 x 10/5 — 8' Clg.

Br. #2 10 x 12 — 8' Clg.

Family Room 21/8 x 15/7 — 12' Clg.

W D

Front Porch 49 x 6 — 8' Clg.

MAIN FLOOR

Design 97152

Units	Single
Price Code	B
Total Finished	1,557 sq. ft.
Main Finished	1,557 sq. ft.
Basement Unfinished	1,557 sq. ft.
Garage Unfinished	400 sq. ft.
Dimensions	40'x61'
Foundation	Basement
Bedrooms	3
Full Baths	1
3/4 Baths	1
Max Ridge Height	26'4"
Roof Framing	Truss
Exterior Walls	2x6

MBR. 15'8" X 13'0"

LIV. 10'-1 1/8" CLG. HGT. 17'8" X 13'4"

BUILT-IN CAB.

BR. #3 12'2" X 11'0"

DIN. 10'-1 1/8" CLG. HGT. 17'8" X 10'2"

BR. #2 12'2" X 11'0"

DN.

KIT. 11'4" X 16'4"

NK. 10'-1 1/8" CLG. HGT

2 CAR GAR. 19'10" X 21'8"

MAIN FLOOR

Units	Single
Price Code	B
Total Finished	1,562 sq. ft.
Main Finished	1,562 sq. ft.
Basement Unfinished	1,562 sq. ft.
Garage Unfinished	506 sq. ft.
Deck Unfinished	19 sq. ft.
Porch Unfinished	83 sq. ft.
Dimensions	73'7"x50'9"
Foundation	Basement
Bedrooms	3
Full Baths	2
Main Ceiling	8'
Vaulted Ceiling	12'
Tray Ceiling	9'
Max Ridge Height	23'
Roof Framing	Stick
Exterior Walls	2x4

MAIN FLOOR

Design 20220

1,501-2,000 sq.ft. HOME PLANS

Units	Single
Price Code	B
Total Finished	1,568 sq. ft.
Main Finished	1,568 sq. ft.
Basement Unfinished	1,568 sq. ft.
Garage Unfinished	509 sq. ft.
Dimensions	54'x48'4"
Foundation	Basement
	Crawlspace
	Slab
Bedrooms	3
Full Baths	2
Main Ceiling	8'
Vaulted Ceiling	10'
Max Ridge Height	19'
Roof Framing	Stick
Exterior Walls	2x4, 2x6

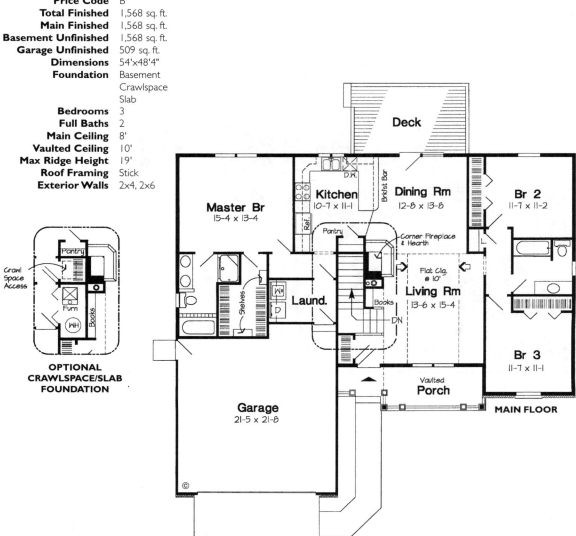

OPTIONAL CRAWLSPACE/SLAB FOUNDATION

MAIN FLOOR

Design 97615

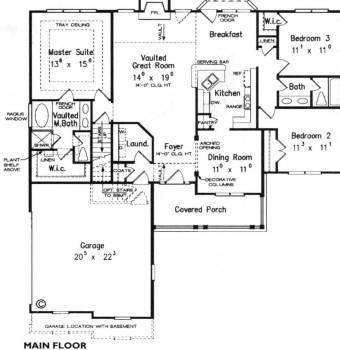

Units	Single
Price Code	B
Total Finished	1,571 sq. ft.
Main Finished	1,571 sq. ft.
Bonus Unfinished	334 sq. ft.
Basement Unfinished	1,642 sq. ft.
Garage Unfinished	483 sq. ft.
Dimensions	53'6"x55'10"
Foundation	Basement
Bedrooms	3
Full Baths	2
Max Ridge Height	23'6"
Roof Framing	Stick
Exterior Walls	2x4

BONUS

MAIN FLOOR

Design 98414

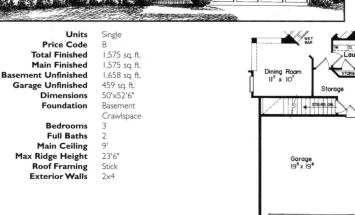

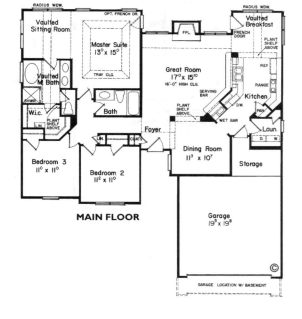

Units	Single
Price Code	B
Total Finished	1,575 sq. ft.
Main Finished	1,575 sq. ft.
Basement Unfinished	1,658 sq. ft.
Garage Unfinished	459 sq. ft.
Dimensions	50'x52'6"
Foundation	Basement
	Crawlspace
Bedrooms	3
Full Baths	2
Main Ceiling	9'
Max Ridge Height	23'6"
Roof Framing	Stick
Exterior Walls	2x4

OPTIONAL BASEMENT STAIR LOCATION

MAIN FLOOR

Design 98479

Units	Single
Price Code	B
Total Finished	1,575 sq. ft.
Main Finished	1,575 sq. ft.
Basement Unfinished	1,612 sq. ft.
Garage Unfinished	456 sq. ft.
Dimensions	52'×52'6"
Foundation	Basement
	Crawlspace
Bedrooms	3
Full Baths	2
Max Ridge Height	25'6"
Roof Framing	Stick
Exterior Walls	2x4

Garage
19⁵ x 20⁹

OPTIONAL BASEMENT STAIR LOCATION

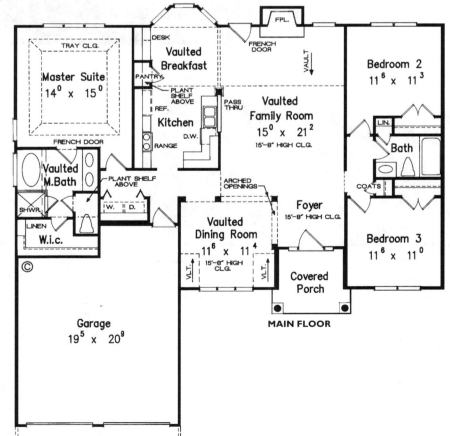

Master Suite
14⁰ x 15⁰

Vaulted Breakfast

Kitchen

Vaulted Family Room
15⁰ x 21²
15'-8" HIGH CLG.

Bedroom 2
11⁶ x 11³

Bath

Vaulted M.Bath

Foyer
15'-8" HIGH CLG.

Vaulted Dining Room
11⁶ x 11⁴
15'-8" HIGH CLG.

Bedroom 3
11⁶ x 11⁰

Covered Porch

Garage
19⁵ x 20⁹

MAIN FLOOR

GARAGE LOCATION WITH BASEMENT

Design 24708

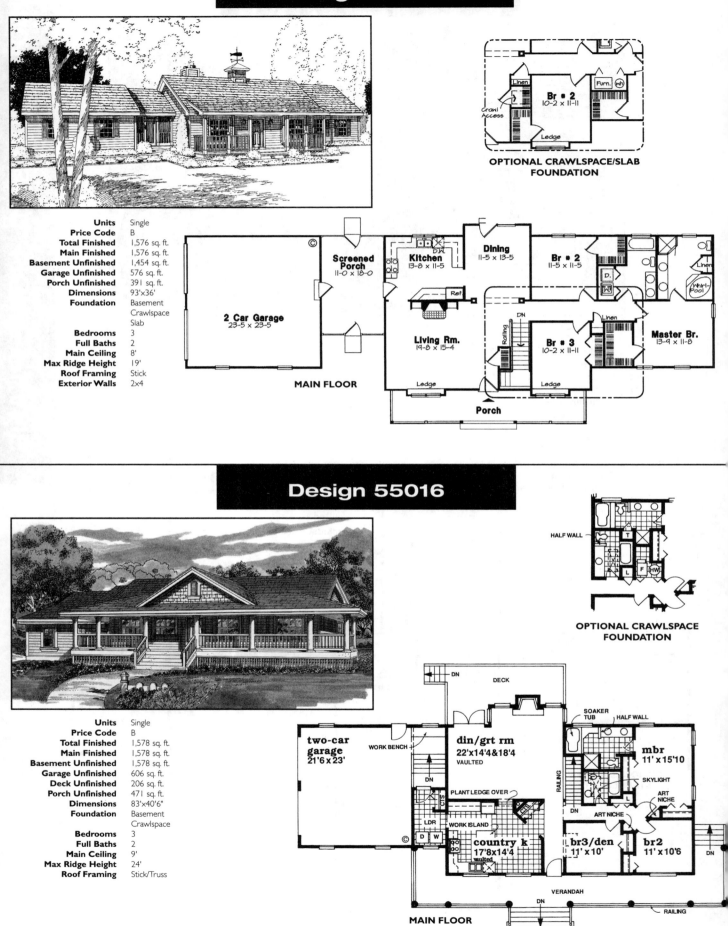

OPTIONAL CRAWLSPACE/SLAB FOUNDATION

Br # 2
10-2 x 11-11

Linen
Furn.
wh
Crawl Access
Ledge

Units	Single
Price Code	B
Total Finished	1,576 sq. ft.
Main Finished	1,576 sq. ft.
Basement Unfinished	1,454 sq. ft.
Garage Unfinished	576 sq. ft.
Porch Unfinished	391 sq. ft.
Dimensions	93'x36'
Foundation	Basement Crawlspace Slab
Bedrooms	3
Full Baths	2
Main Ceiling	8'
Max Ridge Height	19'
Roof Framing	Stick
Exterior Walls	2x4

MAIN FLOOR

2 Car Garage
23-5 x 23-5

Screened Porch
11-0 x 18-0

Kitchen
13-8 x 11-5

Dining
11-5 x 13-5

Br # 2
11-5 x 11-5

Ref.

Living Rm.
19-8 x 15-4

DN
Railing

Br # 3
10-2 x 11-11

Master Br.
13-9 x 11-8

Linen
Whirl-Pool
D.

Ledge

Porch

Design 55016

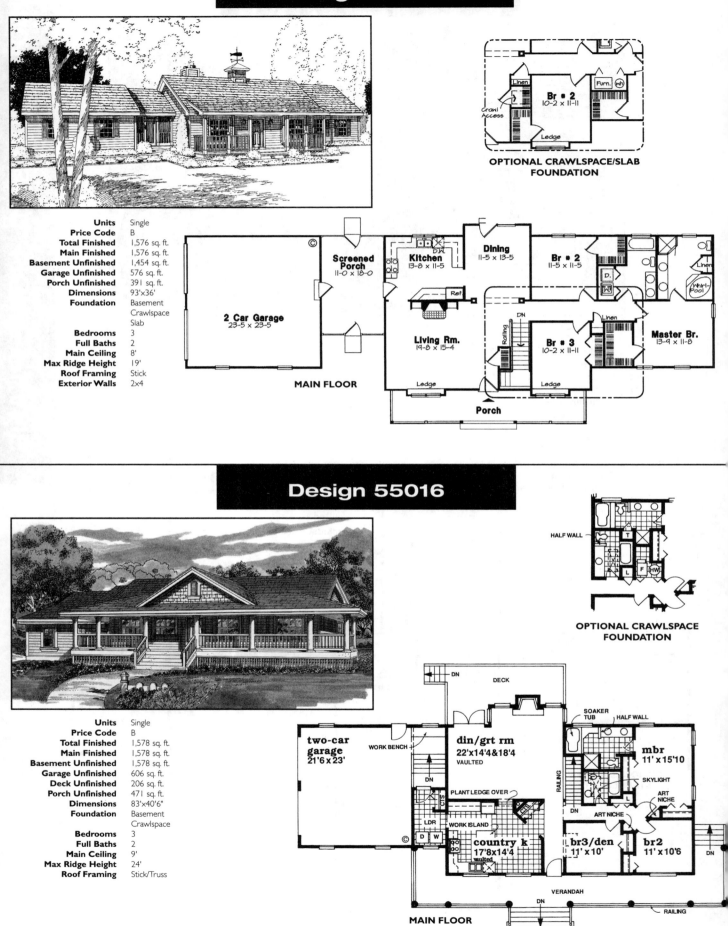

OPTIONAL CRAWLSPACE FOUNDATION

HALF WALL
T
F
L
HW

Units	Single
Price Code	B
Total Finished	1,578 sq. ft.
Main Finished	1,578 sq. ft.
Basement Unfinished	1,578 sq. ft.
Garage Unfinished	606 sq. ft.
Deck Unfinished	206 sq. ft.
Porch Unfinished	471 sq. ft.
Dimensions	83'x40'6"
Foundation	Basement Crawlspace
Bedrooms	3
Full Baths	2
Main Ceiling	9'
Max Ridge Height	24'
Roof Framing	Stick/Truss

DECK
DN

two-car garage
21'6 x 23'

WORK BENCH
DN

LDR
D W

WORK ISLAND

PLANT LEDGE OVER

country k
17'8x14'4
vaulted

din/grt rm
22'x14'4&18'4
VAULTED

SOAKER TUB
HALF WALL

mbr
11' x 15'10

SKYLIGHT

ART NICHE

RAILING

DN
ART NICHE

br3/den
11' x 10'

br2
11' x 10'6

DN

VERANDAH
DN
RAILING

MAIN FLOOR

Design 81009

Units	Single
Price Code	B
Total Finished	1,580 sq. ft.
Main Finished	1,580 sq. ft.
Garage Unfinished	452 sq. ft.
Dimensions	48'x50'
Foundation	Crawlspace
Bedrooms	3
Full Baths	2
Half Baths	1

MAIN FLOOR

Units	Single
Price Code	B
Total Finished	1,581 sq. ft.
Main Finished	1,581 sq. ft.
Garage Unfinished	489 sq. ft.
Dimensions	40'x60'
Foundation	Slab
Bedrooms	3
Full Baths	2
Main Ceiling	8'
Vaulted Ceiling	12'
Max Ridge Height	18'6"

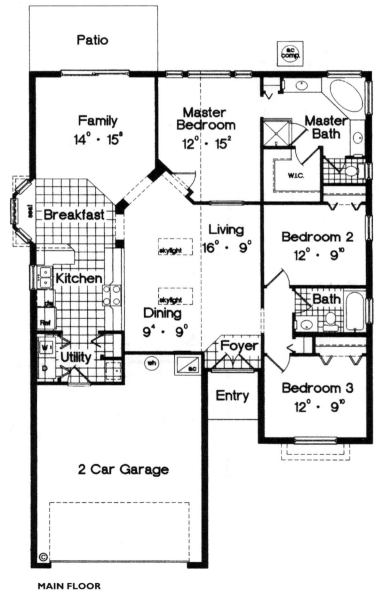

MAIN FLOOR

Design 91165

Units	Single
Price Code	B
Total Finished	1,589 sq. ft.
Main Finished	1,589 sq. ft.
Garage Unfinished	481 sq. ft.
Porch Unfinished	168 sq. ft.
Dimensions	59'10"x57'9"
Foundation	Crawlspace
Bedrooms	3
Full Baths	2

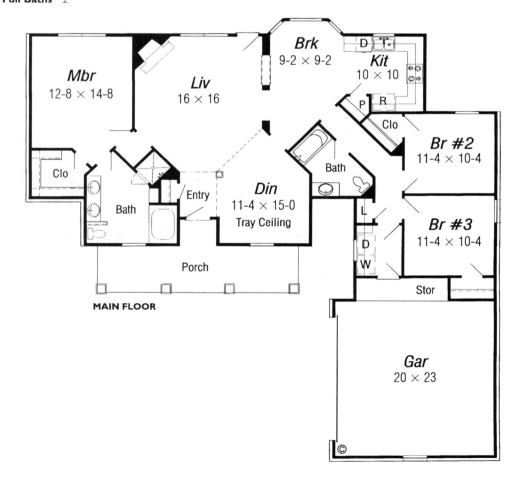

MAIN FLOOR

Units	Single
Price Code	B
Total Finished	1,591 sq. ft.
Main Finished	1,591 sq. ft.
Garage Unfinished	412 sq. ft.
Dimensions	53'x50'6"
Foundation	Basement
	Crawlspace
Bedrooms	3
Full Baths	2
Main Ceiling	9'
Max Ridge Height	22'
Roof Framing	Stick
Exterior Walls	2x4

CAD FILES AVAILABLE For more information call 800-235-5700

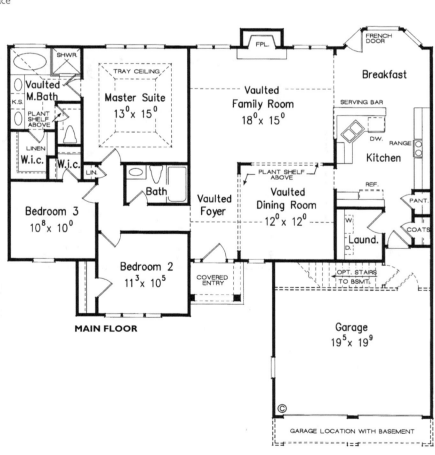

MAIN FLOOR

Design 97762

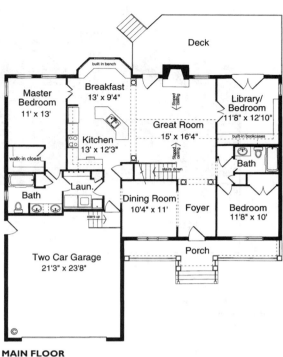

Master Bedroom 11' x 13'

Breakfast 13' x 9'4"

Deck

built in bench

Great Room 15' x 16'4"

Library/Bedroom 11'8" x 12'10"

built-in bookcases

Kitchen 13' x 12'3"

walk-in closet

Bath

Laun.

Bath

stairs down

Sloped ceiling

Bath

Dining Room 10'4" x 11'

Foyer

Bedroom 11'8" x 10'

stairs up

Two Car Garage 21'3" x 23'8"

Porch

MAIN FLOOR

Bedroom 11'8" x 10'5"

THIRD BEDROOM OPTION

Units	Single
Price Code	B
Total Finished	1,594 sq. ft.
Main Finished	1,594 sq. ft.
Basement Unfinished	1,594 sq. ft.
Garage Unfinished	512 sq. ft.
Deck Unfinished	328 sq. ft.
Porch Unfinished	125 sq. ft.
Dimensions	52'8"x55'5"
Foundation	Basement
Bedrooms	3
Full Baths	2
Main Ceiling	8'
Vaulted Ceiling	10'
Max Ridge Height	23'6"
Roof Framing	Truss
Exterior Walls	2x4

Design 94827

Units	Single
Price Code	B
Total Finished	1,595 sq. ft.
Main Finished	1,595 sq. ft.
Basement Unfinished	1,595 sq. ft.
Garage Unfinished	491 sq. ft.
Dimensions	63'x50'6"
Foundation	Basement
	Crawlspace
	Slab
Bedrooms	3
Full Baths	2
Max Ridge Height	22'
Roof Framing	Stick
Exterior Walls	2x4

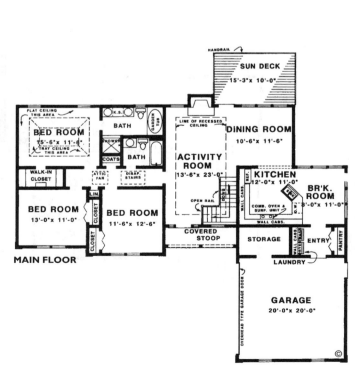

SUN DECK 15'-3"x 10'-0"

HANDRAIL

FLAT CEILING THIS AREA

BED ROOM 15'-6"x 11'-6" TRAY CEILING THIS AREA

BATH

GARDEN TUB

LINE OF RECESSED CEILING

DINING ROOM 10'-6"x 11'-6"

WALK-IN CLOSET

COATS

BATH

ATTIC FAN

DISAP. STAIRS

ACTIVITY ROOM 13'-6"x 23'-0"

KITCHEN 12'-0"x 11'-0"

REF.

BR'K. ROOM 8'-0"x 11'-0"

LIN.

CLOSET

BED ROOM 13'-0"x 11'-0"

CLOSET

BED ROOM 11'-6"x 12'-6"

OPEN RAIL

COMB. OVEN & SURF. UNIT

WALL CABS.

WALL CABS.

COVERED STOOP

STORAGE

ENTRY

PANTRY

LAUNDRY

MAIN FLOOR

GARAGE 20'-0"x 20'-0"

OVERHEAD TYPE GARAGE DOOR

Units	Single
Price Code	B
Total Finished	1,595 sq. ft.
Main Finished	1,595 sq. ft.
Basement Unfinished	1,595 sq. ft.
Garage Unfinished	548 sq. ft.
Dimensions	70'x37'4"
Foundation	Basement
Bedrooms	3
Full Baths	2
Main Ceiling	9'1"
Vaulted Ceiling	10'9"
Tray Ceiling	14'
Max Ridge Height	22'
Roof Framing	Stick
Exterior Walls	2x4

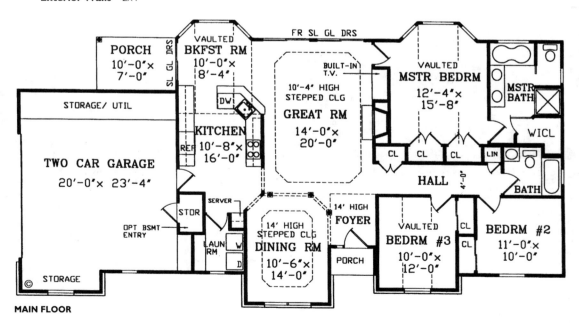

MAIN FLOOR

Design 10674

1,501-2,000 sq.ft. HOME PLANS

Units	Single
Price Code	B
Total Finished	1,600 sq. ft.
Main Finished	1,600 sq. ft.
Garage Unfinished	465 sq. ft.
Dimensions	58'x51'
Foundation	Slab
Bedrooms	3
Full Baths	2
Max Ridge Height	15'
Roof Framing	Stick
Exterior Walls	2x6

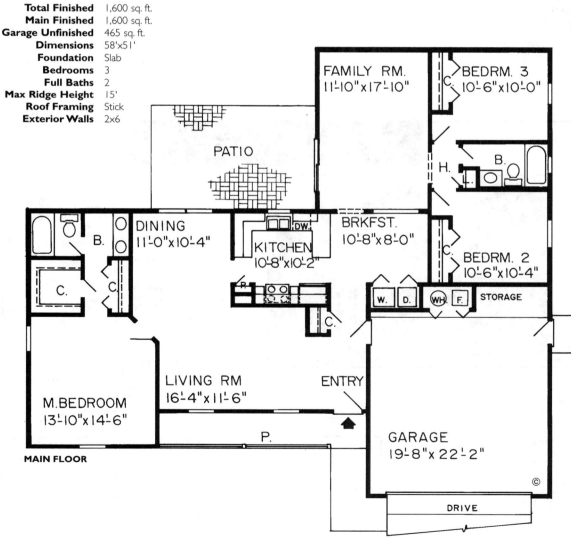

MAIN FLOOR

Units	Single
Price Code	C
Total Finished	1,601 sq. ft.
Main Finished	1,601 sq. ft.
Garage Unfinished	771 sq. ft.
Porch Unfinished	279 sq. ft.
Dimensions	39'x77'2"
Foundation	Crawlspace
	Slab
Bedrooms	3
Full Baths	2
Main Ceiling	9'
Max Ridge Height	22'
Roof Framing	Stick
Exterior Walls	2x4

MAIN FLOOR

Units	Single
Price Code	B
Total Finished	1,604 sq. ft.
Main Finished	1,604 sq. ft.
Bonus Unfinished	316 sq. ft.
Garage Unfinished	529 sq. ft.
Deck Unfinished	718 sq. ft.
Dimensions	57'x59'
Foundation	Crawlspace
	Slab
Bedrooms	3
Full Baths	2
Main Ceiling	9'
Max Ridge Height	28'
Exterior Walls	2x4

* Alternate foundation options available at an additional charge.
Please call 1-800-235-5700 for more information.

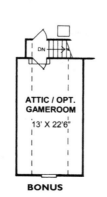

ATTIC / OPT. GAMEROOM
13' X 22'6"

BONUS

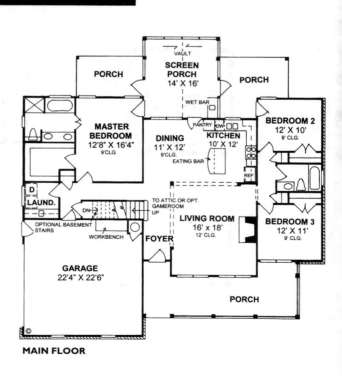

MAIN FLOOR

Design 97760

Units	Single
Price Code	B
Total Finished	1,611 sq. ft.
Main Finished	1,611 sq. ft.
Garage Unfinished	430 sq. ft.
Deck Unfinished	228 sq. ft.
Porch Unfinished	163 sq. ft.
Dimensions	66'4"x43'10"
Foundation	Basement
Bedrooms	3
Full Baths	2
Main Ceiling	8'
Vaulted Ceiling	10'
Tray Ceiling	10'
Max Ridge Height	22'6"
Roof Framing	Truss
Exterior Walls	2x4

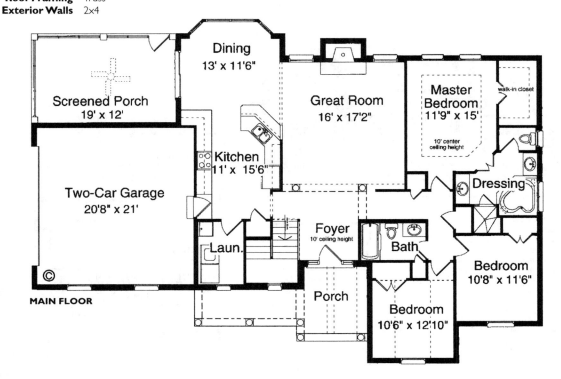

MAIN FLOOR

Screened Porch 19' x 12'

Two-Car Garage 20'8" x 21'

Dining 13' x 11'6"

Kitchen 11' x 15'6"

Great Room 16' x 17'2"

Master Bedroom 11'9" x 15'
10' center ceiling height
walk-in closet

Dressing

Laun.

Foyer 10' ceiling height

Bath

Bedroom 10'8" x 11'6"

Porch

Bedroom 10'6" x 12'10"

Design 90601

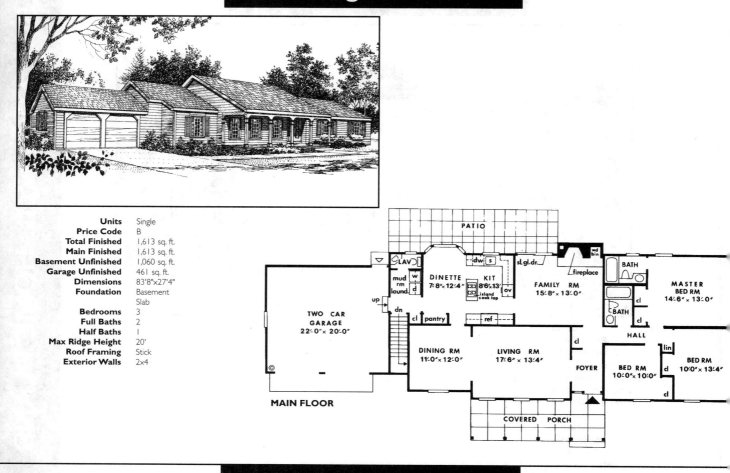

Units	Single
Price Code	B
Total Finished	1,613 sq. ft.
Main Finished	1,613 sq. ft.
Basement Unfinished	1,060 sq. ft.
Garage Unfinished	461 sq. ft.
Dimensions	83'8"x27'4"
Foundation	Basement
	Slab
Bedrooms	3
Full Baths	2
Half Baths	1
Max Ridge Height	20'
Roof Framing	Stick
Exterior Walls	2x4

MAIN FLOOR

PATIO

LAV

mud rm laund. w d

DINETTE 7'8" x 12'4"

dw s

KIT 8'6" x 13'

SL gl.dr.

wd bin

fireplace

BATH

MASTER BED RM 14'6" x 13'0"

TWO CAR GARAGE 22'0" x 20'0"

up dn

cl pantry

FAMILY RM 15'8" x 13'0"

cl

BATH

island cook top

ov

ref

cl

HALL

lin

BED RM 10'0" x 13'4"

DINING RM 11'0" x 12'0"

LIVING RM 17'6" x 13'4"

cl

FOYER

BED RM 10'0" x 10'0"

cl

COVERED PORCH

Design 50051

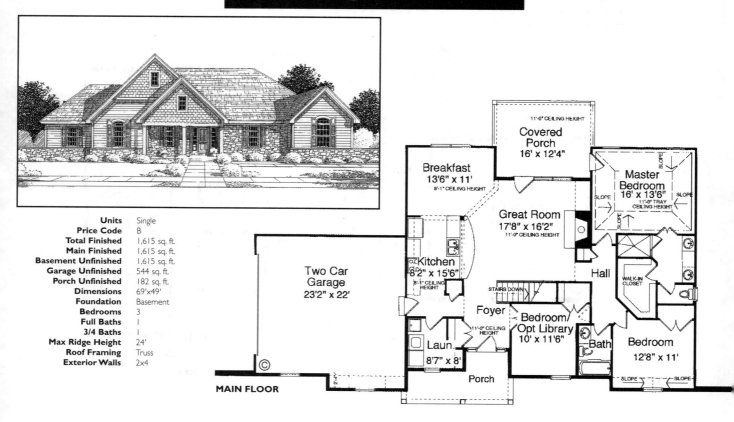

Units	Single
Price Code	B
Total Finished	1,615 sq. ft.
Main Finished	1,615 sq. ft.
Basement Unfinished	1,615 sq. ft.
Garage Unfinished	544 sq. ft.
Porch Unfinished	182 sq. ft.
Dimensions	69'x49'
Foundation	Basement
Bedrooms	3
Full Baths	1
3/4 Baths	1
Max Ridge Height	24'
Roof Framing	Truss
Exterior Walls	2x4

MAIN FLOOR

Covered Porch 16' x 12'4" — 11'-0" CEILING HEIGHT

Breakfast 13'6" x 11' — 8'-1" CEILING HEIGHT

Master Bedroom 16' x 13'6" — 11'-0" TRAY CEILING HEIGHT

SLOPE

Two Car Garage 23'2" x 22'

Kitchen 16'2" x 15'6" — 8'-1" CEILING HEIGHT

Great Room 17'8" x 16'2" — 11'-0" CEILING HEIGHT

Hall

WALK-IN CLOSET

STAIRS DOWN

Foyer

Bedroom/Opt Library 10' x 11'6" — 11'-0" CEILING HEIGHT

Bath

Bedroom 12'8" x 11'

SLOPE

Laun. 8'7" x 8'

Porch

Design 94624

Units	Single
Price Code	B
Total Finished	1,615 sq. ft.
Main Finished	1,615 sq. ft.
Garage Unfinished	451 sq. ft.
Porch Unfinished	145 sq. ft.
Dimensions	38'x62'5"
Foundation	Slab
Bedrooms	3
Full Baths	2
Main Ceiling	9'
Max Ridge Height	23'1"
Roof Framing	Stick
Exterior Walls	2x4

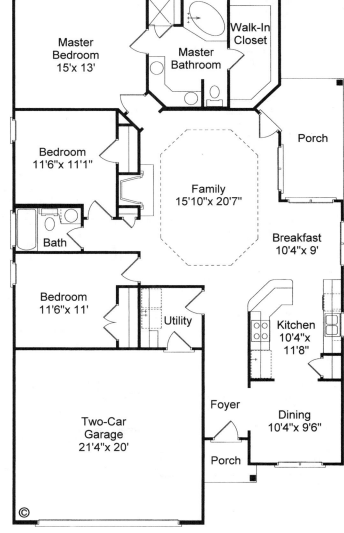

MAIN FLOOR

Units	Single
Price Code	B
Total Finished	1,615 sq. ft.
Main Finished	1,615 sq. ft.
Basement Unfinished	1,615 sq. ft.
Garage Unfinished	415 sq. ft.
Dimensions	72'4"x32'4"
Foundation	Basement
	Crawlspace
	Slab
Bedrooms	3
Full Baths	2
Main Ceiling	8'
Max Ridge Height	18'
Roof Framing	Stick
Exterior Walls	2x4

OPTIONAL
BASEMENT STAIR
LOCATION

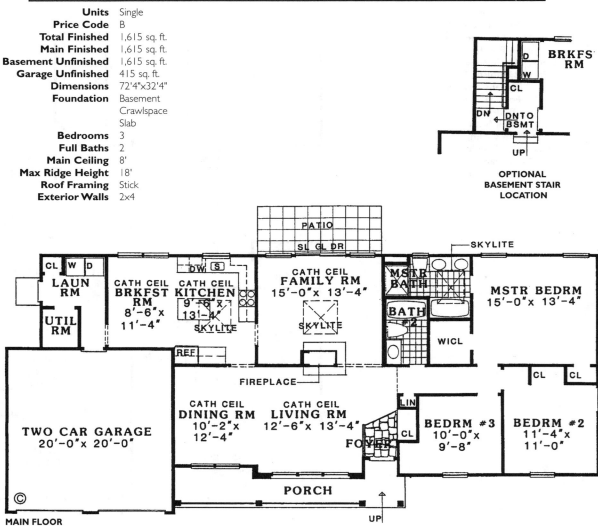

Design 64196

BONUS

Bath

Bonus Room
21'-8" x 12'-10"

Dn

Units	Single
Price Code	G
Total Finished	1,616 sq. ft.
Main Finished	1,616 sq. ft.
Bonus Unfinished	362 sq. ft.
Garage Unfinished	534 sq. ft.
Dimensions	64'x54'6"
Foundation	Crawlspace
Bedrooms	3
Full Baths	2
Max Ridge Height	23'2"
Roof Framing	Stick/Truss
Exterior Walls	2x6

* Alternate foundation options available at an additional charge.
Please call 1-800-235-5700 for more information.

MAIN FLOOR

Porch 26'-6" x 8'-6"

Garage 21'-6" x 21'-6"

St

Master Bedroom 11'-0" x 14'-8" Tray Clg.

entertainment center

Great Room 15'-4" x 17'-4" Stepped Ceiling

Dining 11'-0" x 13'-6" Stepped Clg.

Up

© Sater Design Collection

WIC

Master Bath

Foyer

Kitchen 14'-10" x 11'-8"

Utility

Bath

Porch 18'-0" x 8'-0"

CL

CL

Bedroom 1 10'-0" x 11'-8"

Bedroom 2 11'-0" x 11'-10"

Design 64197

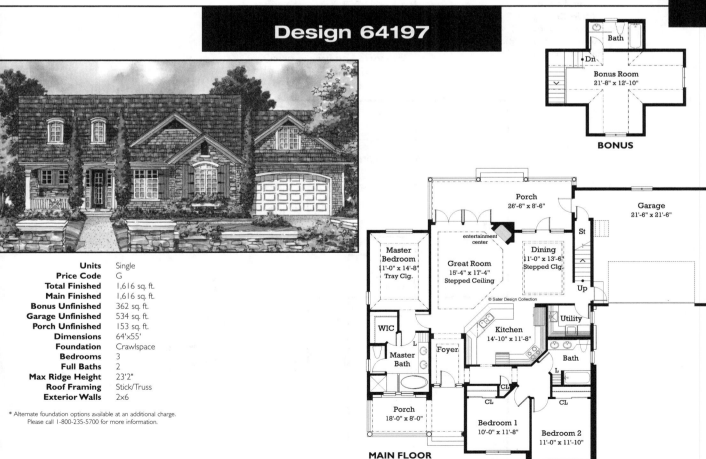

BONUS

Bath

Bonus Room
21'-8" x 12'-10"

Dn

Units	Single
Price Code	G
Total Finished	1,616 sq. ft.
Main Finished	1,616 sq. ft.
Bonus Unfinished	362 sq. ft.
Garage Unfinished	534 sq. ft.
Porch Unfinished	153 sq. ft.
Dimensions	64'x55'
Foundation	Crawlspace
Bedrooms	3
Full Baths	2
Max Ridge Height	23'2"
Roof Framing	Stick/Truss
Exterior Walls	2x6

* Alternate foundation options available at an additional charge.
Please call 1-800-235-5700 for more information.

MAIN FLOOR

Porch 26'-6" x 8'-6"

Garage 21'-6" x 21'-6"

St

Master Bedroom 11'-0" x 14'-8" Tray Clg.

entertainment center

Great Room 15'-4" x 17'-4" Stepped Ceiling

Dining 11'-0" x 13'-6" Stepped Clg.

Up

© Sater Design Collection

WIC

Master Bath

Foyer

Kitchen 14'-10" x 11'-8"

Utility

Bath

Porch 18'-0" x 8'-0"

CL

CL

Bedroom 1 10'-0" x 11'-8"

Bedroom 2 11'-0" x 11'-10"

Design 24701

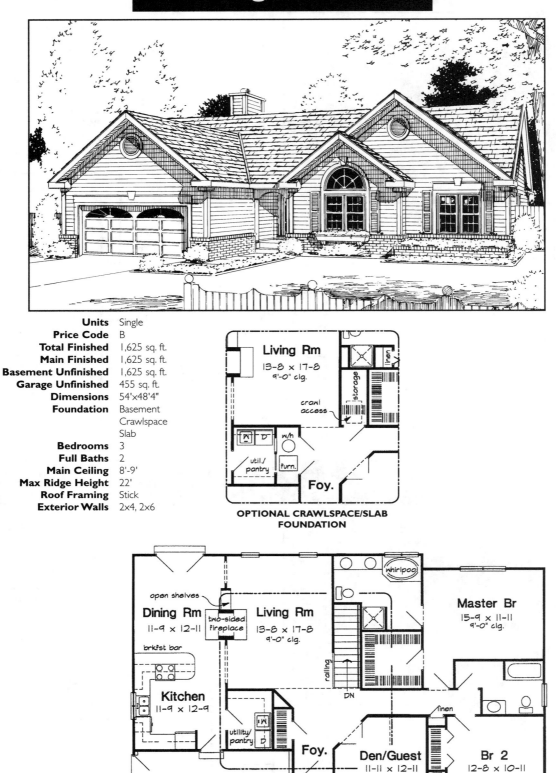

Units	Single
Price Code	B
Total Finished	1,625 sq. ft.
Main Finished	1,625 sq. ft.
Basement Unfinished	1,625 sq. ft.
Garage Unfinished	455 sq. ft.
Dimensions	54'x48'4"
Foundation	Basement
	Crawlspace
	Slab
Bedrooms	3
Full Baths	2
Main Ceiling	8'-9'
Max Ridge Height	22'
Roof Framing	Stick
Exterior Walls	2x4, 2x6

Living Rm 13-8 x 17-8 9'-0" clg.

linen

storage

crawl access

util/ pantry

w/h

Furn.

Foy.

OPTIONAL CRAWLSPACE/SLAB FOUNDATION

open shelves

Dining Rm 11-9 x 12-11

two-sided fireplace

Living Rm 13-8 x 17-8 9'-0" clg.

whirlpool

Master Br 15-9 x 11-11 9'-0" clg.

brkfst bar

railing

DN

Kitchen 11-9 x 12-9

utility/ pantry

linen

Foy.

Den/Guest 11-11 x 12-11

Br 2 12-8 x 10-11

planter

MAIN FLOOR

Garage 20-5 x 21-5

Design 63091

Units	Single
Price Code	B
Total Finished	1,627 sq. ft.
Main Finished	1,627 sq. ft.
Garage Unfinished	420 sq. ft.
Dimensions	46'x70'
Foundation	Slab
Bedrooms	3
Full Baths	2
Main Ceiling	10'
Max Ridge Height	25'8"
Exterior Walls	2x4

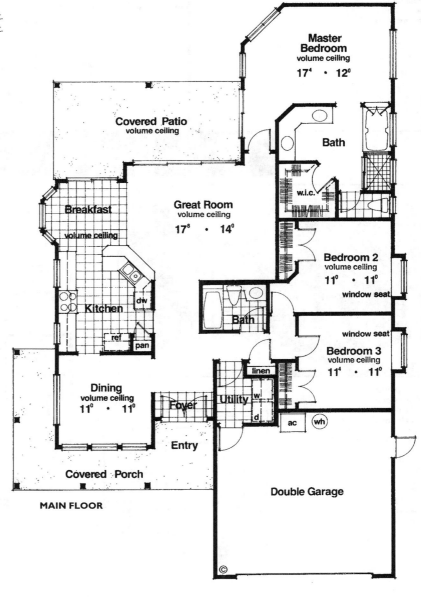

Master Bedroom
volume ceiling
17⁴ • 12⁰

Covered Patio
volume ceiling

Bath

w.i.c.

Breakfast
volume ceiling

Great Room
volume ceiling
17⁸ • 14⁰

Bedroom 2
volume ceiling
11⁰ • 11⁰
window seat

Kitchen

dw

ref

pan

Bath

window seat

Bedroom 3
volume ceiling
11⁴ • 11⁰

Dining
volume ceiling
11⁰ • 11⁰

Foyer

Utility

linen

w

d

ac

wh

Entry

Covered Porch

Double Garage

MAIN FLOOR

Design 82012

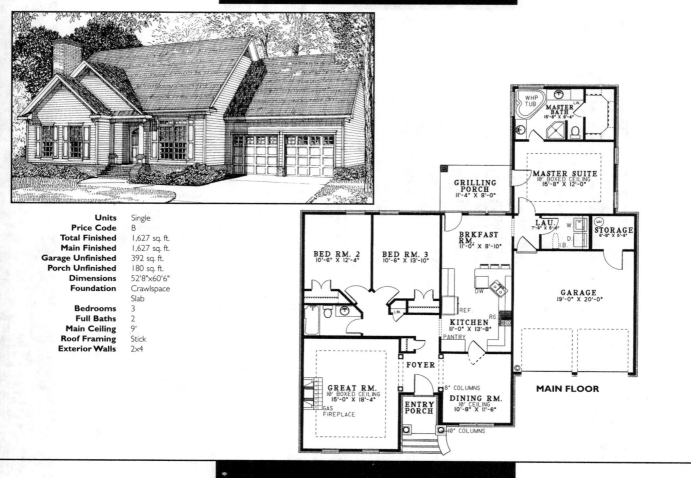

Units	Single
Price Code	B
Total Finished	1,627 sq. ft.
Main Finished	1,627 sq. ft.
Garage Unfinished	392 sq. ft.
Porch Unfinished	180 sq. ft.
Dimensions	52'8"x60'6"
Foundation	Crawlspace
	Slab
Bedrooms	3
Full Baths	2
Main Ceiling	9'
Roof Framing	Stick
Exterior Walls	2x4

Design 94831

Units	Single
Price Code	B
Total Finished	1,639 sq. ft.
Main Finished	1,639 sq. ft.
Bonus Unfinished	318 sq. ft.
Garage Unfinished	495 sq. ft.
Deck Unfinished	192 sq. ft.
Porch Unfinished	125 sq. ft.
Dimensions	58'10"x56'2"
Foundation	Crawlspace
Bedrooms	3
Full Baths	2
Max Ridge Height	23'
Exterior Walls	2x4

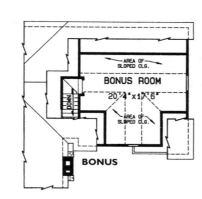

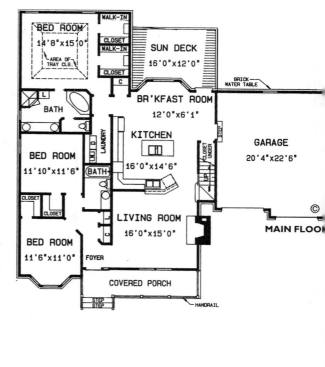

Design 98580

Units	Single
Price Code	B
Total Finished	1,640 sq. ft.
Main Finished	1,640 sq. ft.
Garage Unfinished	408 sq. ft.
Deck Unfinished	72 sq. ft.
Porch Unfinished	60 sq. ft.
Dimensions	50'x56'4"
Foundation	Slab
Bedrooms	3
Full Baths	2
Max Ridge Height	24'2"
Roof Framing	Stick
Exterior Walls	2x4

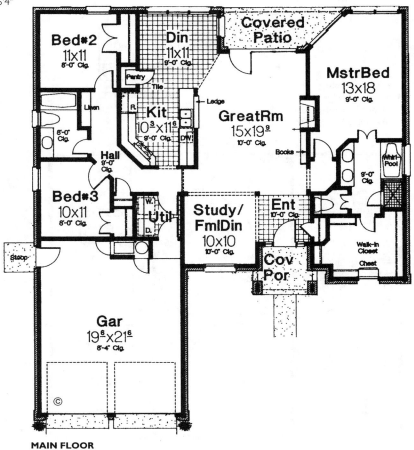

MAIN FLOOR

Units	Single
Price Code	B
Total Finished	1,642 sq. ft.
Main Finished	1,642 sq. ft.
Basement Unfinished	1,642 sq. ft.
Garage Unfinished	430 sq. ft.
Porch Unfinished	156 sq. ft.
Dimensions	59'x44'
Foundation	Basement
	Crawlspace
	Slab
Bedrooms	3
Full Baths	2
Main Ceiling	9'
Vaulted Ceiling	13'6"
Max Ridge Height	24'
Roof Framing	Stick
Exterior Walls	2x4

OPTIONAL BASEMENT STAIR LOCATION

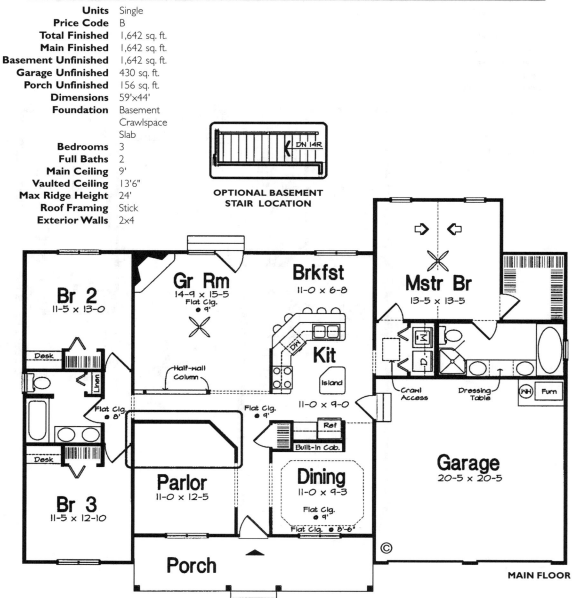

MAIN FLOOR

Design 98920

Units	Single
Price Code	B
Total Finished	1,646 sq. ft.
Main Finished	1,646 sq. ft.
Dimensions	52'x54'
Foundation	Crawlspace
	Slab
Bedrooms	3
Full Baths	2
Max Ridge Height	24'
Roof Framing	Stick
Exterior Walls	2x4

Patio
16-0 x 12-0

Dining
14-2 x 13-6
w/Bay

**Vaulted
Living Area**
17-4 x 17-6

**Master
Bdrm.**
13-6 x 16-2
w/Bay

Kitchen
14-2 x 12-0

Slope

Cab.

Cab.

M.Bath

Seat

Bth.2

Linen

Foyer
6-0 x 13-10

Cts.

St.

W.D.

F.

Wh.

Storage

Bdrm.2
10-2 x 11-6

Bdrm.3
10-6 x 11-6

Double Garage
21-4 x 19-8

MAIN FLOOR

©

Units	Single
Price Code	B
Total Finished	1,648 sq. ft.
Main Finished	1,648 sq. ft.
Basement Unfinished	1,648 sq. ft.
Garage Unfinished	495 sq. ft.
Porch Unfinished	78 sq. ft.
Dimensions	69'x50'10"
Foundation	Basement
Bedrooms	3
Full Baths	2
Main Ceiling	8'
Vaulted Ceiling	11'
Max Ridge Height	24'
Roof Framing	Truss
Exterior Walls	2x4

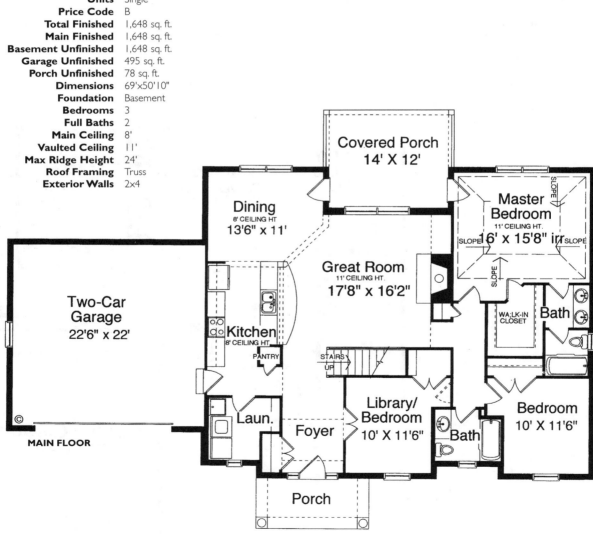

Design 96513

Units	Single
Price Code	B
Total Finished	1,648 sq. ft.
Main Finished	1,648 sq. ft.
Garage Unfinished	479 sq. ft.
Dimensions	68'x50'
Foundation	Crawlspace
	Slab
Bedrooms	3
Full Baths	2
Half Baths	1
Main Ceiling	9'
Max Ridge Height	20'
Roof Framing	Stick
Exterior Walls	2x4

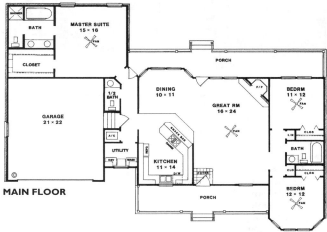

MAIN FLOOR

Design 97442

Units	Single
Price Code	B
Total Finished	1,650 sq. ft.
Main Finished	1,650 sq. ft.
Garage Unfinished	529 sq. ft.
Dimensions	50'8"x48'
Foundation	Basement
Bedrooms	3
Full Baths	2
Main Ceiling	9'
Max Ridge Height	20'6"
Roof Framing	Stick
Exterior Walls	2x4

* Alternate foundation options available at an additional charge.
  Please call 1-800-235-5700 for more information.

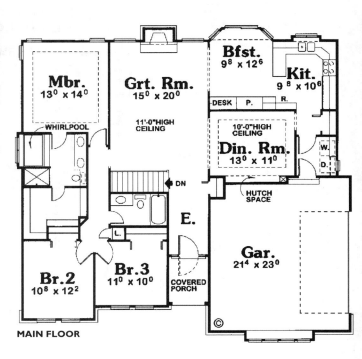

MAIN FLOOR

Design 55021

Units	Single
Price Code	B
Total Finished	1,652 sq. ft.
Main Finished	1,652 sq. ft.
Garage Unfinished	591 sq. ft.
Dimensions	78'6"x48'
Foundation	Basement
Bedrooms	3
Full Baths	2
Main Ceiling	9'
Max Ridge Height	24'
Roof Framing	Truss

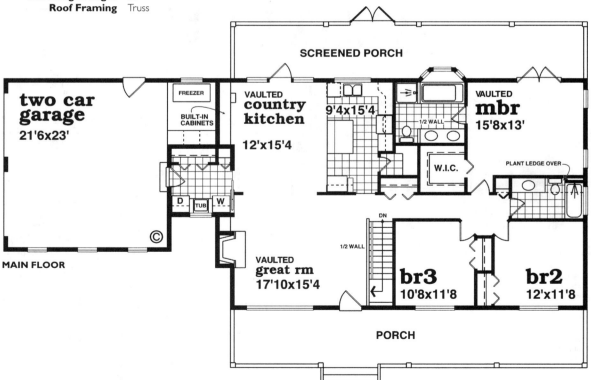

Design 64007

Units	Single
Price Code	B
Total Finished	1,654 sq. ft.
Main Finished	1,654 sq. ft.
Garage Unfinished	576 sq. ft.
Dimensions	66'10"x58'10"
Foundation	Crawlspace
	Slab
Bedrooms	3
Full Baths	2
Main Ceiling	8'
Max Ridge Height	19'3"
Roof Framing	Stick
Exterior Walls	2x4

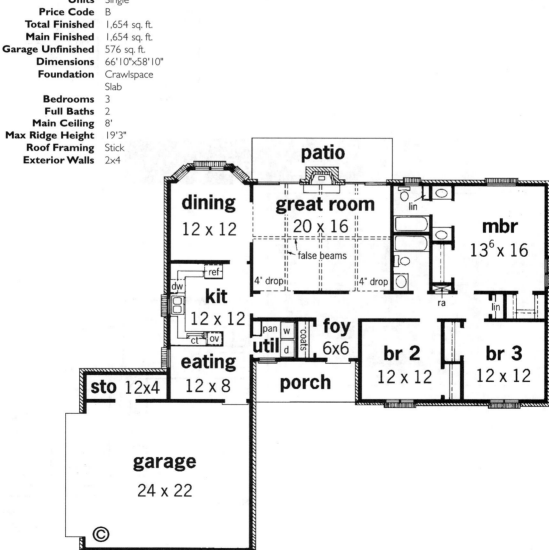

MAIN FLOOR

Design 82011

Units	Single
Price Code	B
Total Finished	1,654 sq. ft.
Main Finished	1,654 sq. ft.
Garage Unfinished	400 sq. ft.
Porch Unfinished	203 sq. ft.
Dimensions	49'x58'6"
Foundation	Basement
	Crawlspace
	Slab
Bedrooms	3
Full Baths	2
Main Ceiling	9'
Roof Framing	Stick
Exterior Walls	2x4

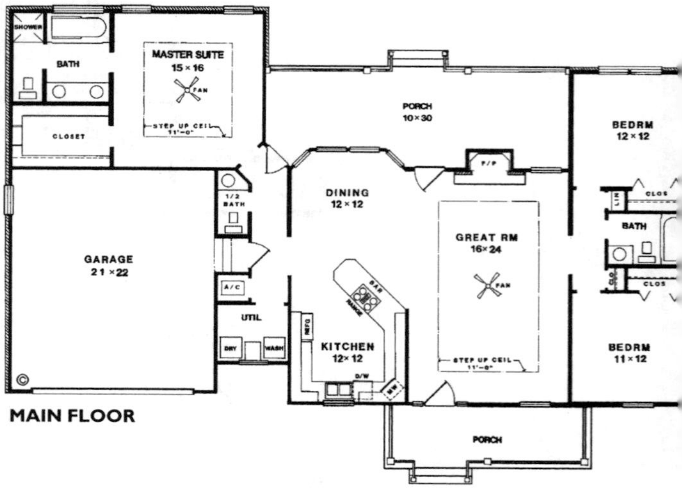

MAIN FLOOR

Floor plan labels:
BED RM. 3 12'-8" X 10'-10", COVERED PORCH 15'-4" X 7'-0", GLASS BLOCKS, WHP TUB, M.BATH, LIN, SHLVS., DINING RM. / HEARTH RM. 15'-4" X 12'-0", MASTER SUITE 10' BOXED CLNG 14'-0" X 13'-0", GAS FIREPLACE, LIN, BED RM. 2 12'-8" X 12'-4", KITCHEN 13'-0" X 13'-0", DW, RG, REF, PAN, STRG. 7'-8" X 5'-6", D., W, GARAGE 19'-8" X 20'-0", 8' COL., FOYER, SLOPED CEILING, GREAT RM. 11' FLAT CEILING 15'-4" X 18'-0", PRCH, MEDIA CENTER

Design 96506

Units	Single
Price Code	B
Total Finished	1,654 sq. ft.
Main Finished	1,654 sq. ft.
Garage Unfinished	480 sq. ft.
Porch Unfinished	401 sq. ft.
Dimensions	68'x46'
Foundation	Crawlspace
	Slab
Bedrooms	3
Full Baths	2
Half Baths	1
Main Ceiling	9'
Max Ridge Height	21'
Roof Framing	Stick
Exterior Walls	2x4

MAIN FLOOR

Floor plan labels:
SHOWER, BATH, CLOSET, MASTER SUITE 15 x 16, STEP UP CEIL 11'-0", PORCH 10 x 30, BEDRM 12 x 12, 1/2 BATH, DINING 12 x 12, GREAT RM 16 x 24, BATH, CLOS, GARAGE 21 x 22, A/C, UTIL, DRY, WASH, KITCHEN 12 x 12, D/W, STEP UP CEIL 11'-0", BEDRM 11 x 12, CLOS, PORCH

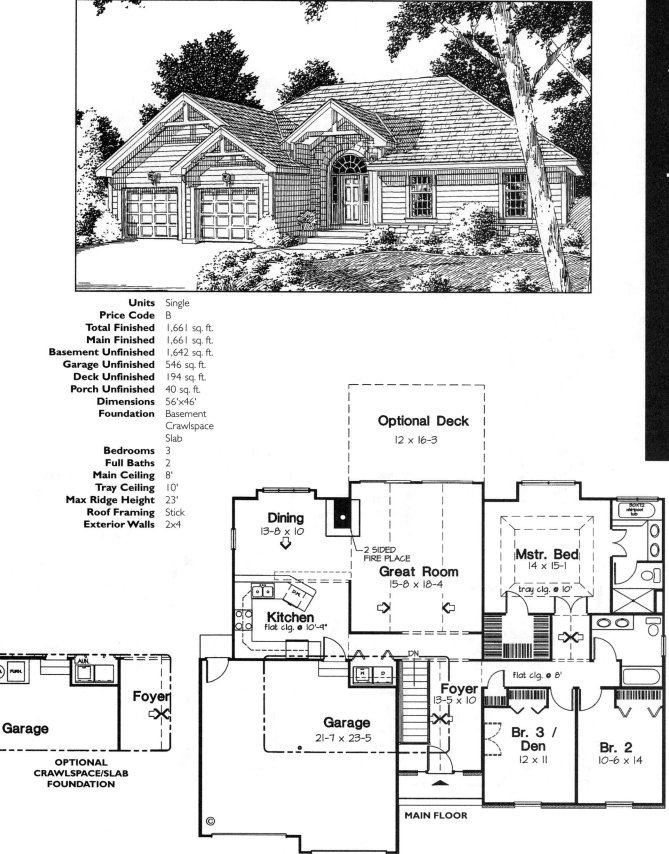

Units	Single
Price Code	B
Total Finished	1,661 sq. ft.
Main Finished	1,661 sq. ft.
Basement Unfinished	1,642 sq. ft.
Garage Unfinished	546 sq. ft.
Deck Unfinished	194 sq. ft.
Porch Unfinished	40 sq. ft.
Dimensions	56'x46'
Foundation	Basement
	Crawlspace
	Slab
Bedrooms	3
Full Baths	2
Main Ceiling	8'
Tray Ceiling	10'
Max Ridge Height	23'
Roof Framing	Stick
Exterior Walls	2x4

Optional Deck
12 x 16-3

Dining
13-8 x 10

2 SIDED FIRE PLACE

Great Room
15-8 x 18-4

Kitchen
flat clg. @ 10'-9"

Mstr. Bed
14 x 15-1
tray clg. @ 10'

50x12 whirlpool tub

flat clg. @ 8'

Foyer
13-5 x 10

Garage
21-7 x 23-5

Br. 3 / Den
12 x 11

Br. 2
10-6 x 14

MAIN FLOOR

Garage

Foyer

OPTIONAL CRAWLSPACE/SLAB FOUNDATION

Units	Single
Price Code	B
Total Finished	1,663 sq. ft.
Main Finished	1,663 sq. ft.
Basement Unfinished	1,663 sq. ft.
Garage Unfinished	539 sq. ft.
Porch Unfinished	176 sq. ft.
Dimensions	69'8"x49'
Foundation	Basement
Bedrooms	3
Full Baths	1
3/4 Baths	1
Main Ceiling	8'
Vaulted Ceiling	11'
Tray Ceiling	11'
Max Ridge Height	24'
Roof Framing	Truss
Exterior Walls	2x4

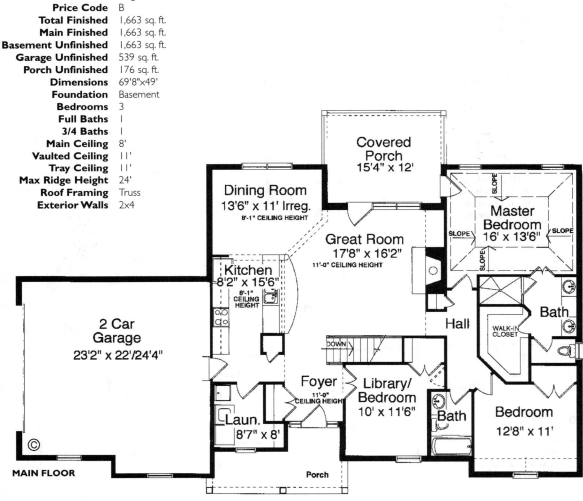

Covered Porch
15'4" x 12'

Dining Room
13'6" X 11' Irreg.
8'-1" CEILING HEIGHT

Great Room
17'8" x 16'2"
11'-0" CEILING HEIGHT

Master Bedroom
16' x 13'6"

Kitchen
8'2" x 15'6"
8'-1" CEILING HEIGHT

Bath

2 Car Garage
23'2" x 22'/24'4"

Hall

WALK-IN CLOSET

DOWN

Foyer
11'-0" CEILING HEIGHT

Library/Bedroom
10' x 11'6"

Bath

Bedroom
12'8" x 11'

Laun.
8'7" x 8'

MAIN FLOOR

Porch

Design 94923

PHOTOGRAPHY: COURTESY OF THE DESIGNER

Units	Single
Price Code	B
Total Finished	1,666 sq. ft.
Main Finished	1,666 sq. ft.
Basement Unfinished	1,666 sq. ft.
Garage Unfinished	496 sq. ft.
Dimensions	55'4"x48'
Foundation	Basement
Bedrooms	3
Full Baths	2
Max Ridge Height	22'9"
Roof Framing	Stick
Exterior Walls	2x4

* Alternate foundation options available at an additional charge.
Please call 1-800-235-5700 for more information.

Please note: The photographed home may have been modified to suit homeowner preferences. If you order plans, have a builder or design professional check them against the photograph to confirm actual construction details.

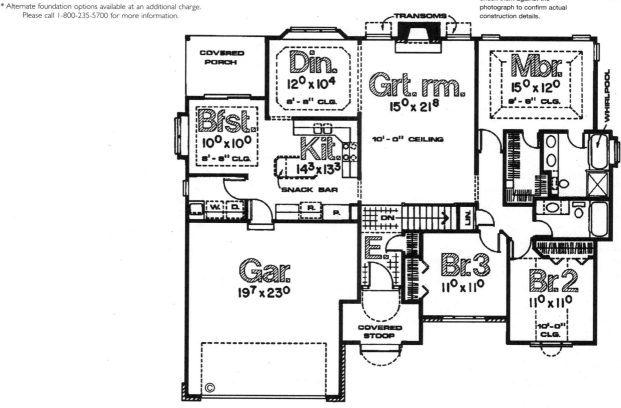

MAIN FLOOR

Units	Single
Price Code	B
Total Finished	1,670 sq. ft.
Main Finished	1,670 sq. ft.
Garage Unfinished	240 sq. ft.
Dimensions	54'x52'
Foundation	Basement
	Crawlspace
	Slab
Bedrooms	3
Full Baths	2
Main Ceiling	9'
Max Ridge Height	24'6"
Roof Framing	Stick
Exterior Walls	2x4

CAD FILES AVAILABLE
For more information call
800-235-5700

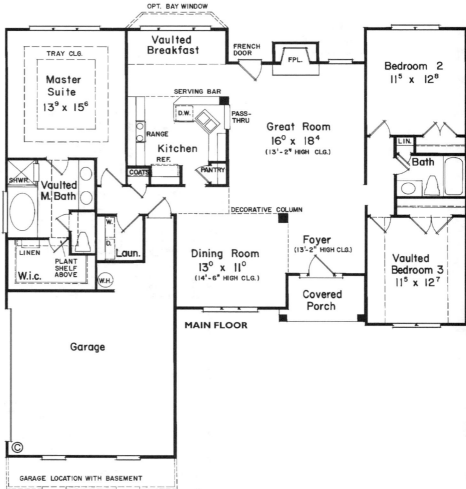

Design 98423

Units	Single
Price Code	B
Total Finished	1,671 sq. ft.
Main Finished	1,671 sq. ft.
Basement Unfinished	1,685 sq. ft.
Garage Unfinished	400 sq. ft.
Dimensions	50'x51'
Foundation	Basement
	Crawlspace
	Slab
Bedrooms	3
Full Baths	2
Main Ceiling	9'
Max Ridge Height	22'6"
Roof Framing	Stick
Exterior Walls	2x4

MAIN FLOOR

Design 34011

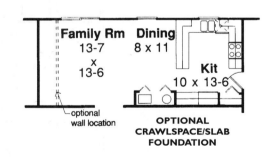

OPTIONAL CRAWLSPACE/SLAB FOUNDATION

Units	Single
Price Code	B
Total Finished	1,672 sq. ft.
Main Finished	1,672 sq. ft.
Garage Unfinished	566 sq. ft.
Dimensions	80'x32'
Foundation	Basement
	Crawlspace
	Slab
Bedrooms	3
Full Baths	2
Max Ridge Height	19'
Roof Framing	Stick
Exterior Walls	2x4, 2x6

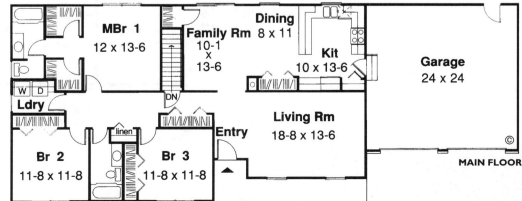

MAIN FLOOR

Units	Single
Price Code	B
Total Finished	1,672 sq. ft.
Main Finished	1,672 sq. ft.
Garage Unfinished	650 sq. ft.
Porch Unfinished	320 sq. ft.
Dimensions	52'10"x66'9"
Foundation	Crawlspace
	Slab
Bedrooms	3
Full Baths	2
Max Ridge Height	22'10"
Roof Framing	Stick
Exterior Walls	2x4

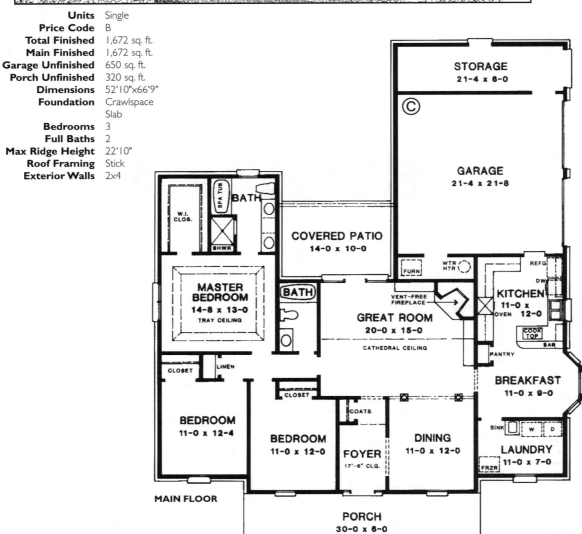

Design 98922

Units	Single
Price Code	B
Total Finished	1,675 sq. ft.
Main Finished	1,675 sq. ft.
Dimensions	56'x60'
Foundation	Crawlspace
	Slab
Bedrooms	3
Full Baths	2
Max Ridge Height	23'
Roof Framing	Stick
Exterior Walls	2x4

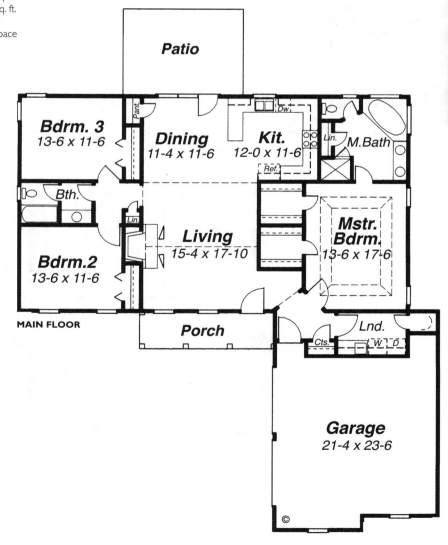

MAIN FLOOR

Design 10760

Units	Single
Price Code	B
Total Finished	1,676 sq. ft.
Main Finished	1,676 sq. ft.
Basement Unfinished	592 sq. ft.
Garage Unfinished	697 sq. ft.
Dimensions	55'2"x32'
Foundation	Basement
Bedrooms	3
Full Baths	1
3/4 Baths	1
Max Ridge Height	26'
Roof Framing	Stick
Exterior Walls	2x6

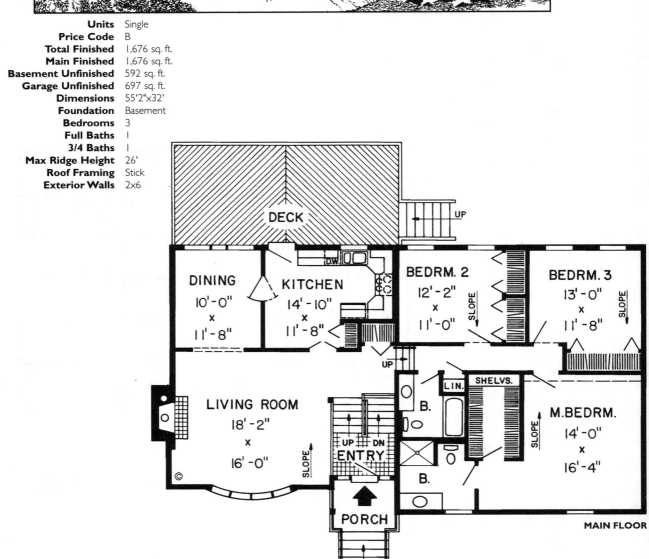

DECK

UP

DINING
10'-0"
x
11'-8"

KITCHEN
14'-10"
x
11'-8"

D.W.

BEDRM. 2
12'-2"
x
11'-0"

SLOPE

BEDRM. 3
13'-0"
x
11'-8"

SLOPE

UP

LIVING ROOM
18'-2"
x
16'-0"

SLOPE

UP   DN

ENTRY

B.

LIN.   SHELVS.

B.

SLOPE

M.BEDRM.
14'-0"
x
16'-4"

PORCH

UP

MAIN FLOOR

Design 98960

1,501-2,000 sq. ft. HOME PLANS

Units	Single
Price Code	B
Total Finished	1,676 sq. ft.
Main Finished	1,676 sq. ft.
Garage Unfinished	552 sq. ft.
Deck Unfinished	192 sq. ft.
Porch Unfinished	89 sq. ft.
Dimensions	56'x62'
Foundation	Basement
Bedrooms	3
Full Baths	2
Main Ceiling	9'
Max Ridge Height	23'
Roof Framing	Stick
Exterior Walls	2x4

Patio
16-0 x 12-0

Pant.

Dw.

Sh.

Bdrm.3
13-6 x 11-0

Dining
11-4 x 11-6

Kit.
12-0 x 11-6

Lin.

M.Bath

Ref.

Bth.2

T-Turn

Hers

His

Master Bdrm.
13-6 x 17-6

L

Vaulted

Living
15-4 x 17-10

Bdrm.2
13-6 x 11-0

Entry

Trav. Ceil.

MAIN FLOOR

Porch

Lnd.

Handicap Ramp

Wh.

Cts.

W.

D.

Double Garage
21-4 x 24-10

©

Design 68201

Units	Single
Price Code	C
Total Finished	1,678 sq. ft.
Main Finished	1,678 sq. ft.
Basement Unfinished	1,678 sq. ft.
Dimensions	46'x55'
Foundation	Basement
	Crawlspace
	Slab
Bedrooms	3
Full Baths	2
Main Ceiling	9'
Max Ridge Height	23'
Roof Framing	Stick
Exterior Walls	2x4

* Alternate foundation options available at an additional charge.
Please call 1-800-235-5700 for more information.

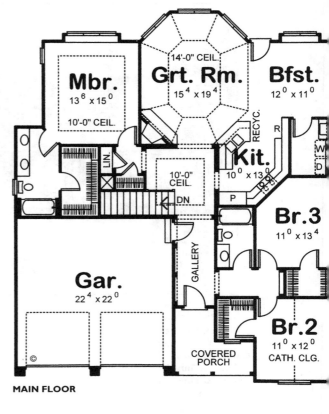

MAIN FLOOR

Design 68202

Units	Single
Price Code	B
Total Finished	1,678 sq. ft.
Main Finished	1,678 sq. ft.
Basement Unfinished	1,678 sq. ft.
Garage Unfinished	509 sq. ft.
Dimensions	46'x55'
Foundation	Basement
	Crawlspace
	Slab
Bedrooms	3
Full Baths	2
Main Ceiling	9'
Max Ridge Height	24'11"
Roof Framing	Stick
Exterior Walls	2x4

* Alternate foundation options available at an additional charge.
Please call 1-800-235-5700 for more information.

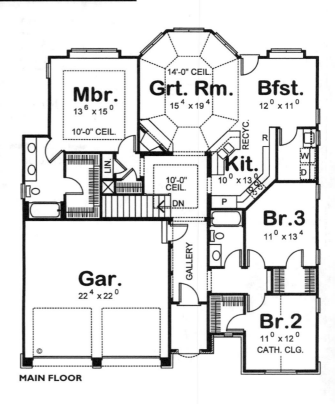

MAIN FLOOR

Design 96543

1,501-2,000 sq.ft. HOME PLANS

Units	Single
Price Code	B
Total Finished	1,680 sq. ft.
Main Finished	1,680 sq. ft.
Garage Unfinished	592 sq. ft.
Porch Unfinished	259 sq. ft.
Dimensions	54'x61'
Foundation	Crawlspace
	Slab
Bedrooms	3
Full Baths	2
Main Ceiling	9'
Vaulted Ceiling	14'
Tray Ceiling	12'
Max Ridge Height	23'
Roof Framing	Stick
Exterior Walls	2x4

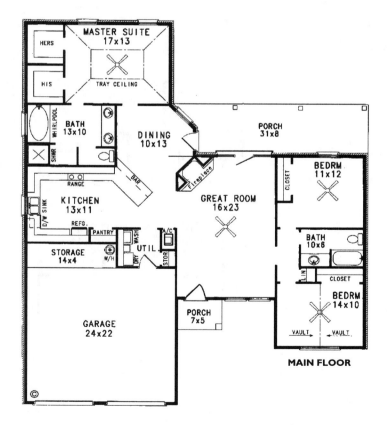

MAIN FLOOR

Design 92434

Units	Single
Price Code	B
Total Finished	1,681 sq. ft.
Main Finished	1,681 sq. ft.
Garage Unfinished	427 sq. ft.
Dimensions	55'8"x53'2"
Foundation	Slab
Bedrooms	3
Full Baths	2
Main Ceiling	9'
Vaulted Ceiling	11'
Tray Ceiling	11'
Max Ridge Height	21'8"
Roof Framing	Stick

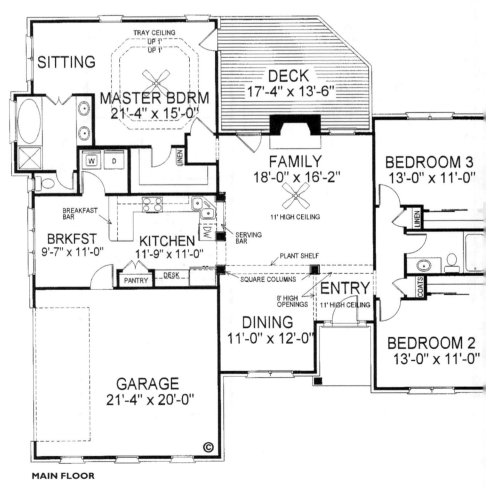

SITTING

TRAY CEILING
UP 1'
UP 1'

MASTER BDRM
21'-4" x 15'-0"

DECK
17'-4" x 13'-6"

W   D

LINEN

FAMILY
18'-0" x 16'-2"

BEDROOM 3
13'-0" x 11'-0"

11' HIGH CEILING

BREAKFAST
BAR

BRKFST
9'-7" x 11'-0"

KITCHEN
11'-9" x 11'-0"

DW

SERVING
BAR

LINEN

PANTRY   DESK

PLANT SHELF

SQUARE COLUMNS

COATS

ENTRY
11' HIGH CEILING

8' HIGH
OPENINGS

DINING
11'-0" x 12'-0"

BEDROOM 2
13'-0" x 11'-0"

GARAGE
21'-4" x 20'-0"

©

MAIN FLOOR

O sq.ft. HOME PLANS

Units	Single
Price Code	B
Total Finished	1,681 sq. ft.
Main Finished	1,681 sq. ft.
Basement Unfinished	1,681 sq. ft.
Garage Unfinished	484 sq. ft.
Porch Unfinished	79 sq. ft.
Dimensions	58'x58'
Foundation	Basement
Bedrooms	3
Full Baths	2
Main Ceiling	8'
Vaulted Ceiling	11'9"
Tray Ceiling	10'
Max Ridge Height	18'7"
Roof Framing	Stick
Exterior Walls	2x4

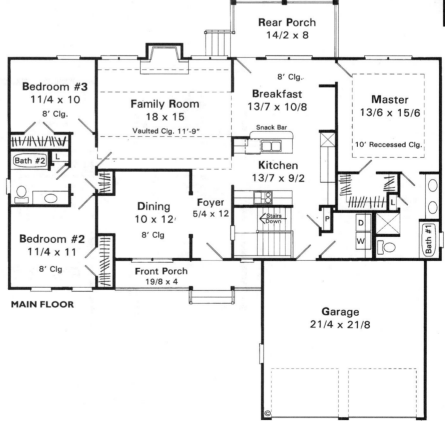

MAIN FLOOR

Units	Single
Price Code	B
Total Finished	1,682 sq. ft.
Main Finished	1,682 sq. ft.
Dimensions	52'6"x59'
Foundation	Crawlspace
Bedrooms	3
Full Baths	2
Max Ridge Height	20'
Roof Framing	Truss
Exterior Walls	2x8

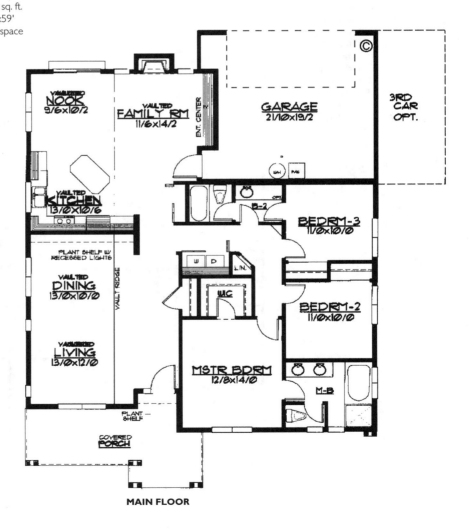

MAIN FLOOR

Design 82104

MAIN FLOOR

Units	Single
Price Code	B
Total Finished	1,683 sq. ft.
Main Finished	1,683 sq. ft.
Garage Unfinished	538 sq. ft.
Porch Unfinished	357 sq. ft.
Dimensions	59'x69'
Foundation	Basement
	Crawlspace
	Slab
Bedrooms	3
Full Baths	2
Main Ceiling	9'
Max Ridge Height	21'8"
Roof Framing	Stick
Exterior Walls	2x4, 2x6

Design 97617

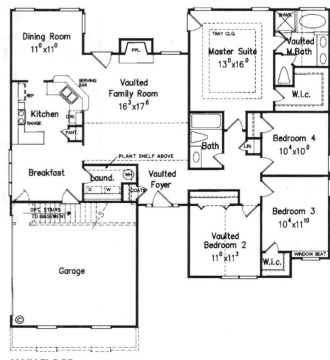

MAIN FLOOR

CAD FILES AVAILABLE
For more information call
800-235-5700

Units	Single
Price Code	B
Total Finished	1,688 sq. ft.
Main Finished	1,688 sq. ft.
Basement Unfinished	1,702 sq. ft.
Garage Unfinished	402 sq. ft.
Dimensions	50'x51'
Foundation	Basement
	Crawlspace
	Slab
Bedrooms	4
Full Baths	2
Max Ridge Height	24'6"
Roof Framing	Stick
Exterior Walls	2x4

Units	Single
Price Code	B
Total Finished	1,691 sq. ft.
Main Finished	1,691 sq. ft.
Garage Unfinished	467 sq. ft.
Porch Unfinished	11 sq. ft.
Dimensions	51'2"x44'7"
Foundation	Slab
Bedrooms	3
Full Baths	2
Main Ceiling	8'
Max Ridge Height	26'
Roof Framing	Stick
Exterior Walls	2x4

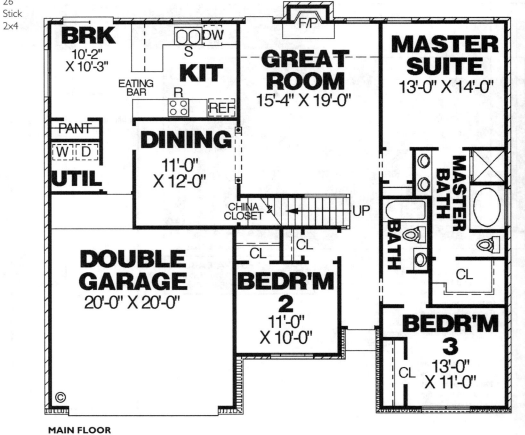

MAIN FLOOR

Units	Single
Price Code	B
Total Finished	1,692 sq. ft.
Main Finished	1,692 sq. ft.
Garage Unfinished	539 sq. ft.
Porch Unfinished	350 sq. ft.
Dimensions	46'x69'
Foundation	Basement
	Crawlspace
	Slab
Bedrooms	3
Full Baths	2
Main Ceiling	9'
Max Ridge Height	27'
Roof Framing	Stick
Exterior Walls	2x4

* Alternate foundation options available at an additional charge.
Please call 1-800-235-5700 for more information.

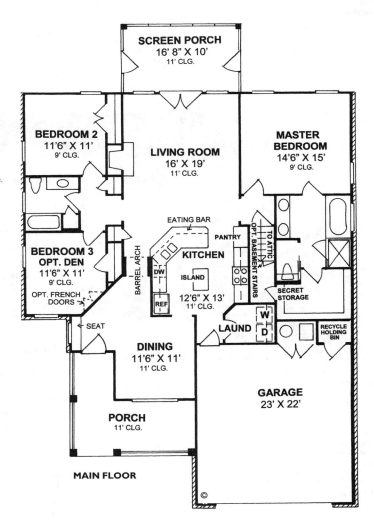

SCREEN PORCH
16' 8" X 10'
11' CLG.

BEDROOM 2
11'6" X 11'
9' CLG.

LIVING ROOM
16' X 19'
11' CLG.

MASTER BEDROOM
14'6" X 15'
9' CLG.

EATING BAR

PANTRY

OPT. BASEMENT STAIRS

TO ATTIC

KITCHEN
12'6" X 13'
11' CLG.

ISLAND

DW

REF

BEDROOM 3 OPT. DEN
11'6" X 11'
9' CLG.

OPT. FRENCH DOORS

BARREL ARCH

SECRET STORAGE

LAUND

W D

RECYCLE HOLDING BIN

SEAT

DINING
11'6" X 11'
11' CLG.

GARAGE
23' X 22'

PORCH
11' CLG.

MAIN FLOOR

Design 97254

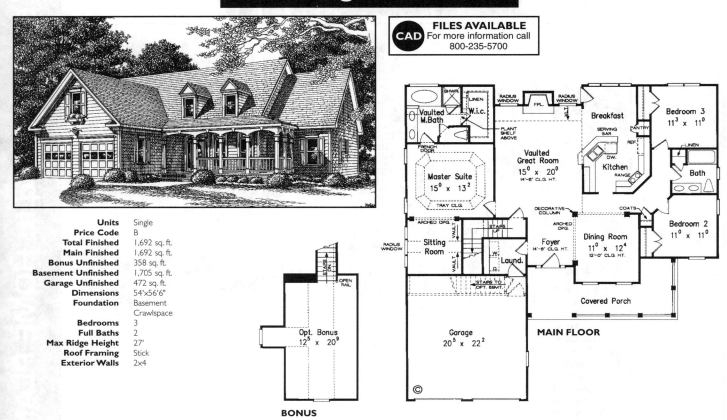

Units	Single
Price Code	B
Total Finished	1,692 sq. ft.
Main Finished	1,692 sq. ft.
Bonus Unfinished	358 sq. ft.
Basement Unfinished	1,705 sq. ft.
Garage Unfinished	472 sq. ft.
Dimensions	54'x56'6"
Foundation	Basement
	Crawlspace
Bedrooms	3
Full Baths	2
Max Ridge Height	27'
Roof Framing	Stick
Exterior Walls	2x4

Design 92290

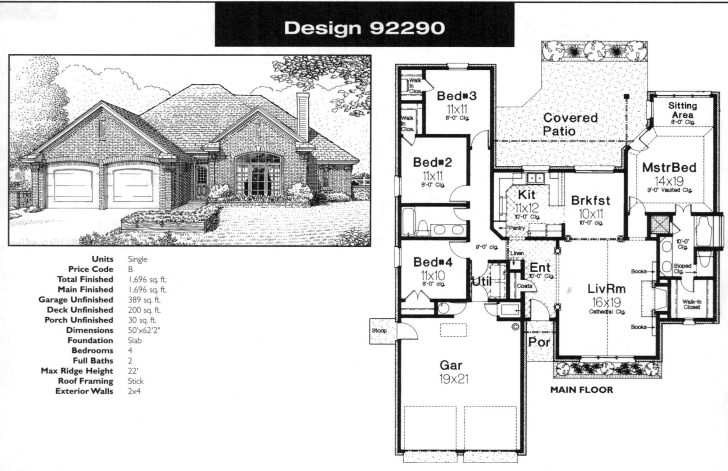

Units	Single
Price Code	B
Total Finished	1,696 sq. ft.
Main Finished	1,696 sq. ft.
Garage Unfinished	389 sq. ft.
Deck Unfinished	200 sq. ft.
Porch Unfinished	30 sq. ft.
Dimensions	50'x62'2"
Foundation	Slab
Bedrooms	4
Full Baths	2
Max Ridge Height	22'
Roof Framing	Stick
Exterior Walls	2x4

Design 97607

Units	Single
Price Code	B
Total Finished	1,696 sq. ft.
Main Finished	1,696 sq. ft.
Basement Unfinished	1,720 sq. ft.
Garage Unfinished	475 sq. ft.
Dimensions	52'x59'
Foundation	Basement
	Crawlspace
Bedrooms	3
Full Baths	2
Main Ceiling	9'
Max Ridge Height	24'4"
Exterior Walls	2x4

CAD FILES AVAILABLE
For more information call
800-235-5700

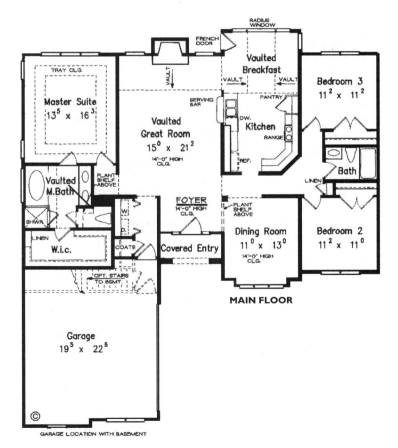

MAIN FLOOR

GARAGE LOCATION WITH BASEMENT

Units	Single
Price Code	B
Total Finished	1,698 sq. ft.
Main Finished	1,698 sq. ft.
Basement Unfinished	1,698 sq. ft.
Garage Unfinished	483 sq. ft.
Porch Unfinished	200 sq. ft.
Dimensions	59'x61'
Foundation	Basement
	Crawlspace
	Slab
Bedrooms	3
Full Baths	2
Half Baths	1
Main Ceiling	8'
Second Ceiling	9'
Vaulted Ceiling	10'
Max Ridge Height	24'
Roof Framing	Truss
Exterior Walls	2x4

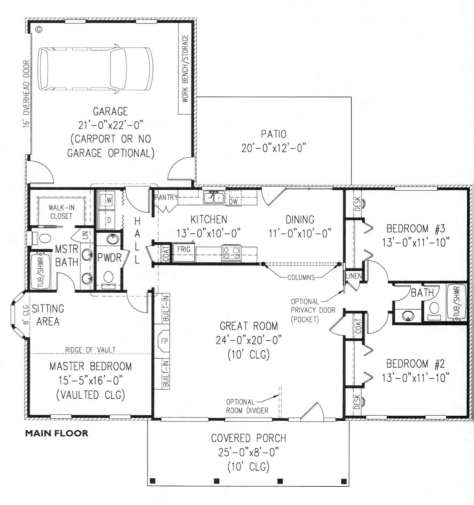

MAIN FLOOR

Design 81010

Units	Single
Price Code	B
Total Finished	1,699 sq. ft.
Main Finished	1,699 sq. ft.
Dimensions	50'x51'
Foundation	Crawlspace
Bedrooms	3
Full Baths	2
Main Ceiling	9'
Max Ridge Height	23'
Roof Framing	Truss
Exterior Walls	2x6

VAULTED
MASTER
11/0 X 15/0 +

PORCH

NOOK
8/0 X 10/0 +/-
(9' CLG.)

10/2 x 10/4 +/-

REF.

W. D.

FAMILY
11/0 X 13/4
(9' CLG.)

BR. 2
11/0 X 10/0
(9' CLG.)

DINING
13/0 X 10/0
(9' CLG.)

GARAGE
20/0 X 23/6 +/-

LIVING
13/0 X 12/0 +/-
(9' CLG.)

BR. 3
11/0 X 10/0
(9' CLG.)

MAIN FLOOR

Units	Single
Price Code	D
Total Finished	1,700 sq. ft.
Main Finished	1,700 sq. ft.
Dimensions	50'x42'
Foundation	Crawlspace
Bedrooms	3
Full Baths	2
Main Ceiling	9'
Max Ridge Height	24'
Roof Framing	Truss
Exterior Walls	2x4

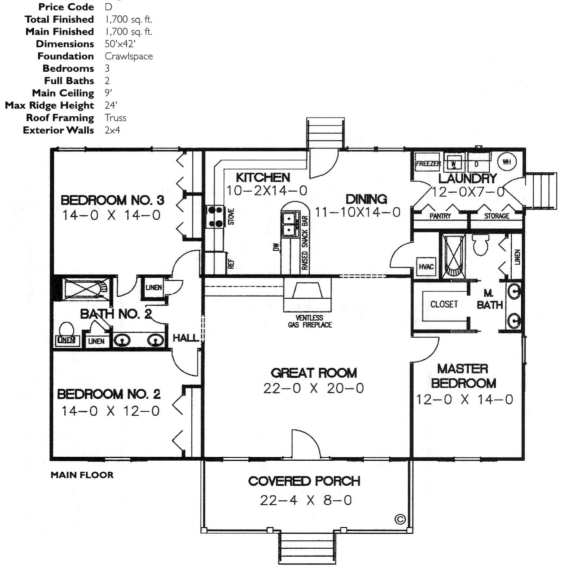

MAIN FLOOR

Design 24719

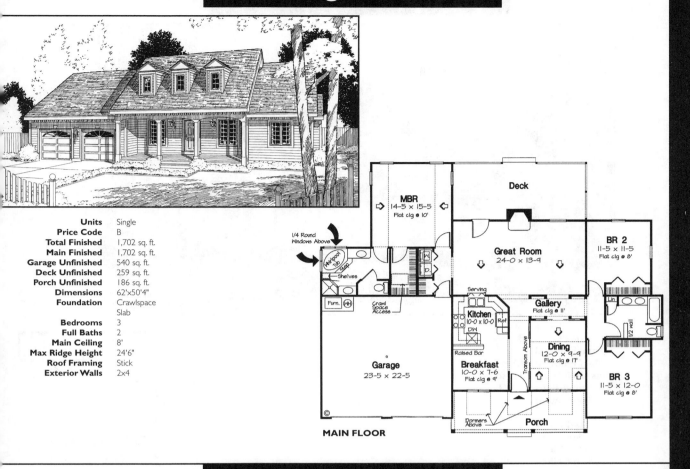

Units	Single
Price Code	B
Total Finished	1,702 sq. ft.
Main Finished	1,702 sq. ft.
Garage Unfinished	540 sq. ft.
Deck Unfinished	259 sq. ft.
Porch Unfinished	186 sq. ft.
Dimensions	62'x50'4"
Foundation	Crawlspace
	Slab
Bedrooms	3
Full Baths	2
Main Ceiling	8'
Max Ridge Height	24'6"
Roof Framing	Stick
Exterior Walls	2x4

MAIN FLOOR

Design 52183

BONUS

Units	Single
Price Code	B
Total Finished	1,704 sq. ft.
Main Finished	1,704 sq. ft.
Basement Unfinished	1,704 sq. ft.
Garage Unfinished	470 sq. ft.
Dimensions	54'x53'4"
Foundation	Basement
	Crawlspace
Bedrooms	3
Full Baths	2
Main Ceiling	9'
Second Ceiling	8'
Max Ridge Height	26'
Roof Framing	Stick
Exterior Walls	2x4

MAIN FLOOR

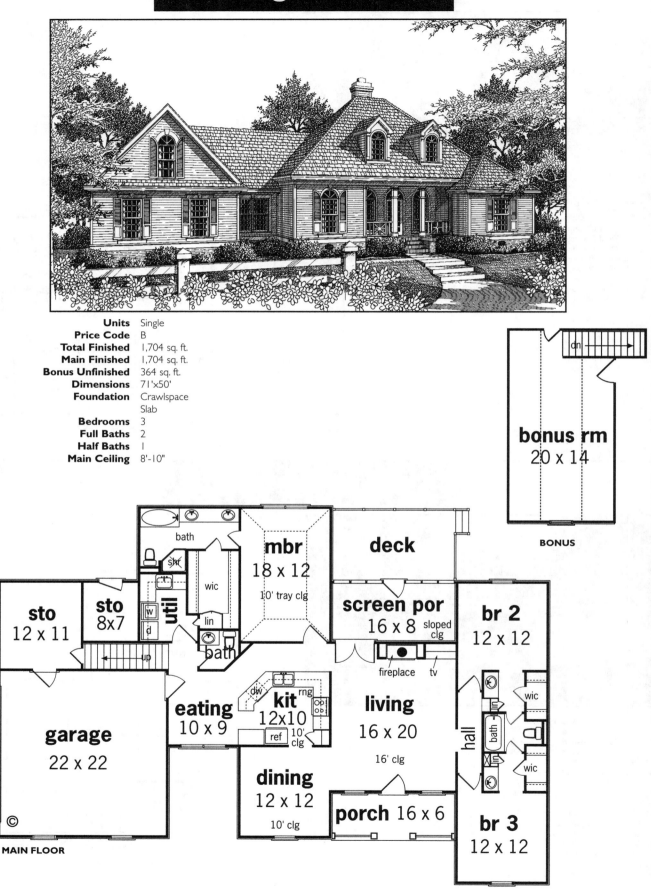

Units	Single
Price Code	B
Total Finished	1,704 sq. ft.
Main Finished	1,704 sq. ft.
Bonus Unfinished	364 sq. ft.
Dimensions	71'x50'
Foundation	Crawlspace
	Slab
Bedrooms	3
Full Baths	2
Half Baths	1
Main Ceiling	8'-10"

bonus rm 20 x 14

BONUS

mbr 18 x 12 — 10' tray clg

deck

screen por 16 x 8 — sloped clg

br 2 12 x 12

bath — sht — wic — lin — util — w — d

sto 12 x 11

sto 8x7

garage 22 x 22

eating 10 x 9

dw — **kit** 12x10 — rng — 10' clg — ref

up

fireplace — tv

living 16 x 20 — 16' clg

hall — bath — wic — wic

dining 12 x 12 — 10' clg

porch 16 x 6

br 3 12 x 12

MAIN FLOOR

Design 94602

Units	Single
Price Code	B
Total Finished	1,704 sq. ft.
Main Finished	1,704 sq. ft.
Porch Unfinished	146 sq. ft.
Dimensions	45'x58'4"
Foundation	Crawlspace
	Slab
Bedrooms	3
Full Baths	2
Main Ceiling	9'
Max Ridge Height	20'3"
Roof Framing	Truss
Exterior Walls	2x4, 2x6

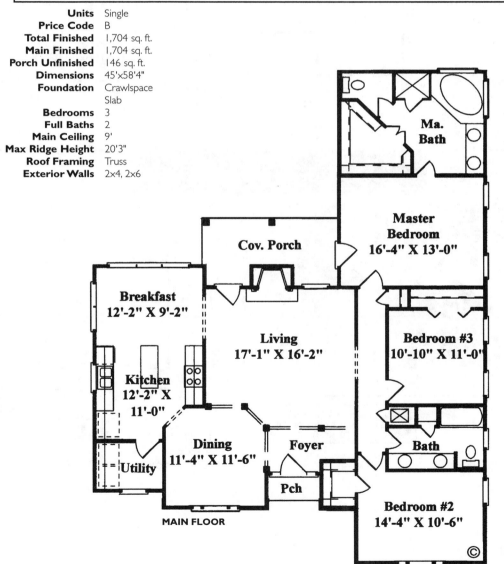

Ma. Bath

Master Bedroom
16'-4" X 13'-0"

Cov. Porch

Breakfast
12'-2" X 9'-2"

Living
17'-1" X 16'-2"

Bedroom #3
10'-10" X 11'-0"

Kitchen
12'-2" X 11'-0"

Bath

Dining
11'-4" X 11'-6"

Foyer

Utility

Pch

Bedroom #2
14'-4" X 10'-6"

MAIN FLOOR

Design 69016

Units	Single
Price Code	B
Total Finished	1,708 sq. ft.
Main Finished	1,708 sq. ft.
Dimensions	80'x42'
Foundation	Basement
	Crawlspace
Bedrooms	3
Full Baths	2
Main Ceiling	8'
Max Ridge Height	21'6"
Roof Framing	Truss
Exterior Walls	2x4

Porch

Family
15-5x20-3

Garage
23-8x23-5

Br 3
10-4x12-4

Dn

P

R

Kit
9-8x
10-0

MBr
13-7x15-11

W D

Dining
10-0x11-6

Brk
9-8x
8-0

Foyer

Br 2
11-5x12-11

MAIN FLOOR

Porch depth 4-0

Design 98456

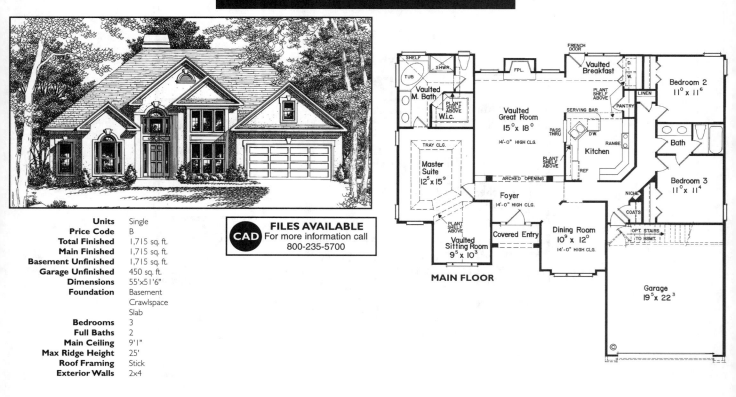

Units	Single
Price Code	B
Total Finished	1,715 sq. ft.
Main Finished	1,715 sq. ft.
Basement Unfinished	1,715 sq. ft.
Garage Unfinished	450 sq. ft.
Dimensions	55'x51'6"
Foundation	Basement
	Crawlspace
	Slab
Bedrooms	3
Full Baths	2
Main Ceiling	9'1"
Max Ridge Height	25'
Roof Framing	Stick
Exterior Walls	2x4

CAD **FILES AVAILABLE** For more information call 800-235-5700

SHELF
SHWR.
TUB
Vaulted
M. Bath
W.i.c.

FPL.

FRENCH DOOR
Vaulted Breakfast
D.
W.

Bedroom 2
11⁰ x 11⁶

Vaulted Great Room
15⁰ x 18⁰
14'-0" HIGH CLG.

PLANT SHELF ABOVE

SERVING BAR
PANTRY
LINEN
PLANT SHELF ABOVE

Kitchen
RANGE
DW.
REF.

Bath

TRAY CLG.
Master Suite
12⁵ x 15⁹

PASS THRU

PLANT SHELF ABOVE

Bedroom 3
11⁰ x 11⁴

ARCHED OPENING

NICHE
COATS

Foyer
14'-0" HIGH CLG.

PLANT SHELF ABOVE

Vaulted Sitting Room
9⁵ x 10³

Covered Entry

Dining Room
10⁹ x 12⁰
14'-0" HIGH CLG.

OPT. STAIRS TO BSMT.

Garage
19⁵ x 22³

MAIN FLOOR

Design 64502

Units	Single
Price Code	B
Total Finished	1,716 sq. ft.
Main Finished	1,716 sq. ft.
Garage Unfinished	500 sq. ft.
Porch Unfinished	624 sq. ft.
Dimensions	44'x65'
Foundation	Basement
	Crawlspace
	Slab
Bedrooms	3
Full Baths	2
Main Ceiling	9'
Max Ridge Height	24'
Roof Framing	Truss
Exterior Walls	2x4

MASTER BEDROOM 16'8 X 16'0

7' DEEP PORCH

CLOSET 6'0 X 10'0

BD RM 3 12'0 X 11'8

11' DEEP PORCH

GREAT ROOM 19'6 X 22'0

BD RM 2 11'10 X 11'0

KITCHEN/ BREAKFAST 12'8 X 21'10

SNACK BAR   COOKTOP

REF.   OVEN   P

6' DEEP PORCH

MAIN FLOOR

STOR   STOR

DETACHED GARAGE 24'0 X 20'0

GARAGE

Units	Single
Price Code	B
Total Finished	1,721 sq. ft.
Main Finished	1,721 sq. ft.
Dimensions	83'x42'
Foundation	Basement
	Crawlspace
	Slab
Bedrooms	3
Full Baths	2
Main Ceiling	8'
Max Ridge Height	22'
Roof Framing	Truss
Exterior Walls	2x4

MAIN FLOOR

Atrium Below

Dn

Brk
11-5x12-0

Great Rm
16-0x16-10
vaulted

MBr
16-0x14-0
vaulted

Covered
Porch

Kit
11-5x
12-0

vaulted

P

R

Garage
29-4x21-4

Dining
11-0x11-6

Br 3
11-1x13-3

Br 2
11-0x12-9

W
D

Porch
27-8x5-0

Design 52059

Units	Single
Price Code	B
Total Finished	1,727 sq. ft.
Main Finished	1,727 sq. ft.
Bonus Unfinished	318 sq. ft.
Basement Unfinished	1,727 sq. ft.
Garage Unfinished	555 sq. ft.
Dimensions	55'x62'
Foundation	Basement
	Crawlspace
Bedrooms	3
Full Baths	2
Main Ceiling	9'
Max Ridge Height	23'9"
Roof Framing	Stick
Exterior Walls	2x4

CAD **FILES AVAILABLE**
For more information call
800-235-5700

BONUS

MAIN FLOOR

Design 50052

Units	Single
Price Code	B
Total Finished	1,729 sq. ft.
Main Finished	1,729 sq. ft.
Basement Unfinished	1,729 sq. ft.
Garage Unfinished	544 sq. ft.
Porch Unfinished	110 sq. ft.
Dimensions	70'6"x50'2"
Foundation	Basement
Bedrooms	3
Full Baths	2
Main Ceiling	8'
Vaulted Ceiling	11'
Tray Ceiling	11'
Max Ridge Height	24'
Roof Framing	Truss
Exterior Walls	2x4

MAIN FLOOR

Design 99923

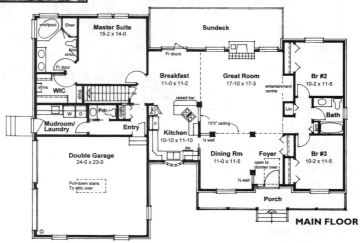

Units	Single
Price Code	B
Total Finished	1,734 sq. ft.
Main Finished	1,734 sq. ft.
Basement Unfinished	1,842 sq. ft.
Garage Unfinished	528 sq. ft.
Deck Unfinished	252 sq. ft.
Porch Unfinished	132 sq. ft.
Dimensions	66'x48'
Foundation	Basement
Bedrooms	3
Full Baths	2
Half Baths	1
Main Ceiling	8'
Vaulted Ceiling	10'
Max Ridge Height	22'
Roof Framing	Truss
Exterior Walls	2x6

MAIN FLOOR

Design 97352

Units	Single
Price Code	C
Total Finished	1,735 sq. ft.
Main Finished	1,735 sq. ft.
Basement Unfinished	1,314 sq. ft.
Dimensions	49'4"x63'8"
Foundation	Basement
Bedrooms	3
Full Baths	2
Main Ceiling	9'
Max Ridge Height	24'3"
Roof Framing	Truss
Exterior Walls	2x6

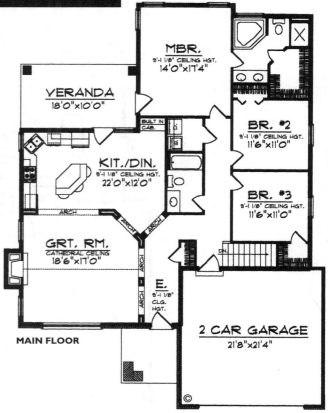

MAIN FLOOR

Units	Single
Price Code	B
Total Finished	1,735 sq. ft.
Main Finished	1,735 sq. ft.
Garage Unfinished	488 sq. ft.
Dimensions	60'x50'
Foundation	Basement
Bedrooms	3
Full Baths	2
Max Ridge Height	19'4"
Roof Framing	Stick
Exterior Walls	2x4

* Alternate foundation options available at an additional charge.
Please call 1-800-235-5700 for more information.

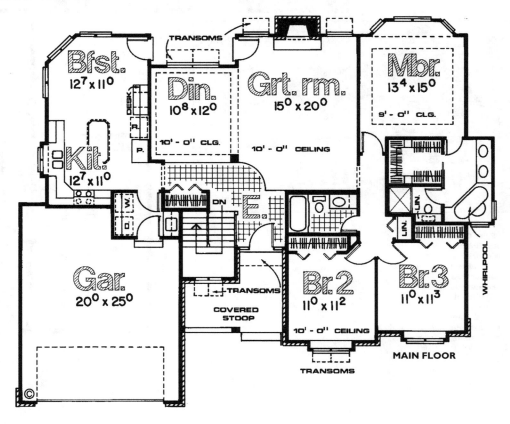

Design 93402

Units	Single
Price Code	B
Total Finished	1,739 sq. ft.
Main Finished	1,739 sq. ft.
Garage Unfinished	509 sq. ft.
Porch Unfinished	144 sq. ft.
Dimensions	64'x49'
Foundation	Crawlspace
	Slab
Bedrooms	3
Full Baths	2
Max Ridge Height	24'
Roof Framing	Stick
Exterior Walls	2x4

MAIN FLOOR

Design 65083

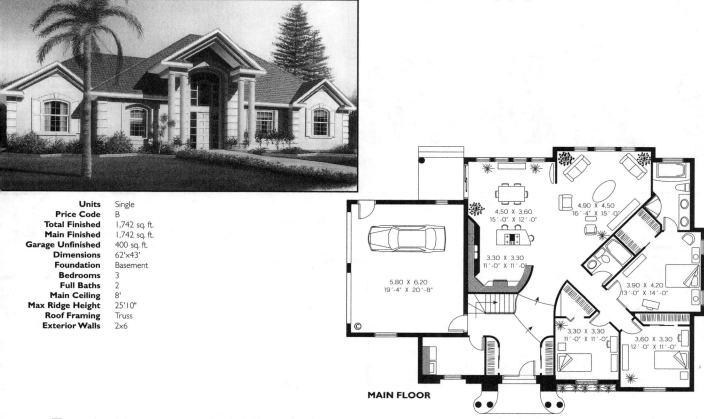

Units	Single
Price Code	B
Total Finished	1,742 sq. ft.
Main Finished	1,742 sq. ft.
Garage Unfinished	400 sq. ft.
Dimensions	62'x43'
Foundation	Basement
Bedrooms	3
Full Baths	2
Main Ceiling	8'
Max Ridge Height	25'10"
Roof Framing	Truss
Exterior Walls	2x6

MAIN FLOOR

Design 92625

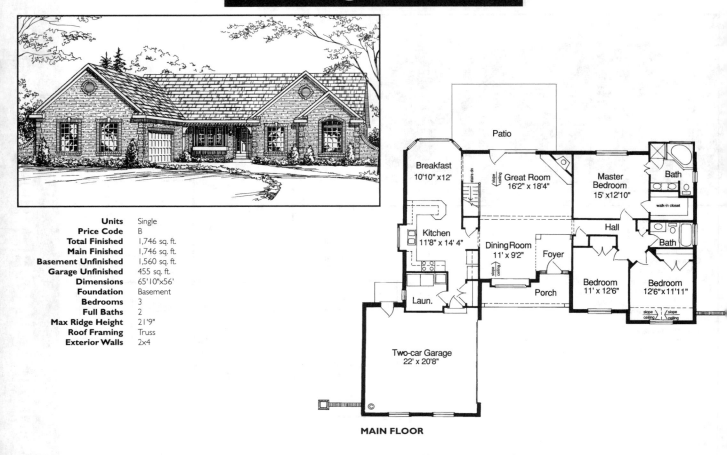

Units	Single
Price Code	B
Total Finished	1,746 sq. ft.
Main Finished	1,746 sq. ft.
Basement Unfinished	1,560 sq. ft.
Garage Unfinished	455 sq. ft.
Dimensions	65'10"×56'
Foundation	Basement
Bedrooms	3
Full Baths	2
Max Ridge Height	21'9"
Roof Framing	Truss
Exterior Walls	2×4

MAIN FLOOR

Design 92655

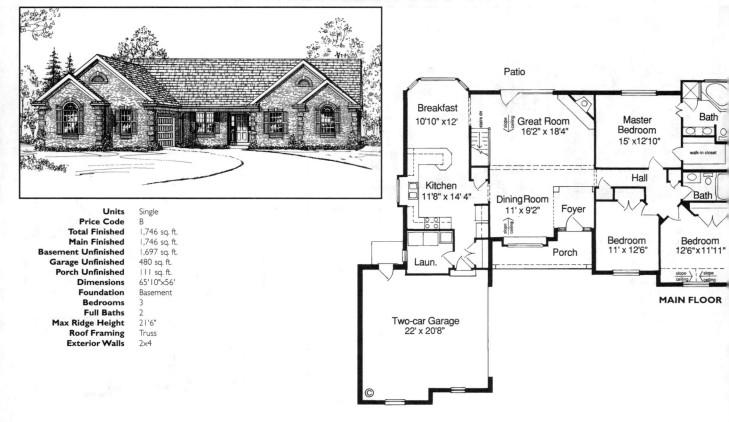

Units	Single
Price Code	B
Total Finished	1,746 sq. ft.
Main Finished	1,746 sq. ft.
Basement Unfinished	1,697 sq. ft.
Garage Unfinished	480 sq. ft.
Porch Unfinished	111 sq. ft.
Dimensions	65'10"×56'
Foundation	Basement
Bedrooms	3
Full Baths	2
Max Ridge Height	21'6"
Roof Framing	Truss
Exterior Walls	2×4

MAIN FLOOR

Design 52018

Units	Single
Price Code	B
Total Finished	1,748 sq. ft.
Main Finished	1,748 sq. ft.
Bonus Unfinished	303 sq. ft.
Basement Unfinished	1,748 sq. ft.
Garage Unfinished	436 sq. ft.
Dimensions	55'x55'
Foundation	Basement
	Crawlspace
Bedrooms	3
Full Baths	2
Main Ceiling	9'
Second Ceiling	8'
Max Ridge Height	24'
Roof Framing	Stick
Exterior Walls	2x4

CAD FILES AVAILABLE
For more information call
800-235-5700

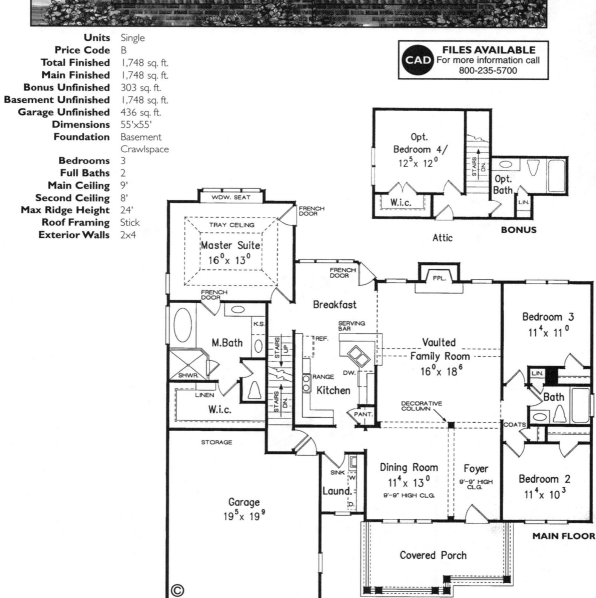

Opt. Bedroom 4/ 12⁵ x 12⁰

W.i.c.

Opt. Bath

LIN.

Attic

BONUS

WDW. SEAT

TRAY CEILING

FRENCH DOOR

Master Suite 16⁰ x 13⁰

FRENCH DOOR

K.S.

M.Bath

SHWR.

LINEN

W.i.c.

STORAGE

Garage 19⁵ x 19⁹

FRENCH DOOR

Breakfast

SERVING BAR

REF.

RANGE

Kitchen

DW.

PANT.

FPL.

Vaulted Family Room 16⁰ x 18⁶

DECORATIVE COLUMN

COATS

Bedroom 3 11⁴ x 11⁰

LIN.

Bath

SINK

Laund.

Dining Room 11⁴ x 13⁰
9'-9" HIGH CLG.

Foyer 9'-9" HIGH CLG.

Bedroom 2 11⁴ x 10³

MAIN FLOOR

Covered Porch

Design 10839

PHOTOGRAPHY: JOHN EHRENCLOU

Units	Single
Price Code	B
Total Finished	1,750 sq. ft.
Main Finished	1,750 sq. ft.
Basement Unfinished	1,083 sq. ft.
Garage Unfinished	796 sq. ft.
Porch Unfinished	100 sq. ft.
Dimensions	66'x50'
Foundation	Basement
	Crawlspace
	Slab
Bedrooms	2
Full Baths	2
Main Ceiling	8'
Max Ridge Height	24'6"
Roof Framing	Stick
Exterior Walls	2x4, 2x6

Please note: The photographed home may have been modified to suit homeowner preferences. If you order plans, have a builder or design professional check them against the photograph to confirm actual construction details.

OPTIONAL CRAWLSPACE/SLAB FOUNDATION

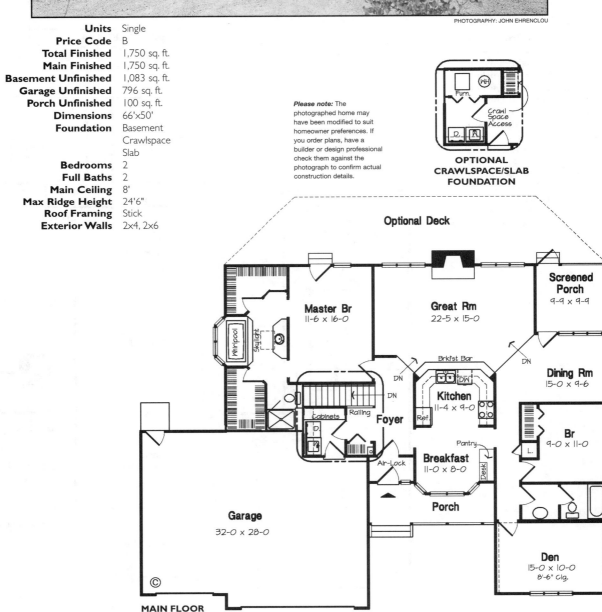

Design 50031

Units	Single
Price Code	C
Total Finished	1,751 sq. ft.
Main Finished	1,751 sq. ft.
Basement Unfinished	1,751 sq. ft.
Garage Unfinished	500 sq. ft.
Porch Unfinished	136 sq. ft.
Dimensions	72'6"x42'3"
Foundation	Basement
Bedrooms	3
Full Baths	2
Main Ceiling	8'
Max Ridge Height	42'
Roof Framing	Truss
Exterior Walls	2x4

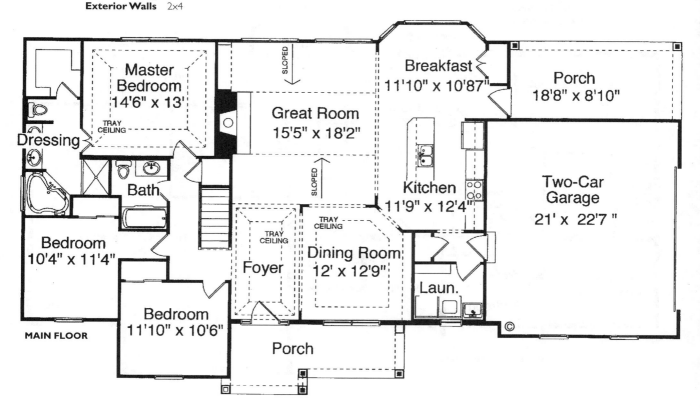

MAIN FLOOR

Units	Single
Price Code	B
Total Finished	1,755 sq. ft.
Main Finished	1,755 sq. ft.
Basement Unfinished	1,725 sq. ft.
Garage Unfinished	796 sq. ft.
Deck Unfinished	44 sq. ft.
Porch Unfinished	138 sq. ft.
Dimensions	78'6"x47'7"
Foundation	Basement
Bedrooms	3
Full Baths	2
Main Ceiling	8'
Max Ridge Height	22'
Roof Framing	Truss
Exterior Walls	2x4

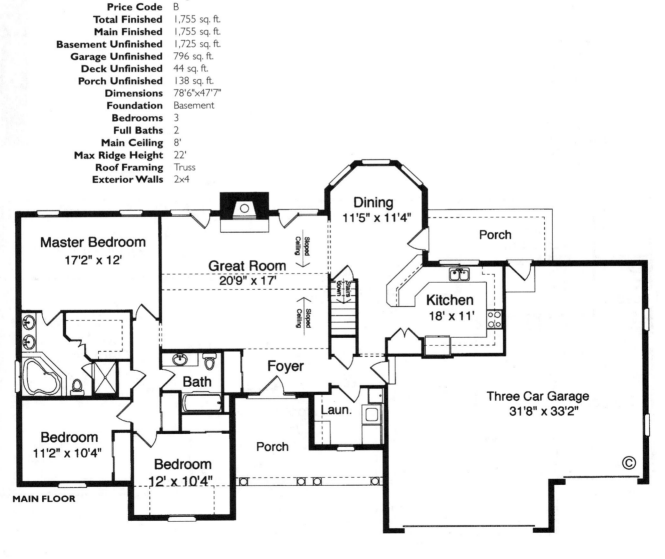

MAIN FLOOR

Design 60078

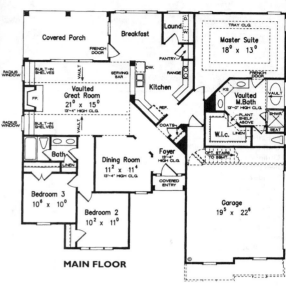

FILES AVAILABLE
CAD For more information call
800-235-5700

Units	Single
Price Code	C
Total Finished	1,756 sq. ft.
Main Finished	1,756 sq. ft.
Basement Unfinished	1,756 sq. ft.
Garage Unfinished	481 sq. ft.
Dimensions	52'6"x51'6"
Foundation	Basement
	Crawlspace
Bedrooms	3
Full Baths	2
Main Ceiling	9'
Roof Framing	Stick
Exterior Walls	2x4

MAIN FLOOR

Design 97456

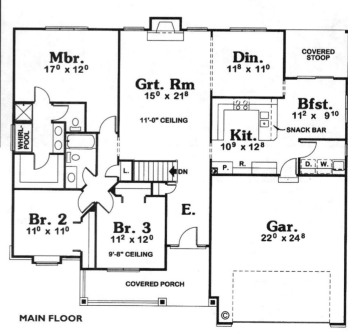

Units	Single
Price Code	C
Total Finished	1,758 sq. ft.
Main Finished	1,758 sq. ft.
Garage Unfinished	494 sq. ft.
Dimensions	55'4"x49'8"
Foundation	Basement
Bedrooms	3
Full Baths	2
Main Ceiling	9'
Max Ridge Height	26'
Roof Framing	Stick
Exterior Walls	2x4

* Alternate foundation options available at an additional charge.
  Please call 1-800-235-5700 for more information.

MAIN FLOOR

Design 93133

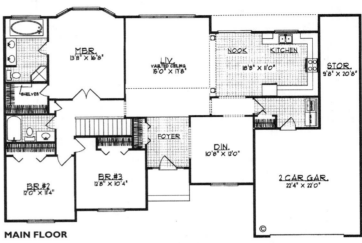

Units	Single
Price Code	C
Total Finished	1,763 sq. ft.
Main Finished	1,763 sq. ft.
Basement Unfinished	1,763 sq. ft.
Garage Unfinished	658 sq. ft.
Dimensions	67'8"x42'8"
Foundation	Basement
Bedrooms	3
Full Baths	2
Main Ceiling	8'
Vaulted Ceiling	14'
Max Ridge Height	22'
Roof Framing	Truss
Exterior Walls	2x6

MAIN FLOOR

Design 50046

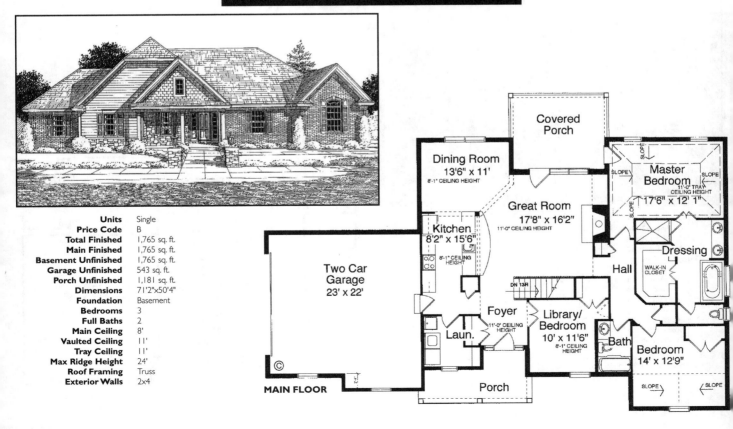

Units	Single
Price Code	B
Total Finished	1,765 sq. ft.
Main Finished	1,765 sq. ft.
Basement Unfinished	1,765 sq. ft.
Garage Unfinished	543 sq. ft.
Porch Unfinished	1,181 sq. ft.
Dimensions	71'2"x50'4"
Foundation	Basement
Bedrooms	3
Full Baths	2
Main Ceiling	8'
Vaulted Ceiling	11'
Tray Ceiling	11'
Max Ridge Height	24'
Roof Framing	Truss
Exterior Walls	2x4

MAIN FLOOR

Design 96534

1,501–2,000 sq. ft. HOME PLANS

Units	Single
Price Code	C
Total Finished	1,765 sq. ft.
Main Finished	1,765 sq. ft.
Garage Unfinished	440 sq. ft.
Porch Unfinished	435 sq. ft.
Dimensions	68'x47'
Foundation	Crawlspace
Bedrooms	3
Full Baths	2
Main Ceiling	9'
Max Ridge Height	21'
Roof Framing	Stick
Exterior Walls	2x4

MAIN FLOOR

Units	Single
Price Code	C
Total Finished	1,768 sq. ft.
Main Finished	1,768 sq. ft.
Bonus Unfinished	347 sq. ft.
Garage Unfinished	524 sq. ft.
Dimensions	54'x59'6"
Foundation	Basement
	Crawlspace
	Slab
Bedrooms	3
Full Baths	2
Main Ceiling	9'
Second Ceiling	8'
Max Ridge Height	25'6"
Roof Framing	Stick
Exterior Walls	2x4

CAD FILES AVAILABLE
For more information call
800-235-5700

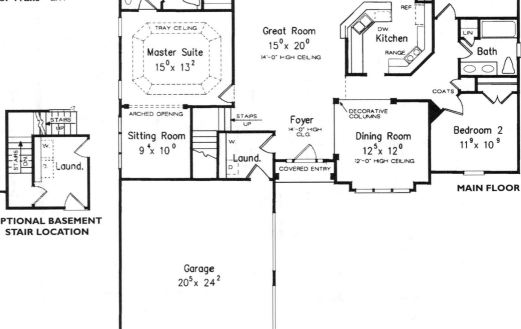

OPTIONAL BASEMENT STAIR LOCATION

MAIN FLOOR

Design 52058

Units	Single
Price Code	C
Total Finished	1,769 sq. ft.
Main Finished	1,769 sq. ft.
Bonus Unfinished	324 sq. ft.
Basement Unfinished	1,769 sq. ft.
Garage Unfinished	460 sq. ft.
Dimensions	61'x47'8"
Foundation	Basement
	Crawlspace
Bedrooms	3
Full Baths	2
Main Ceiling	9'
Second Ceiling	8'
Max Ridge Height	23'6"
Roof Framing	Stick
Exterior Walls	2x4

CAD FILES AVAILABLE
For more information call
800-235-5700

BONUS

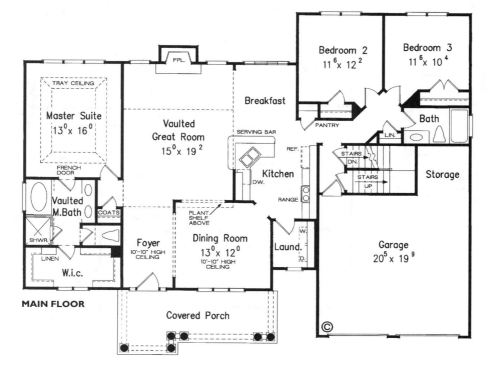

MAIN FLOOR

Units	Single
Price Code	C
Total Finished	1,771 sq. ft.
Main Finished	1,771 sq. ft.
Basement Unfinished	1,194 sq. ft.
Garage Unfinished	517 sq. ft.
Porch Unfinished	106 sq. ft.
Dimensions	54'x50'
Foundation	Combo Basement/Crawlspace Crawlspace Slab
Bedrooms	2
Full Baths	2
Main Ceiling	8'
Vaulted Ceiling	13'6"
Max Ridge Height	23'6"
Roof Framing	Stick
Exterior Walls	2x4

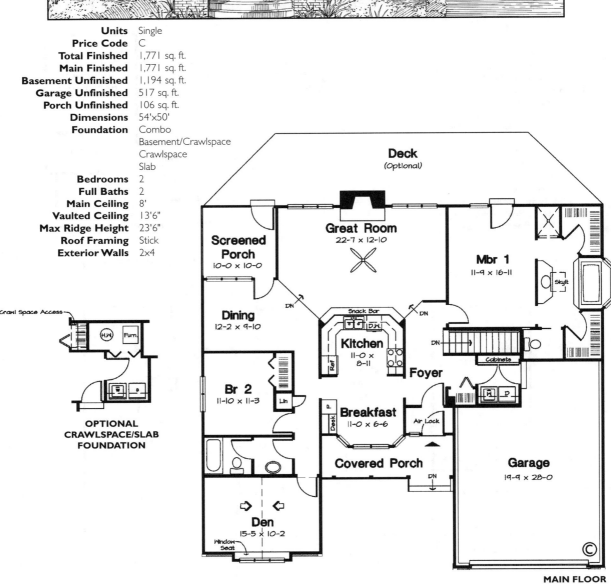

OPTIONAL
CRAWLSPACE/SLAB
FOUNDATION

MAIN FLOOR

Design 24715

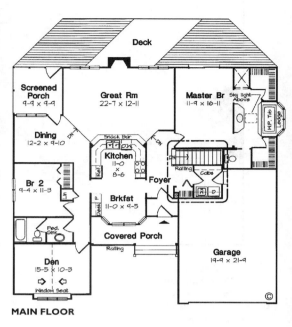

Units	Single
Price Code	C
Total Finished	1,771 sq. ft.
Main Finished	1,771 sq. ft.
Basement Unfinished	1,194 sq. ft.
Garage Unfinished	517 sq. ft.
Deck Unfinished	390 sq. ft.
Porch Unfinished	106 sq. ft.
Dimensions	55'5"x52'
Foundation	Crawlspace
	Slab
	Combo
	Basement/
	Crawlspace
Bedrooms	2
Full Baths	2
Main Ceiling	8'
Vaulted Ceiling	13'6"
Max Ridge Height	23'
Roof Framing	Stick
Exterior Walls	2x4

OPTIONAL CRAWLSPACE/SLAB FOUNDATION

MAIN FLOOR

Design 96525

Units	Single
Price Code	C
Total Finished	1,771 sq. ft.
Main Finished	1,771 sq. ft.
Garage Unfinished	480 sq. ft.
Dimensions	68'x50'
Foundation	Crawlspace
	Slab
Bedrooms	3
Full Baths	2
Main Ceiling	9'
Max Ridge Height	21'
Roof Framing	Stick

MAIN FLOOR

9' CEILINGS TYPICAL

Design 24716

Units	Single
Price Code	C
Total Finished	1,772 sq. ft.
Main Finished	1,772 sq. ft.
Basement Unfinished	1,764 sq. ft.
Garage Unfinished	568 sq. ft.
Porch Unfinished	117 sq. ft.
Dimensions	56'x56'4"
Foundation	Basement
	Crawlspace
	Slab
Bedrooms	3
Full Baths	2
Main Ceiling	9'
Max Ridge Height	26'
Roof Framing	Stick
Exterior Walls	2x4

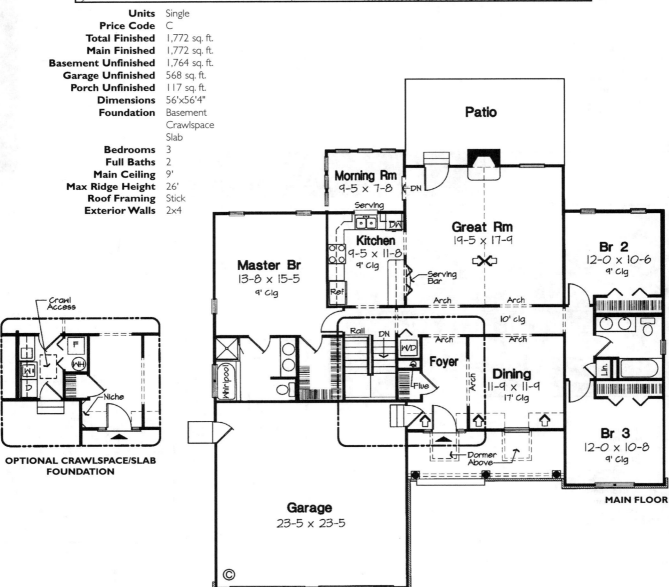

OPTIONAL CRAWLSPACE/SLAB
FOUNDATION

Patio

Morning Rm
9-5 x 7-8

Kitchen
9-5 x 11-8
9' Clg

Great Rm
19-5 x 17-9

Br 2
12-0 x 10-6
9' Clg

Master Br
13-8 x 15-5
9' Clg

Foyer

Dining
11-9 x 11-9
17' Clg

Br 3
12-0 x 10-8
9' Clg

MAIN FLOOR

Garage
23-5 x 23-5

Design 98936

Units	Single
Price Code	C
Total Finished	1,772 sq. ft.
Main Finished	1,772 sq. ft.
Basement Unfinished	845 sq. ft.
Garage Unfinished	888 sq. ft.
Deck Unfinished	220 sq. ft.
Porch Unfinished	136 sq. ft.
Dimensions	57'x38'
Foundation	Basement
Bedrooms	3
Full Baths	2
Main Ceiling	9'

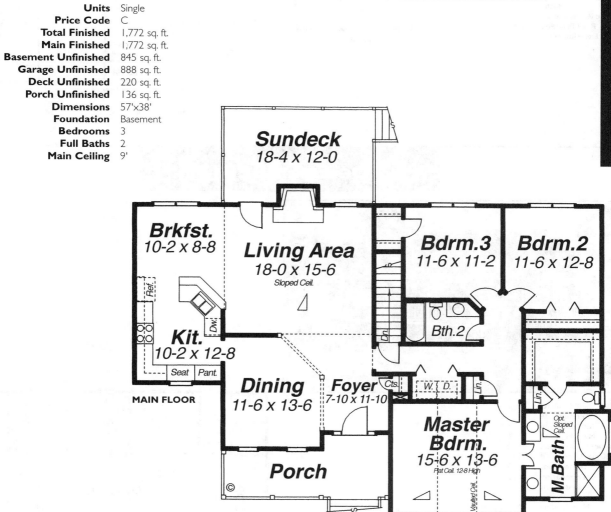

Sundeck
18-4 x 12-0

Brkfst.
10-2 x 8-8

Living Area
18-0 x 15-6
Sloped Ceil.

Bdrm.3
11-6 x 11-2

Bdrm.2
11-6 x 12-8

Ref.

Kit.
10-2 x 12-8

Dw.

Seat | Pant.

Bth.2

Dining
11-6 x 13-6

Foyer
7-10 x 11-10

Cts.

W. | D.

Ln.

Ln.

Opt.
Sloped
Ceil.

MAIN FLOOR

**Master
Bdrm.**
15-6 x 13-6
Flat Ceil. 12-8 High

M.Bath

Porch

Vaulted Ceil.

Design 90423

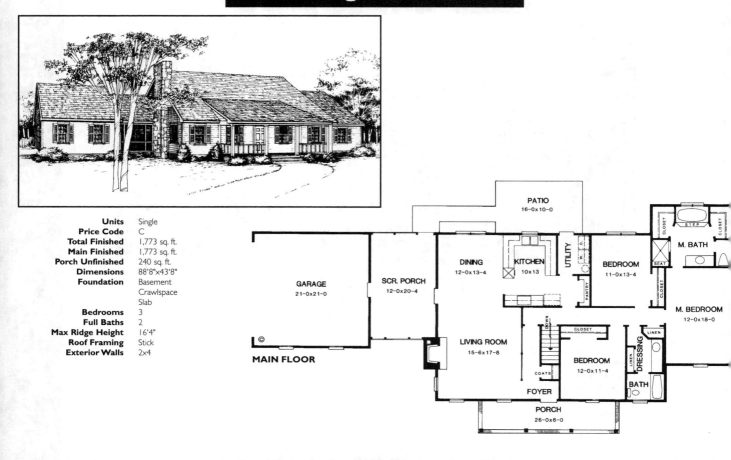

Units	Single
Price Code	C
Total Finished	1,773 sq. ft.
Main Finished	1,773 sq. ft.
Porch Unfinished	240 sq. ft.
Dimensions	88'8"x43'8"
Foundation	Basement
	Crawlspace
	Slab
Bedrooms	3
Full Baths	2
Max Ridge Height	16'4"
Roof Framing	Stick
Exterior Walls	2x4

MAIN FLOOR

- GARAGE 21-0x21-0
- SCR. PORCH 12-0x20-4
- PATIO 16-0x10-0
- DINING 12-0x13-4
- KITCHEN 10x13
- UTILITY
- BEDROOM 11-0x13-4
- M. BATH
- M. BEDROOM 12-0x18-0
- LIVING ROOM 15-6x17-8
- CLOSET
- DRESSING
- LINEN
- BEDROOM 12-0x11-4
- BATH
- FOYER
- PORCH 26-0x6-0

Design 93261

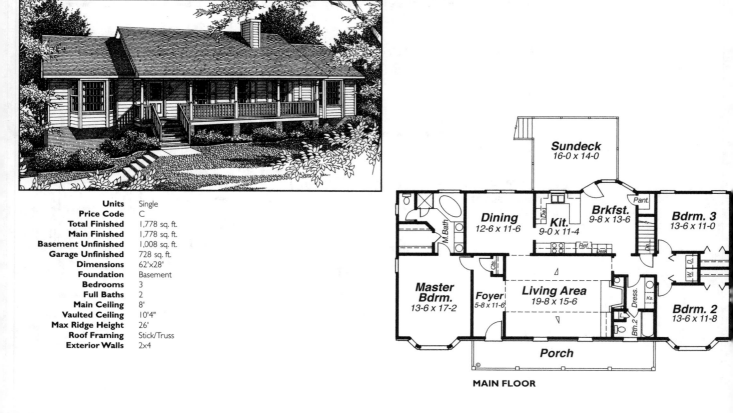

Units	Single
Price Code	C
Total Finished	1,778 sq. ft.
Main Finished	1,778 sq. ft.
Basement Unfinished	1,008 sq. ft.
Garage Unfinished	728 sq. ft.
Dimensions	62'x28'
Foundation	Basement
Bedrooms	3
Full Baths	2
Main Ceiling	8'
Vaulted Ceiling	10'4"
Max Ridge Height	26'
Roof Framing	Stick/Truss
Exterior Walls	2x4

- Sundeck 16-0 x 14-0
- Dining 12-6 x 11-6
- Kit. 9-0 x 11-4
- Brkfst. 9-8 x 13-6
- Bdrm. 3 13-6 x 11-0
- M. Bath
- Master Bdrm. 13-6 x 17-2
- Foyer 5-8 x 11-6
- Living Area 19-8 x 15-6
- Bth. 2
- Dress.
- Bdrm. 2 13-6 x 11-8
- Porch

MAIN FLOOR

Design 98464

1,501-2,000 sq.ft. HOME PLANS

Units	Single
Price Code	C
Total Finished	1,779 sq. ft.
Main Finished	1,779 sq. ft.
Basement Unfinished	1,818 sq. ft.
Garage Unfinished	499 sq. ft.
Dimensions	57'x56'4"
Foundation	Basement
	Crawlspace
Bedrooms	3
Full Baths	2
Main Ceiling	9'
Max Ridge Height	24'6"
Roof Framing	Stick
Exterior Walls	2x4

CAD **FILES AVAILABLE**
For more information call
800-235-5700

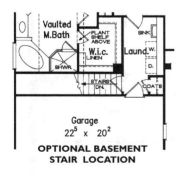

**OPTIONAL BASEMENT
STAIR LOCATION**

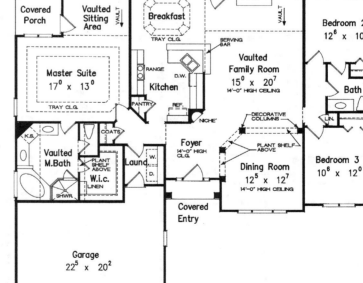

MAIN FLOOR

Design 92630

Units	Single
Price Code	C
Total Finished	1,782 sq. ft.
Main Finished	1,782 sq. ft.
Basement Unfinished	1,735 sq. ft.
Garage Unfinished	407 sq. ft.
Dimensions	67'2"x47'
Foundation	Basement
Bedrooms	3
Full Baths	2
Max Ridge Height	20'
Roof Framing	Truss
Exterior Walls	2x4

Please note: The photographed home may have been modified to suit homeowner preferences. If you order plans, have a builder or design professional check them against the photograph to confirm actual construction details.

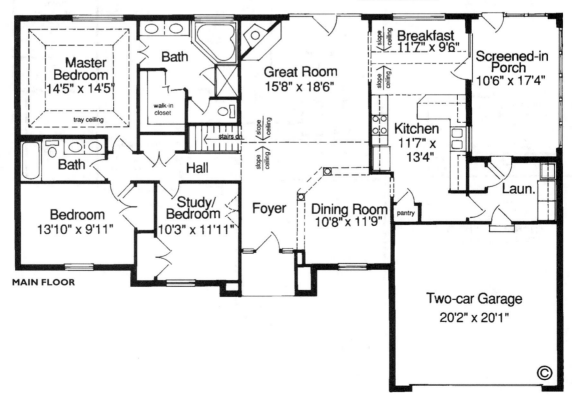

MAIN FLOOR

Units	Single
Price Code	C
Total Finished	1,782 sq. ft.
Main Finished	1,782 sq. ft.
Bonus Unfinished	432 sq. ft.
Basement Unfinished	288 sq. ft.
Garage Unfinished	828 sq. ft.
Deck Unfinished	430 sq. ft.
Dimensions	50'x42'
Foundation	Basement
Bedrooms	3
Full Baths	2
Max Ridge Height	33'
Roof Framing	Stick
Exterior Walls	2x4

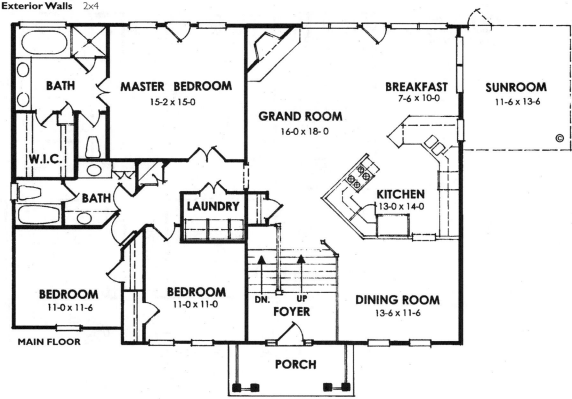

MASTER BEDROOM 15-2 x 15-0

BATH

W.I.C.

BATH

LAUNDRY

BEDROOM 11-0 x 11-6

BEDROOM 11-0 x 11-0

FOYER

DN. UP

GRAND ROOM 16-0 x 18-0

BREAKFAST 7-6 x 10-0

SUNROOM 11-6 x 13-6

KITCHEN 13-0 x 14-0

DINING ROOM 13-6 x 11-6

MAIN FLOOR

PORCH

Units	Single
Price Code	C
Total Finished	1,785 sq. ft.
Main Finished	1,785 sq. ft.
Basement Unfinished	1,785 sq. ft.
Garage Unfinished	528 sq. ft.
Porch Unfinished	334 sq. ft.
Dimensions	56'x32'
Foundation	Basement
	Crawlspace
	Slab
Bedrooms	3
Full Baths	2
3/4 Baths	1
Main Ceiling	9'
Max Ridge Height	24'
Roof Framing	Stick
Exterior Walls	2x4

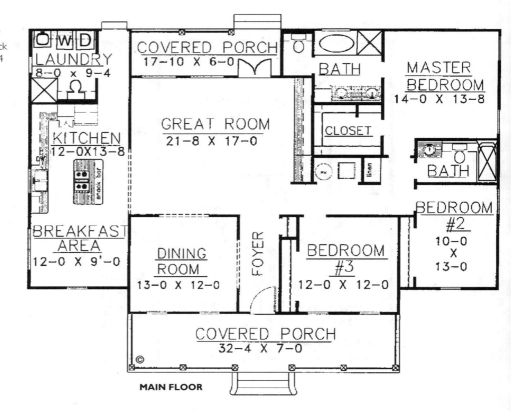

MAIN FLOOR

Design 34976

OPTIONAL BASEMENT FOUNDATION

Units	Single
Price Code	C
Total Finished	1,786 sq. ft.
Main Finished	1,786 sq. ft.
Basement Unfinished	1,775 sq. ft.
Garage Unfinished	426 sq. ft.
Porch Unfinished	223 sq. ft.
Dimensions	75'6"x46'11"
Foundation	Basement
	Crawlspace
	Slab
Bedrooms	3
Full Baths	2
Max Ridge Height	18'
Roof Framing	Stick
Exterior Walls	2x4, 2x6

Screened Porch

Brkfst 8 x 10-5

MBr 1 15-11 x 13-8

Family Rm 13-5 x 15-6

Kit 10 x 10-5

Garage 21-4 x 18-4

Living Rm 12 x 13-5

Dining 15-10 x 10-5

Br 2 12 x 10

Br 3 12 x 10

Foy

MAIN FLOOR

Design 82038

Units	Single
Price Code	C
Total Finished	1,787 sq. ft.
Main Finished	1,787 sq. ft.
Garage Unfinished	417 sq. ft.
Porch Unfinished	196 sq. ft.
Dimensions	54'2"x56'2"
Foundation	Basement
	Crawlspace
	Slab
Bedrooms	3
Full Baths	2
Main Ceiling	8'
Roof Framing	Stick
Exterior Walls	2x4

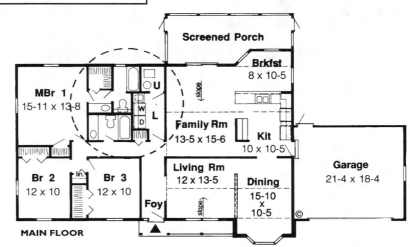

BRKFAST RM. 10'-0" X 9'-5"

MASTER SUITE 14'-6" X 14'-0" 9' PAN CEILING

GREAT RM. 15'-11" X 16'-7" 9' BOXED CEILING

GRILLING PORCH 11'-4" X 5'-10"

BED RM. 2 12'-0" X 11'-0"

M. BATH. 10'-8" X 15'-7"

KITCHEN 10'-0" X 12'-8"

WHP TUB

GLASS BLOCKS

STORAGE

LAU

DINING RM. 12'-8" X 12'-0" 10' CEILING

FOYER 10' CEILING

BATH

PORCH

GARAGE 20'-10" X 20'-0"

BED RM. 1 12'-0" X 11'-0"

MAIN FLOOR

Units	Single
Price Code	B
Total Finished	1,787 sq. ft.
Main Finished	1,787 sq. ft.
Bonus Unfinished	263 sq. ft.
Basement Unfinished	1,787 sq. ft.
Dimensions	55'8"x56'6"
Foundation	Basement
	Crawlspace
Bedrooms	3
Full Baths	2
Main Ceiling	9'
Vaulted Ceiling	11'
Tray Ceiling	11'
Max Ridge Height	21'
Roof Framing	Stick
Exterior Walls	2x4

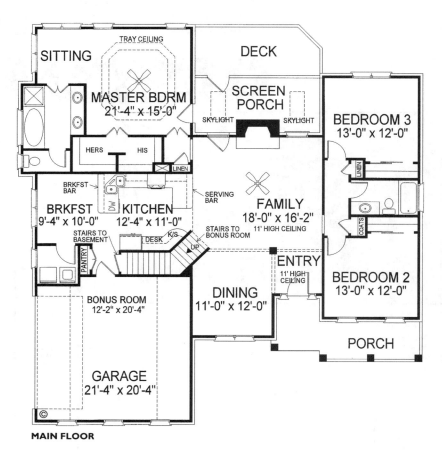

MAIN FLOOR

Design 50047

Units	Single
Price Code	C
Total Finished	1,788 sq. ft.
Main Finished	1,788 sq. ft.
Basement Unfinished	1,788 sq. ft.
Garage Unfinished	545 sq. ft.
Porch Unfinished	135 sq. ft.
Dimensions	66'x69'
Foundation	Basement
Bedrooms	3
Full Baths	2
Main Ceiling	8'
Vaulted Ceiling	12'
Max Ridge Height	21'
Exterior Walls	2x4

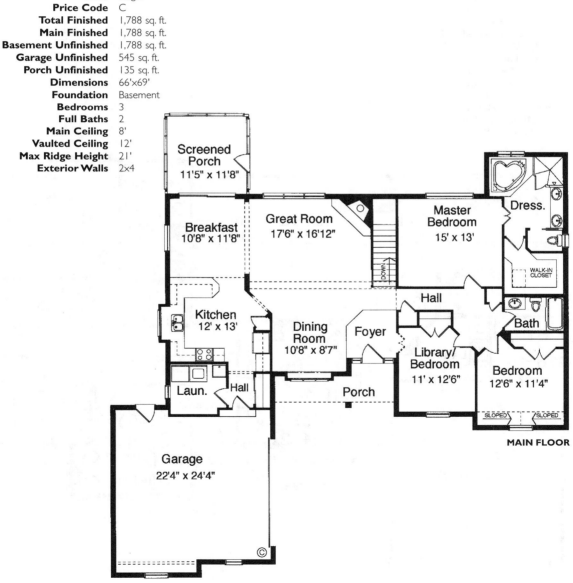

MAIN FLOOR

Units	Single
Price Code	C
Total Finished	1,791 sq. ft.
Main Finished	1,791 sq. ft.
Dimensions	67'4"x48'4"
Foundation	Basement
Bedrooms	4
Full Baths	2
Main Ceiling	8'
Max Ridge Height	22'
Roof Framing	Truss
Exterior Walls	2x4

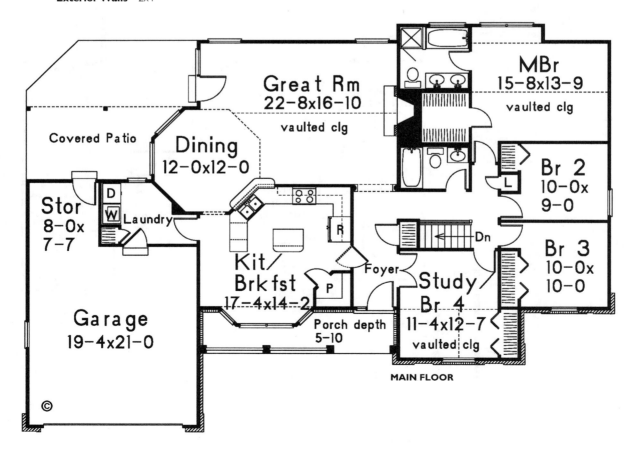

MAIN FLOOR

Design 20198

Units	Single
Price Code	C
Total Finished	1,792 sq. ft.
Main Finished	1,792 sq. ft.
Basement Unfinished	818 sq. ft.
Garage Unfinished	857 sq. ft.
Porch Unfinished	336 sq. ft.
Dimensions	56'x32'
Foundation	Basement
Bedrooms	3
Full Baths	2
Main Ceiling	8'
Max Ridge Height	25'
Roof Framing	Stick
Exterior Walls	2×4, 2×6

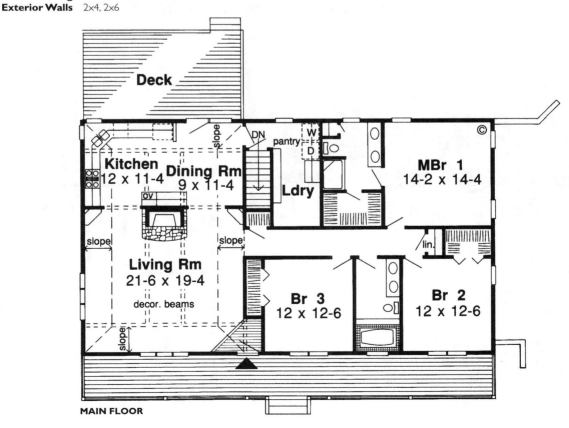

Deck

Kitchen
12 x 11-4

Dining Rm
9 x 11-4

pantry

Ldry

MBr 1
14-2 x 14-4

Living Rm
21-6 x 19-4

decor. beams

Br 3
12 x 12-6

Br 2
12 x 12-6

lin.

MAIN FLOOR

Design 99680

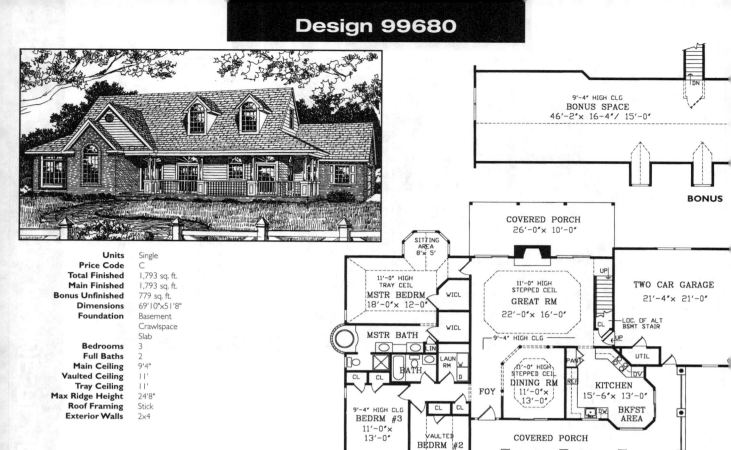

BONUS

9'-4" HIGH CLG
BONUS SPACE
46'-2"x 16'-4"/ 15'-0"

Units	Single
Price Code	C
Total Finished	1,793 sq. ft.
Main Finished	1,793 sq. ft.
Bonus Unfinished	779 sq. ft.
Dimensions	69'10"x51'8"
Foundation	Basement
	Crawlspace
	Slab
Bedrooms	3
Full Baths	2
Main Ceiling	9'4"
Vaulted Ceiling	11'
Tray Ceiling	11'
Max Ridge Height	24'8"
Roof Framing	Stick
Exterior Walls	2x4

COVERED PORCH
26'-0"x 10'-0"

SITTING AREA
8'x 5'

11'-0" HIGH TRAY CEIL
MSTR BEDRM
18'-0"x 12'-0"

WICL

WICL

MSTR BATH

LIN

BATH

LAUN RM

CL CL

9'-4" HIGH CLG
BEDRM #3
11'-0"x 13'-0"

CL CL

VAULTED
BEDRM #2
10'-6"x 12'-0"

FOY

11'-0" HIGH STEPPED CEIL
GREAT RM
22'-0"x 16'-0"

9'-4" HIGH CLG

11'-0" HIGH STEPPED CEIL
DINING RM
11'-0"x 13'-0"

PANT

KITCHEN
15'-6"x 13'-0"

BKFST AREA

UP

TWO CAR GARAGE
21'-4"x 21'-0"

LOC. OF ALT BSMT STAIR

UTIL

COVERED PORCH

MAIN FLOOR

Design 66019

Units	Single
Price Code	C
Total Finished	1,795 sq. ft.
Main Finished	1,795 sq. ft.
Garage Unfinished	482 sq. ft.
Deck Unfinished	240 sq. ft.
Porch Unfinished	42 sq. ft.
Dimensions	53'x61'
Foundation	Slab
Bedrooms	3
Full Baths	2
Main Ceiling	8'-10'
Max Ridge Height	24'6"
Roof Framing	Stick
Exterior Walls	2x4

COVERED PATIO

BRKFST AREA
11'6 X 10
9'-0" CEILING

COVERED PATIO

MASTER BEDROOM
14 X 14'6
VAULTED CEILING
8'-0" TO 10'-0"

KITCHEN

PANTRY

GREAT ROOM
14 X 20
10'-0" CEILING

BEDRM. TWO
11 X 13
8'-0" CEILING

CLOSET

LINEN

BATH TWO

HALL

MSTR BATH

WHIRLPOOL

W.I. CLOSET

HALLWAY

DRY WASH

UTILITY

HW

STUDY
10 X 11'6
10'-0" CEILING

ENTRY

COATS

CLOSET

BEDRM. THREE
12 X 11
8'-0" CEILING

SEAT

DOUBLE GARAGE

COVERED PORCH

MAIN FLOOR

Design 61048

Units	Single
Price Code	C
Total Finished	1,798 sq. ft.
Main Finished	1,798 sq. ft.
Garage Unfinished	417 sq. ft.
Porch Unfinished	196 sq. ft.
Dimensions	54'2"x56'2"
Foundation	Basement
	Crawlspace
	Slab
Bedrooms	3
Full Baths	2
Main Ceiling	8'
Roof Framing	Stick
Exterior Walls	2x4

MAIN FLOOR

Design 93293

Units	Single
Price Code	C
Total Finished	1,803 sq. ft.
Main Finished	1,718 sq. ft.
Lower Finished	85 sq. ft.
Basement Unfinished	483 sq. ft.
Garage Unfinished	500 sq. ft.
Deck Unfinished	192 sq. ft.
Dimensions	54'x34'
Foundation	Basement
Bedrooms	3
Full Baths	2
Max Ridge Height	30'
Roof Framing	Truss
Exterior Wall	2x4

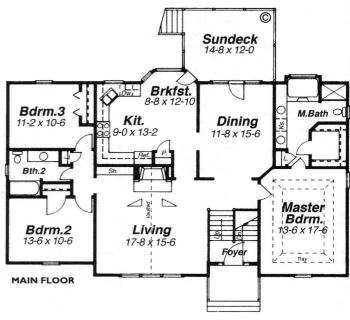

Sundeck
14-8 x 12-0

Bdrm.3
11-2 x 10-6

Brkfst.
8-8 x 12-10

Kit.
9-0 x 13-2

Dining
11-8 x 15-6

M.Bath

Bth.2

Ref.

Sh.

Bdrm.2
13-6 x 10-6

Living
17-8 x 15-6

Master Bdrm.
13-6 x 17-6

Vaulted

Foyer

Tray

MAIN FLOOR

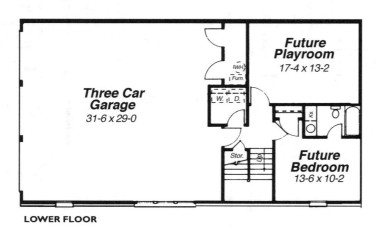

Three Car Garage
31-6 x 29-0

Future Playroom
17-4 x 13-2

WH
Furn.

W. D.

Future Bedroom
13-6 x 10-2

Stor.

LOWER FLOOR

Design 90476

Units	Single
Price Code	C
Total Finished	1,804 sq. ft.
Main Finished	1,804 sq. ft.
Basement Unfinished	1,804 sq. ft.
Garage Unfinished	506 sq. ft.
Deck Unfinished	220 sq. ft.
Porch Unfinished	156 sq. ft.
Dimensions	62'x55'8"
Foundation	Basement
	Crawlspace
	Slab
Bedrooms	3
Full Baths	2
Main Ceiling	8'
Max Ridge Height	22'1"
Roof Framing	Stick
Exterior Walls	2x4

MAIN FLOOR

Design 90441

Units	Single
Price Code	C
Total Finished	1,811 sq. ft.
Main Finished	1,811 sq. ft.
Basement Unfinished	1,811 sq. ft.
Garage Unfinished	484 sq. ft.
Deck Unfinished	336 sq. ft.
Porch Unfinished	390 sq. ft.
Dimensions	89'6"x44'4"
Foundation	Basement
	Crawlspace
	Slab
Bedrooms	3
Full Baths	2
Main Ceiling	8'
Max Ridge Height	16'4"
Roof Framing	Stick
Exterior Walls	2x4

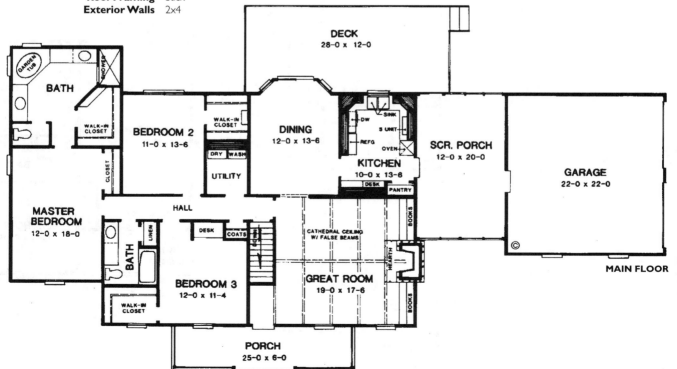

Design 67000

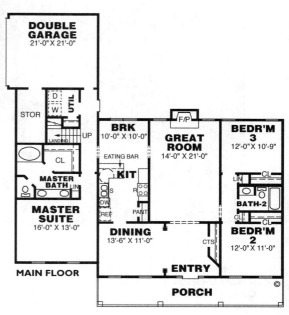

Units	Single
Price Code	C
Total Finished	1,815 sq. ft.
Main Finished	1,815 sq. ft.
Dimensions	58'3"x66'1"
Foundation	Slab
Bedrooms	3
Full Baths	2
Main Ceiling	8'
Max Ridge Height	24'
Roof Framing	Stick
Exterior Walls	2x4

Design 98914

Units	Single
Price Code	C
Total Finished	1,817 sq. ft.
Main Finished	1,817 sq. ft.
Garage Unfinished	440 sq. ft.
Deck Unfinished	222 sq. ft.
Porch Unfinished	60 sq. ft.
Dimensions	58'x55'5"
Foundation	Slab
Bedrooms	4
Full Baths	2
Max Ridge Height	20'
Roof Framing	Truss
Exterior Walls	2x4

Units	Single
Price Code	G
Total Finished	1,822 sq. ft.
Main Finished	1,822 sq. ft.
Basement Unfinished	1,822 sq. ft.
Garage Unfinished	537 sq. ft.
Deck Unfinished	264 sq. ft.
Porch Unfinished	287 sq. ft.
Dimensions	58'x66'8"
Foundation	Basement
Bedrooms	3
Full Baths	2
Max Ridge Height	26'10"
Exterior Walls	2x6
Roof Framing	Stick/Truss

* Alternate foundation options available at an additional charge.
Please call 1-800-235-5700 for more information.

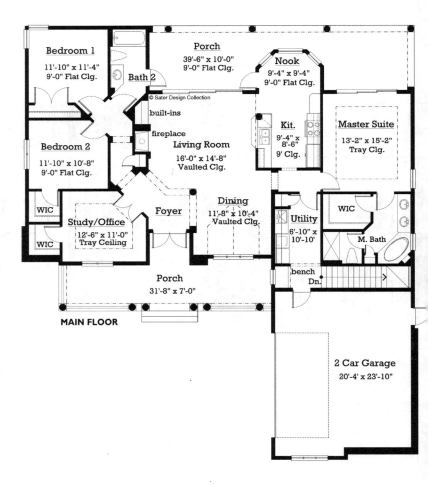

MAIN FLOOR

Design 90007

Units	Single
Price Code	C
Total Finished	1,830 sq. ft.
Main Finished	1,830 sq. ft.
Basement Unfinished	1,830 sq. ft.
Garage Unfinished	540 sq. ft.
Dimensions	86'x65'
Foundation	Basement
Bedrooms	4
Full Baths	2
3/4 Baths	1
Max Ridge Height	18'
Roof Framing	Stick
Exterior Walls	2x4

MAIN FLOOR

Design 92220

Units	Single
Price Code	C
Total Finished	1,830 sq. ft.
Main Finished	1,830 sq. ft.
Garage Unfinished	759 sq. ft.
Deck Unfinished	315 sq. ft.
Porch Unfinished	390 sq. ft.
Dimensions	75'x52'3"
Foundation	Basement
	Crawlspace
	Slab
Bedrooms	3
Full Baths	2
Max Ridge Height	27'3"
Roof Framing	Stick
Exterior Walls	2x4

COVERED VERANDA

KITCHEN/DINING 21 X 15

MSTR. BDRM. 14 X 16 VAULTED CLG. 9" TO 11"

SLOPED CLGS. 9" TO 11"

WALK-IN-CLOS.

HALL 9" CLGS.

LAUND.

3 CAR GARAGE 23 X 33

GREAT ROOM 22 X 16 CATHEDRAL CLGS.

ENT 10" CLGS.

BDRM #2 12 X 13 10" CLGS.

BDRM. #3 11 X 12 9" CLGS.

PANTRY

SERVICE PORCH

COVERED VERANDA

MAIN FLOOR

Design 34031

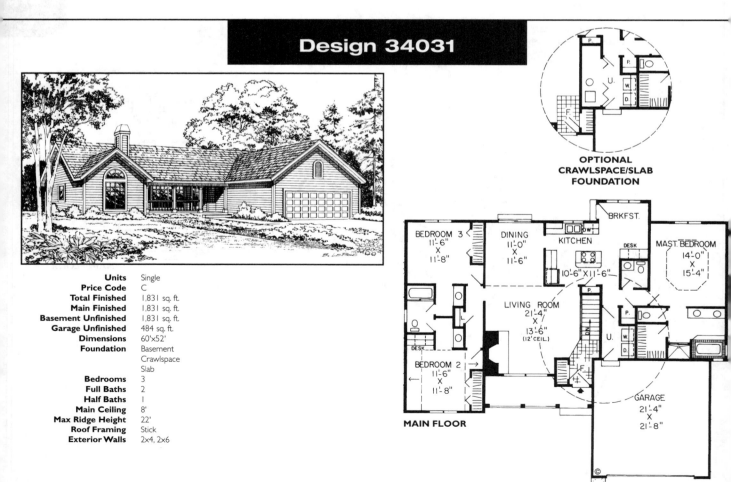

Units	Single
Price Code	C
Total Finished	1,831 sq. ft.
Main Finished	1,831 sq. ft.
Basement Unfinished	1,831 sq. ft.
Garage Unfinished	484 sq. ft.
Dimensions	60'x52'
Foundation	Basement
	Crawlspace
	Slab
Bedrooms	3
Full Baths	2
Half Baths	1
Main Ceiling	8'
Max Ridge Height	22'
Roof Framing	Stick
Exterior Walls	2x4, 2x6

OPTIONAL CRAWLSPACE/SLAB FOUNDATION

BRKFST.

BEDROOM 3 11'-6" X 11'-8"

DINING 11'-0" X 11'-6"

KITCHEN 10'-6" X 11'-6"

DESK

MAST. BEDROOM 14'-0" X 15'-4"

LIVING ROOM 21'-4" X 13'-6" (12' CEIL.)

BEDROOM 2 11'-6" X 11'-8"

GARAGE 21'-4" X 21'-8"

MAIN FLOOR

Design 24254

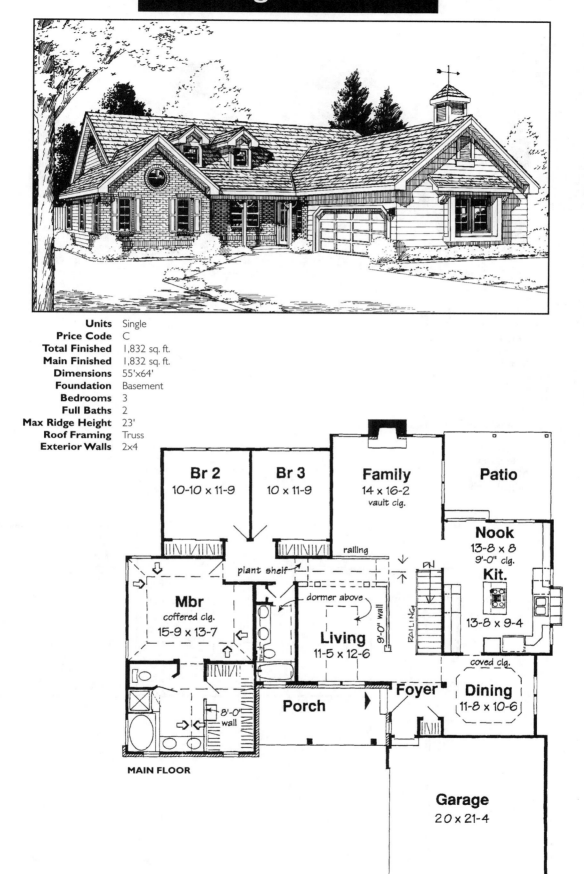

Units	Single
Price Code	C
Total Finished	1,832 sq. ft.
Main Finished	1,832 sq. ft.
Dimensions	55'x64'
Foundation	Basement
Bedrooms	3
Full Baths	2
Max Ridge Height	23'
Roof Framing	Truss
Exterior Walls	2x4

Br 2
10-10 x 11-9

Br 3
10 x 11-9

Family
14 x 16-2
vault clg.

Patio

Nook
13-8 x 8
9'-0" clg.

Kit.
13-8 x 9-4

Mbr
coffered clg.
15-9 x 13-7

plant shelf

railing

dormer above

9'-0" wall

Living
11-5 x 12-6

DN

RAILING

coved clg.

Dining
11-8 x 10-6

8'-0" wall

Porch

Foyer

Garage
20 x 21-4

MAIN FLOOR

Units	Single
Price Code	C
Total Finished	1,838 sq. ft.
Main Finished	1,838 sq. ft.
Bonus Unfinished	394 sq. ft.
Garage Unfinished	568 sq. ft.
Deck Unfinished	936 sq. ft.
Dimensions	65'×56'
Foundation	Crawlspace
	Slab
Bedrooms	3
Full Baths	2
Main Ceiling	9'
Max Ridge Height	24'
Exterior Walls	2×4

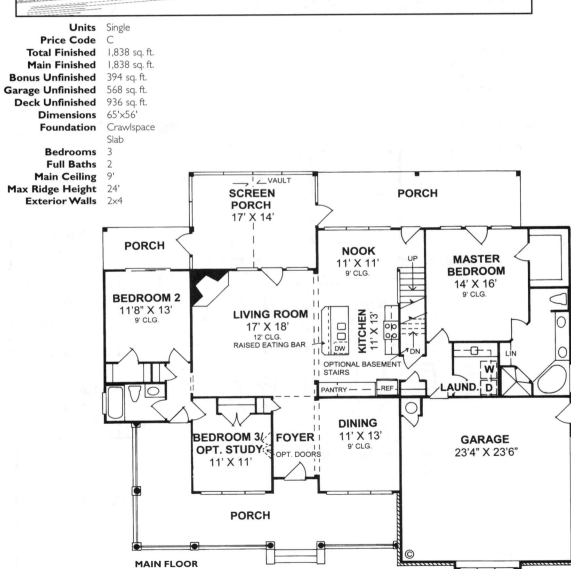

MAIN FLOOR

Design 90466

1,501-2,000 sq.ft. HOME PLANS

Units	Single
Price Code	C
Total Finished	1,845 sq. ft.
Main Finished	1,845 sq. ft.
Garage Unfinished	512 sq. ft.
Deck Unfinished	216 sq. ft.
Porch Unfinished	38 sq. ft.
Dimensions	57'2"x54'10"
Foundation	Crawlspace
	Slab
Bedrooms	3
Full Baths	2
Half Baths	1
Main Ceiling	8'
Max Ridge Height	23'10"
Roof Framing	Stick
Exterior Walls	2x4

Units	Single
Price Code	C
Total Finished	1,845 sq. ft.
Main Finished	1,845 sq. ft.
Bonus Unfinished	409 sq. ft.
Basement Unfinished	1,845 sq. ft.
Garage Unfinished	529 sq. ft.
Dimensions	56'x60'
Foundation	Basement
	Crawlspace
Bedrooms	3
Full Baths	2
Half Baths	1
Main Ceiling	9'
Max Ridge Height	26'6"
Roof Framing	Stick
Exterior Walls	2x4

CAD FILES AVAILABLE
For more information call
800-235-5700

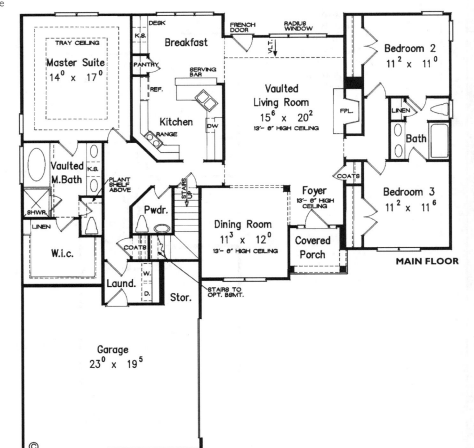

MAIN FLOOR

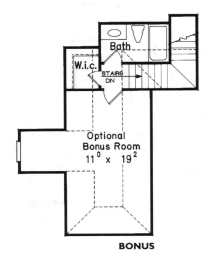

BONUS

Design 94692

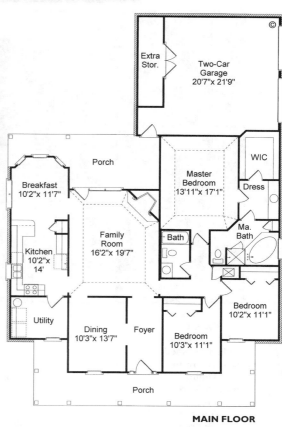

MAIN FLOOR

Units	Single
Price Code	C
Total Finished	1,847 sq. ft.
Main Finished	1,847 sq. ft.
Garage Unfinished	593 sq. ft.
Porch Unfinished	528 sq. ft.
Dimensions	49'6"x72'5"
Foundation	Slab
Bedrooms	3
Full Baths	2
Max Ridge Height	24'8"
Roof Framing	Stick
Exterior Walls	2x4

Design 64122

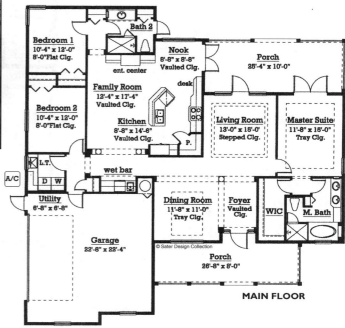

MAIN FLOOR

Units	Single
Price Code	G
Total Finished	1,848 sq. ft.
Main Finished	1,848 sq. ft.
Garage Unfinished	571 sq. ft.
Deck Unfinished	254 sq. ft.
Porch Unfinished	217 sq. ft.
Dimensions	58'x58'6"
Foundation	Slab
Bedrooms	3
Full Baths	1
3/4 Baths	1
Max Ridge Height	30'6"
Roof Framing	Stick/Truss
Exterior Walls	2x6

Alternate foundation options available at an additional charge.
Please call 1-800-235-5700 for more information.

Units	Single
Price Code	G
Total Finished	1,848 sq. ft.
Main Finished	1,848 sq. ft.
Garage Unfinished	571 sq. ft.
Deck Unfinished	254 sq. ft.
Porch Unfinished	217 sq. ft.
Dimensions	58'x60'
Foundation	Crawlspace
Bedrooms	3
Full Baths	1
3/4 Baths	1
Max Ridge Height	30'6"
Exterior Walls	2×6
Roof Framing	Stick/Truss

* Alternate foundation options available at an additional charge.
Please call 1-800-235-5700 for more information.

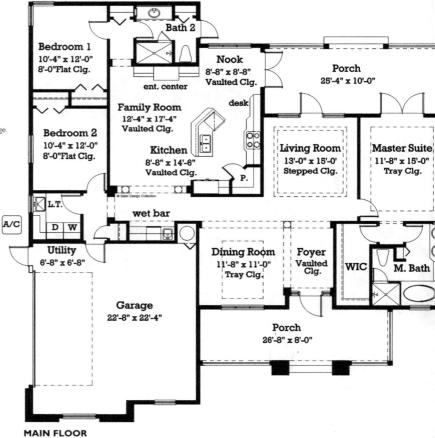

MAIN FLOOR

Design 64124

Units	Single
Price Code	G
Total Finished	1,848 sq. ft.
Main Finished	1,848 sq. ft.
Garage Unfinished	571 sq. ft.
Deck Unfinished	217 sq. ft.
Porch Unfinished	254 sq. ft.
Dimensions	58'x59'6"
Foundation	Slab
Bedrooms	3
Full Baths	1
3/4 Baths	1
Max Ridge Height	30'6"
Exterior Walls	2x6
Roof Framing	Stick/Truss

* Alternate foundation options available at an additional charge.
Please call 1-800-235-5700 for more information.

MAIN FLOOR

Units	Single
Price Code	C
Total Finished	1,848 sq. ft.
Main Finished	1,848 sq. ft.
Garage Unfinished	429 sq. ft.
Porch Unfinished	430 sq. ft.
Dimensions	38'x79'6"
Foundation	Basement
	Crawlspace
	Slab
Bedrooms	3
Full Baths	2
Main Ceiling	9'
Roof Framing	Stick
Exterior Walls	2x4

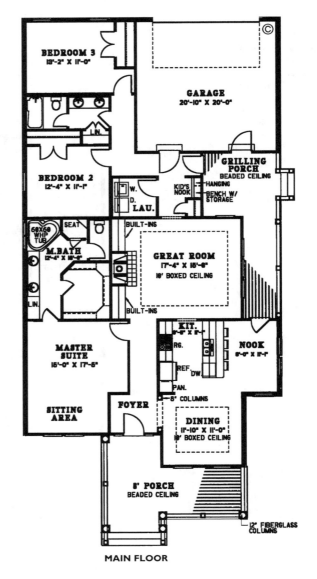

MAIN FLOOR

Design 98919

Units	Single
Price Code	C
Total Finished	1,850 sq. ft.
Main Finished	1,850 sq. ft.
Porch Unfinished	100 sq. ft.
Dimensions	60'x64'
Foundation	Crawlspace
	Slab
Bedrooms	3
Full Baths	2
Half Baths	I
Max Ridge Height	23'
Roof Framing	Stick
Exterior Walls	2x4

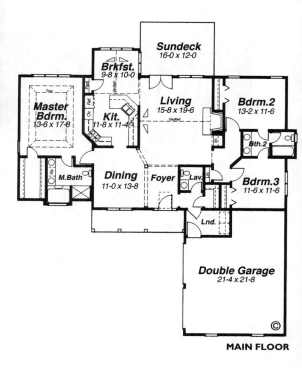

Sundeck
16-0 x 12-0

Brkfst.
9-8 x 10-0

Living
15-8 x 19-6
Vaulted

Bdrm.2
13-2 x 11-6

Master
Bdrm.
13-6 x 17-8

Kit.
11-8 x 11-4

Bth.2

M.Bath

Dining
11-0 x 13-8

Foyer

Lav.

Bdrm.3
11-6 x 11-6

Lnd.

Double Garage
21-4 x 21-8

MAIN FLOOR

Design 81008

Units	Single
Price Code	C
Total Finished	1,852 sq. ft.
Main Finished	1,852 sq. ft.
Garage Unfinished	757 sq. ft.
Dimensions	70'x45'
Foundation	Crawlspace
Bedrooms	3
Full Baths	2

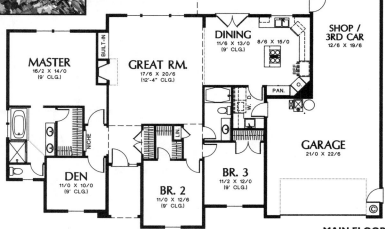

DINING
11/6 X 13/0
(9' CLG.)

SHOP /
3RD CAR
12/6 X 19/6

8/6 X 15/0

MASTER
16/2 X 14/0
(9' CLG.)

GREAT RM.
17/6 X 20/6
(12'-4" CLG.)

PAN.

DEN
11/0 X 10/0
(9' CLG.)

NICHE

LIN.

BR. 2
11/0 X 12/6
(9' CLG.)

BR. 3
11/2 X 12/0
(9' CLG.)

GARAGE
21/0 X 22/6

MAIN FLOOR

Units	Single
Price Code	C
Total Finished	1,856 sq. ft.
Main Finished	1,856 sq. ft.
Garage Unfinished	627 sq. ft.
Porch Unfinished	367 sq. ft.
Dimensions	58'x68'
Foundation	Crawlspace Slab
Bedrooms	4
Full Baths	3
Main Ceiling	10'
Roof Framing	Truss
Exterior Walls	2x4

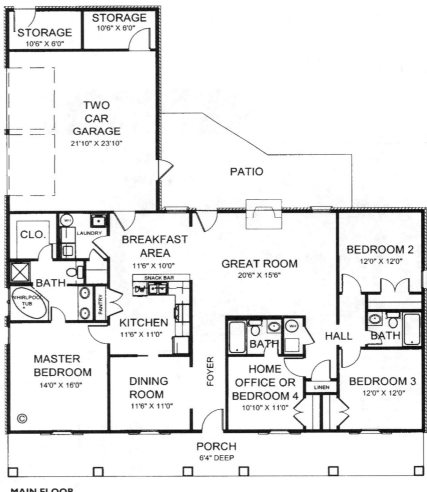

MAIN FLOOR

Design 98408

Units	Single
Price Code	C
Total Finished	1,856 sq. ft.
Main Finished	1,856 sq. ft.
Basement Unfinished	1,856 sq. ft.
Garage Unfinished	429 sq. ft.
Dimensions	59'x54'6"
Foundation	Basement
	Crawlspace
	Slab
Bedrooms	3
Full Baths	2
Main Ceiling	9'
Max Ridge Height	25'6"
Roof Framing	Stick
Exterior Walls	2x4

CAD FILES AVAILABLE
For more information call
800-235-5700

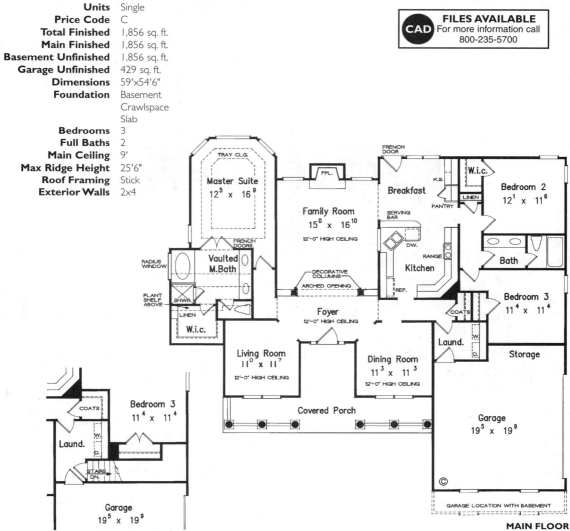

OPTIONAL BASEMENT STAIR LOCATION

MAIN FLOOR

Design 99174

Units	Single
Price Code	C
Total Finished	1,859 sq. ft.
Main Finished	1,859 sq. ft.
Basement Unfinished	1,859 sq. ft.
Garage Unfinished	750 sq. ft.
Dimensions	69'8"x43'
Foundation	Basement
Bedrooms	3
Full Baths	2
Half Baths	1
Main Ceiling	8'2"
Max Ridge Height	23'7"
Roof Framing	Truss
Exterior Walls	2x6

Design 98316

Units	Single
Price Code	C
Total Finished	1,859 sq. ft.
Main Finished	1,859 sq. ft.
Garage Unfinished	393 sq. ft.
Dimensions	54'x57'
Foundation	Slab
Bedrooms	3
Full Baths	2
Max Ridge Height	20'
Roof Framing	Truss
Exterior Walls	2x6

Design 97797

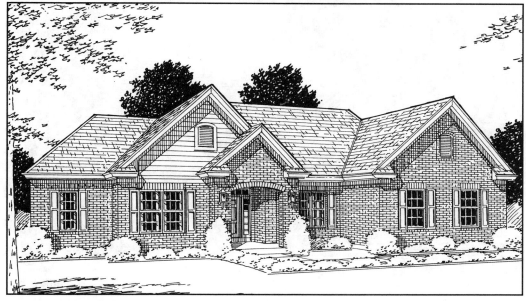

Units	Single
Price Code	C
Total Finished	1,860 sq. ft.
Main Finished	1,860 sq. ft.
Basement Unfinished	1,860 sq. ft.
Porch Unfinished	129 sq. ft.
Dimensions	64'2"x46'6"
Foundation	Basement
Bedrooms	3
Full Baths	2
Main Ceiling	9'
Max Ridge Height	23'
Roof Framing	Truss
Exterior Walls	2x4

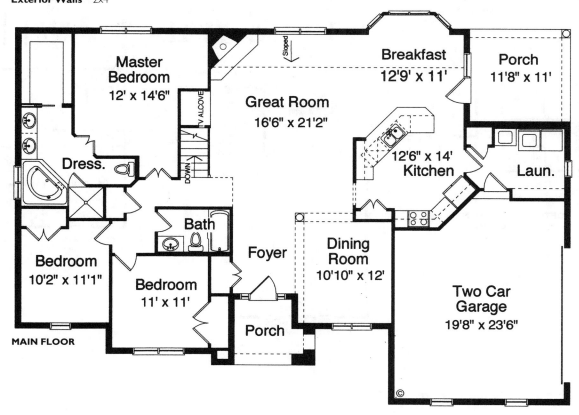

Design 97616

Units	Single
Price Code	C
Total Finished	1,861 sq. ft.
Main Finished	1,861 sq. ft.
Basement Unfinished	1,898 sq. ft.
Garage Unfinished	450 sq. ft.
Dimensions	58'6"x56'
Foundation	Basement Crawlspace
Bedrooms	3
Full Baths	2
Half Baths	1
Max Ridge Height	24'6"
Roof Framing	Stick
Exterior Walls	2x4

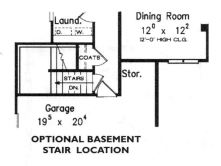

OPTIONAL BASEMENT STAIR LOCATION

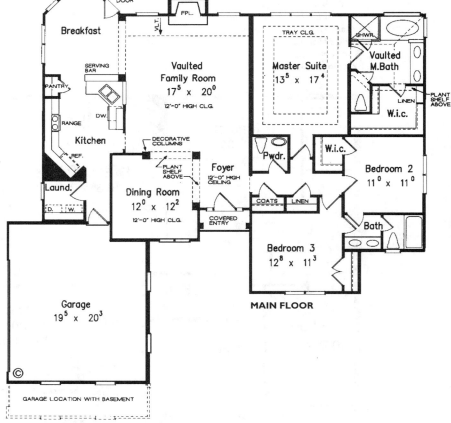

MAIN FLOOR

Design 66101

Units	Single
Price Code	C
Total Finished	1,862 sq. ft.
Main Finished	1,862 sq. ft.
Garage Unfinished	495 sq. ft.
Deck Unfinished	180 sq. ft.
Dimensions	50'x66'4"
Foundation	Slab
Bedrooms	3
Full Baths	2
Main Ceiling	9'
Max Ridge Height	24'
Roof Framing	Stick
Exterior Walls	2x4

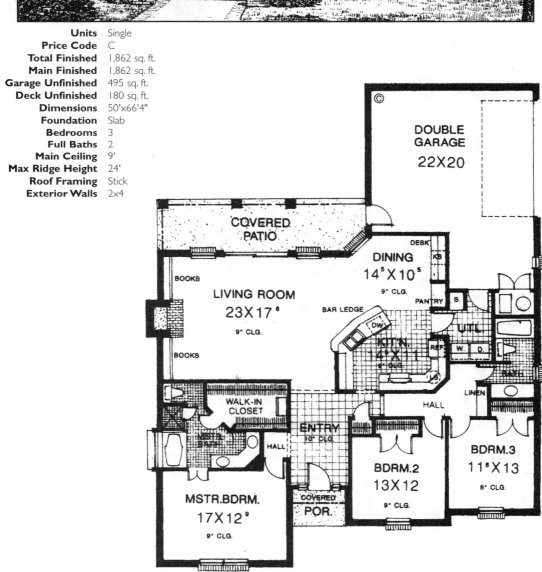

MAIN FLOOR

Units	Single
Price Code	C
Total Finished	1,868 sq. ft.
Main Finished	1,868 sq. ft.
Garage Unfinished	400 sq. ft.
Dimensions	45'x66'
Foundation	Slab
Bedrooms	4
Full Baths	2
Max Ridge Height	19'10"
Roof Framing	Truss

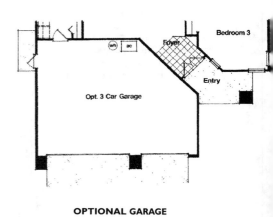

OPTIONAL GARAGE

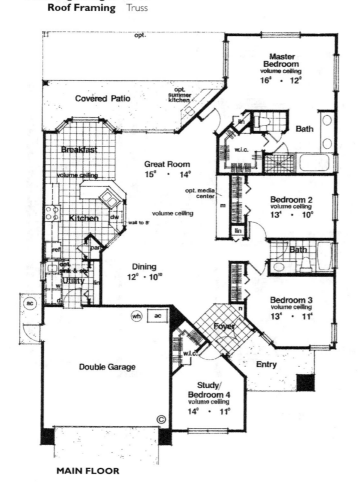

MAIN FLOOR

Design 63144

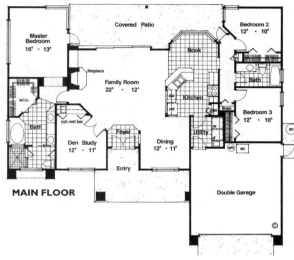

Units	Single
Price Code	C
Total Finished	1,869 sq. ft.
Main Finished	1,869 sq. ft.
Garage Unfinished	470 sq. ft.
Dimensions	61'8"x53'
Foundation	Slab
Bedrooms	3
Full Baths	2
Main Ceiling	10'
Max Ridge Height	19'8"
Roof Framing	Truss
Exterior Walls	2x4

Design 61037

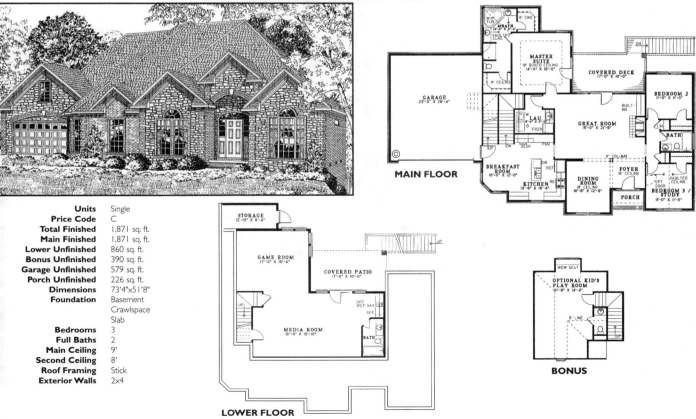

Units	Single
Price Code	C
Total Finished	1,871 sq. ft.
Main Finished	1,871 sq. ft.
Lower Unfinished	860 sq. ft.
Bonus Unfinished	390 sq. ft.
Garage Unfinished	579 sq. ft.
Porch Unfinished	226 sq. ft.
Dimensions	73'4"x51'8"
Foundation	Basement
	Crawlspace
	Slab
Bedrooms	3
Full Baths	2
Main Ceiling	9'
Second Ceiling	8'
Roof Framing	Stick
Exterior Walls	2x4

Design 92552

Units	Single
Price Code	C
Total Finished	1,873 sq. ft.
Main Finished	1,873 sq. ft.
Bonus Unfinished	145 sq. ft.
Garage Unfinished	613 sq. ft.
Dimensions	72'10"x54'5"
Foundation	Crawlspace
	Slab
Bedrooms	3
Full Baths	2
Main Ceiling	9'
Max Ridge Height	23'5"
Roof Framing	Stick
Exterior Walls	2x4

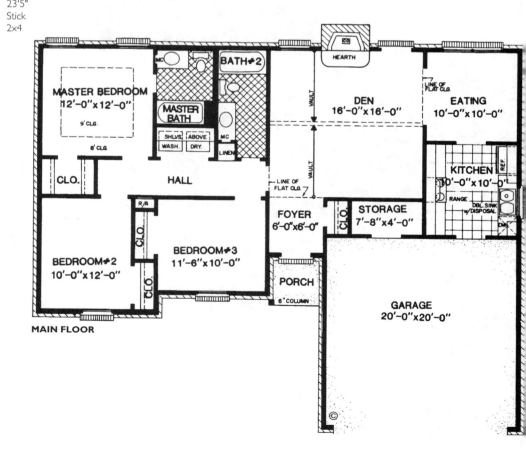

MAIN FLOOR

Design 98430

1,501-2,000 sq.ft. HOME PLANS

Units	Single
Price Code	C
Total Finished	1,884 sq. ft.
Main Finished	1,884 sq. ft.
Basement Unfinished	1,908 sq. ft.
Garage Unfinished	495 sq. ft.
Dimensions	50'x55'4"
Foundation	Basement
	Crawlspace
	Slab
Bedrooms	3
Full Baths	2
Half Baths	1
Main Ceiling	9'
Max Ridge Height	25'
Roof Framing	Stick
Exterior Walls	2x4

CAD FILES AVAILABLE
For more information call
800-235-5700

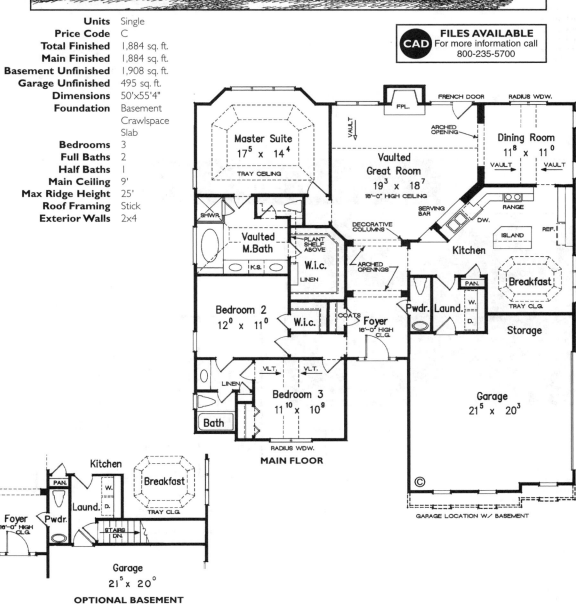

MAIN FLOOR

Master Suite 17⁵ x 14⁴ TRAY CEILING

Vaulted Great Room 19³ x 18⁷ 18'-0" HIGH CEILING

Dining Room 11⁸ x 11⁰

Vaulted M.Bath

Kitchen

Breakfast TRAY CLG.

Bedroom 2 12⁰ x 11⁰

Foyer 16'-0" HIGH CLG.

Pwdr. Laund.

Storage

Bedroom 3 11¹⁰ x 10⁹

Bath

Garage 21⁵ x 20³

RADIUS WDW.

GARAGE LOCATION W/ BASEMENT

OPTIONAL BASEMENT STAIR LOCATION

Foyer 16'-0" HIGH CLG.

Kitchen

Breakfast TRAY CLG.

Laund.

Pwdr.

Garage 21⁵ x 20⁰

STAIRS DN.

Design 93080

Units	Single
Price Code	C
Total Finished	1,890 sq. ft.
Main Finished	1,890 sq. ft.
Garage Unfinished	565 sq. ft.
Porch Unfinished	241 sq. ft.
Dimensions	65'10"x53'5"
Foundation	Crawlspace
	Slab
Bedrooms	3
Full Baths	2
Main Ceiling	10'
Max Ridge Height	21'6"
Roof Framing	Stick
Exterior Walls	2x4

MAIN FLOOR

Design 69503

Units	Single
Price Code	C
Total Finished	1,892 sq. ft.
Main Finished	1,892 sq. ft.
Bonus Unfinished	285 sq. ft.
Garage Unfinished	461 sq. ft.
Porch Unfinished	215 sq. ft.
Dimensions	65'x44'
Foundation	Basement
	Crawlspace
	Slab
Bedrooms	3
Full Baths	2
Half Baths	1
Main Ceiling	9'1⁄16"
Second Ceiling	8'1⁄16"
Max Ridge Height	25'4"
Roof Framing	Stick
Exterior Walls	2x4

8'-1" HIGH VAULTED CLG

BONUS RM
10'-6"x
23'-0"

BONUS

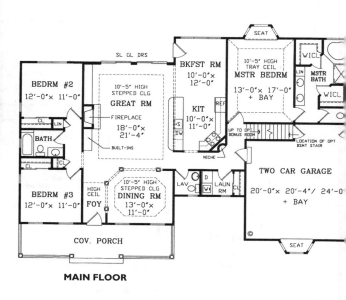

MAIN FLOOR

Design 63142

Units	Single
Price Code	C
Total Finished	1,901 sq. ft.
Main Finished	1,901 sq. ft.
Garage Unfinished	484 sq. ft.
Dimensions	64'x53'8"
Foundation	Slab
Bedrooms	3
Full Baths	2
Max Ridge Height	20'
Roof Framing	Truss
Exterior Walls	2x4

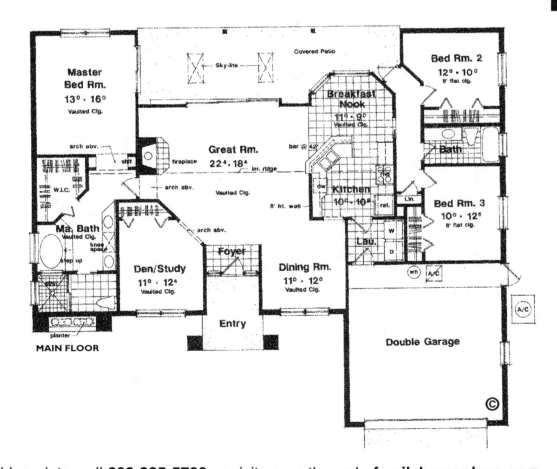

MAIN FLOOR

Design 84014

Units	Single
Price Code	C
Total Finished	1,901 sq. ft.
Main Finished	1,901 sq. ft.
Garage Unfinished	420 sq. ft.
Dimensions	68'x34'
Foundation	Basement
	Crawlspace
	Slab
Bedrooms	4
Full Baths	2
Max Ridge Height	17'
Roof Framing	Stick
Exterior Walls	2x4, 2x6

**OPTIONAL
CRAWLSPACE/SLAB
FOUNDATION**

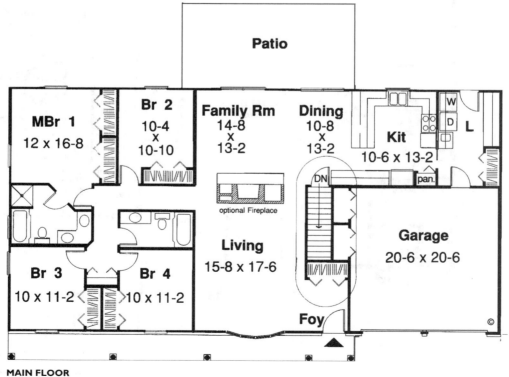

MAIN FLOOR

Design 98589

1,501-2,000 sq.ft. HOME PLANS

Units	Single
Price Code	C
Total Finished	1,902 sq. ft.
Main Finished	1,902 sq. ft.
Garage Unfinished	636 sq. ft.
Deck Unfinished	210 sq. ft.
Porch Unfinished	185 sq. ft.
Dimensions	84'7"x34'5"
Foundation	Slab
Bedrooms	3
Full Baths	2
Half Baths	1
Roof Framing	Stick
Exterior Walls	2x4

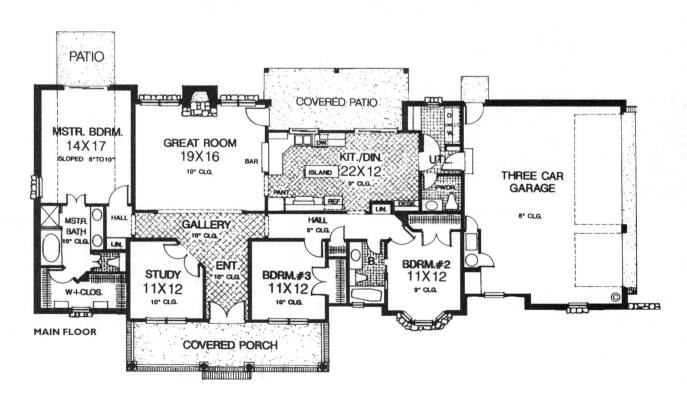

Units	Single
Price Code	C
Total Finished	1,906 sq. ft.
Main Finished	1,906 sq. ft.
Garage Unfinished	444 sq. ft.
Dimensions	58'2"×59'10"
Foundation	Slab
Bedrooms	4
Full Baths	2
Main Ceiling	8'
Max Ridge Height	18'5"
Roof Framing	Truss

MAIN FLOOR

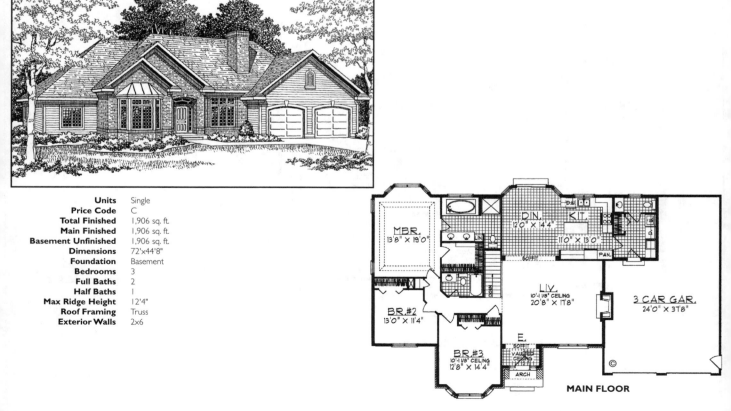

Units	Single
Price Code	C
Total Finished	1,906 sq. ft.
Main Finished	1,906 sq. ft.
Basement Unfinished	1,906 sq. ft.
Dimensions	72'×44'8"
Foundation	Basement
Bedrooms	3
Full Baths	2
Half Baths	1
Max Ridge Height	12'4"
Roof Framing	Truss
Exterior Walls	2x6

MAIN FLOOR

Design 91105

Units	Single
Price Code	C
Total Finished	1,908 sq. ft.
Main Finished	1,908 sq. ft.
Bonus Unfinished	262 sq. ft.
Garage Unfinished	562 sq. ft.
Porch Unfinished	95 sq. ft.
Dimensions	58'5½"×58'11½"
Foundation	Slab
Bedrooms	3
Full Baths	2
Main Ceiling	8'
Vaulted Ceiling	13'7"
Max Ridge Height	21'
Roof Framing	Stick
Exterior Walls	2x4

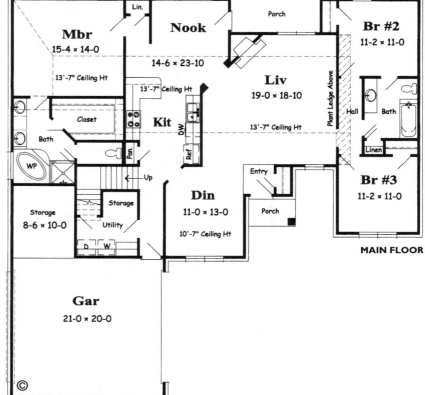

Bonus
10-0 × 20-0

BONUS

Mbr
15-4 × 14-0

13'-7" Ceiling Ht

Lin.

Nook

14-6 × 23-10

13'-7" Ceiling Ht

Closet

Kit

Bath

WP

Pan.

Up

Storage
8-6 × 10-0

Storage

Utility

D W

Gar
21-0 × 20-0

Attic

Down

Closet

Porch

Liv
19-0 × 18-10

13'-7" Ceiling Ht

dW

Ref

Plant Ledge Above

Din
11-0 × 13-0

10'-7" Ceiling Ht

Entry

Porch

Hall

Br #2
11-2 × 11-0

Bath

Linen

Br #3
11-2 × 11-0

MAIN FLOOR

Units	Single
Price Code	C
Total Finished	1,911 sq. ft.
Main Finished	1,911 sq. ft.
Garage Unfinished	481 sq. ft.
Dimensions	56'x58'
Foundation	Basement
Bedrooms	3
Full Baths	2
Max Ridge Height	22'7"
Roof Framing	Stick
Exterior Walls	2x4

* Alternate foundation options available at an additional charge. Please call 1-800-235-5700 for more information.

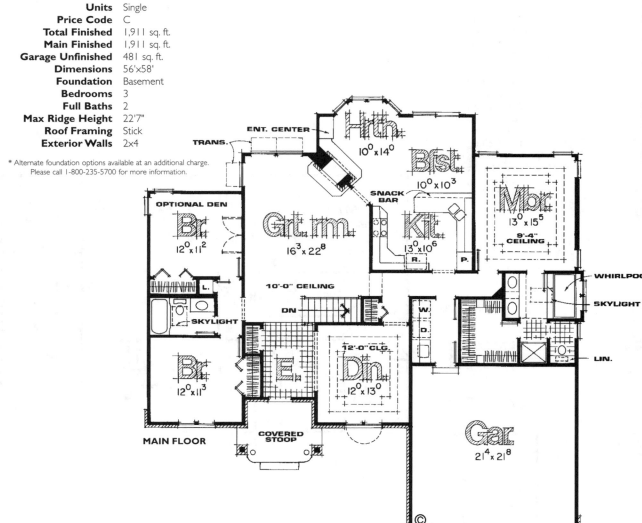

Design 66020

Units	Single
Price Code	B
Total Finished	1,912 sq. ft.
Main Finished	1,912 sq. ft.
Garage Unfinished	502 sq. ft.
Deck Unfinished	212 sq. ft.
Porch Unfinished	62 sq. ft.
Dimensions	57'×61'
Foundation	Slab
Bedrooms	3
Full Baths	2
Main Ceiling	8'-10'
Max Ridge Height	26'
Roof Framing	Stick
Exterior Walls	2x4

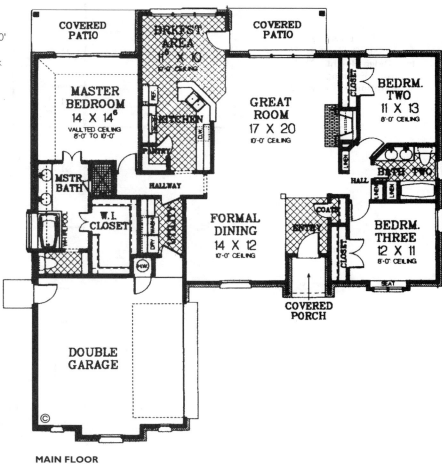

MAIN FLOOR

Units	Single
Price Code	C
Total Finished	1,914 sq. ft.
Main Finished	1,914 sq. ft.
Garage Unfinished	473 sq. ft.
Porch Unfinished	345 sq. ft.
Dimensions	59'8"x69'
Foundation	Basement
	Crawlspace
	Slab
Bedrooms	3
Full Baths	2
Main Ceiling	9'
Max Ridge Height	21'4"
Roof Framing	Stick
Exterior Walls	2x4, 2x6

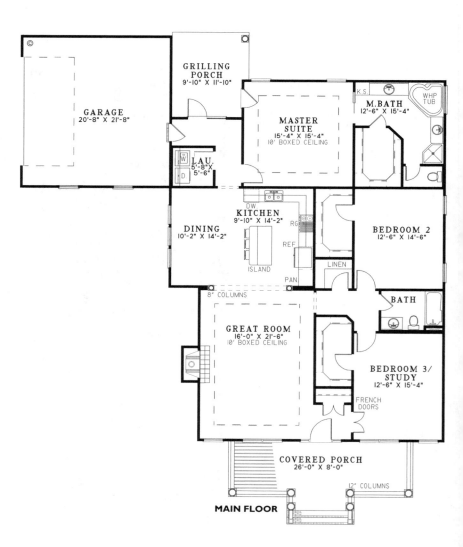

GARAGE
20'-8" X 21'-8"

GRILLING PORCH
9'-10" X 11'-10"

MASTER SUITE
15'-4" X 15'-4"
10' BOXED CEILING

M.BATH
12'-6" X 15'-4"

WHP TUB

K.S.

LAU.
5'-8"X 5'-6"

KITCHEN
9'-10" X 14'-2"

DW

RG

REF

DINING
10'-2" X 14'-2"

ISLAND

PAN

LINEN

BEDROOM 2
12'-6" X 14'-6"

8" COLUMNS

GREAT ROOM
16'-0" X 21'-6"
10' BOXED CEILING

BATH

BEDROOM 3/ STUDY
12'-6" X 15'-4"

FRENCH DOORS

COVERED PORCH
26'-0" X 8'-0"

12" COLUMNS

MAIN FLOOR

Design 68175

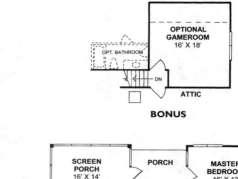

OPTIONAL GAMEROOM
16' X 18'

OPT. BATHROOM

DN

ATTIC

BONUS

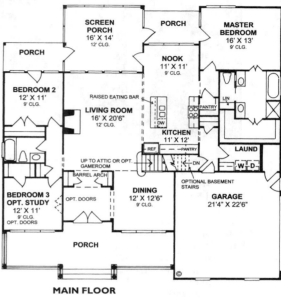

Units	Single
Price Code	C
Total Finished	1,915 sq. ft.
Main Finished	1,915 sq. ft.
Bonus Unfinished	308 sq. ft.
Garage Unfinished	530 sq. ft.
Deck Unfinished	680 sq. ft.
Dimensions	57'x58'
Foundation	Crawlspace
	Slab
Bedrooms	3
Full Baths	2
Main Ceiling	9'
Max Ridge Height	26'
Exterior Walls	2x4

* Alternate foundation options available at an additional charge.
Please call 1-800-235-5700 for more information.

MAIN FLOOR

SCREEN PORCH 16' X 14' 12' CLG.
PORCH
MASTER BEDROOM 16' X 13' 9' CLG.
PORCH
NOOK 11' X 11' 9' CLG.
BEDROOM 2 12' X 11' 9' CLG.
RAISED EATING BAR
LIVING ROOM 16' X 20'6" 12' CLG.
KITCHEN 11' X 12'
PANTRY
LIN
LAUND. W D
REF PANTRY DW
UP TO ATTIC OR OPT. GAMEROOM
DN
BARREL ARCH
BEDROOM 3 OPT. STUDY 12' X 11' 9' CLG. OPT. DOORS
OPT. DOORS
DINING 12' X 12'6" 9' CLG.
OPTIONAL BASEMENT STAIRS
GARAGE 21'4" X 22'6"
PORCH

Design 97618

Units	Single
Price Code	C
Total Finished	1,915 sq. ft.
Main Finished	1,915 sq. ft.
Basement Unfinished	1,932 sq. ft.
Garage Unfinished	489 sq. ft.
Dimensions	56'6"x57'6"
Foundation	Basement
	Crawlspace
Bedrooms	4
Full Baths	3
Max Ridge Height	22'6"
Roof Framing	Stick
Exterior Walls	2x4

CAD FILES AVAILABLE For more information call 800-235-5700

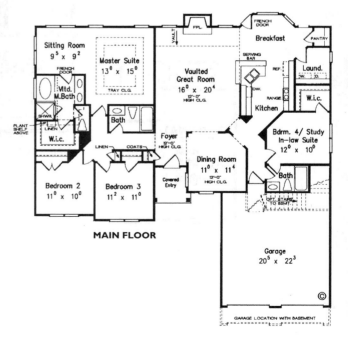

Sitting Room 9⁵ x 9²
Master Suite 13⁰ x 15⁰ TRAY CLG.
Breakfast
PANTRY
FPL
FRENCH DOOR
VAULT
SERVING BAR
Laund. W D
Mtd. M.Bath
Vaulted Great Room 16⁰ x 20⁴ 12'-0" HIGH CLG.
REF.
DW.
RANGE
Kitchen
W.i.c.
Bath
PLANT SHELF ABOVE
W.i.c.
Foyer 12'-0" HIGH CLG.
Bdrm. 4/ Study In-law Suite 12⁰ x 10⁰
LINEN
COATS
LINEN
Bedroom 2 11⁰ x 10⁰
Bedroom 3 11² x 11⁰
Covered Entry
Dining Room 11⁰ x 11⁴ 12'-0" HIGH CLG.
Bath
OPT. STAIRS TO BSMT.
Garage 20⁵ x 22³
GARAGE LOCATION WITH BASEMENT

MAIN FLOOR

Units	Single
Price Code	C
Total Finished	1,919 sq. ft.
Main Finished	1,919 sq. ft.
Bonus Unfinished	281 sq. ft.
Garage Unfinished	456 sq. ft.
Porch Unfinished	111 sq. ft.
Dimensions	53'4"x66'3"
Foundation	Crawlspace
Bedrooms	3
Full Baths	2
Main Ceiling	8'
Vaulted Ceiling	11'
Max Ridge Height	23'3"
Roof Framing	Stick
Exterior Walls	2x4

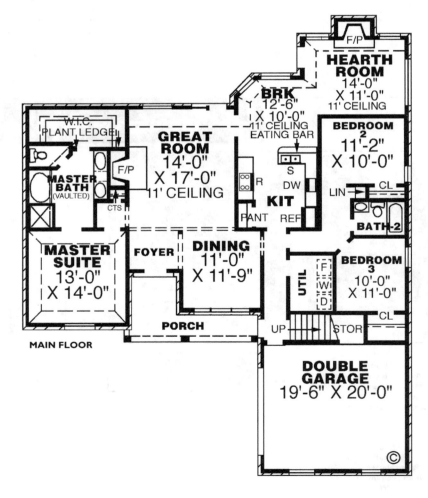

MAIN FLOOR

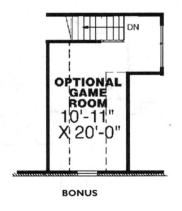

OPTIONAL GAME ROOM 10'-11" X 20'-0"

BONUS

Design 94978

1,501-2,000 sq.ft. HOME PLANS

Units	Single
Price Code	C
Total Finished	1,919 sq. ft.
Main Finished	1,919 sq. ft.
Basement Unfinished	1,919 sq. ft.
Garage Unfinished	481 sq. ft.
Dimensions	56'x58'
Foundation	Basement
Bedrooms	3
Full Baths	2
Max Ridge Height	21'
Roof Framing	Stick
Exterior Walls	2x4

* Alternate foundation options available at an additional charge.
Please call 1-800-235-5700 for more information.

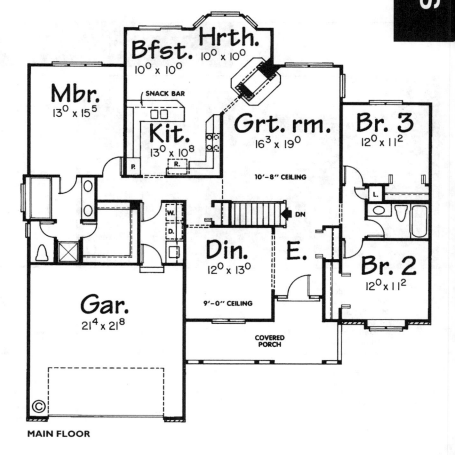

MAIN FLOOR

Design 97894

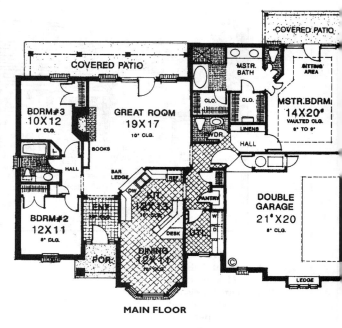

MAIN FLOOR

Units	Single
Price Code	C
Total Finished	1,920 sq. ft.
Main Finished	1,920 sq. ft.
Garage Unfinished	430 sq. ft.
Deck Unfinished	162 sq. ft.
Porch Unfinished	46 sq. ft.
Dimensions	61'x48'7"
Foundation	Slab
Bedrooms	3
Full Baths	2
Half Baths	1
Main Ceiling	10'
Max Ridge Height	29'6"
Roof Framing	Stick
Exterior Walls	2x4

Design 52011

MAIN FLOOR

GARAGE LOCATION WITH BASEMENT

Units	Single
Price Code	C
Total Finished	1,927 sq. ft.
Main Finished	1,927 sq. ft.
Basement Unfinished	1,941 sq. ft.
Garage Unfinished	440 sq. ft.
Dimensions	54'x55'
Foundation	Basement
	Crawlspace
Bedrooms	3
Full Baths	2
Main Ceiling	9'
Max Ridge Height	24'
Roof Framing	Stick
Exterior Walls	2x4

Design 97353

Units	Single
Price Code	C
Total Finished	1,929 sq. ft.
Main Finished	1,929 sq. ft.
Dimensions	68'x49'
Foundation	Basement
Bedrooms	3
Full Baths	2
Max Ridge Height	23'8"
Roof Framing	Truss
Exterior Walls	2x6

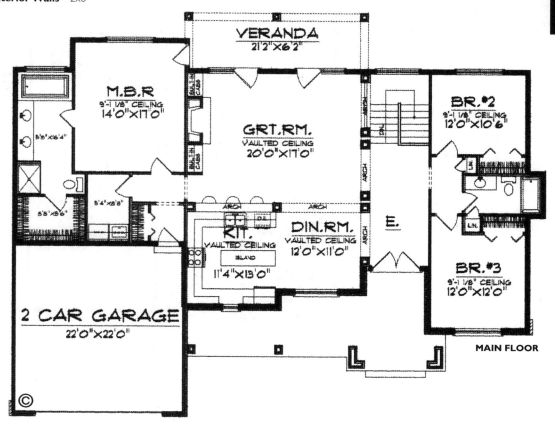

MAIN FLOOR

Design 93098

Units	Single
Price Code	C
Total Finished	1,932 sq. ft.
Main Finished	1,932 sq. ft.
Garage Unfinished	552 sq. ft.
Deck Unfinished	225 sq. ft.
Dimensions	65'10"x53'5"
Foundation	Crawlspace
	Slab
Bedrooms	3
Full Baths	2
Max Ridge Height	22'4"
Roof Framing	Stick
Exterior Walls	2x4

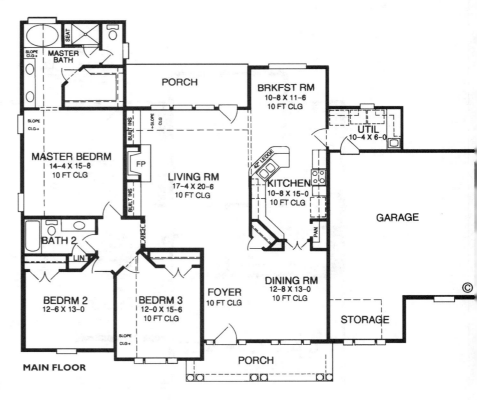

MAIN FLOOR

Design 52028

FILES AVAILABLE
CAD
For more information call
800-235-5700

Units	Single
Price Code	C
Total Finished	1,933 sq. ft.
Main Finished	1,933 sq. ft.
Bonus Unfinished	519 sq. ft.
Basement Unfinished	1,933 sq. ft.
Garage Unfinished	468 sq. ft.
Dimensions	62'x50'
Foundation	Basement
	Crawlspace
Bedrooms	3
Full Baths	2
Half Baths	1
Main Ceiling	9'
Second Ceiling	8'
Max Ridge Height	26'
Roof Framing	Stick
Exterior Walls	2x4

BONUS

MAIN FLOOR

Units	Single
Price Code	C
Total Finished	1,934 sq. ft.
Main Finished	1,934 sq. ft.
Garage Unfinished	489 sq. ft.
Porch Unfinished	239 sq. ft.
Dimensions	36'8"x85'
Foundation	Crawlspace
	Slab
Bedrooms	3
Full Baths	2
Roof Framing	Stick
Exterior Walls	2x4

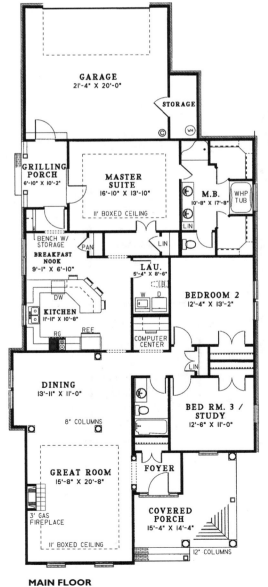

GARAGE
21'-4" X 20'-0"

STORAGE

WH

GRILLING PORCH
6'-10" X 10'-2"

MASTER SUITE
16'-10" X 13'-10"
11' BOXED CEILING

M.B.
10'-8" X 17'-8"

WHP TUB

LIN

BENCH W/ STORAGE

PAN

LIN

BREAKFAST NOOK
9'-1" X 6'-10"

LAU.
5'-4" X 8'-6"

BEDROOM 2
12'-4" X 13'-2"

DW

W D

KITCHEN
11'-11" X 10'-8"

RG

REF

COMPUTER CENTER

LIN

DINING
13'-11" X 11'-0"

8" COLUMNS

BED RM. 3 / STUDY
12'-6" X 11'-0"

GREAT ROOM
15'-8" X 20'-8"

FOYER

3' GAS FIREPLACE

11' BOXED CEILING

COVERED PORCH
15'-4" X 14'-4"

12" COLUMNS

MAIN FLOOR

Design 82034

MAIN FLOOR

Units	Single
Price Code	C
Total Finished	1,940 sq. ft.
Main Finished	1,940 sq. ft.
Garage Unfinished	417 sq. ft.
Porch Unfinished	188 sq. ft.
Dimensions	58'x54'10"
Foundation	Crawlspace
	Slab
Bedrooms	4
Full Baths	2
Main Ceiling	8'
Roof Framing	Stick
Exterior Walls	2x4

Design 98435

CAD FILES AVAILABLE
For more information call
800-235-5700

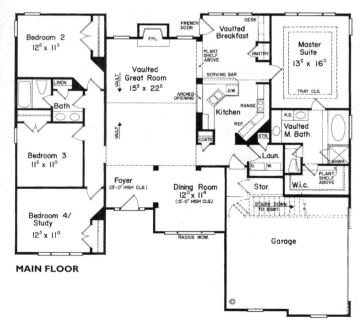

MAIN FLOOR

Units	Single
Price Code	C
Total Finished	1,945 sq. ft.
Main Finished	1,945 sq. ft.
Dimensions	56'6"x52'6"
Foundation	Basement
	Crawlspace
Bedrooms	4
Full Baths	2
Main Ceiling	9'
Max Ridge Height	26'4"
Roof Framing	Stick
Exterior Walls	2x4

Units	Single
Price Code	C
Total Finished	1,947 sq. ft.
Main Finished	1,947 sq. ft.
Basement Unfinished	1,947 sq. ft.
Dimensions	69'8"x46'
Foundation	Basement
Bedrooms	3
Full Baths	2
Half Baths	1
Main Ceiling	8'
Max Ridge Height	22'4"
Roof Framing	Truss
Exterior Walls	2x6

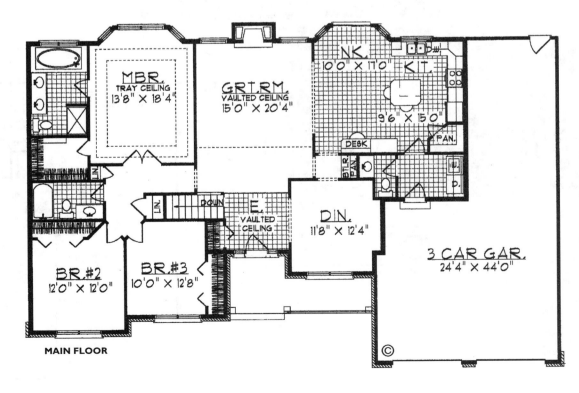

MAIN FLOOR

Design 64006

Units	Single
Price Code	C
Total Finished	1,949 sq. ft.
Main Finished	1,949 sq. ft.
Garage Unfinished	462 sq. ft.
Porch Unfinished	512 sq. ft.
Dimensions	82'10"x46'10"
Foundation	Crawlspace
	Slab
Bedrooms	3
Full Baths	2
Main Ceiling	8'
Max Ridge Height	20'9"
Roof Framing	Stick
Exterior Walls	2x4

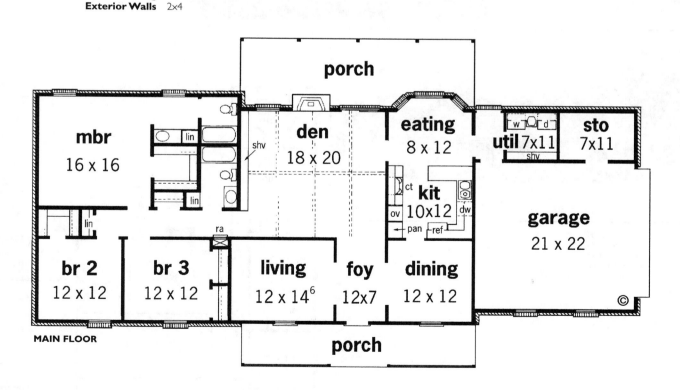

MAIN FLOOR

Design 82077

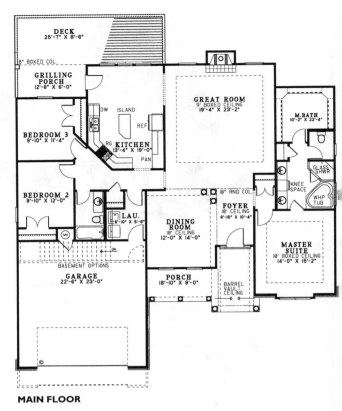

Units	Single
Price Code	C
Total Finished	1,950 sq. ft.
Main Finished	1,950 sq. ft.
Garage Unfinished	518 sq. ft.
Porch Unfinished	298 sq. ft.
Dimensions	56'8"x58'4"
Foundation	Basement
	Crawlspace
	Slab
Bedrooms	3
Full Baths	2
Exterior Walls	2x4

MAIN FLOOR

Design 90407

Units	Single
Price Code	C
Total Finished	1,950 sq. ft.
Main Finished	1,950 sq. ft.
Dimensions	67'1"x60'4"
Foundation	Basement
	Crawlspace
	Slab
Bedrooms	3
Full Baths	2

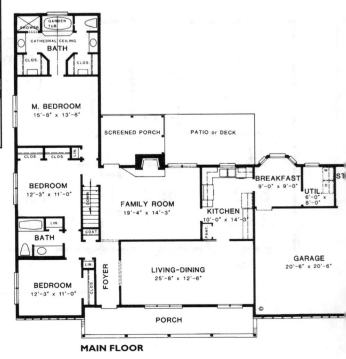

MAIN FLOOR

Units	Single
Price Code	E
Total Finished	1,953 sq. ft.
Main Finished	1,953 sq. ft.
Porch Unfinished	256 sq. ft.
Garage Unfinished	516 sq. ft.
Dimensions	49'10"x68'
Foundation	Slab
Bedrooms	3
Full Baths	2
Roof Framing	Truss

* Alternate foundation options available at an additional charge.
Please call 1-800-235-5700 for more information.

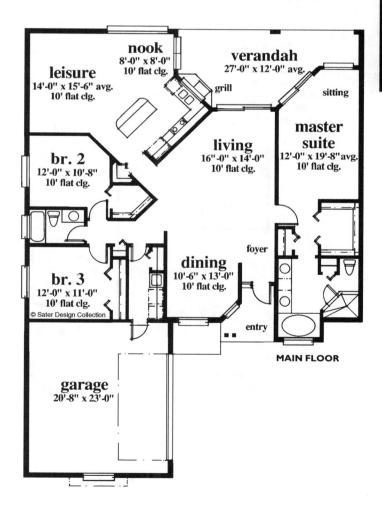

MAIN FLOOR

Units	Single
Price Code	C
Total Finished	1,954 sq. ft.
Main Finished	1,954 sq. ft.
Garage Unfinished	411 sq. ft.
Porch Unfinished	325 sq. ft.
Dimensions	74'6"x43'
Foundation	Crawlspace
	Slab
Bedrooms	3
Full Baths	2
Half Baths	1
Main Ceiling	8'
Max Ridge Height	23'4"
Roof Framing	Truss
Exterior Walls	2x4

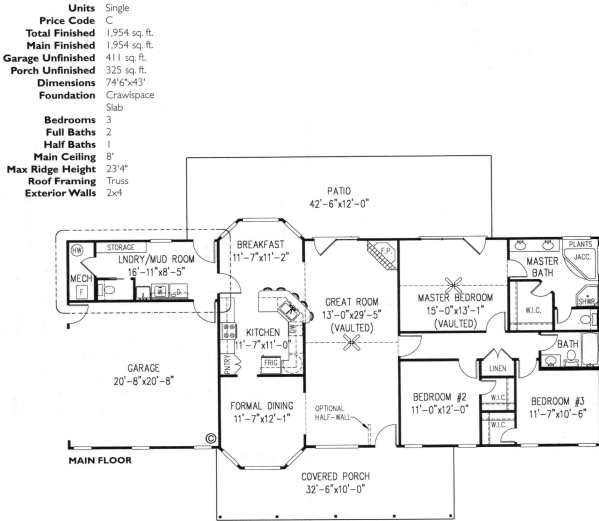

MAIN FLOOR

Design 93085

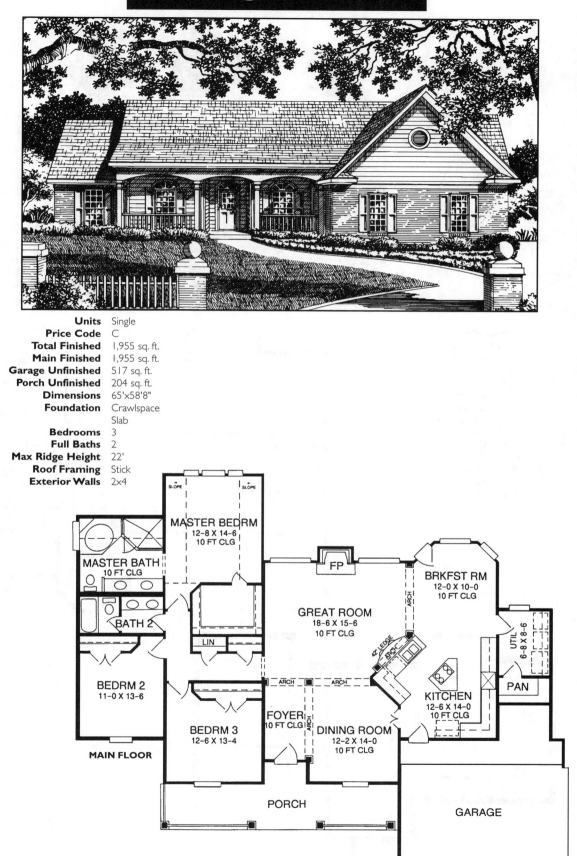

Units	Single
Price Code	C
Total Finished	1,955 sq. ft.
Main Finished	1,955 sq. ft.
Garage Unfinished	517 sq. ft.
Porch Unfinished	204 sq. ft.
Dimensions	65'x58'8"
Foundation	Crawlspace
	Slab
Bedrooms	3
Full Baths	2
Max Ridge Height	22'
Roof Framing	Stick
Exterior Walls	2x4

MASTER BEDRM
12-8 X 14-6
10 FT CLG

MASTER BATH
10 FT CLG

BATH 2

BEDRM 2
11-0 X 13-6

BEDRM 3
12-6 X 13-4

FOYER
10 FT CLG

DINING ROOM
12-2 X 14-0
10 FT CLG

GREAT ROOM
18-6 X 15-6
10 FT CLG

BRKFST RM
12-0 X 10-0
10 FT CLG

KITCHEN
12-6 X 14-0
10 FT CLG

UTIL
6-8 X 8-6

PAN

MAIN FLOOR

PORCH

GARAGE

Design 97703

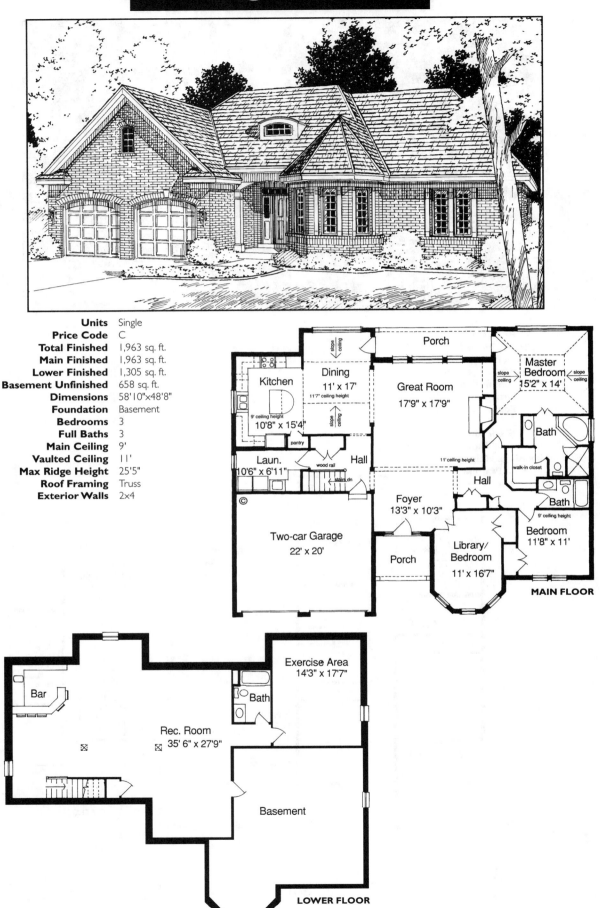

Units	Single
Price Code	C
Total Finished	1,963 sq. ft.
Main Finished	1,963 sq. ft.
Lower Finished	1,305 sq. ft.
Basement Unfinished	658 sq. ft.
Dimensions	58'10"x48'8"
Foundation	Basement
Bedrooms	3
Full Baths	3
Main Ceiling	9'
Vaulted Ceiling	11'
Max Ridge Height	25'5"
Roof Framing	Truss
Exterior Walls	2x4

MAIN FLOOR

Porch

Dining
11' x 17'
11'7" ceiling height

Kitchen
10'8" x 15'4"
9' ceiling height

pantry

Laun.
10'6" x 6'11"

wood rail

Hall

stairs dn

Two-car Garage
22' x 20'

Great Room
17'9" x 17'9"

11' ceiling height

Foyer
13'3" x 10'3"

Porch

Library/
Bedroom
11' x 16'7"

Hall

Master
Bedroom
15'2" x 14'

slope ceiling

Bath

walk-in closet

Bath
9' ceiling height

Bedroom
11'8" x 11'

LOWER FLOOR

Bar

Rec. Room
35' 6" x 27'9"

Bath

Exercise Area
14'3" x 17'7"

Basement

Design 62056

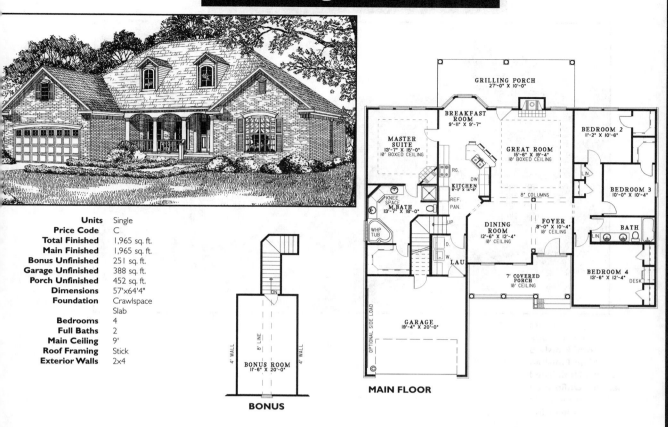

Units	Single
Price Code	C
Total Finished	1,965 sq. ft.
Main Finished	1,965 sq. ft.
Bonus Unfinished	251 sq. ft.
Garage Unfinished	388 sq. ft.
Porch Unfinished	452 sq. ft.
Dimensions	57'x64'4"
Foundation	Crawlspace
	Slab
Bedrooms	4
Full Baths	2
Main Ceiling	9'
Roof Framing	Stick
Exterior Walls	2x4

BONUS

MAIN FLOOR

Design 69103

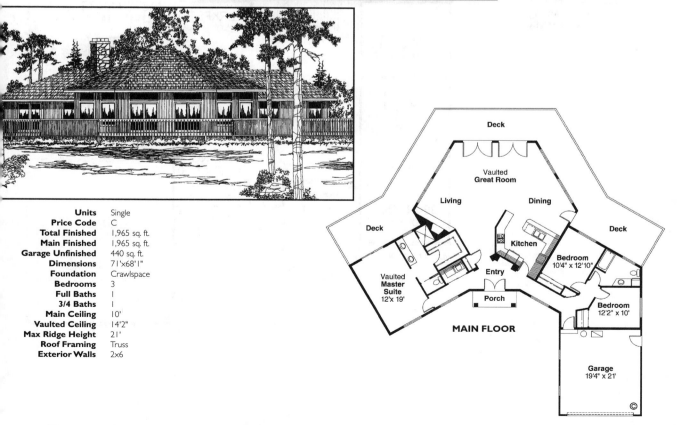

Units	Single
Price Code	C
Total Finished	1,965 sq. ft.
Main Finished	1,965 sq. ft.
Garage Unfinished	440 sq. ft.
Dimensions	71'x68'1"
Foundation	Crawlspace
Bedrooms	3
Full Baths	1
3/4 Baths	1
Main Ceiling	10'
Vaulted Ceiling	14'2"
Max Ridge Height	21'
Roof Framing	Truss
Exterior Walls	2x6

MAIN FLOOR

Units	Single
Price Code	C
Total Finished	1,982 sq. ft.
Main Finished	1,982 sq. ft.
Bonus Unfinished	386 sq. ft.
Basement Unfinished	1,982 sq. ft.
Dimensions	63'x58'
Foundation	Basement
	Crawlspace
Bedrooms	3
Full Baths	2
Half Baths	1
Main Ceiling	9'
Vaulted Ceiling	14'4"
Tray Ceiling	12'4"
Max Ridge Height	21'10"
Roof Framing	Stick
Exterior Walls	2x4

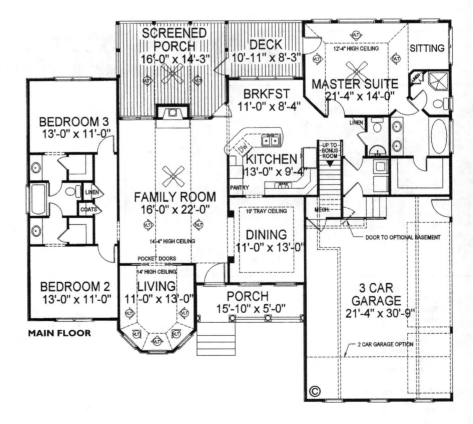

MAIN FLOOR

Design 64173

Units	Single
Price Code	H
Total Finished	1,989 sq. ft.
Main Finished	1,989 sq. ft.
Bonus Unfinished	274 sq. ft.
Garage Unfinished	525 sq. ft.
Dimensions	81'x50'
Foundation	Crawlspace
Bedrooms	3
Full Baths	2
Max Ridge Height	27'
Exterior Walls	2x6
Roof Framing	Stick/Truss

* Alternate foundation options available at an additional charge.
Please call 1-800-235-5700 for more information.

BONUS

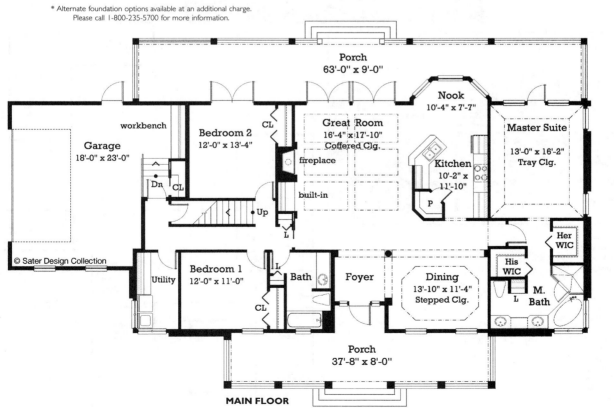

MAIN FLOOR

© Sater Design Collection

Design 64174

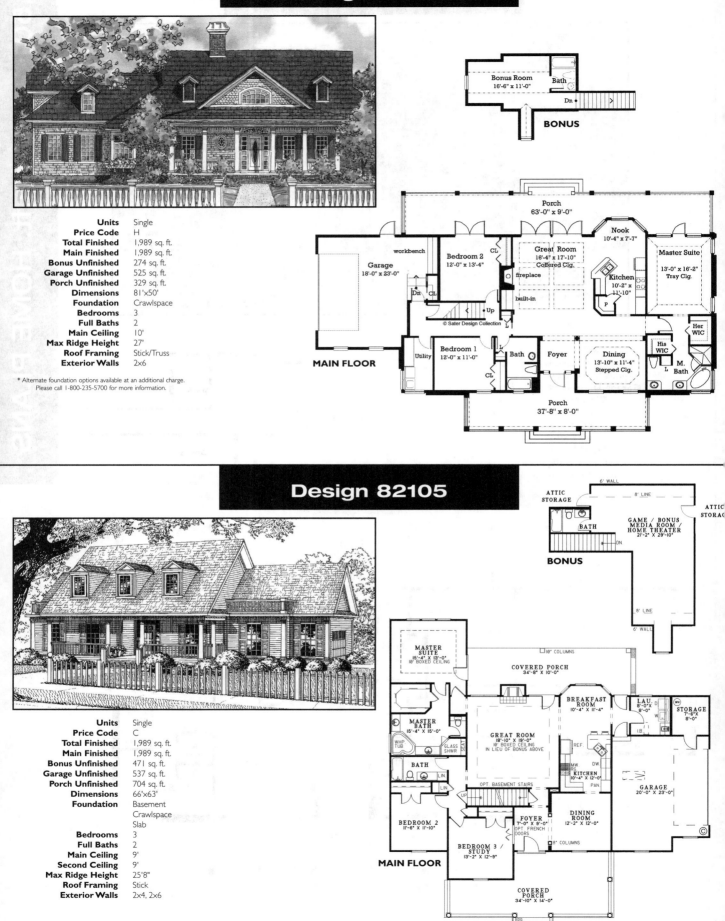

BONUS

Bonus Room
16'-6" x 11'-0"

Bath

Dn

MAIN FLOOR

Porch
63'-0" x 9'-0"

Garage
18'-0" x 23'-0"

workbench

Bedroom 2
12'-0" x 13'-4"

Great Room
16'-4" x 17'-10"
Coffered Clg.

fireplace

built-in

Nook
10'-4" x 7'-7"

Kitchen
10'-2" x 11'-10"

Master Suite
13'-0" x 16'-2"
Tray Clg.

Her WIC

Bedroom 1
12'-0" x 11'-0"

Utility

Bath

Foyer

Dining
13'-10" x 11'-4"
Stepped Clg.

His WIC

M. Bath

Porch
37'-8" x 8'-0"

© Sater Design Collection

Units	Single
Price Code	H
Total Finished	1,989 sq. ft.
Main Finished	1,989 sq. ft.
Bonus Unfinished	274 sq. ft.
Garage Unfinished	525 sq. ft.
Porch Unfinished	329 sq. ft.
Dimensions	81'x50'
Foundation	Crawlspace
Bedrooms	3
Full Baths	2
Main Ceiling	10'
Max Ridge Height	27'
Roof Framing	Stick/Truss
Exterior Walls	2x6

* Alternate foundation options available at an additional charge.
Please call 1-800-235-5700 for more information.

Design 82105

BONUS

ATTIC STORAGE

ATTIC STORAGE

6' WALL

8' LINE

BATH

GAME / BONUS
MEDIA ROOM /
HOME THEATER
21'-2" X 29'-0"

DN

8' LINE

6' WALL

MAIN FLOOR

MASTER SUITE
15'-4" X 13'-0"
10' BOXED CEILING

10" COLUMNS

COVERED PORCH
34'-8" X 10'-0"

MASTER BATH
15'-4" X 15'-0"

WHP TUB

GLASS SHWR

BATH

BEDROOM 2
11'-6" X 11'-10"

OPT. BASEMENT STAIRS

UP

GREAT ROOM
18'-10" X 19'-0"
10' BOXED CEILING
IN LIEU OF BONUS ABOVE

BREAKFAST ROOM
10'-4" X 11'-4"

LAU.
8'-0" X 8'-0"

STORAGE
7'-6" X 8'-0"

KITCHEN
10'-4" X 12'-0"

REF.

MW. FRG.

DW

PAN

GARAGE
20'-0" X 23'-0"

FOYER
7'-0" X 9'-0"
OPT FRENCH DOORS

DINING ROOM
12'-2" X 12'-0"

BEDROOM 3 / STUDY
13'-2" X 12'-9"

8" COLUMNS

COVERED PORCH
34'-10" X 14'-0"

Units	Single
Price Code	C
Total Finished	1,989 sq. ft.
Main Finished	1,989 sq. ft.
Bonus Unfinished	471 sq. ft.
Garage Unfinished	537 sq. ft.
Porch Unfinished	704 sq. ft.
Dimensions	66'x63'
Foundation	Basement
	Crawlspace
	Slab
Bedrooms	3
Full Baths	2
Main Ceiling	9'
Second Ceiling	9'
Max Ridge Height	25'8"
Roof Framing	Stick
Exterior Walls	2x4, 2x6

Design 24743

Units	Single
Price Code	C
Total Finished	1,990 sq. ft.
Main Finished	1,990 sq. ft.
Basement Unfinished	1,338 sq. ft.
Garage Unfinished	660 sq. ft.
Porch Unfinished	212 sq. ft.
Dimensions	62'x43'
Foundation	Basement
Bedrooms	3
Full Baths	2
Main Ceiling	8'
Vaulted Ceiling	12'
Max Ridge Height	22'6"
Roof Framing	Stick
Exterior Walls	2x4

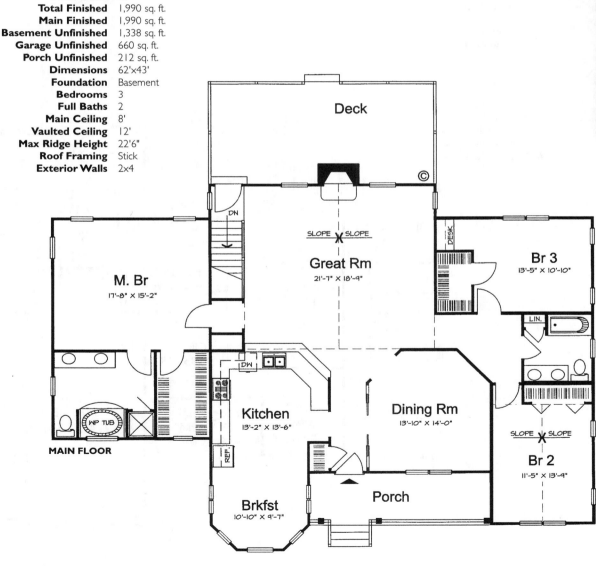

MAIN FLOOR

Units	Single
Price Code	C
Total Finished	1,992 sq. ft.
Main Finished	1,992 sq. ft.
Dimensions	63'×57'2"
Foundation	Basement
	Crawlspace
	Slab
Bedrooms	3
Full Baths	2
Half Baths	1
Main Ceiling	9'
Vaulted Ceiling	13'10"
Tray Ceiling	12'
Max Ridge Height	20'

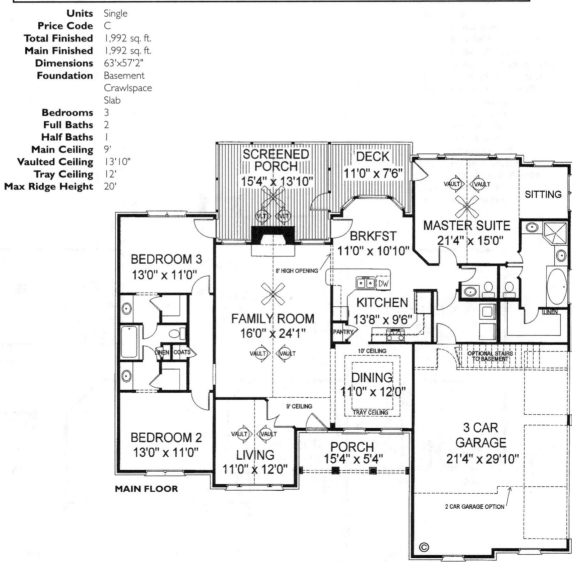

SCREENED PORCH 15'4" x 13'10"

DECK 11'0" x 7'6"

SITTING

MASTER SUITE 21'4" x 15'0"

BEDROOM 3 13'0" x 11'0"

BRKFST 11'0" x 10'10"

8' HIGH OPENING

LINEN

FAMILY ROOM 16'0" x 24'1"

KITCHEN 13'8" x 9'6"

PANTRY

VAULT VAULT

LINEN COATS

10' CEILING

OPTIONAL STAIRS TO BASEMENT

DINING 11'0" x 12'0"

TRAY CEILING

9' CEILING

3 CAR GARAGE 21'4" x 29'10"

BEDROOM 2 13'0" x 11'0"

VAULT VAULT

LIVING 11'0" x 12'0"

PORCH 15'4" x 5'4"

MAIN FLOOR

2 CAR GARAGE OPTION

Design 51017

1,501-2,000 sq. ft. HOME PLANS

PHOTOGRAPHY: MARK ENGLUND

Units	Single
Price Code	C
Total Finished	1,993 sq. ft.
Main Finished	1,993 sq. ft.
Basement Unfinished	1,993 sq. ft.
Garage Unfinished	521 sq. ft.
Deck Unfinished	180 sq. ft.
Dimensions	60'x48'4"
Foundation	Basement
Bedrooms	3
Full Baths	2
Main Ceiling	8'
Max Ridge Height	23'3"
Roof Framing	Truss
Exterior Walls	2x4

Please note: The photographed home may have been modified to suit homeowner preferences. If you order plans, have a builder or design professional check them against the photograph to confirm actual construction details.

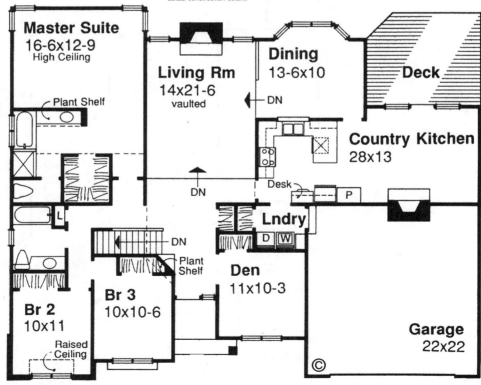

MAIN FLOOR

Units	Single
Price Code	C
Total Finished	1,994 sq. ft.
Main Finished	1,994 sq. ft.
Garage Unfinished	417 sq. ft.
Porch Unfinished	118 sq. ft.
Dimensions	65'2"x63'
Foundation	Basement
	Crawlspace
	Slab
Bedrooms	3
Full Baths	2
Roof Framing	Stick
Exterior Walls	2x4

MAIN FLOOR

Design 52075

CAD FILES AVAILABLE
For more information call
800-235-5700

Units	Single
Price Code	B
Total Finished	1,996 sq. ft.
Main Finished	1,996 sq. ft.
Basement Unfinished	1,996 sq. ft.
Garage Unfinished	476 sq. ft.
Dimensions	60'x47'6"
Foundation	Combo Basement/ Crawlspace
Bedrooms	4
Full Baths	3
Main Ceiling	9'
Second Ceiling	8'
Max Ridge Height	26'9"
Roof Framing	Stick
Exterior Walls	2x4

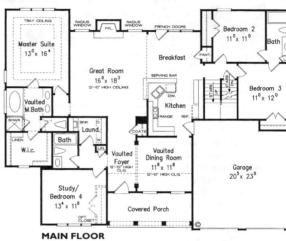

MAIN FLOOR

Design 63049

Units	Single
Price Code	C
Total Finished	1,997 sq. ft.
Main Finished	1,997 sq. ft.
Bonus Unfinished	310 sq. ft.
Garage Unfinished	502 sq. ft.
Dimensions	64'x57'
Foundation	Basement
Bedrooms	2
Full Baths	2
Half Baths	1
Main Ceiling	10'
Max Ridge Height	23'
Roof Framing	Truss
Exterior Walls	2x4

BONUS

MAIN FLOOR

Units	Single
Price Code	C
Total Finished	1,999 sq. ft.
Main Finished	1,999 sq. ft.
Garage Unfinished	561 sq. ft.
Porch Unfinished	299 sq. ft.
Dimensions	70'x57'10"
Foundation	Crawlspace
	Slab
Bedrooms	3
Full Baths	2
Main Ceiling	9'
Max Ridge Height	24'6"
Roof Framing	Stick
Exterior Walls	2x4, 2x6

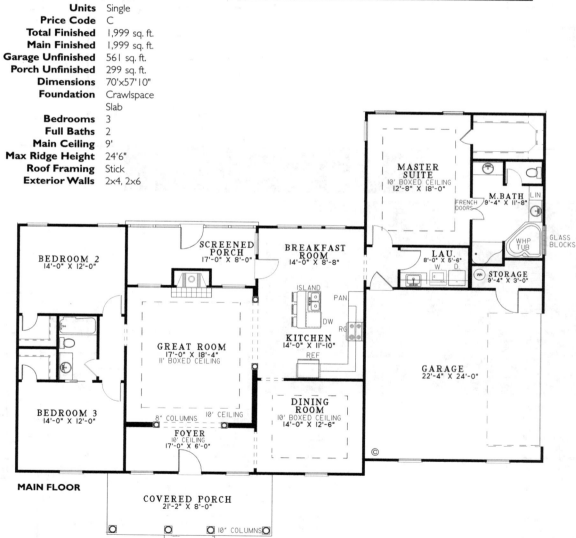

MASTER SUITE
10' BOXED CEILING
12'-8" X 18'-0"

M. BATH
9'-4" X 11'-8"

FRENCH DOORS

WHP TUB

GLASS BLOCKS

LIN

LAU.
8'-0" X 5'-6"

STORAGE
9'-4" X 3'-0"

WH

BEDROOM 2
14'-0" X 12'-0"

SCREENED PORCH
17'-0" X 8'-0"

BREAKFAST ROOM
14'-0" X 8'-8"

ISLAND

PAN

DW

KITCHEN
14'-0" X 11'-10"

REF

GREAT ROOM
17'-0" X 18'-4"
11' BOXED CEILING

GARAGE
22'-4" X 24'-0"

BEDROOM 3
14'-0" X 12'-0"

8" COLUMNS   10' CEILING

10' CEILING

FOYER
10' CEILING
17'-0" X 6'-0"

DINING ROOM
10' BOXED CEILING
14'-0" X 12'-6"

©

MAIN FLOOR

COVERED PORCH
21'-2" X 8'-0"

10" COLUMNS

Design 99681

Units	Single
Price Code	D
Total Finished	2,003 sq. ft.
Main Finished	2,003 sq. ft.
Basement Unfinished	2,003 sq. ft.
Garage Unfinished	485 sq. ft.
Dimensions	67'x57'
Foundation	Basement
	Crawlspace
	Slab
Bedrooms	3
Full Baths	2
Main Ceiling	8'
Max Ridge Height	18'
Roof Framing	Stick
Exterior Walls	2x4

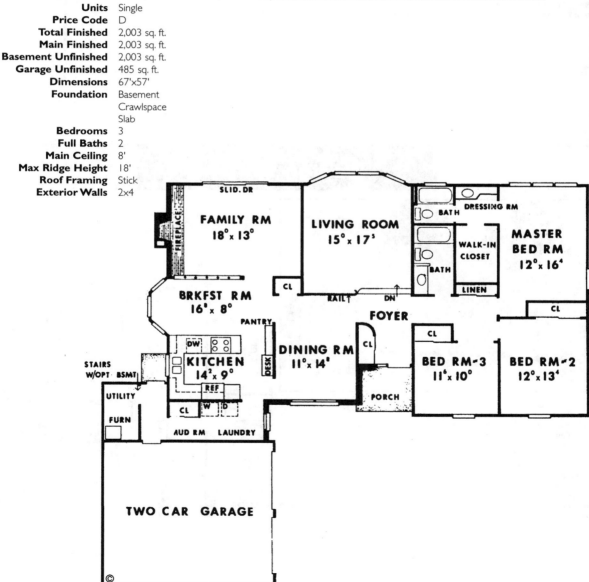

MAIN FLOOR

Design 63125

MAIN FLOOR

Units	Single
Price Code	D
Total Finished	2,005 sq. ft.
Main Finished	2,005 sq. ft.
Garage Unfinished	466 sq. ft.
Dimensions	58'x60'
Foundation	Slab
Bedrooms	3
Full Baths	2
Main Ceiling	10'
Max Ridge Height	20'10"
Roof Framing	Truss

Design 97151

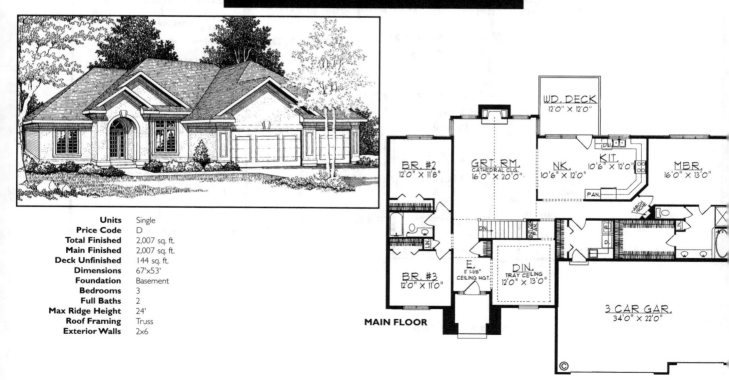

Units	Single
Price Code	D
Total Finished	2,007 sq. ft.
Main Finished	2,007 sq. ft.
Deck Unfinished	144 sq. ft.
Dimensions	67'x53'
Foundation	Basement
Bedrooms	3
Full Baths	2
Max Ridge Height	24'
Roof Framing	Truss
Exterior Walls	2x6

MAIN FLOOR

Design 62064

Units	Single
Price Code	D
Total Finished	2,014 sq. ft.
Main Finished	2,014 sq. ft.
Garage Unfinished	428 sq. ft.
Porch Unfinished	231 sq. ft.
Dimensions	59'10"x62'10"
Foundation	Crawlspace
	Slab
Bedrooms	3
Full Baths	2
Main Ceiling	9'
Max Ridge Height	22'10"
Exterior Walls	2x4

GARAGE 21'-4" X 23'-2"

OPTIONAL COURTYARD GARAGE

MAIN FLOOR

Design 62063

Units	Single
Price Code	D
Total Finished	2,026 sq. ft.
Main Finished	2,026 sq. ft.
Garage Unfinished	421 sq. ft.
Porch Unfinished	479 sq. ft.
Dimensions	58'x79'6"
Foundation	Crawlspace
	Slab
Bedrooms	3
Full Baths	2
Max Ridge Height	28'6'
Roof Framing	Stick
Exterior Walls	2x6

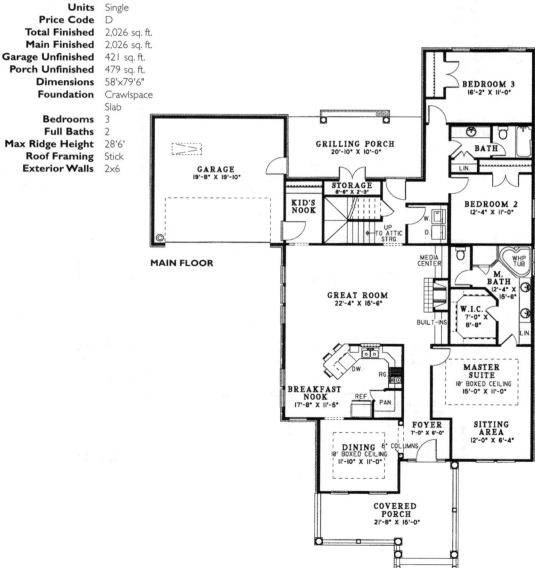

MAIN FLOOR

Design 67001

Units	Single
Price Code	D
Total Finished	2,028 sq. ft.
Main Finished	2,028 sq. ft.
Garage Unfinished	442 sq. ft.
Porch Unfinished	232 sq. ft.
Dimensions	60'x58'
Foundation	Slab
Bedrooms	3
Full Baths	2
Main Ceiling	10'
Max Ridge Height	23'3"
Roof Framing	Stick
Exterior Walls	2x4

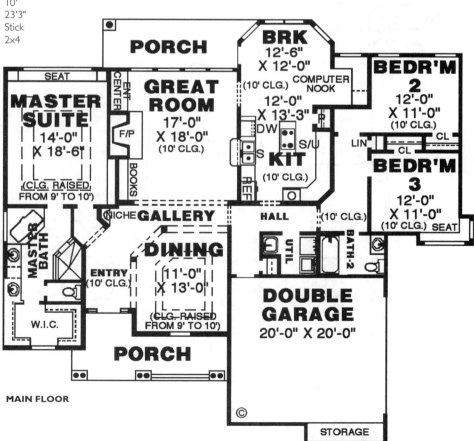

MAIN FLOOR

Units	Single
Price Code	D
Total Finished	2,032 sq. ft.
Main Finished	2,032 sq. ft.
Basement Unfinished	1,471 sq. ft.
Garage Unfinished	561 sq. ft.
Dimensions	58'6"x43'1"
Foundation	Basement
Bedrooms	4
Full Baths	2
Main Ceiling	9'
Max Ridge Height	24'
Roof Framing	Stick
Exterior Walls	2x4

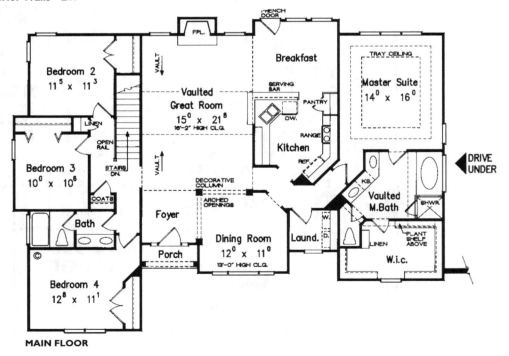

MAIN FLOOR

Design 63120

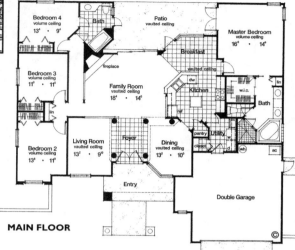

Units	Single
Price Code	D
Total Finished	2,060 sq. ft.
Main Finished	2,060 sq. ft.
Garage Unfinished	478 sq. ft.
Dimensions	60'4"x56'
Foundation	Slab
Bedrooms	4
Full Baths	2
Main Ceiling	10'
Max Ridge Height	24'
Roof Framing	Truss
Exterior Walls	2x4

Design 96505

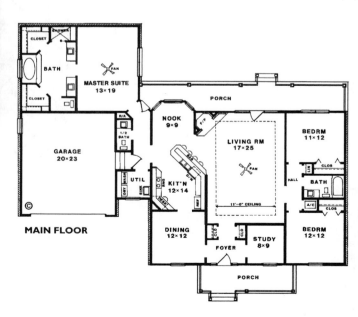

Units	Single
Price Code	D
Total Finished	2,069 sq. ft.
Main Finished	2,069 sq. ft.
Garage Unfinished	481 sq. ft.
Porch Unfinished	374 sq. ft.
Dimensions	70'x58'
Foundation	Crawlspace
	Slab
Bedrooms	3
Full Baths	2
Half Baths	1
Main Ceiling	9'
Max Ridge Height	23'
Exterior Walls	2x4

Units	Single
Price Code	D
Total Finished	2,070 sq. ft.
Main Finished	2,070 sq. ft.
Garage Unfinished	474 sq. ft.
Dimensions	52'x68'6"
Foundation	Slab
Bedrooms	4
Full Baths	2
3/4 Baths	I
Max Ridge Height	21'
Roof Framing	Stick
Exterior Walls	2x4

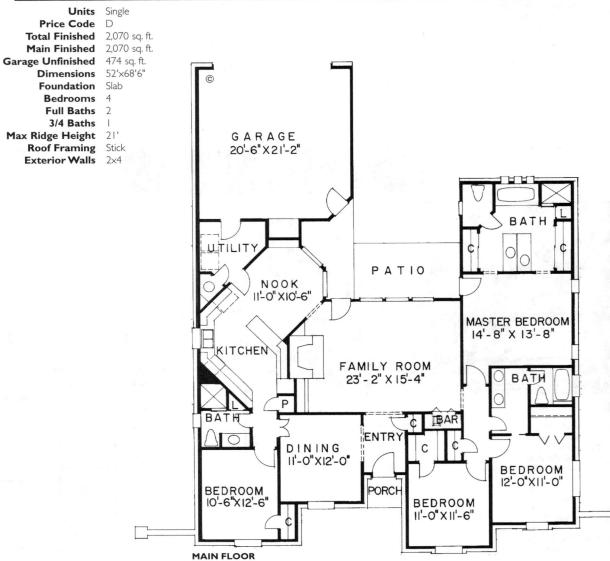

GARAGE
20'-6" X 21'-2"

UTILITY

NOOK
11'-0" X10'-6"

KITCHEN

PATIO

BATH

MASTER BEDROOM
14'-8" X 13'-8"

FAMILY ROOM
23'-2" X 15'-4"

BATH

BATH

DINING
11'-0" X12'-0"

ENTRY

BAR

BEDROOM
10'-6" X12'-6"

PORCH

BEDROOM
11'-0" X11'-6"

BEDROOM
12'-0" X11'-0"

MAIN FLOOR

Design 63136

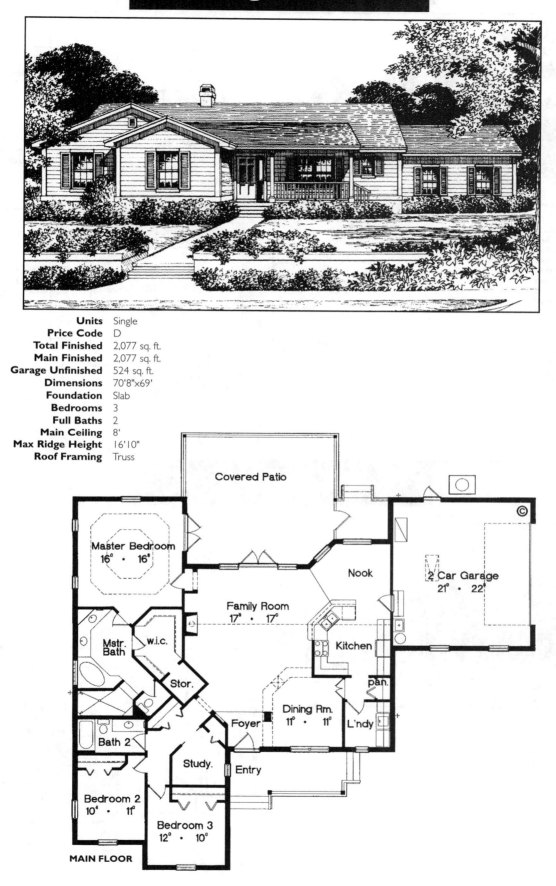

Units	Single
Price Code	D
Total Finished	2,077 sq. ft.
Main Finished	2,077 sq. ft.
Garage Unfinished	524 sq. ft.
Dimensions	70'8"x69'
Foundation	Slab
Bedrooms	3
Full Baths	2
Main Ceiling	8'
Max Ridge Height	16'10"
Roof Framing	Truss

Covered Patio

Master Bedroom
16⁰ · 16⁸

Mstr. Bath

w.i.c.

Stor.

Bath 2

Study.

Family Room
17⁸ · 17⁰

Nook

Kitchen

2 Car Garage
21⁰ · 22⁰

pan.

Foyer

Dining Rm.
11⁰ · 11⁰

L'ndy

Entry

Bedroom 2
10⁴ · 11⁰

Bedroom 3
12⁰ · 10⁰

MAIN FLOOR

Design 24982

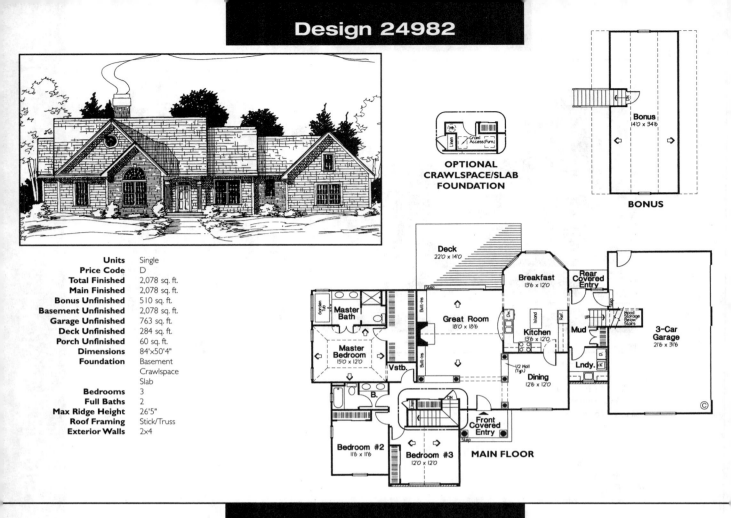

OPTIONAL CRAWLSPACE/SLAB FOUNDATION

BONUS
Bonus 14'0 x 34'6

Units	Single
Price Code	D
Total Finished	2,078 sq. ft.
Main Finished	2,078 sq. ft.
Bonus Unfinished	510 sq. ft.
Basement Unfinished	2,078 sq. ft.
Garage Unfinished	763 sq. ft.
Deck Unfinished	284 sq. ft.
Porch Unfinished	60 sq. ft.
Dimensions	84'x50'4"
Foundation	Basement
	Crawlspace
	Slab
Bedrooms	3
Full Baths	2
Max Ridge Height	26'5"
Roof Framing	Stick/Truss
Exterior Walls	2x4

MAIN FLOOR

Deck 22'0 x 14'0
Great Room 18'0 x 18'6
Breakfast 13'6 x 12'0
Rear Covered Entry
Master Bath
Master Bedroom 15'0 x 12'0
Vstb.
Kitchen 13'6 x 12'0
Mud
3-Car Garage 21'6 x 31'6
Dining 12'6 x 12'0
Lndy.
Front Covered Entry
Bedroom #2 11'6 x 11'6
Bedroom #3 12'0 x 12'0

Design 98583

Units	Single
Price Code	D
Total Finished	2,078 sq. ft.
Main Finished	2,078 sq. ft.
Garage Unfinished	734 sq. ft.
Deck Unfinished	140 sq. ft.
Porch Unfinished	240 sq. ft.
Dimensions	75'x47'10"
Foundation	Crawlspace
	Slab
Bedrooms	4
Full Baths	2
Max Ridge Height	27'
Roof Framing	Stick
Exterior Walls	2x4

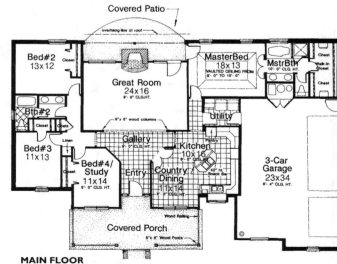

Covered Patio
Bed#2 13x12
Great Room 24x16
MasterBed 18x13
MstrBth
Bth#2
Bed#3 11x13
Gallery
Kitchen 10x16
Utility
Bed#4/ Study 11x14
Entry
Country Dining 11x14
3-Car Garage 23x34
Covered Porch

MAIN FLOOR

Design 98559

Units	Single
Price Code	D
Total Finished	2,081 sq. ft.
Main Finished	2,081 sq. ft.
Garage Unfinished	422 sq. ft.
Porch Unfinished	240 sq. ft.
Dimensions	55'x57'10"
Foundation	Slab
Bedrooms	3
Full Baths	2
3/4 Baths	1
Max Ridge Height	24'6"
Roof Framing	Stick
Exterior Walls	2x4

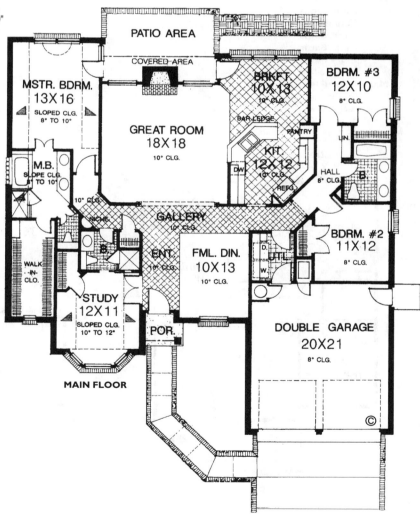

MAIN FLOOR

Units	Single
Price Code	D
Total Finished	2,083 sq. ft.
Main Finished	2,083 sq. ft.
Garage Unfinished	533 sq. ft.
Dimensions	84'x43'9"
Foundation	Crawlspace
Bedrooms	3
Full Baths	1
3/4 Baths	1
Main Ceiling	9'
Max Ridge Height	20'10"
Roof Framing	Truss
Exterior Walls	2x6

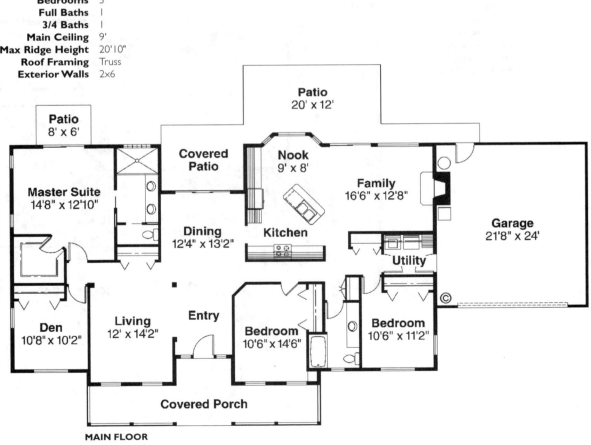

Patio 20' x 12'

Patio 8' x 6'

Covered Patio

Nook 9' x 8'

Family 16'6" x 12'8"

Garage 21'8" x 24'

Master Suite 14'8" x 12'10"

Dining 12'4" x 13'2"

Kitchen

Utility

Den 10'8" x 10'2"

Living 12' x 14'2"

Entry

Bedroom 10'6" x 14'6"

Bedroom 10'6" x 11'2"

Covered Porch

MAIN FLOOR

Design 66017

Units	Single
Price Code	D
Total Finished	2,088 sq. ft.
Main Finished	2,088 sq. ft.
Bonus Unfinished	320 sq. ft.
Garage Unfinished	520 sq. ft.
Deck Unfinished	140 sq. ft.
Porch Unfinished	42 sq. ft.
Dimensions	44'10"x79'10"
Foundation	Slab
Bedrooms	3
Full Baths	2
Main Ceiling	9'-10'
Max Ridge Height	27'6"
Roof Framing	Stick
Exterior Walls	2x4

BONUS

MAIN FLOOR

Units	Single
Price Code	D
Total Finished	2,089 sq. ft.
Main Finished	2,089 sq. ft.
Bonus Unfinished	497 sq. ft.
Garage Unfinished	541 sq. ft.
Dimensions	79'×52'
Foundation	Crawlspace
	Slab
Bedrooms	3
Full Baths	2
Half Baths	I
Main Ceiling	9'
Max Ridge Height	22'
Roof Framing	Stick
Exterior Walls	2x4

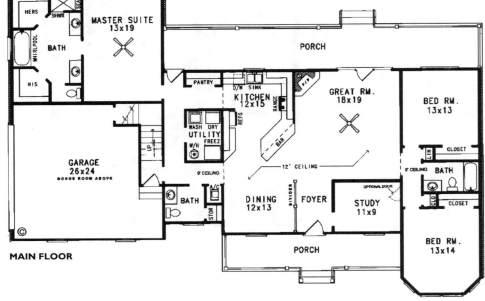

BONUS

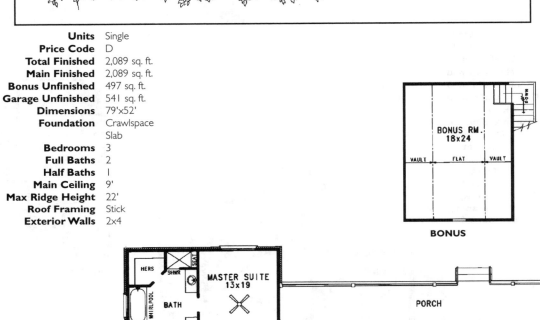

MAIN FLOOR

Design 96550

Units	Single
Price Code	D
Total Finished	2,104 sq. ft.
Main Finished	2,104 sq. ft.
Garage Unfinished	564 sq. ft.
Porch Unfinished	305 sq. ft.
Dimensions	75'x56'
Foundation	Crawlspace
	Slab
Bedrooms	3
Full Baths	2
Half Baths	1
Main Ceiling	9'
Max Ridge Height	24'6"
Roof Framing	Stick
Exterior Walls	2x4

MAIN FLOOR

Design 64519

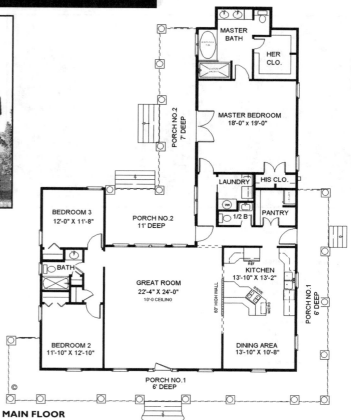

Units	Single
Price Code	D
Total Finished	2,123 sq. ft.
Main Finished	2,123 sq. ft.
Porch Unfinished	1,008 sq. ft.
Dimensions	60'x76'
Foundation	Crawlspace
Bedrooms	3
Full Baths	2
Half Baths	1
Main Ceiling	9'
Roof Framing	Truss
Exterior Walls	2x4

MAIN FLOOR

Design 66018

Units	Single
Price Code	C
Total Finished	2,128 sq. ft.
Main Finished	2,128 sq. ft.
Garage Unfinished	602 sq. ft.
Deck Unfinished	200 sq. ft.
Porch Unfinished	40 sq. ft.
Dimensions	60'x67'
Foundation	Slab
Bedrooms	3
Full Baths	2
Half Baths	1
Main Ceiling	9'-10'
Max Ridge Height	27'
Roof Framing	Stick
Exterior Walls	2x4

Design 61095

Units	Single
Price Code	D
Total Finished	2,140 sq. ft.
Main Finished	2,140 sq. ft.
Garage Unfinished	394 sq. ft.
Porch Unfinished	235 sq. ft.
Dimensions	40'x84'4"
Foundation	Basement
	Combo
	Basement/Slab
Bedrooms	3
Full Baths	2
Main Ceiling	9'
Roof Framing	Stick
Exterior Walls	2x6

Design 52107

Units	Single
Price Code	D
Total Finished	2,141 sq. ft.
Main Finished	2,141 sq. ft.
Bonus Unfinished	296 sq. ft.
Basement Unfinished	2,141 sq. ft.
Garage Unfinished	487 sq. ft.
Dimensions	70'6"x67'
Foundation	Basement
	Crawlspace
Bedrooms	3
Full Baths	2
Half Baths	1
Main Ceiling	9'
Second Ceiling	8'
Max Ridge Height	28'6"
Roof Framing	Stick
Exterior Walls	2x4

CAD FILES AVAILABLE
For more information call
800-235-5700

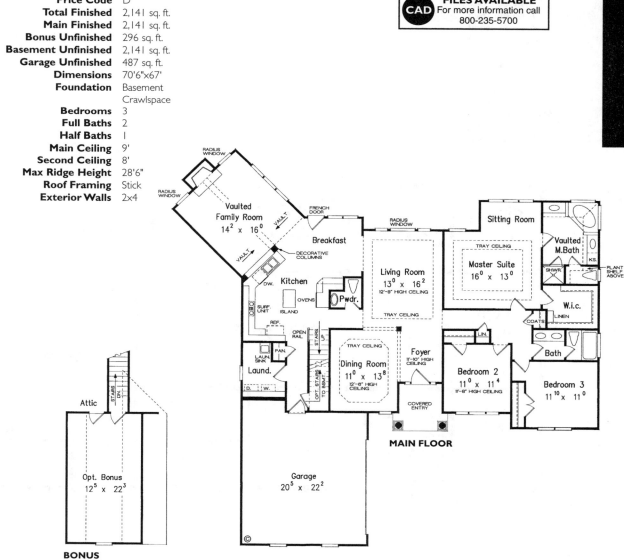

MAIN FLOOR

BONUS

Units	Single
Price Code	D
Total Finished	2,142 sq. ft.
Main Finished	2,142 sq. ft.
Garage Unfinished	574 sq. ft.
Dimensions	55'x84'
Foundation	Slab
Bedrooms	2
Full Baths	2
Main Ceiling	9'
Max Ridge Height	21'
Roof Framing	Stick
Exterior Walls	2×6

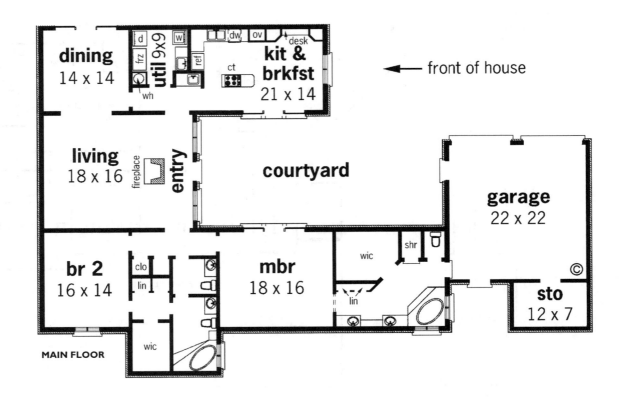

← front of house

MAIN FLOOR

Design 50037

Units	Single
Price Code	D
Total Finished	2,143 sq. ft.
Main Finished	2,143 sq. ft.
Basement Unfinished	2,143 sq. ft.
Garage Unfinished	529 sq. ft.
Porch Unfinished	217 sq. ft.
Dimensions	76'8"x44'
Foundation	Basement
Bedrooms	3
Full Baths	2
Main Ceiling	9'
Max Ridge Height	26'
Roof Framing	Truss
Exterior Walls	2x4

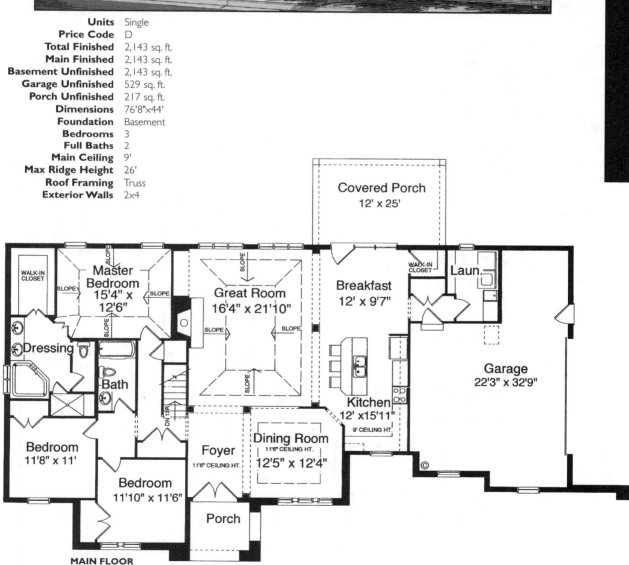

MAIN FLOOR

Units	Single
Price Code	D
Total Finished	2,148 sq. ft.
Main Finished	2,148 sq. ft.
Garage Unfinished	477 sq. ft.
Porch Unfinished	190 sq. ft.
Dimensions	63'x52'8"
Foundation	Crawlspace
	Slab
Bedrooms	4
Full Baths	2
Main Ceiling	9'
Roof Framing	Stick
Exterior Walls	2x4

Design 99479

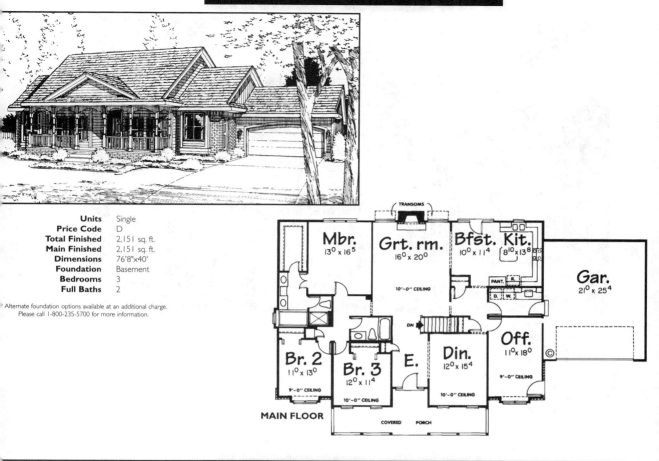

Units	Single
Price Code	D
Total Finished	2,151 sq. ft.
Main Finished	2,151 sq. ft.
Dimensions	76'8"x40'
Foundation	Basement
Bedrooms	3
Full Baths	2

Alternate foundation options available at an additional charge.
Please call 1-800-235-5700 for more information.

Design 66022

Units	Single
Price Code	D
Total Finished	2,158 sq. ft.
Main Finished	2,158 sq. ft.
Garage Unfinished	420 sq. ft.
Deck Unfinished	160 sq. ft.
Porch Unfinished	40 sq. ft.
Dimensions	61'x50'6"
Foundation	Crawlspace
	Slab
Bedrooms	4
Full Baths	2
Half Baths	1
Main Ceiling	9'-10'
Max Ridge Height	24'
Roof Framing	Stick
Exterior Walls	2x4

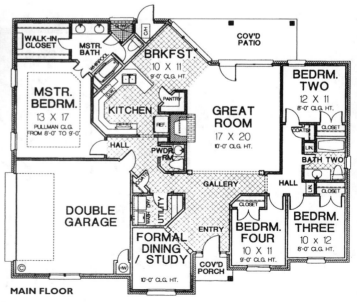

Design 24748

Units	Single
Price Code	C
Total Finished	2,161 sq. ft.
Main Finished	2,161 sq. ft.
Basement Unfinished	2,161 sq. ft.
Garage Unfinished	590 sq. ft.
Deck Unfinished	170 sq. ft.
Porch Unfinished	72 sq. ft.
Dimensions	82'1½"x45'
Foundation	Basement
	Crawlspace
	Slab
Bedrooms	3
Full Baths	2
Half Baths	1
Main Ceiling	9'
Max Ridge Height	29'
Roof Framing	Stick/Truss
Exterior Walls	2x4

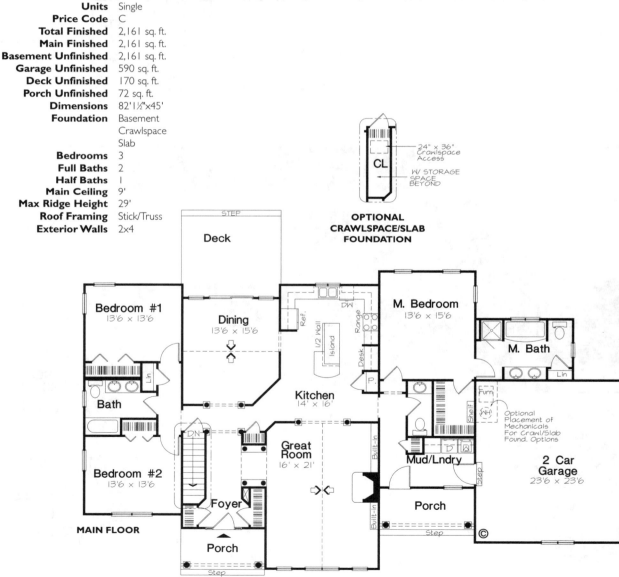

OPTIONAL CRAWLSPACE/SLAB FOUNDATION

24" x 36" Crawlspace Access

W/ STORAGE SPACE BEYOND

MAIN FLOOR

Bedroom #1 13'6 x 13'6

Bath

Bedroom #2 13'6 x 13'6

Foyer

Porch

Deck

Dining 13'6 x 15'6

Kitchen 14' x 16'

Great Room 16' x 21'

M. Bedroom 13'6 x 15'6

M. Bath

Mud/Lndry

Porch

2 Car Garage 23'6 x 23'6

Optional Placement of Mechanicals For Crawl/Slab Found. Options

Design 96504

Units	Single
Price Code	D
Total Finished	2,162 sq. ft.
Main Finished	2,162 sq. ft.
Garage Unfinished	498 sq. ft.
Porch Unfinished	343 sq. ft.
Dimensions	70'x50'
Foundation	Crawlspace
	Slab
Bedrooms	3
Full Baths	2
Main Ceiling	8'
Tray Ceiling	10'
Max Ridge Height	25'
Roof Framing	Stick
Exterior Walls	2x4

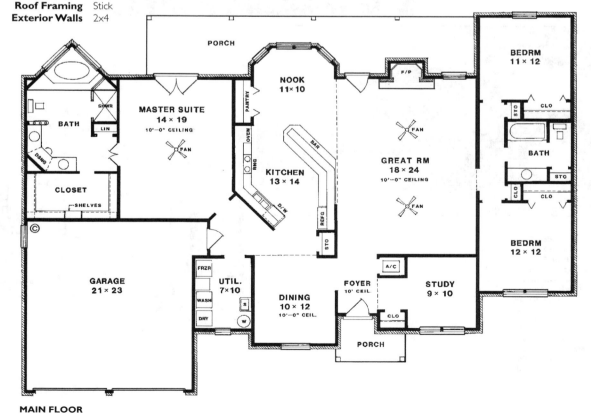

MAIN FLOOR

Design 82106

Units	Single
Price Code	C
Total Finished	2,163 sq. ft.
Main Finished	2,163 sq. ft.
Garage Unfinished	512 sq. ft.
Porch Unfinished	516 sq. ft.
Dimensions	66'4"x58'7"
Foundation	Basement
	Crawlspace
	Slab
Bedrooms	3
Full Baths	2
Main Ceiling	9'
Max Ridge Height	25'
Roof Framing	Stick
Exterior Walls	2x4, 2x6

MAIN FLOOR

GRILLING PORCH 25'-10" X 8'-0"
M. BATH 12'-8" X 15'-4"
MASTER SUITE 13'-6" X 15'-4" 10" BOXED CEILING
GREAT ROOM 13'-10" X 19'-2"
BREAKFAST ROOM 12'-10" X 9'-8"
HEARTH ROOM 11'-10" X 16'-5"
BATH
KITCHEN 11'-8" X 12'-3"
PANTRY
ATTIC STORAGE
LAU. 8'-6" X 5'-10"
FOYER 7'-6" X 9'-0"
BEDROOM 3 10'-8" X 11'-0"
BEDROOM 2 / STUDY 11'-2" X 11'-2"
DINING ROOM 12'-4" X 16'-4"
OPTIONAL BASEMENT STAIRS
COVERED PORCH 32'-4" X 8'-0"
GARAGE 22'-0" X 23'-6"

Design 98512

Units	Single
Price Code	D
Total Finished	2,167 sq. ft.
Main Finished	2,167 sq. ft.
Garage Unfinished	690 sq. ft.
Deck Unfinished	162 sq. ft.
Porch Unfinished	22 sq. ft.
Dimensions	64'x58'1"
Foundation	Slab
Bedrooms	3
Full Baths	2
Main Ceiling	8'-10'
Max Ridge Height	26'3"
Roof Framing	Stick
Exterior Walls	2x4

Covered Patio
MstrBed 13'x17' Vaulted Clg.
Brkfst 13'8x9'8
Bed#2 15'x11'6
GreatRm 21x17
Kit 13'8x12'8
Gallery
Bed#3 11x11'8
Util
FmlDin 11'8x11
Ent
Por.
3-Car Gar. 30'8x23

MAIN FLOOR

Design 98554

Units	Single
Price Code	D
Total Finished	2,169 sq. ft.
Main Finished	2,169 sq. ft.
Garage Unfinished	542 sq. ft.
Deck Unfinished	160 sq. ft.
Dimensions	76'6"x44'4"
Foundation	Slab
Bedrooms	4
Full Baths	3
Main Ceiling	8'-10'
Max Ridge Height	24'6"
Roof Framing	Stick
Exterior Walls	2×4

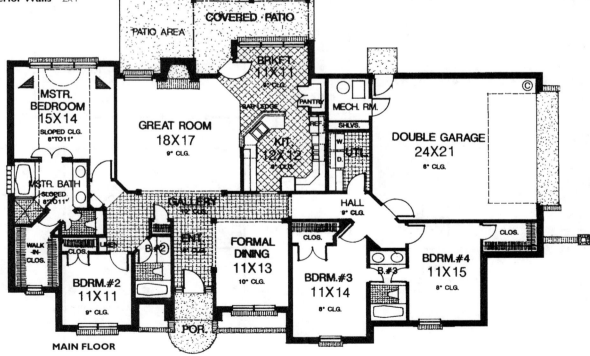

MAIN FLOOR

Units	Single
Price Code	D
Total Finished	2,172 sq. ft.
Main Finished	2,172 sq. ft.
Basement Unfinished	2,172 sq. ft.
Garage Unfinished	623 sq. ft.
Porch Unfinished	151 sq. ft.
Dimensions	64'6"x56'10"
Foundation	Basement
	Crawlspace
	Slab
Bedrooms	3
Full Baths	2
Main Ceiling	9'
Max Ridge Height	27'6"
Roof Framing	Stick
Exterior Walls	2x4

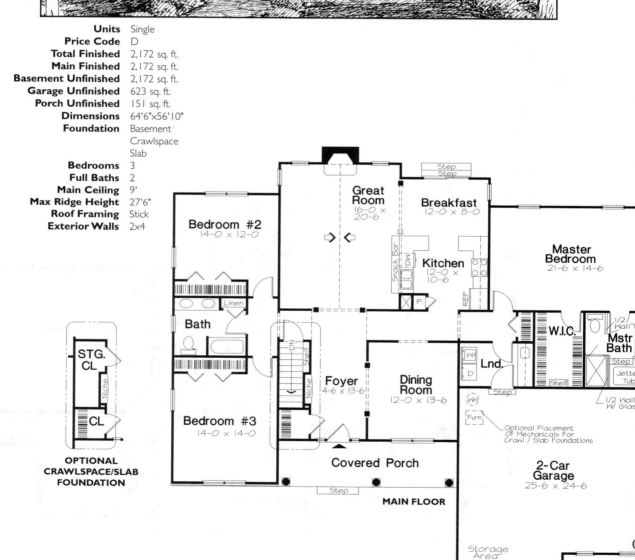

OPTIONAL CRAWLSPACE/SLAB FOUNDATION

MAIN FLOOR

Design 94971

Units	Single
Price Code	D
Total Finished	2,172 sq. ft.
Main Finished	2,172 sq. ft.
Garage Unfinished	680 sq. ft.
Dimensions	76'x46'
Foundation	Basement
Bedrooms	4
Full Baths	2
3/4 Baths	1
Max Ridge Height	21'6"
Roof Framing	Stick
Exterior Walls	2x4

* Alternate foundation options available at an additional charge.
Please call 1-800-235-5700 for more information.

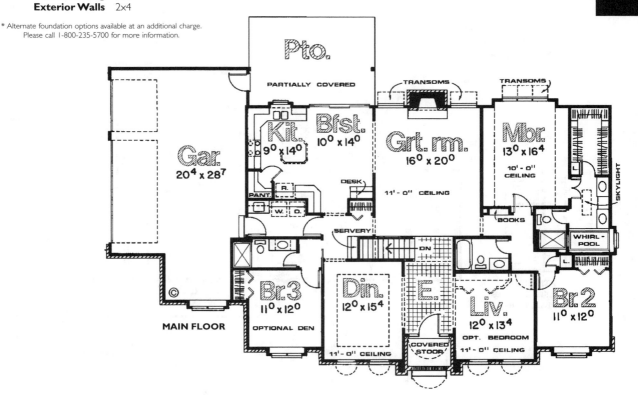

Design 24952

Units	Single
Price Code	D
Total Finished	2,179 sq. ft.
Main Finished	2,179 sq. ft.
Bonus Unfinished	644 sq. ft.
Basement Unfinished	2,179 sq. ft.
Garage Unfinished	671 sq. ft.
Deck Unfinished	162 sq. ft.
Porch Unfinished	120 sq. ft.
Dimensions	78'x54'4"
Foundation	Basement
	Crawlspace
	Slab
Bedrooms	3
Full Baths	2
Main Ceiling	9'
Max Ridge Height	27'10"
Roof Framing	Stick
Exterior Walls	2x4

BONUS

Bonus Rm. 23-5 x 12-0
12-0 x 9-8
14-0 x 9-8

OPTIONAL CRAWLSPACE/SLAB FOUNDATION

MAIN FLOOR

Deck · Brkfst 8-6 x 14-1 · Kitchen 9-9 x 16-5 · Util. · Garage 23-5 x 25-5 · Great Room 15-5 x 19-5 · Three Sided Fireplace · Dining 13-9 x 10-9 · Storage 4-10 x 10-8 · Glass Block · Gallery · Master Br 17-5 x 13-9 · Sitting 11-5 x 5-6 · Porch · Br 2 11-8 x 11-8 · Br 3 13-5 x 13-9

Design 68174

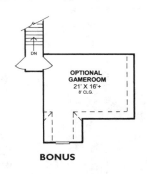

OPTIONAL GAMEROOM
21' X 16'+
8' CLG.

DN

BONUS

Units	Single
Price Code	D
Total Finished	2,184 sq. ft.
Main Finished	2,184 sq. ft.
Bonus Unfinished	436 sq. ft.
Garage Unfinished	621 sq. ft.
Deck Unfinished	1,127 sq. ft.
Dimensions	98'x57'
Foundation	Crawlspace
	Slab
Bedrooms	3
Full Baths	2
Main Ceiling	9'
Max Ridge Height	30'
Exterior Walls	2x4

Alternate foundation options available at an additional charge.
Please call 1-800-235-5700 for more information.

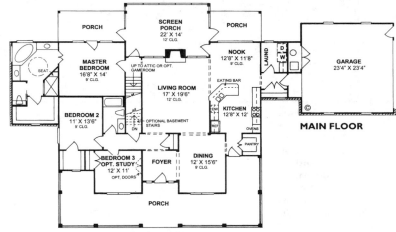

PORCH • **SCREEN PORCH** 22' X 14' 12' CLG. • **PORCH**

MASTER BEDROOM 16'8" X 14' 9' CLG.

NOOK 12'8" X 11'8" 9' CLG.

LAUND

GARAGE 23'4" X 23'4"

SEAT

UP TO ATTIC OR OPT. GAMEROOM

LIVING ROOM 17' X 19'6" 12' CLG.

EATING BAR

BEDROOM 2 11' X 13'6" 9' CLG.

OPTIONAL BASEMENT STAIRS

DN

KITCHEN 12'8" X 12'

MAIN FLOOR

OVENS

PANTRY

BEDROOM 3 OPT. STUDY 12' X 11' OPT. DOORS

FOYER

DINING 12' X 15'6" 9' CLG.

PORCH

Design 93722

Units	Single
Price Code	D
Total Finished	2,184 sq. ft.
Main Finished	2,184 sq. ft.
Dimensions	67'8"x49'2"
Foundation	Basement
	Crawlspace
	Slab
Bedrooms	4
Full Baths	2
Half Baths	1
Max Ridge Height	25'8"
Roof Framing	Stick
Exterior Walls	2x4

Skylights **Porch** Seat

Bdrm 3 11'6" x 11'6"

M. Bedroom 13'6" x 16'8"

Kitchen 12'8" x 15'4"

Breakfast 9'3" x 11'6"

Great Room 15'7" x 19'6" 11'7" h. Ceiling

Utility 6'0"x7'10"

Foyer 11'7" h. Ceiling

Garage 21'6" x 21'6"

Dining 11'8" x 13'6" 11'7" h. Ceiling

Office Bdrm 4 10'0" x 10'2"

Bdrm 2 11'6" x 11'6"

Porch

MAIN FLOOR

Units	Single
Price Code	D
Total Finished	2,185 sq. ft.
First Finished	2,185 sq. ft.
Dimensions	58'x60'
Foundation	Crawlspace
Bedrooms	4
Full Baths	2
Max Ridge Height	18'2"
Roof Framing	Stick/Truss
Exterior Walls	2x6

MAIN FLOOR

Design 97494

Units	Single
Price Code	D
Total Finished	2,186 sq. ft.
Main Finished	2,186 sq. ft.
Garage Unfinished	720 sq. ft.
Dimensions	64'x66'
Foundation	Basement
Bedrooms	3
Full Baths	2
Half Baths	1
Main Ceiling	8'
Max Ridge Height	25'
Roof Framing	Stick
Exterior Walls	2x4

* Alternate foundation options available at an additional charge.
Please call 1-800-235-5700 for more information.

Din.
14⁰ x 12⁰
9'-0" CLG.

Bfst.
13⁰ x 12⁰

TRANSOMS   TRANSOMS

SNACK BAR

Mbr.
14⁰ x 14⁰
10'-0" CEILING

Grt. rm.
15⁰ x 20⁰
10'-0" CEILING

WET BAR
P.
LIN.

Kit.
13⁶ x 14⁸

WHIRLPOOL

LIN.

SEAT

ENT. CENTER

SEAT

LIN.

DN

COMPUTER DEN/
OPT. WALK - IN
PANTRY

Br. 2
11⁰ x 12⁰

Br. 3
11⁰ x 12⁰
OPT. DEN
10'-0" CLG.

D.W.

WORK BENCH

Gar.
20⁸ x 32⁰

COVERED STOOP

TRANSOMS

MAIN FLOOR

Design 62060

Units	Single
Price Code	D
Total Finished	2,189 sq. ft.
Main Finished	2,189 sq. ft.
Garage Unfinished	550 sq. ft.
Porch Unfinished	225 sq. ft.
Dimensions	58'x69'6"
Foundation	Crawlspace
	Slab
Bedrooms	4
Full Baths	2
Main Ceiling	9'
Roof Framing	Stick
Exterior Walls	2x4

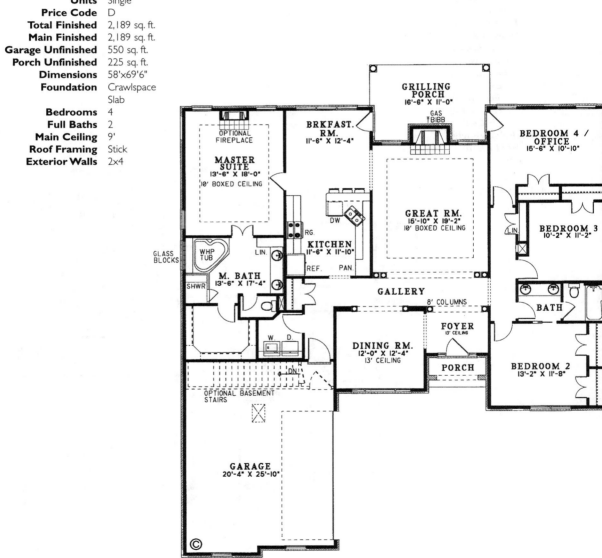

MAIN FLOOR

Design 99284

2,001-2,500 sq.ft. HOME PLANS

Units	Single
Price Code	D
Total Finished	2,189 sq. ft.
Main Finished	2,189 sq. ft.
Dimensions	56'x72'
Foundation	Slab
Bedrooms	3
Full Baths	2
Max Ridge Height	23'
Roof Framing	Truss
Exterior Walls	2x6

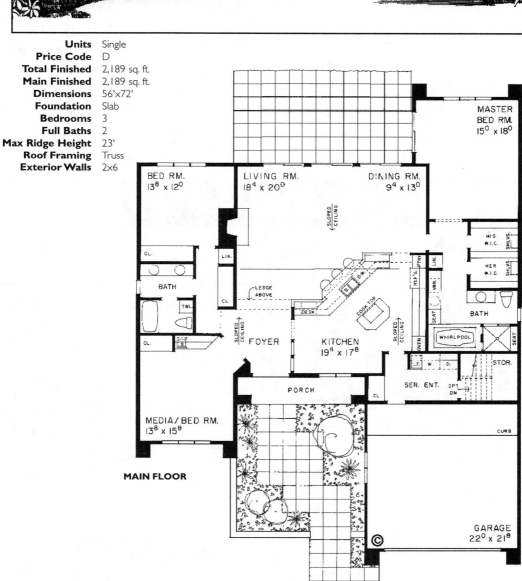

MAIN FLOOR

Design 66104

Units	Single
Price Code	D
Total Finished	2,192 sq. ft.
Main Finished	2,192 sq. ft.
Bonus Unfinished	403 sq. ft.
Garage Unfinished	440 sq. ft.
Dimensions	49'10"x75'11"
Foundation	Slab
Bedrooms	3
Full Baths	2
Main Ceiling	10'
Second Ceiling	8'
Max Ridge Height	27'
Roof Framing	Stick
Exterior Walls	2x4

BONUS

MAIN FLOOR

Design 98466

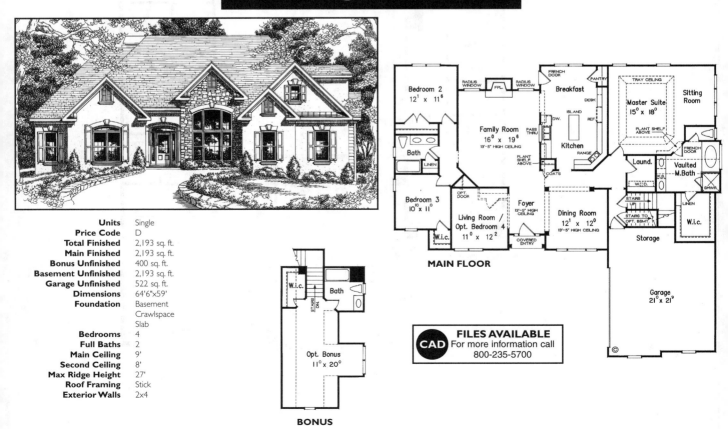

Units	Single
Price Code	D
Total Finished	2,193 sq. ft.
Main Finished	2,193 sq. ft.
Bonus Unfinished	400 sq. ft.
Basement Unfinished	2,193 sq. ft.
Garage Unfinished	522 sq. ft.
Dimensions	64'6"x59'
Foundation	Basement
	Crawlspace
	Slab
Bedrooms	4
Full Baths	2
Main Ceiling	9'
Second Ceiling	8'
Max Ridge Height	27'
Roof Framing	Stick
Exterior Walls	2x4

MAIN FLOOR

BONUS

CAD FILES AVAILABLE For more information call 800-235-5700

Design 10507

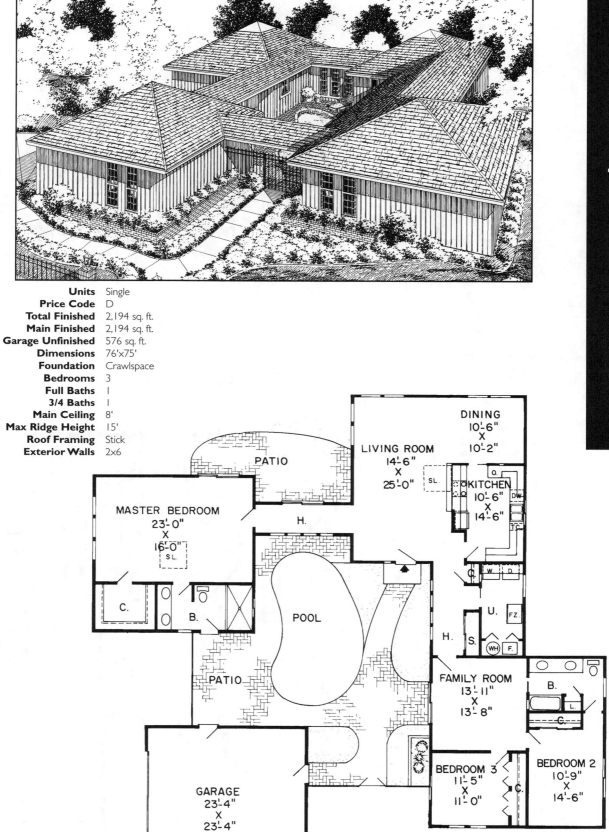

Units	Single
Price Code	D
Total Finished	2,194 sq. ft.
Main Finished	2,194 sq. ft.
Garage Unfinished	576 sq. ft.
Dimensions	76'x75'
Foundation	Crawlspace
Bedrooms	3
Full Baths	1
3/4 Baths	1
Main Ceiling	8'
Max Ridge Height	15'
Roof Framing	Stick
Exterior Walls	2x6

DINING
10'-6"
X
10'-2"

LIVING ROOM
14'-6"
X
25'-0"

KITCHEN
10'-6"
X
14'-6"

PATIO

MASTER BEDROOM
23'-0"
X
16'-0"

H.

POOL

U.

FAMILY ROOM
13'-11"
X
13'-8"

B.

PATIO

GARAGE
23'-4"
X
23'-4"

BEDROOM 3
11'-5"
X
11'-0"

BEDROOM 2
10'-9"
X
14'-6"

MAIN FLOOR

Units	Single
Price Code	D
Total Finished	2,194 sq. ft.
Main Finished	2,194 sq. ft.
Garage Unfinished	462 sq. ft.
Deck Unfinished	422 sq. ft.
Porch Unfinished	32 sq. ft.
Dimensions	60'x57'
Foundation	Slab
Bedrooms	4
Full Baths	2
Half Baths	1
Max Ridge Height	25'
Roof Framing	Stick
Exterior Walls	2x4

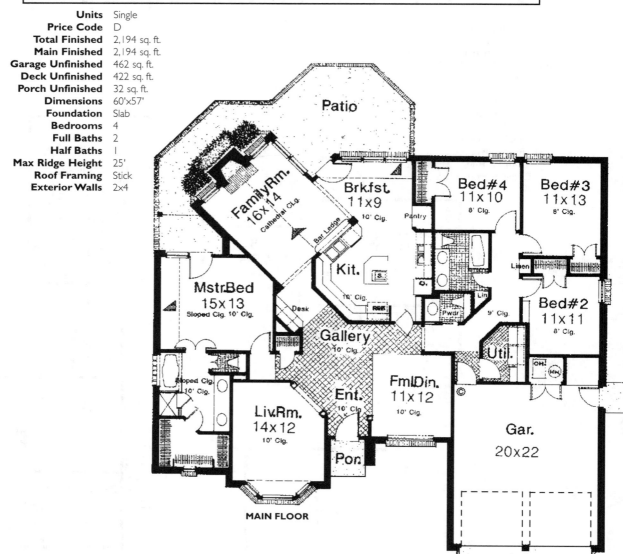

MAIN FLOOR

Design 93190

Units	Single
Price Code	D
Total Finished	2,196 sq. ft.
Main Finished	2,196 sq. ft.
Basement Unfinished	2,196 sq. ft.
Dimensions	73'x58'8"
Foundation	Basement
Bedrooms	3
Full Baths	2
Half Baths	1
Max Ridge Height	23'6"
Roof Framing	Truss
Exterior Walls	2x6

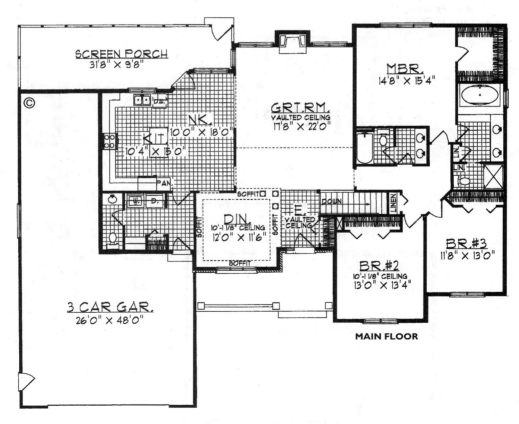

SCREEN PORCH
31'8" X 9'8"

MBR.
14'8" X 15'4"

GRT. RM.
VAULTED CEILING
17'8" X 22'0"

NK.
10'0" X 18'0"

KIT.
10'4" X 15'0"

PAN.

DIN.
10'-1 1/8" CEILING
12'0" X 11'6"

SOFFIT

DOWN

LINEN

BR. #3
11'8" X 13'0"

BR. #2
10'-1 1/8" CEILING
13'0" X 13'4"

3 CAR GAR.
26'0" X 48'0"

MAIN FLOOR

Design 97303

Units	Single
Price Code	D
Total Finished	2,198 sq. ft.
Main Finished	2,198 sq. ft.
Garage Unfinished	1,128 sq. ft.
Deck Unfinished	128 sq. ft.
Porch Unfinished	126 sq. ft.
Dimensions	84'8"x59'
Foundation	Basement
Bedrooms	3
Full Baths	2
Main Ceiling	9'1⅛"
Max Ridge Height	26'4"
Roof Framing	Truss
Exterior Walls	2×6

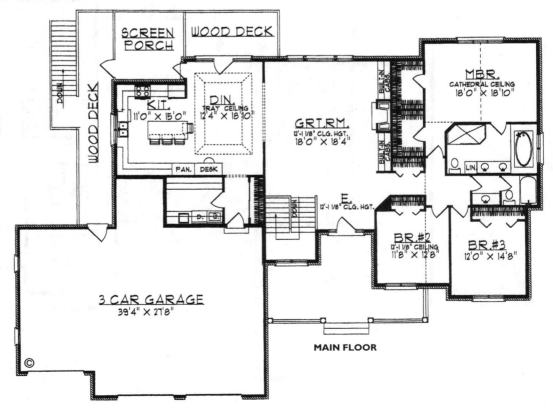

MAIN FLOOR

Design 97228

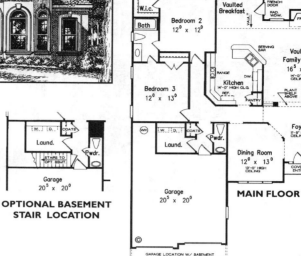

CAD FILES AVAILABLE
For more information call
800-235-5700

Units	Single
Price Code	D
Total Finished	2,201 sq. ft.
Main Finished	2,201 sq. ft.
Basement Unfinished	2,201 sq. ft.
Garage Unfinished	452 sq. ft.
Dimensions	59'6"x62'
Foundation	Basement
	Crawlspace
Bedrooms	3
Full Baths	2
Half Baths	1
Max Ridge Height	25'
Roof Framing	Stick
Exterior Walls	2x4

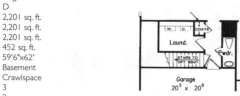

OPTIONAL BASEMENT STAIR LOCATION

MAIN FLOOR

Design 97858

Units	Single
Price Code	D
Total Finished	2,214 sq. ft.
Main Finished	2,214 sq. ft.
Garage Unfinished	599 sq. ft.
Deck Unfinished	136 sq. ft.
Porch Unfinished	42 sq. ft.
Dimensions	55'x77'11"
Foundation	Slab
Bedrooms	3
Full Baths	2
Half Baths	1
Main Ceiling	9'-10'
Max Ridge Height	27'
Roof Framing	Stick
Exterior Walls	2x4

MAIN FLOOR

Design 90454

Units	Single
Price Code	D
Total Finished	2,218 sq. ft.
Main Finished	2,218 sq. ft.
Basement Unfinished	1,658 sq. ft.
Garage Unfinished	528 sq. ft.
Deck Unfinished	342 sq. ft.
Porch Unfinished	216 sq. ft.
Dimensions	72'x64'
Foundation	Basement
	Crawlspace
Bedrooms	3
Full Baths	2
Main Ceiling	9'
Max Ridge Height	20'10"
Roof Framing	Stick
Exterior Walls	2x4

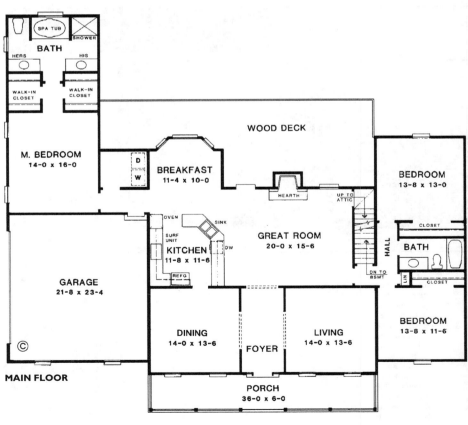

MAIN FLOOR

Design 97135

Units	Single
Price Code	D
Total Finished	2,229 sq. ft.
Main Finished	2,229 sq. ft.
Basement Unfinished	2,229 sq. ft.
Garage Unfinished	551 sq. ft.
Dimensions	65'x56'
Foundation	Basement
Bedrooms	3
Full Baths	2
Max Ridge Height	26'
Roof Framing	Truss
Exterior Walls	2x6

MAIN FLOOR

Design 94673

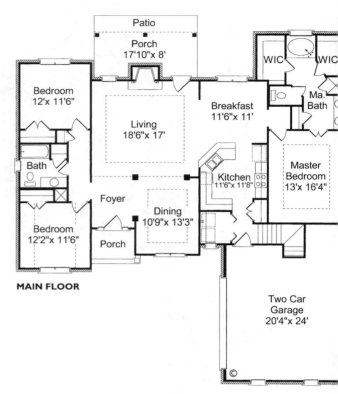

Units	Single
Price Code	D
Total Finished	2,232 sq. ft.
Main Finished	2,232 sq. ft.
Dimensions	57'6"x37'10"
Foundation	Slab
Bedrooms	3
Full Baths	2
Roof Framing	Stick

Gameroom 21'8"x 16'

BONUS

Patio

Porch 17'10"x 8'

Bedroom 12'x 11'6"

Living 18'6"x 17'

Breakfast 11'6"x 11'

WIC WIC

Ma. Bath

Bath

Kitchen 11'6"x 11'8"

Master Bedroom 13'x 16'4"

Foyer

Bedroom 12'2"x 11'6"

Dining 10'9"x 13'3"

Porch

MAIN FLOOR

Two Car Garage 20'4"x 24'

Design 98521

Units	Single
Price Code	D
Total Finished	2,233 sq. ft.
Main Finished	2,233 sq. ft.
Garage Unfinished	635 sq. ft.
Deck Unfinished	120 sq. ft.
Porch Unfinished	72 sq. ft.
Dimensions	63'10"x56'10"
Foundation	Slab
Bedrooms	4
Full Baths	3
Main Ceiling	9'
Max Ridge Height	26'
Roof Framing	Stick
Exterior Walls	2x4

PATIO AREA

BRKFT. 12X11 9' CLG. HT.

BED THREE 11X11 8' CLG.HT.

BOOKS

LIVING ROOM 20X16 10' CLG. HT.

BAR LEDGE

KIT. 13X12 9' CLG. HT.

MSTR.BED 15X16 9' CLG. HT.

BOOKS

LINEN LIN

GALLERY 10' CLG. HT.

PANTRY

BED TWO 13X11 8' CLG. HT.

ENT

FORMAL DINING 11X11 10' CLG. HT.

LAUND.

NICHE

BED FOUR 13X10 9' CLG. HT.

PORCH

GARAGE 22X29

MAIN FLOOR

Design 98424

Units	Single
Price Code	D
Total Finished	2,236 sq. ft.
Main Finished	2,236 sq. ft.
Basement Unfinished	2,236 sq. ft.
Garage Unfinished	517 sq. ft.
Dimensions	63'x67'
Foundation	Basement
	Crawlspace
Bedrooms	3
Full Baths	2
Half Baths	I
Max Ridge Height	25'5"
Roof Framing	Stick
Exterior Walls	2x4

CAD **FILES AVAILABLE**
For more information call
800-235-5700

MAIN FLOOR

Design 82103

Units	Single
Price Code	D
Total Finished	2,246 sq. ft.
Main Finished	2,246 sq. ft.
Garage Unfinished	418 sq. ft.
Porch Unfinished	503 sq. ft.
Dimensions	66'x63'8"
Foundation	Basement
	Crawlspace
	Slab
Bedrooms	4
Full Baths	2
Main Ceiling	9'
Max Ridge Height	21'6"
Roof Framing	Stick
Exterior Walls	2x4, 2x6

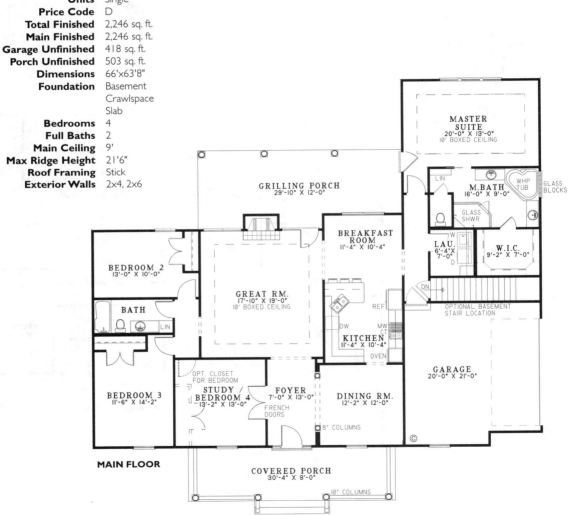

MASTER SUITE
20'-0" X 13'-0"
10' BOXED CEILING

M.BATH
16'-0" X 9'-0"

WHP TUB

GLASS BLOCKS

GLASS SHWR

LIN

LAU.
6'-4" X 7'-0"

W.I.C.
9'-2" X 7'-0"

GRILLING PORCH
29'-10" X 12'-0"

BREAKFAST ROOM
11'-4" X 10'-4"

BEDROOM 2
13'-0" X 10'-0"

GREAT RM.
17'-10" X 19'-0"
10' BOXED CEILING

REF

DN

OPTIONAL BASEMENT STAIR LOCATION

BATH

LIN

DW

MW CT

KITCHEN
11'-4" X 10'-4"

OVEN

GARAGE
20'-0" X 21'-0"

BEDROOM 3
11'-6" X 14'-2"

OPT. CLOSET FOR BEDROOM

STUDY BEDROOM 4
13'-2" X 13'-0"

FOYER
7'-0" X 13'-0"

FRENCH DOORS

DINING RM.
12'-2" X 12'-0"

8" COLUMNS

MAIN FLOOR

COVERED PORCH
30'-4" X 8'-0"

10" COLUMNS

Design 97850

Units	Single
Price Code	E
Total Finished	2,253 sq. ft.
Main Finished	2,253 sq. ft.
Garage Unfinished	602 sq. ft.
Deck Unfinished	205 sq. ft.
Porch Unfinished	110 sq. ft.
Dimensions	63'×60'3"
Foundation	Slab
Bedrooms	4
Full Baths	2
3/4 Baths	1
Main Ceiling	8'-10'
Max Ridge Height	26'
Roof Framing	Stick
Exterior Walls	2×4

MAIN FLOOR

Units	Single
Price Code	E
Total Finished	2,256 sq. ft.
Main Finished	2,256 sq. ft.
Garage Unfinished	514 sq. ft.
Dimensions	72'×52'
Foundation	Crawlspace
	Slab
Bedrooms	3
Full Baths	2
Max Ridge Height	23'
Roof Framing	Stick
Exterior Walls	2x4

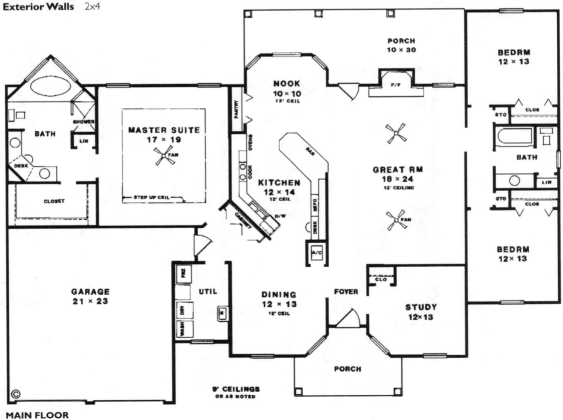

MAIN FLOOR

Design 98548

Units	Single
Price Code	E
Total Finished	2,257 sq. ft.
Main Finished	2,257 sq. ft.
Garage Unfinished	601 sq. ft.
Porch Unfinished	325 sq. ft.
Dimensions	65'x65'10"
Foundation	Crawlspace
	Slab
Bedrooms	4
Full Baths	2
Half Baths	1
Main Ceiling	9'-11'
Max Ridge Height	25'
Roof Framing	Stick
Exterior Walls	2x4

MAIN FLOOR

Units	Single
Price Code	E
Total Finished	2,257 sq. ft.
Main Finished	2,257 sq. ft.
Garage Unfinished	528 sq. ft.
Dimensions	64'7"x77'10"
Foundation	Slab
Bedrooms	3
Full Baths	2
Half Baths	1
Main Ceiling	9'-10'
Max Ridge Height	26'6"
Roof Framing	Stick
Exterior Walls	2x4

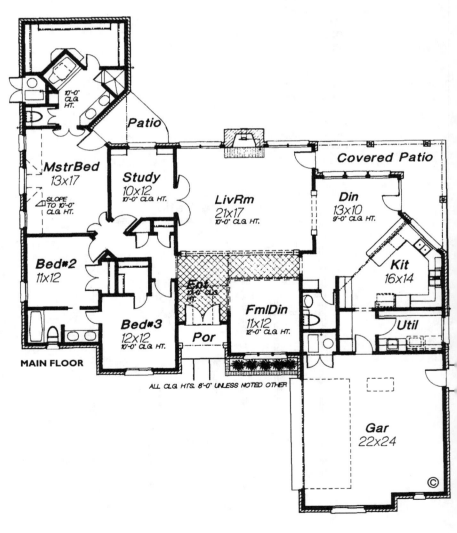

MAIN FLOOR

ALL CLG. HTS. 8'-0" UNLESS NOTED OTHER

Design 92404

Units	Single
Price Code	E
Total Finished	2,275 sq. ft.
Main Finished	2,275 sq. ft.
Basement Unfinished	2,207 sq. ft.
Garage Unfinished	512 sq. ft.
Dimensions	62'x60'
Foundation	Basement
Bedrooms	3
Full Baths	2
Max Ridge Height	22'
Roof Framing	Stick
Exterior Walls	2x4

DECK

BR.#2
14x11

BREAKFAST

MASTER
14x18
Trey Clg.

Vaulted Clg

KITCHEN
10x10

FAMILY ROOM
16X18

BR.#3
13x12

Stairs
Down

DINING
12x13
Trey Clg.

FOYER

LIVING
13x13
Cathedral

Cathedral

UTILITY

WORKSHOP

GARAGE
22x19

MAIN FLOOR

Units	Single
Price Code	E
Total Finished	2,285 sq. ft.
Main Finished	2,285 sq. ft.
Garage Unfinished	653 sq. ft.
Dimensions	74'10"×56'10"
Foundation	Slab
Bedrooms	4
Full Baths	3
Max Ridge Height	22'
Roof Framing	Stick
Exterior Walls	2x4

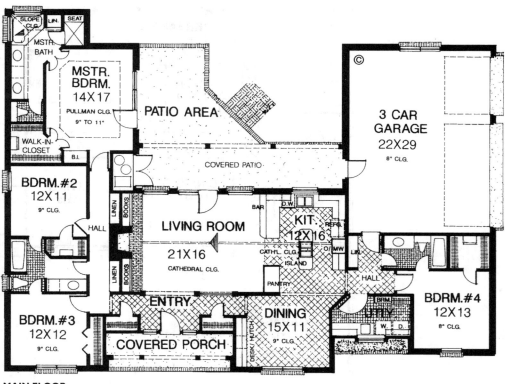

MAIN FLOOR

Design 90467

Units	Single
Price Code	E
Total Finished	2,290 sq. ft.
Main Finished	2,290 sq. ft.
Bonus Unfinished	304 sq. ft.
Basement Unfinished	2,290 sq. ft.
Garage Unfinished	544 sq. ft.
Deck Unfinished	206 sq. ft.
Porch Unfinished	114 sq. ft.
Dimensions	67'4"x54'6"
Foundation	Basement
	Crawlspace
Bedrooms	3
Full Baths	2
Half Baths	1
Main Ceiling	9'
Max Ridge Height	32'4"
Roof Framing	Stick
Exterior Walls	2x4

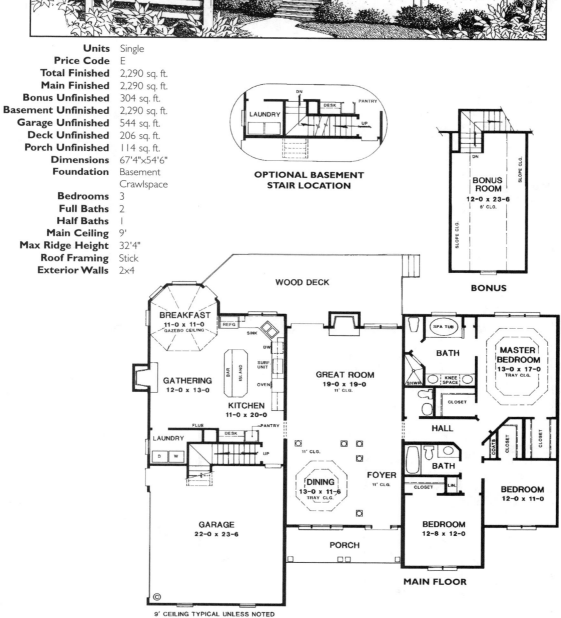

OPTIONAL BASEMENT
STAIR LOCATION

BONUS

MAIN FLOOR

9' CEILING TYPICAL UNLESS NOTED

Units	Single
Price Code	E
Total Finished	2,292 sq. ft.
Main Finished	2,292 sq. ft.
Garage Unfinished	526 sq. ft.
Dimensions	80'7"x50'6"
Foundation	Crawlspace
	Slab
Bedrooms	4
Full Baths	2
Half Baths	1
Max Ridge Height	22'
Roof Framing	Stick
Exterior Walls	2x4

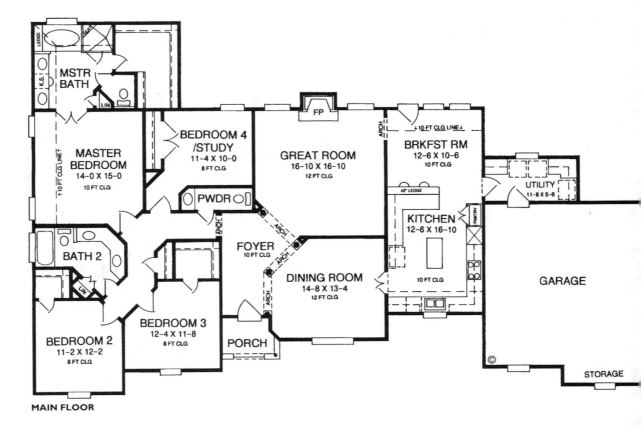

MAIN FLOOR

Design 96551

Units	Single
Price Code	E
Total Finished	2,296 sq. ft.
Main Finished	2,296 sq. ft.
Garage Unfinished	641 sq. ft.
Porch Unfinished	483 sq. ft.
Dimensions	70'x61'
Foundation	Crawlspace
	Slab
Bedrooms	3
Full Baths	2
Main Ceiling	9'
Max Ridge Height	26'8"
Roof Framing	Stick
Exterior Walls	2x4, 2x6

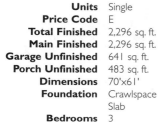

MAIN FLOOR

CLOSET 7' x 8'

DRESSING 8' x 7'

MASTER SUITE 16' x 16'

PORCH 8' x 12'

MASTER BATH 13' x 8'

LAUNDRY CHUTE

FREEZER

UTILITY 8' x 11'

NOOK 12' x 11' (11' CEILING)

PORCH 27' x 8'

BEDRM. #2 12' x 12'

CLOSET

STORAGE

GARAGE 23' x 26'

KITCHEN 12' x 13' (11' CEILING)

GREAT ROOM 16' x 24' (11' CEILING)

FIREPLACE

LIN.

CREDENZA

BATH #2 8' x 11'

LINEN

COAT

R-A

A/C

DINING 12' x 14' (11' CEILING)

FOYER 11' x 7' (11' CLNG.)

STUDY 11' x 12' (11' CEILING)

BEDRM. #3 12' x 12'

9' ceilings typical

PORCH 32' x 6'

Units	Single
Price Code	E
Total Finished	2,306 sq. ft.
Main Finished	2,306 sq. ft.
Basement Unfinished	2,267 sq. ft.
Garage Unfinished	468 sq. ft.
Dimensions	72'x56'1"
Foundation	Basement
	Crawlspace
Bedrooms	4
Full Baths	3
Main Ceiling	9'
Max Ridge Height	26'6"
Roof Framing	Stick
Exterior Walls	2×4

CAD FILES AVAILABLE
For more information call
800-235-5700

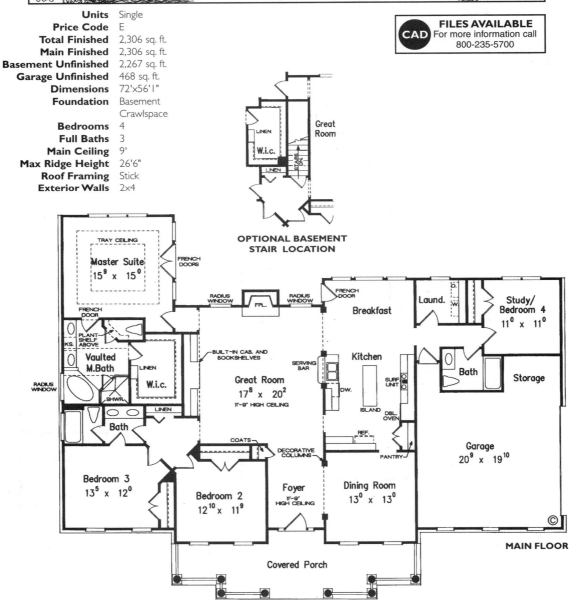

OPTIONAL BASEMENT
STAIR LOCATION

MAIN FLOOR

Design 97869

Units	Single
Price Code	E
Total Finished	2,307 sq. ft.
Main Finished	2,307 sq. ft.
Garage Unfinished	572 sq. ft.
Deck Unfinished	189 sq. ft.
Porch Unfinished	35 sq. ft.
Dimensions	60'10"x70'11"
Foundation	Slab
Bedrooms	3
Full Baths	2
3/4 Baths	1
Main Ceiling	10'
Max Ridge Height	26'
Roof Framing	Stick
Exterior Walls	2x4

MAIN FLOOR

Units	Single
Price Code	E
Total Finished	2,311 sq. ft.
Main Finished	2,311 sq. ft.
Bonus Unfinished	425 sq. ft.
Basement Unfinished	2,311 sq. ft.
Garage Unfinished	500 sq. ft.
Dimensions	61'x65'4"
Foundation	Basement Crawlspace
Bedrooms	4
Full Baths	2
Half Baths	1
Main Ceiling	9'
Second Ceiling	8'
Max Ridge Height	26'8"
Roof Framing	Stick
Exterior Walls	2x4

CAD FILES AVAILABLE
For more information call
800-235-5700

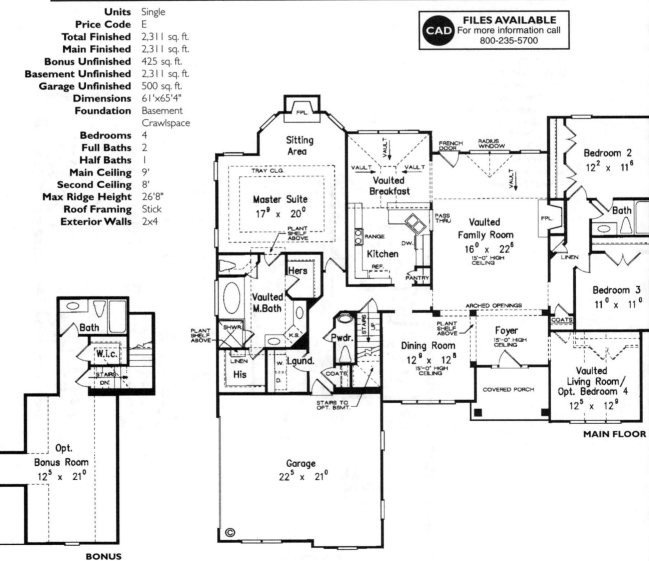

BONUS

MAIN FLOOR

Design 97621

Units	Single
Price Code	E
Total Finished	2,322 sq. ft.
Main Finished	2,322 sq. ft.
Basement Unfinished	2,322 sq. ft.
Garage Unfinished	453 sq. ft.
Dimensions	62'x61'
Foundation	Basement
	Crawlspace
	Slab
Bedrooms	3
Full Baths	2
Half Baths	1
Main Ceiling	9'
Max Ridge Height	30'
Roof Framing	Stick
Exterior Walls	2x4

CAD FILES AVAILABLE
For more information call
800-235-5700

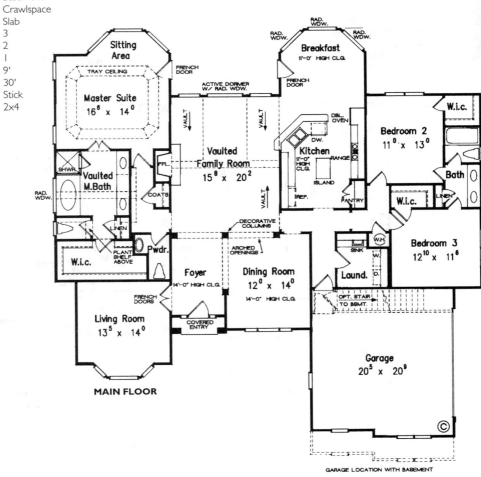

MAIN FLOOR

Units	Single
Price Code	E
Total Finished	2,326 sq. ft.
Main Finished	2,326 sq. ft.
Garage Unfinished	808 sq. ft.
Dimensions	74'x69'
Foundation	Crawlspace
Bedrooms	4
Full Baths	2
Main Ceiling	9'
Vaulted Ceiling	15'
Max Ridge Height	21'
Roof Framing	Truss
Exterior Walls	2x6

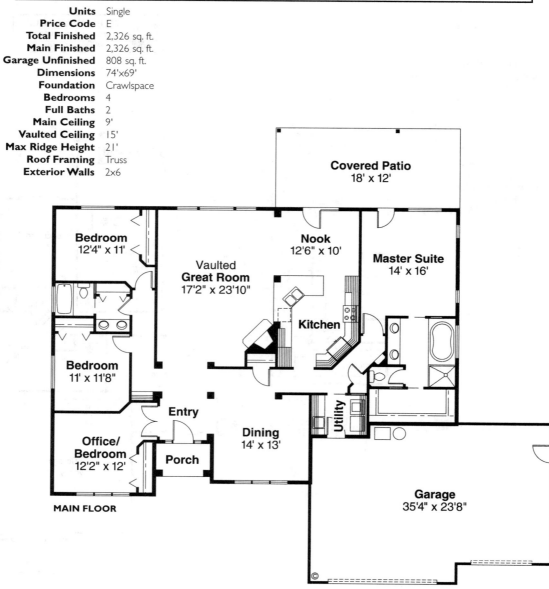

Covered Patio
18' x 12'

Bedroom
12'4" x 11'

Nook
12'6" x 10'

Master Suite
14' x 16'

Vaulted
Great Room
17'2" x 23'10"

Kitchen

Bedroom
11' x 11'8"

Entry

Utility

Office/
Bedroom
12'2" x 12'

Porch

Dining
14' x 13'

Garage
35'4" x 23'8"

MAIN FLOOR

Design 64165

Units	Single
Price Code	H
Total Finished	2,329 sq. ft.
Main Finished	2,329 sq. ft.
Garage Unfinished	528 sq. ft.
Porch Unfinished	215 sq. ft.
Dimensions	72'x73'
Foundation	Crawlspace
Bedrooms	3
Full Baths	2
Half Baths	1
Max Ridge Height	25'4"
Exterior Walls	2x6
Roof Framing	Stick/Truss

* Alternate foundation options available at an additional charge.
Please call 1-800-235-5700 for more information.

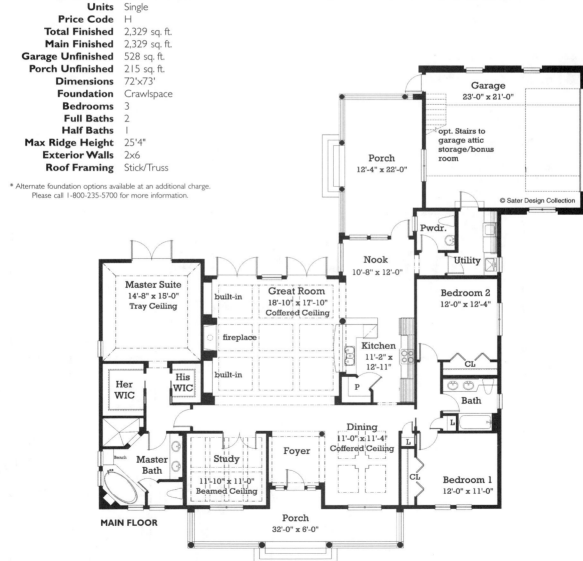

Garage
23'-0" x 21'-0"

opt. Stairs to garage attic storage/bonus room

© Sater Design Collection

Porch
12'-4" x 22'-0"

Pwdr.

Utility

Nook
10'-8" x 12'-0"

Bedroom 2
12'-0" x 12'-4"

Master Suite
14'-8" x 15'-0"
Tray Ceiling

built-in

Great Room
18'-10" x 17'-10"
Coffered Ceiling

fireplace

built-in

Kitchen
11'-2" x 12'-11"

P

CL

Bath

Her WIC

His WIC

Master Bath

Bench

Study
11'-10" x 11'-0"
Beamed Ceiling

Foyer

Dining
11'-0" x 11'-4"
Coffered Ceiling

CL

L

L

L

CL

Bedroom 1
12'-0" x 11'-0"

MAIN FLOOR

Porch
32'-0" x 6'-0"

Units	Single
Price Code	E
Total Finished	2,330 sq. ft.
Main Finished	2,330 sq. ft.
Basement Unfinished	2,330 sq. ft.
Garage Unfinished	416 sq. ft.
Deck Unfinished	196 sq. ft.
Dimensions	50'x70'
Foundation	Crawlspace
Bedrooms	3
Full Baths	3
Main Ceiling	9'
Tray Ceiling	14'
Max Ridge Height	32'
Roof Framing	Stick
Exterior Walls	2x4

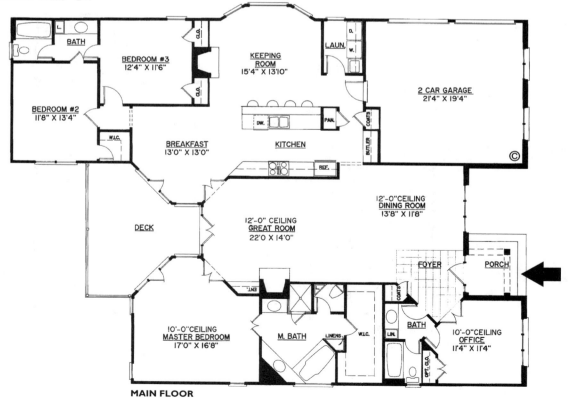

MAIN FLOOR

Design 97945

Units	Single
Price Code	E
Total Finished	2,331 sq. ft.
Main Finished	2,331 sq. ft.
Garage Unfinished	806 sq. ft.
Deck Unfinished	132 sq. ft.
Dimensions	74'11"×68'9½"
Foundation	Slab
Bedrooms	3
Full Baths	2
Half Baths	1
Main Ceiling	9'
Max Ridge Height	24'6½"
Roof Framing	Stick
Exterior Walls	2×4

* Alternate foundation options available at an additional charge.
Please call 1-800-235-5700 for more information.

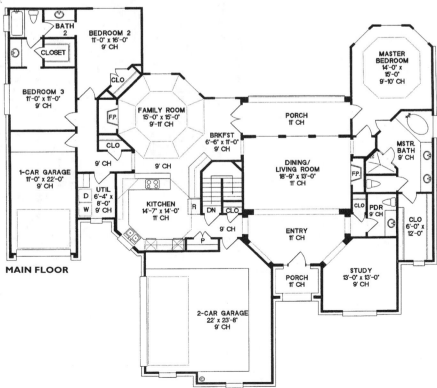

MAIN FLOOR

Units	Single
Price Code	E
Total Finished	2,332 sq. ft.
Main Finished	2,332 sq. ft.
Garage Unfinished	620 sq. ft.
Deck Unfinished	80 sq. ft.
Porch Unfinished	48 sq. ft.
Dimensions	82'3"x86'6"
Foundation	Slab
Bedrooms	3
Full Baths	2
Half Baths	1
Main Ceiling	9'-10'
Max Ridge Height	29'
Roof Framing	Stick
Exterior Walls	2x4

Design 66106

Units	Single
Price Code	E
Total Finished	2,352 sq. ft.
Main Finished	2,352 sq. ft.
Garage Unfinished	726 sq. ft.
Dimensions	77'6"x53'2"
Foundation	Basement
	Crawlspace
	Slab
Bedrooms	4
Full Baths	3
Main Ceiling	9'
Max Ridge Height	25'
Roof Framing	Stick
Exterior Walls	2×4

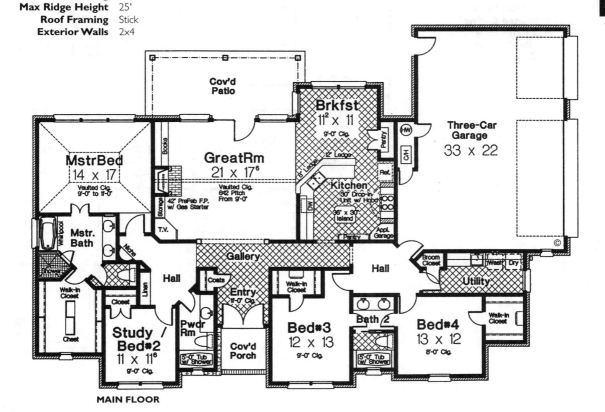

MAIN FLOOR

Units	Single
Price Code	E
Total Finished	2,361 sq. ft.
Main Finished	2,361 sq. ft.
Basement Unfinished	2,361 sq. ft.
Garage Unfinished	490 sq. ft.
Deck Unfinished	128 sq. ft.
Porch Unfinished	168 sq. ft.
Dimensions	67'x69'6"
Foundation	Basement
Bedrooms	3
Full Baths	3
Main Ceiling	9'
Vaulted Ceiling	14'
Max Ridge Height	22'5"
Roof Framing	Stick
Exterior Walls	2×4

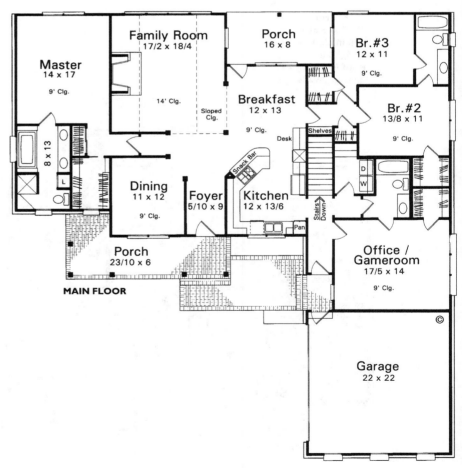

MAIN FLOOR

To order blueprints, call **800-235-5700** or visit us on the web, **familyhomeplans.com**

Design 94632

2,001-2,500 sq. ft. HOME PLANS

Units	Single
Price Code	E
Total Finished	2,365 sq. ft.
Main Finished	2,365 sq. ft.
Dimensions	67'6"x73'
Foundation	Crawlspace
	Slab
Bedrooms	4
Full Baths	2
Main Ceiling	9'
Max Ridge Height	31'6"
Roof Framing	Stick
Exterior Walls	2x4

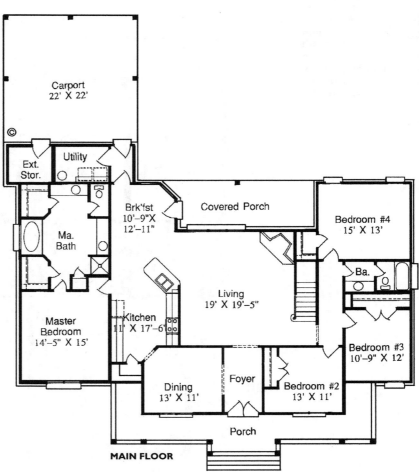

Carport
22' X 22'

Ext. Stor.

Utility

Ma. Bath

Brk'fst
10'-9"X 12'-11"

Covered Porch

Bedroom #4
15' X 13'

Ba.

Living
19' X 19'-5"

Master Bedroom
14'-5" X 15'

Kitchen
11' X 17'-6'

Bedroom #3
10'-9" X 12'

Dining
13' X 11'

Foyer

Bedroom #2
13' X 11'

Porch

MAIN FLOOR

Units	Single
Price Code	E
Total Finished	2,370 sq. ft.
Main Finished	2,370 sq. ft.
Garage Unfinished	638 sq. ft.
Deck Unfinished	132 sq. ft.
Porch Unfinished	30 sq. ft.
Dimensions	55'x63'10"
Foundation	Slab
Bedrooms	4
Full Baths	2
Half Baths	1
Max Ridge Height	26'8"
Roof Framing	Stick
Exterior Walls	2×4

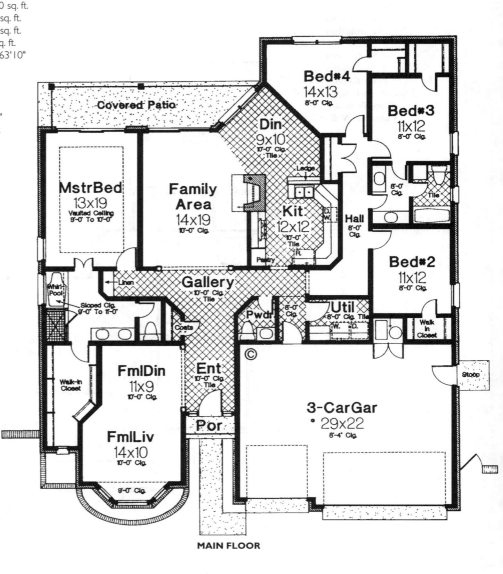

MAIN FLOOR

Design 61098

Units	Single
Price Code	E
Total Finished	2,372 sq. ft.
Main Finished	2,372 sq. ft.
Bonus Unfinished	366 sq. ft.
Garage Unfinished	732 sq. ft.
Porch Unfinished	188 sq. ft.
Dimensions	66'4"x66'10"
Foundation	Basement
	Crawlspace
	Slab
Bedrooms	4
Full Baths	3
Main Ceiling	9'
Roof Framing	Stick

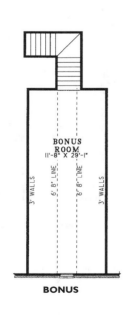

BONUS

MAIN FLOOR

Units	Single
Price Code	E
Total Finished	2,387 sq. ft.
Main Finished	2,387 sq. ft.
Garage Unfinished	505 sq. ft.
Porch Unfinished	194 sq. ft.
Dimensions	64'10"x54'10"
Foundation	Crawlspace
	Slab
Bedrooms	4
Full Baths	2
Half Baths	1
Main Ceiling	9'
Max Ridge Height	28'
Roof Framing	Truss
Exterior Walls	2x4

MAIN FLOOR

Floor plan labels:
- MASTER BEDROOM 15'X14'
- MASTER BATH
- PORCH 19'X8'
- GARAGE 21'X22'
- BEDROOM 4 12'X11'
- DEN 19'X20'
- STO
- UTILITY
- 1/2 BATH
- BATH 2
- KITCHEN 15'X14'
- BEDROOM 2 11'-6"X12'-6"
- FOYER
- DINING 14'X12'-6"
- BEDROOM 3 12'X12'
- PORCH
- BREAKFAST 10'X15'

Design 93033

Units	Single
Price Code	E
Total Finished	2,389 sq. ft.
Main Finished	2,389 sq. ft.
Garage Unfinished	543 sq. ft.
Porch Unfinished	208 sq. ft.
Dimensions	75'2"x61'4"
Foundation	Crawlspace
	Slab
Bedrooms	4
Full Baths	2
Half Baths	1
Max Ridge Height	22'
Roof Framing	Stick
Exterior Walls	2x4

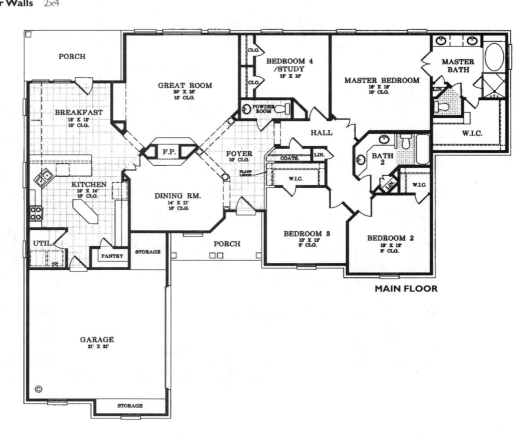

MAIN FLOOR

Units	Single
Price Code	E
Total Finished	2,389 sq. ft.
Main Finished	2,389 sq. ft.
Garage Unfinished	609 sq. ft.
Deck Unfinished	193 sq. ft.
Porch Unfinished	62 sq. ft.
Dimensions	65'x63'10"
Foundation	Slab
Bedrooms	4
Full Baths	2
3/4 Baths	1
Main Ceiling	9'-10'
Max Ridge Height	28'
Roof Framing	Stick
Exterior Walls	2x4

MAIN FLOOR

Design 52224

Units	Single
Price Code	E
Total Finished	3,649 sq. ft.
Main Finished	2,391 sq. ft.
Lower Finished	1,258 sq. ft.
Basement Unfinished	1,133 sq. ft.
Garage Unfinished	484 sq. ft.
Dimensions	54'x66'
Foundation	Basement
Bedrooms	4
Full Baths	4
Main Ceiling	10'
Max Ridge Height	27'4"
Roof Framing	Stick
Exterior Walls	2x4

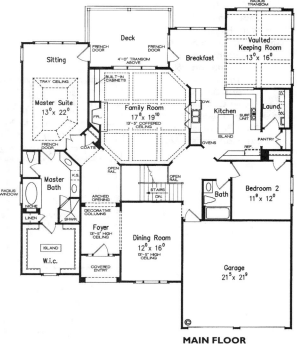

MAIN FLOOR

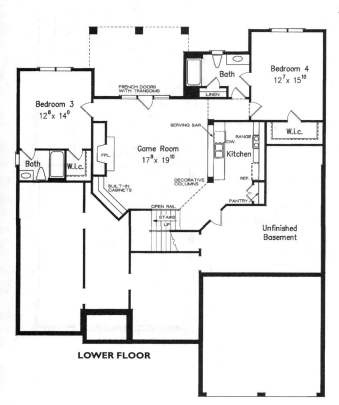

LOWER FLOOR

Design 94672

Units	Single
Price Code	E
Total Finished	2,391 sq. ft.
Main Finished	2,391 sq. ft.
Garage Unfinished	595 sq. ft.
Dimensions	61'10"x64'11"
Foundation	Slab
Bedrooms	4
Full Baths	3
Main Ceiling	9'
Max Ridge Height	31'7"
Roof Framing	Stick
Exterior Walls	2x4

WIC

WIC

Master Bath

Porch
26'4"x 9'

Bedroom
11'5"x 11'3"

Breakfast
12'x 11'

Master Bedroom
15'6"x 16'

Living
15'6"x 19'6"

Bath

Kitchen
12'x 15'4"

Bedroom
8'x 11'3"

Bath

Hall

Utility

Foyer
7'x 12'

Dining
12'x 14'

Bedroom
11'6"x 14'6"

Two Car Garage
21'8"x 23'10"

MAIN FLOOR

Design 97244

Units	Single
Price Code	E
Total Finished	2,403 sq. ft.
Main Finished	2,403 sq. ft.
Bonus Unfinished	285 sq. ft.
Basement Unfinished	2,403 sq. ft.
Garage Unfinished	488 sq. ft.
Dimensions	60'x67'
Foundation	Basement
	Crawlspace
Bedrooms	3
Full Baths	2
Half Baths	1
Main Ceiling	9'
Second Ceiling	8'
Max Ridge Height	29'6"
Roof Framing	Stick
Exterior Walls	2x4

CAD FILES AVAILABLE
For more information call
800-235-5700

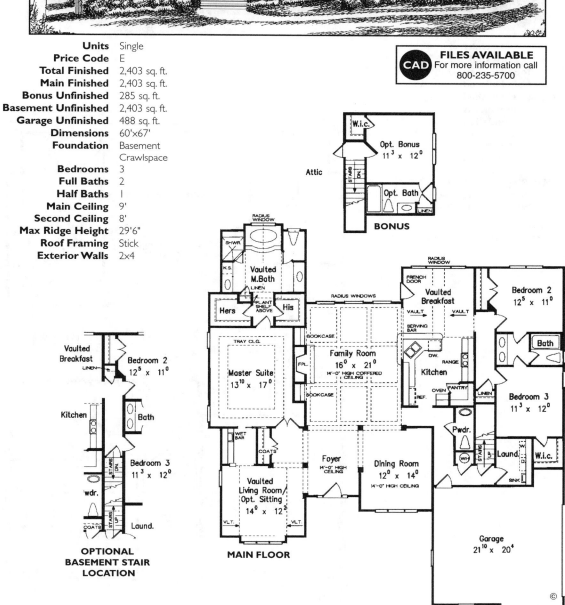

BONUS

OPTIONAL BASEMENT STAIR LOCATION

MAIN FLOOR

Units	Single
Price Code	E
Total Finished	2,404 sq. ft.
Main Finished	2,404 sq. ft.
Garage Unfinished	493 sq. ft.
Dimensions	50'4"x70'8"
Foundation	Slab
Bedrooms	3
Full Baths	2
Half Baths	I
Main Ceiling	9'
Max Ridge Height	25'
Roof Framing	Stick
Exterior Walls	2x4

* Alternate foundation options available at an additional charge.
Please call 1-800-235-5700 for more information.

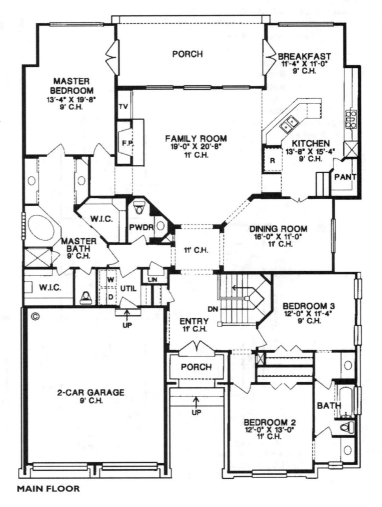

MAIN FLOOR

Design 93095

PHOTOGRAPHY: COURTESY OF THE DESIGNER

Units	Single
Price Code	E
Total Finished	2,409 sq. ft.
Main Finished	2,409 sq. ft.
Bonus Unfinished	709 sq. ft.
Garage Unfinished	644 sq. ft.
Porch Unfinished	392 sq. ft.
Dimensions	85'8"×68'4"
Foundation	Crawlspace
	Slab
Bedrooms	3
Full Baths	2
Half Baths	1
Max Ridge Height	25'8"
Roof Framing	Stick
Exterior Walls	2x4

Please note: The photographed home may have been modified to suit homeowner preferences. If you order plans, have a builder or design professional check them against the photograph to confirm actual construction details.

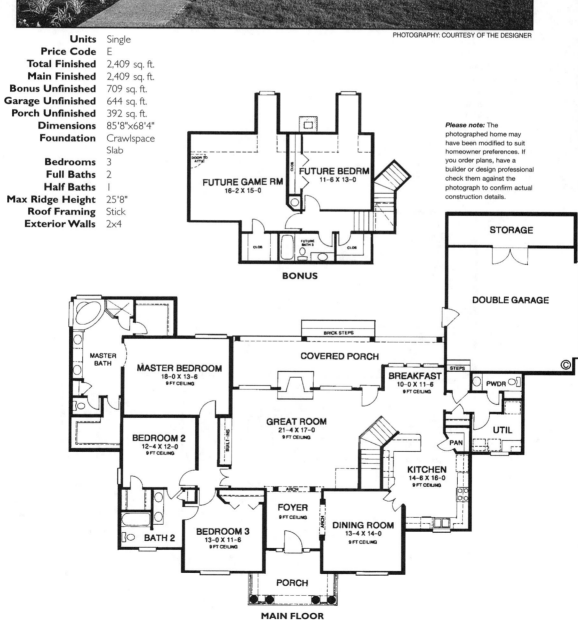

Design 63059

Units	Single
Price Code	E
Total Finished	2,441 sq. ft.
Main Finished	2,441 sq. ft.
Garage Unfinished	477 sq. ft.
Dimensions	74'x64'
Foundation	Slab
Bedrooms	4
Full Baths	3
Half Baths	1
Main Ceiling	10'-12'
Max Ridge Height	21'
Exterior Walls	2x4

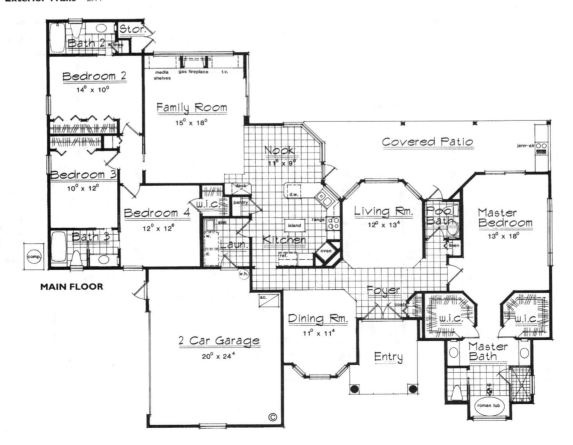

MAIN FLOOR

Design 98511

Units	Single
Price Code	E
Total Finished	2,445 sq. ft.
Main Finished	2,445 sq. ft.
Garage Unfinished	630 sq. ft.
Deck Unfinished	234 sq. ft.
Porch Unfinished	32 sq. ft.
Dimensions	65'x68'8"
Foundation	Crawlspace
	Slab
Bedrooms	4
Full Baths	3
Half Baths	1
Main Ceiling	9'-12'
Max Ridge Height	32'
Roof Framing	Stick
Exterior Walls	2x4

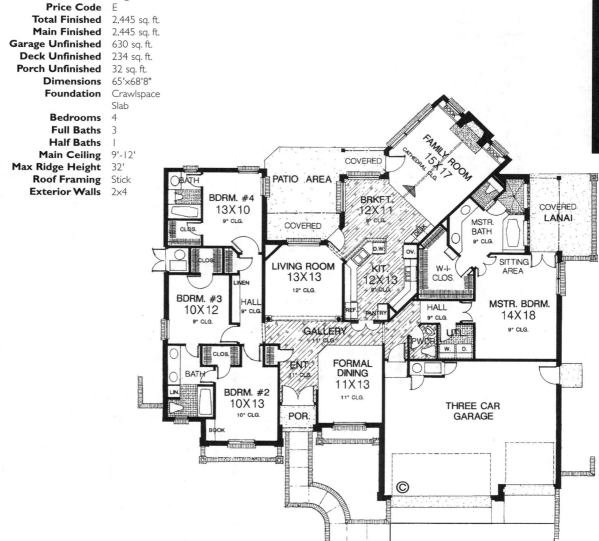

MAIN FLOOR

Design 94669

Units	Single
Price Code	E
Total Finished	2,450 sq. ft.
Main Finished	2,450 sq. ft.
Garage Unfinished	427 sq. ft.
Porch Unfinished	431 sq. ft.
Dimensions	66'10"x64'11"
Foundation	Slab
Bedrooms	4
Full Baths	2
Half Baths	1
Main Ceiling	9'
Max Ridge Height	29'1"
Roof Framing	Stick
Exterior Walls	2×4

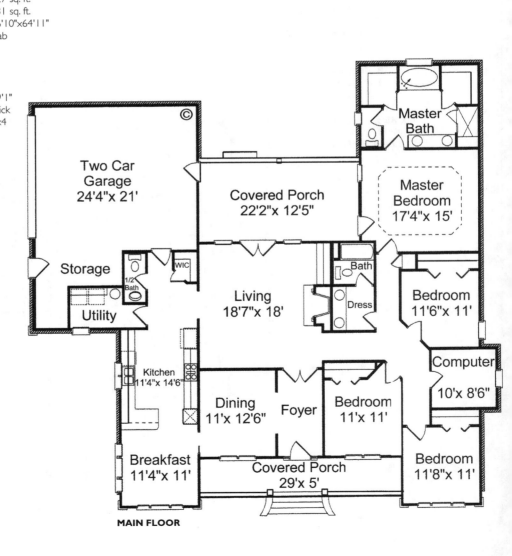

MAIN FLOOR

Design 64195

Units	Single
Price Code	H
Total Finished	2,454 sq. ft.
Main Finished	2,454 sq. ft.
Bonus Unfinished	256 sq. ft.
Porch Unfinished	165 sq. ft.
Dimensions	80'6"x66'6"
Foundation	Crawlspace
Bedrooms	3
Full Baths	2
Door Framing	Stick/Truss
Exterior Walls	2x6

* Alternate foundation options available at an additional charge.
Please call 1-800-235-5700 for more information.

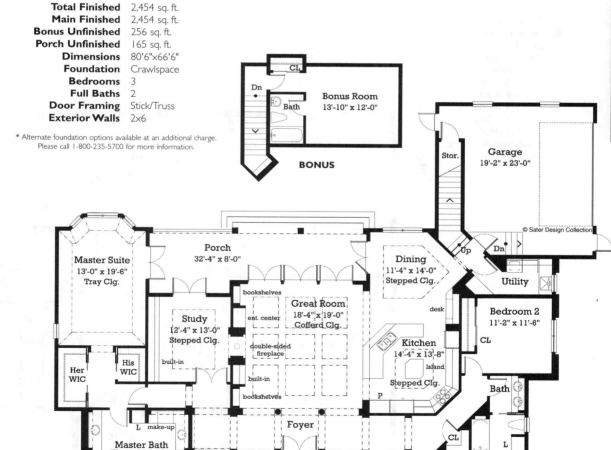

MAIN FLOOR

Design 97750

Units	Single
Price Code	E
Total Finished	2,463 sq. ft.
Main Finished	2,463 sq. ft.
Bonus Unfinished	2,463 sq. ft.
Garage Unfinished	456 sq. ft.
Dimensions	59'x58'
Foundation	Basement
Bedrooms	2
Full Baths	1
3/4 Baths	1
Main Ceiling	9'
Max Ridge Height	26'
Roof Framing	Truss
Exterior Walls	2x6

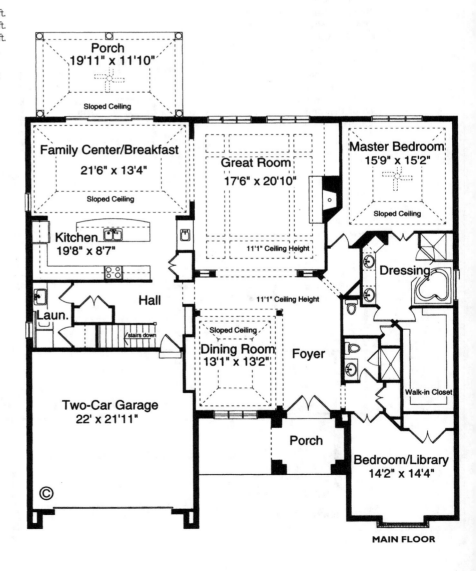

Porch
19'11" x 11'10"
Sloped Ceiling

Family Center/Breakfast
21'6" x 13'4"
Sloped Ceiling

Great Room
17'6" x 20'10"
11'1" Ceiling Height

Master Bedroom
15'9" x 15'2"
Sloped Ceiling

Kitchen
19'8" x 8'7"

Dressing

11'1" Ceiling Height

Hall

Laun.

stairs down

Dining Room
13'1" x 13'2"
Sloped Ceiling

Foyer

Walk-in Closet

Two-Car Garage
22' x 21'11"

Porch

Bedroom/Library
14'2" x 14'4"

MAIN FLOOR

To order blueprints, call **800-235-5700** or visit us on the web, **familyhomeplans.com**

Design 9850

Units	Single
Price Code	E
Total Finished	2,466 sq. ft.
Main Finished	2,466 sq. ft.
Basement Unfinished	1,447 sq. ft.
Garage Unfinished	664 sq. ft.
Dimensions	89'4"x40'
Foundation	Basement
Bedrooms	3
Full Baths	1
3/4 Baths	1
Half Baths	1
Main Ceiling	8'
Max Ridge Height	16'
Roof Framing	Stick
Exterior Walls	2x4

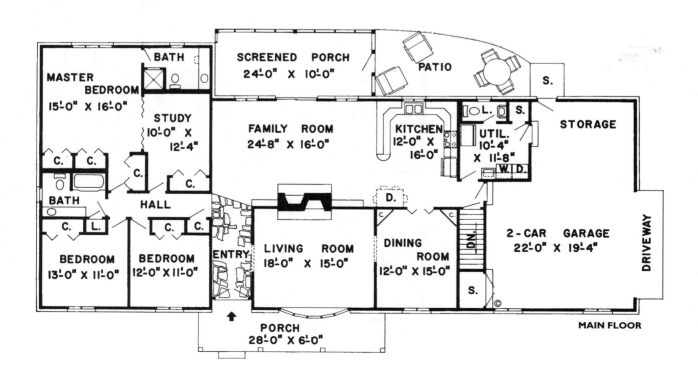

MAIN FLOOR

Units	Single
Price Code	E
Total Finished	2,471 sq. ft.
Main Finished	2,471 sq. ft.
Garage Unfinished	566 sq. ft.
Porch Unfinished	274 sq. ft.
Dimensions	62'10"x75'3"
Foundation	Slab
Bedrooms	4
Full Baths	2
Half Baths	1
Main Ceiling	9'
Max Ridge Height	23'6"
Roof Framing	Stick
Exterior Walls	2x4

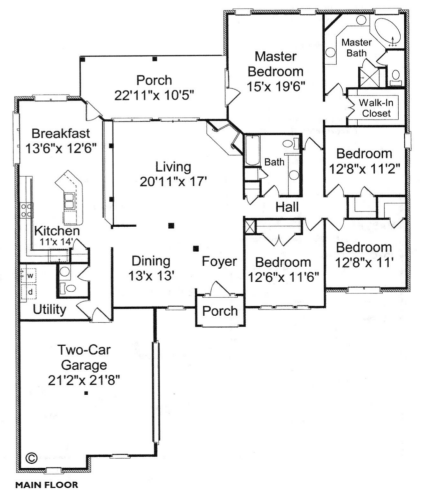

MAIN FLOOR

Design 52098

Units	Single
Price Code	E
Total Finished	2,479 sq. ft.
Main Finished	2,479 sq. ft.
Bonus Unfinished	316 sq. ft.
Basement Unfinished	2,479 sq. ft.
Garage Unfinished	533 sq. ft.
Dimensions	73'x75'6"
Foundation	Basement
	Crawlspace
Bedrooms	3
Full Baths	2
Half Baths	1
Main Ceiling	9'
Second Ceiling	8'
Max Ridge Height	27'10"
Roof Framing	Stick
Exterior Walls	2x4

CAD FILES AVAILABLE
For more information call
800-235-5700

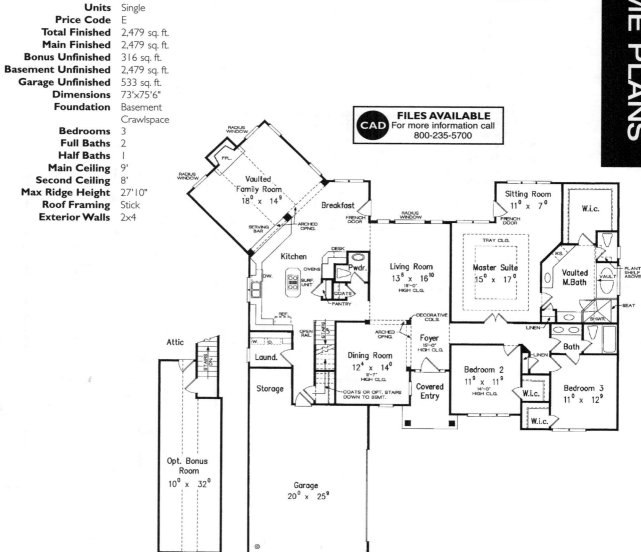

BONUS   **MAIN FLOOR**

Units	Single
Price Code	E
Total Finished	2,483 sq. ft.
Main Finished	2,483 sq. ft.
Garage Unfinished	504 sq. ft.
Dimensions	75'x61'8"
Foundation	Crawlspace
Bedrooms	4
Full Baths	3
Half Baths	1
Main Ceiling	9'
Vaulted Ceiling	11'
Max Ridge Height	23'
Roof Framing	Stick
Exterior Walls	2x4

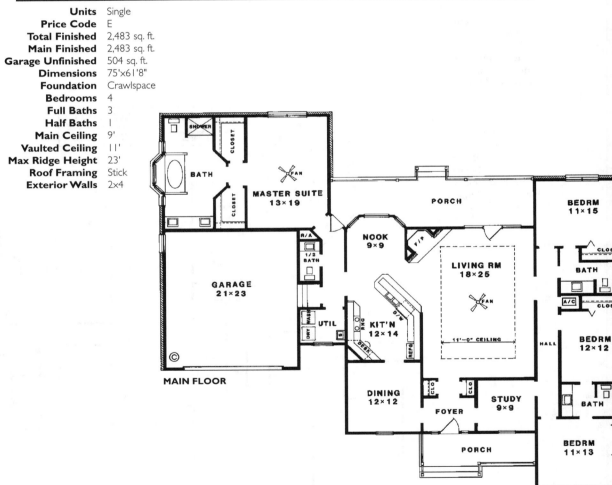

MAIN FLOOR

Design 90461

Units	Single
Price Code	E
Total Finished	2,485 sq. ft.
Main Finished	2,485 sq. ft.
Basement Unfinished	2,485 sq. ft.
Garage Unfinished	484 sq. ft.
Deck Unfinished	328 sq. ft.
Porch Unfinished	320 sq. ft.
Dimensions	84'x55'8"
Foundation	Basement
	Crawlspace
Bedrooms	3
Full Baths	2
Half Baths	I
Main Ceiling	9'
Max Ridge Height	24'8"
Roof Framing	Stick
Exterior Walls	2x4

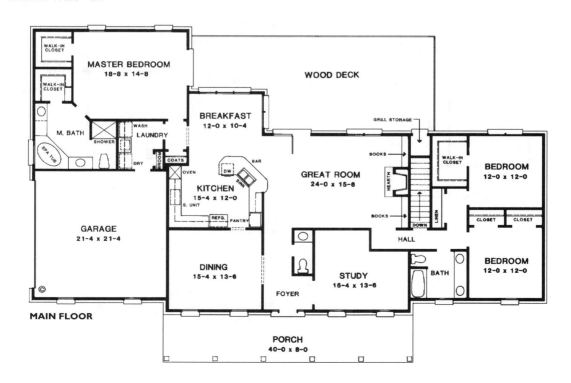

MAIN FLOOR

Units	Single
Price Code	H
Total Finished	2,502 sq. ft.
Main Finished	2,502 sq. ft.
Garage Unfinished	612 sq. ft.
Deck Unfinished	108 sq. ft.
Porch Unfinished	397 sq. ft.
Dimensions	70'x72'
Foundation	Basement
	Slab
Bedrooms	3
Full Baths	2
Max Ridge Height	27'4"
Exterior Walls	2x6
Roof Framing	Stick/Truss

* Alternate foundation options available at an additional charge.
Please call 1-800-235-5700 for more information.

OPTIONAL BASEMENT STAIR LOCATION

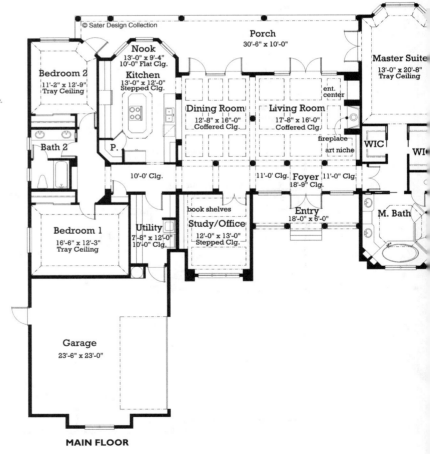

MAIN FLOOR

Design 69137

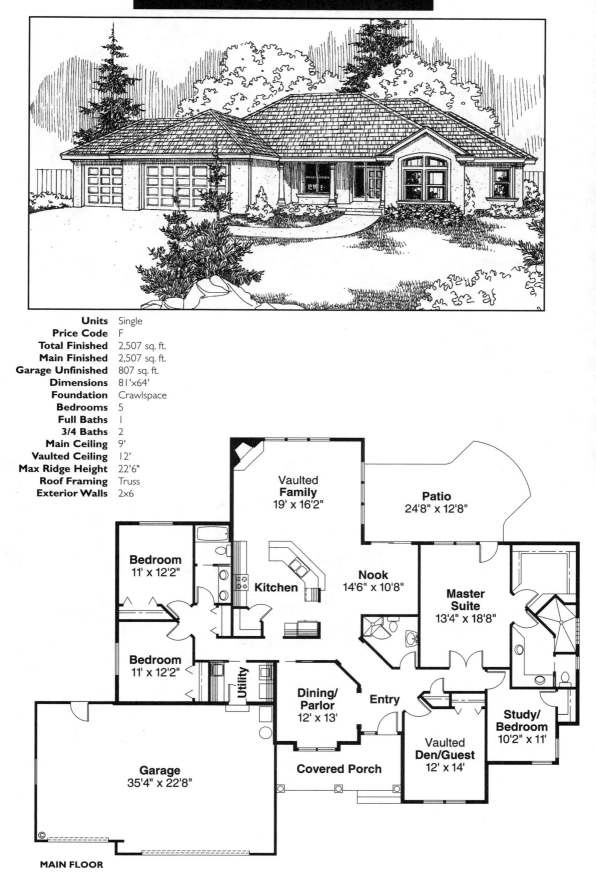

Units	Single
Price Code	F
Total Finished	2,507 sq. ft.
Main Finished	2,507 sq. ft.
Garage Unfinished	807 sq. ft.
Dimensions	81'x64'
Foundation	Crawlspace
Bedrooms	5
Full Baths	1
3/4 Baths	2
Main Ceiling	9'
Vaulted Ceiling	12'
Max Ridge Height	22'6"
Roof Framing	Truss
Exterior Walls	2x6

Vaulted Family 19' x 16'2"

Patio 24'8" x 12'8"

Bedroom 11' x 12'2"

Kitchen

Nook 14'6" x 10'8"

Master Suite 13'4" x 18'8"

Bedroom 11' x 12'2"

Utility

Dining/Parlor 12' x 13'

Entry

Study/Bedroom 10'2" x 11'

Garage 35'4" x 22'8"

Covered Porch

Vaulted Den/Guest 12' x 14'

MAIN FLOOR

Units	Single
Price Code	F
Total Finished	2,512 sq. ft.
Main Finished	2,512 sq. ft.
Garage Unfinished	783 sq. ft.
Dimensions	74'x67'8"
Foundation	Basement
Bedrooms	3
Full Baths	2
Half Baths	1
Max Ridge Height	25'5"
Roof Framing	Stick
Exterior Walls	2x4

* Alternate foundation options available at an additional charge.
Please call 1-800-235-5700 for more information.

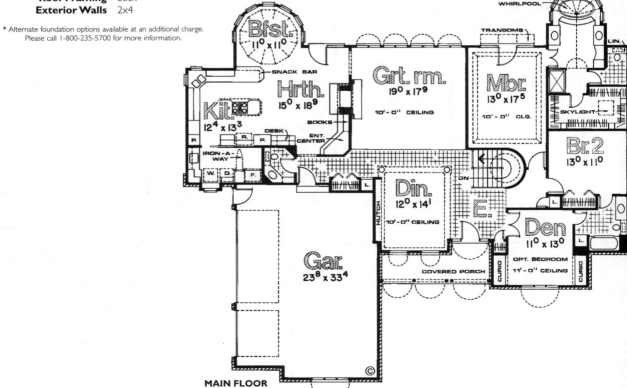

MAIN FLOOR

Design 93253

2,501-3,000 sq. ft. HOME PLANS

Units	Single
Price Code	F
Total Finished	2,542 sq. ft.
Main Finished	2,542 sq. ft.
Garage Unfinished	510 sq. ft.
Dimensions	72'10"x63'5"
Foundation	Slab
Bedrooms	4
Full Baths	2
Half Baths	1
Main Ceiling	8'
Max Ridge Height	25'
Roof Framing	Stick
Exterior Walls	2x4

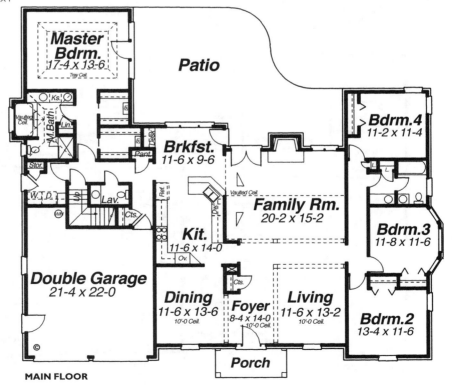

Master Bdrm. 17-4 x 13-6 Tray Ceil.

Patio

Bdrm.4 11-2 x 11-4

Vaulted Ceil.

M.Bath. Lin. KS.

Stor.

Desk Sh.

Pant.

Brkfst. 11-6 x 9-6

Vaulted Ceil.

Family Rm. 20-2 x 15-2

W.T.D. S Lav. Cts.

Ref.

Kit. 11-6 x 14-0

Ov.

Bdrm.3 11-8 x 11-6

Double Garage 21-4 x 22-0

Cts.

Dining 11-6 x 13-6 10'-0 Ceil.

Foyer 8-4 x 14-0 10'-0 Ceil.

Living 11-6 x 13-2 10'-0 Ceil.

Bdrm.2 13-4 x 11-6

Porch

MAIN FLOOR

Units	Single
Price Code	F
Total Finished	2,545 sq. ft.
Main Finished	2,545 sq. ft.
Garage Unfinished	603 sq. ft.
Porch Unfinished	354 sq. ft.
Dimensions	78'x58'
Foundation	Crawlspace
	Slab
Bedrooms	4
Full Baths	3
Half Baths	1
Main Ceiling	9'
Max Ridge Height	27'4"
Roof Framing	Stick
Exterior Walls	2x4

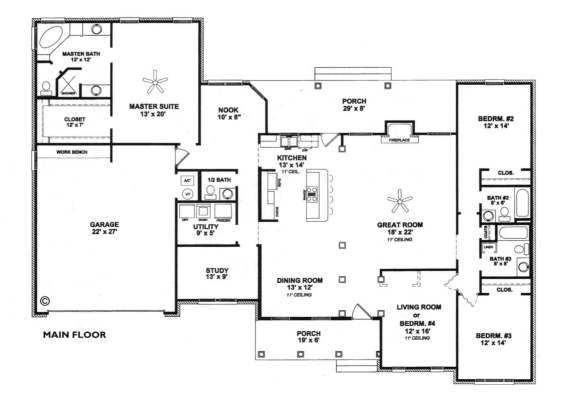

MAIN FLOOR

Design 97837

Units	Single
Price Code	F
Total Finished	2,551 sq. ft.
Main Finished	2,551 sq. ft.
Garage Unfinished	642 sq. ft.
Deck Unfinished	310 sq. ft.
Porch Unfinished	48 sq. ft.
Dimensions	97'10"x52'4"
Foundation	Slab
Bedrooms	3
Full Baths	2
Half Baths	1
Max Ridge Height	29'
Roof Framing	Stick
Exterior Walls	2x4

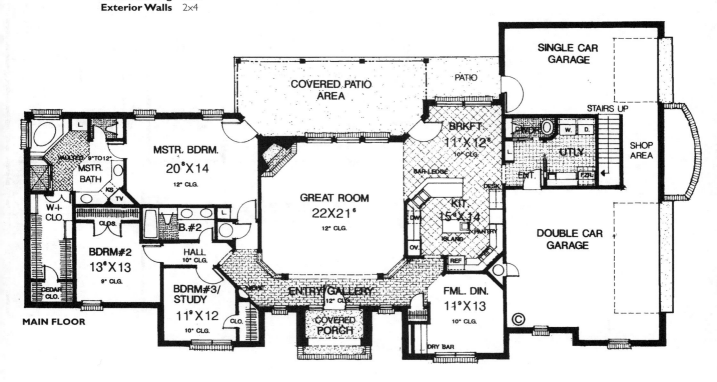

MAIN FLOOR

Design 64178

Units	Single
Price Code	H
Total Finished	2,555 sq. ft.
Main Finished	2,555 sq. ft.
Garage Unfinished	640 sq. ft.
Porch Unfinished	315 sq. ft.
Dimensions	70'x76'6"
Foundation	Crawlspace
Bedrooms	3
Full Baths	2
Half Baths	1
Max Ridge Height	28'4"
Exterior Walls	2x6
Roof Framing	Stick/Truss

* Alternate foundation options available at an additional charge.
Please call 1-800-235-5700 for more information.

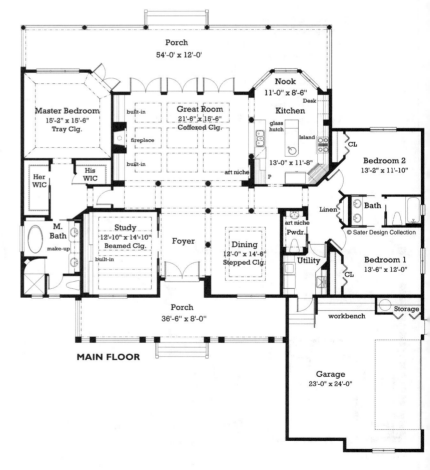

MAIN FLOOR

Design 64180

Units	Single
Price Code	H
Total Finished	2,555 sq. ft.
Main Finished	2,555 sq. ft.
Garage Unfinished	640 sq. ft.
Dimensions	70'6"x76'6"
Foundation	Crawlspace
Bedrooms	3
Full Baths	2
Half Baths	1
Max Ridge Height	28'4"
Exterior Walls	2x6

* Alternate foundation options available at an additional charge.
Please call 1-800-235-5700 for more information.

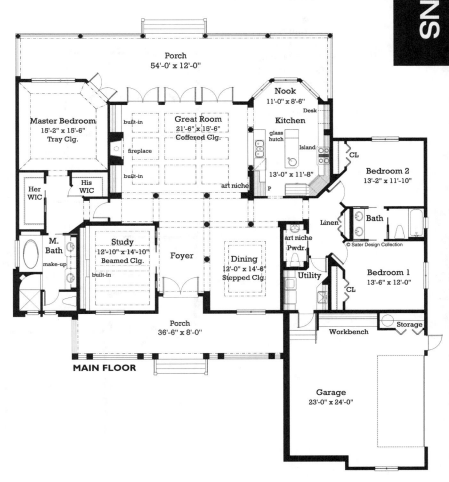

MAIN FLOOR

Design 94640

Units	Single
Price Code	F
Total Finished	2,558 sq. ft.
Main Finished	2,558 sq. ft.
Garage Unfinished	549 sq. ft.
Porch Unfinished	151 sq. ft.
Dimensions	63'6"x71'6"
Foundation	Crawlspace
	Slab
Bedrooms	4
Full Baths	3
Main Ceiling	9'
Max Ridge Height	21'6"
Roof Framing	Stick
Exterior Walls	2x4

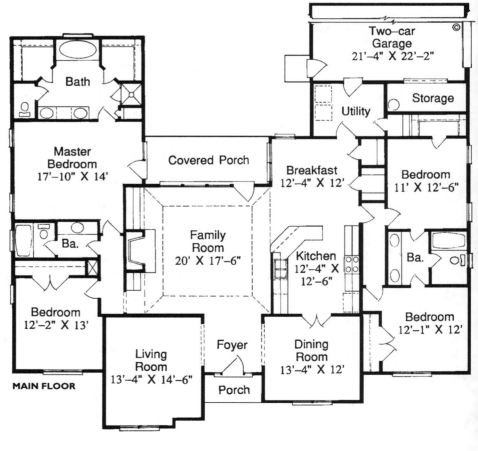

Bath

Master Bedroom
17'-10" X 14'

Covered Porch

Two-car Garage
21'-4" X 22'-2"

Utility

Storage

Breakfast
12'-4" X 12'

Bedroom
11' X 12'-6"

Ba.

Family Room
20' X 17'-6"

Kitchen
12'-4" X 12'-6"

Ba.

Bedroom
12'-2" X 13'

Living Room
13'-4" X 14'-6"

Foyer

Dining Room
13'-4" X 12'

Bedroom
12'-1" X 12'

Porch

MAIN FLOOR

Design 69146

Units	Single
Price Code	F
Total Finished	2,561 sq. ft.
Main Finished	2,561 sq. ft.
Garage Unfinished	739 sq. ft.
Dimensions	64'x63'
Foundation	Crawlspace
Bedrooms	3
Full Baths	2
Half Baths	1
Main Ceiling	9'
Vaulted Ceiling	10'
Max Ridge Height	24'
Roof Framing	Truss
Exterior Walls	2x6

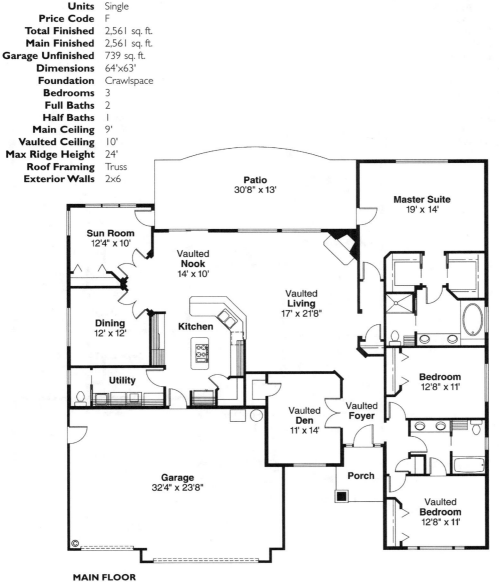

MAIN FLOOR

Units	Single
Price Code	F
Total Finished	2,579 sq. ft.
Main Finished	2,579 sq. ft.
Garage Unfinished	630 sq. ft.
Dimensions	60'x70'
Foundation	Slab
Bedrooms	4
Full Baths	3
Max Ridge Height	26'6"
Roof Framing	Stick
Exterior Walls	2x4

MAIN FLOOR

Design 93708

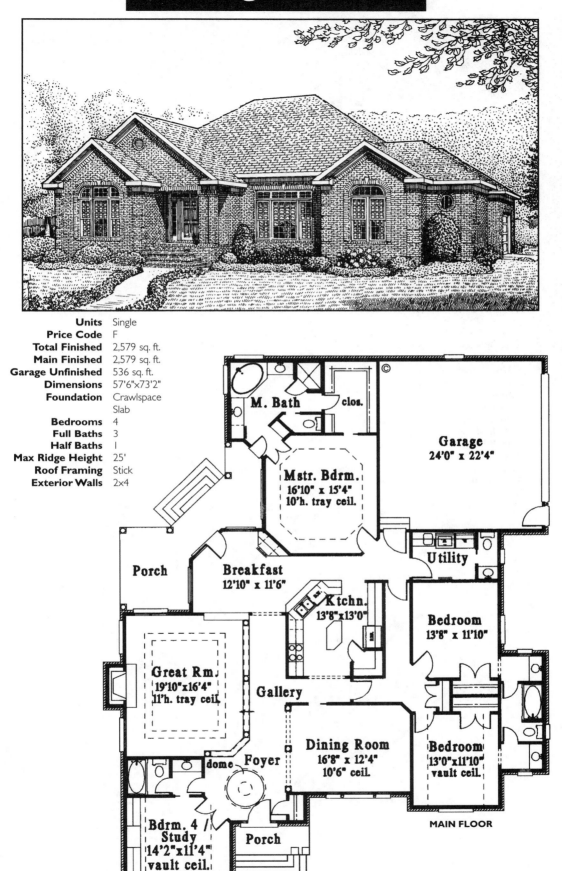

Units	Single
Price Code	F
Total Finished	2,579 sq. ft.
Main Finished	2,579 sq. ft.
Garage Unfinished	536 sq. ft.
Dimensions	57'6"x73'2"
Foundation	Crawlspace
	Slab
Bedrooms	4
Full Baths	3
Half Baths	I
Max Ridge Height	25'
Roof Framing	Stick
Exterior Walls	2x4

M. Bath

clos.

Garage
24'0" x 22'4"

Mstr. Bdrm.
16'10" x 15'4"
10'h. tray ceil.

Utility

Porch

Breakfast
12'10" x 11'6"

Ktchn.
13'8"x13'0"

Bedroom
13'8" x 11'10"

Great Rm.
19'10"x16'4"
11'h. tray ceil.

Gallery

Dining Room
16'8" x 12'4"
10'6" ceil.

Bedroom
13'0"x11'10"
vault ceil.

dome

Foyer

Bdrm. 4 /
Study
14'2"x11'4"
vault ceil.

Porch

MAIN FLOOR

PHOTOGRAPHY: WILLIAM STITES

Units	Single
Price Code	D
Total Finished	2,581 sq. ft.
Main Finished	2,581 sq. ft.
Garage Unfinished	602 sq. ft.
Porch Unfinished	422 sq. ft.
Dimensions	62'x87'8"
Foundation	Slab
Bedrooms	3
Full Baths	2
Half Baths	1
Main Ceiling	10'
Tray Ceiling	13'
Max Ridge Height	31'
Roof Framing	Truss
Exterior Walls	2x6

MAIN FLOOR

Please note: The photographed home may have been modified to suit homeowner preferences. If you order plans, have a builder or design professional check them against the photograph to confirm actual construction details.

Design 96938

Units	Single
Price Code	F
Total Finished	2,585 sq. ft.
Main Finished	2,585 sq. ft.
Bonus Unfinished	519 sq. ft.
Basement Unfinished	2,609 sq. ft.
Garage Unfinished	607 sq. ft.
Dimensions	61'x80'
Foundation	Basement Crawlspace
Bedrooms	3
Full Baths	2
Half Baths	1
Main Ceiling	9'
Vaulted Ceiling	12'
Tray Ceiling	10'6"
Max Ridge Height	31'
Roof Framing	Stick
Exterior Walls	2x4

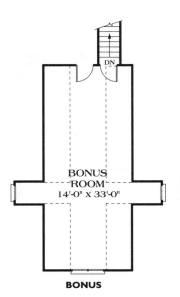

BONUS

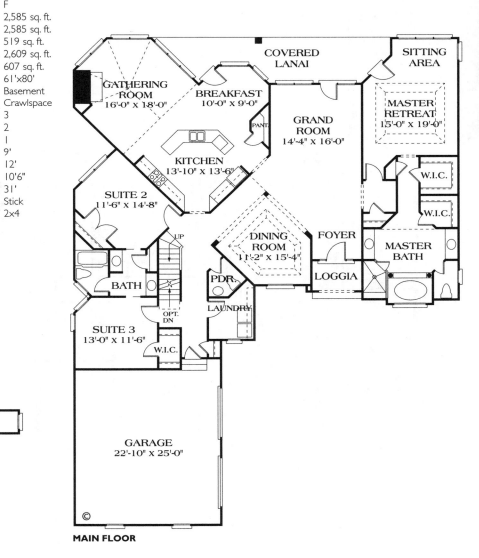

MAIN FLOOR

Units	Single
Price Code	F
Total Finished	2,600 sq. ft.
Main Finished	2,600 sq. ft.
Basement Unfinished	2,600 sq. ft.
Dimensions	87'x60'
Foundation	Basement
Bedrooms	3
Full Baths	2
Half Baths	I
Max Ridge Height	26'8"
Roof Framing	Stick
Exterior Walls	2x6

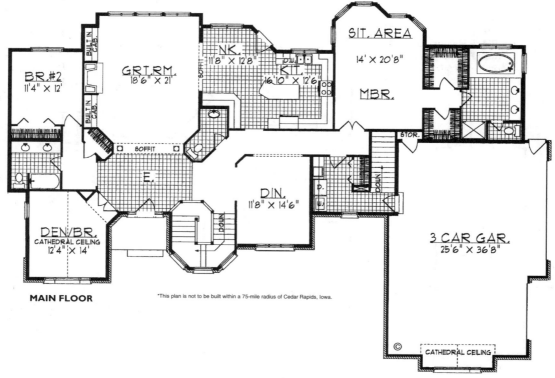

MAIN FLOOR

*This plan is not to be built within a 75-mile radius of Cedar Rapids, Iowa.

Design 66091

Units	Single
Price Code	F
Total Finished	2,606 sq. ft.
Main Finished	2,606 sq. ft.
Garage Unfinished	292 sq. ft.
Deck Unfinished	224 sq. ft.
Dimensions	79'7"x55'10"
Foundation	Slab
Bedrooms	3
Full Baths	2
Half Baths	1
Main Ceiling	9'
Max Ridge Height	26'6"
Roof Framing	Stick
Exterior Walls	2x4

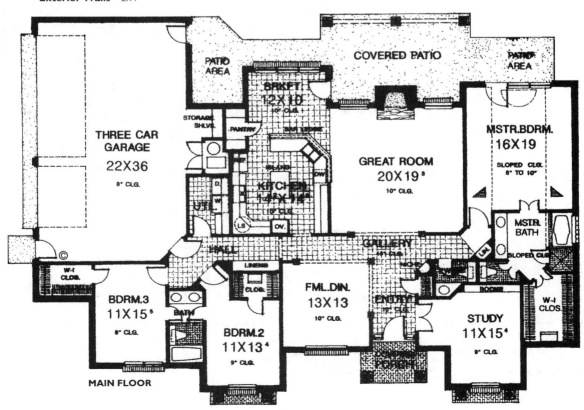

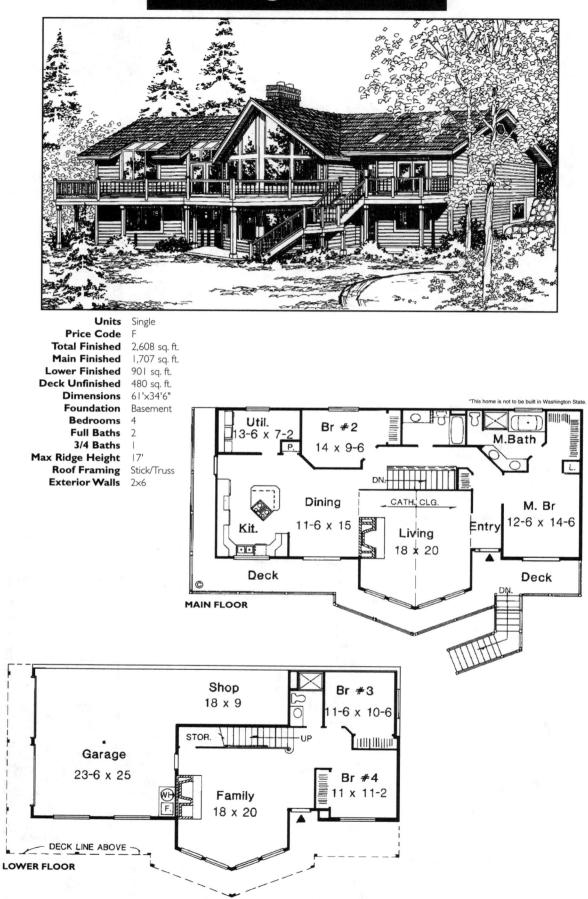

Units	Single
Price Code	F
Total Finished	2,608 sq. ft.
Main Finished	1,707 sq. ft.
Lower Finished	901 sq. ft.
Deck Unfinished	480 sq. ft.
Dimensions	61'x34'6"
Foundation	Basement
Bedrooms	4
Full Baths	2
3/4 Baths	1
Max Ridge Height	17'
Roof Framing	Stick/Truss
Exterior Walls	2x6

*This home is not to be built in Washington State.

MAIN FLOOR

Util. 13-6 x 7-2
Br #2 14 x 9-6
M.Bath
Kit.
Dining 11-6 x 15
DN.
CATH. CLG.
Living 18 x 20
Entry
M. Br 12-6 x 14-6
Deck
Deck
DN.

LOWER FLOOR

Shop 18 x 9
Br #3 11-6 x 10-6
STOR.
UP
Garage 23-6 x 25
Family 18 x 20
Br #4 11 x 11-2
WH
F.
DECK LINE ABOVE

Design 98426

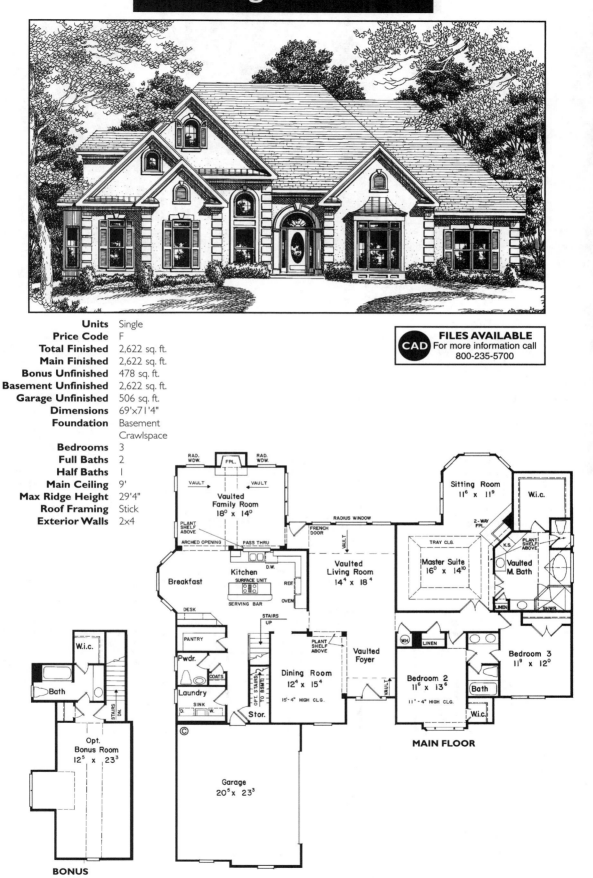

Units	Single
Price Code	F
Total Finished	2,622 sq. ft.
Main Finished	2,622 sq. ft.
Bonus Unfinished	478 sq. ft.
Basement Unfinished	2,622 sq. ft.
Garage Unfinished	506 sq. ft.
Dimensions	69'x71'4"
Foundation	Basement
	Crawlspace
Bedrooms	3
Full Baths	2
Half Baths	1
Main Ceiling	9'
Max Ridge Height	29'4"
Roof Framing	Stick
Exterior Walls	2x4

CAD FILES AVAILABLE
For more information call
800-235-5700

BONUS

MAIN FLOOR

Design 52136

Units	Single
Price Code	F
Total Finished	2,626 sq. ft.
Main Finished	2,626 sq. ft.
Bonus Unfinished	434 sq. ft.
Basement Unfinished	2,626 sq. ft.
Garage Unfinished	549 sq. ft.
Dimensions	65'x69'
Foundation	Basement
	Crawlspace
Bedrooms	3
Full Baths	2
Half Baths	1
Main Ceiling	9'
Second Ceiling	8'
Max Ridge Height	25'8"
Roof Framing	Stick
Exterior Walls	2x4

CAD FILES AVAILABLE For more information ca 800-235-5700

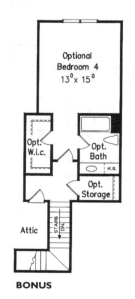

BONUS

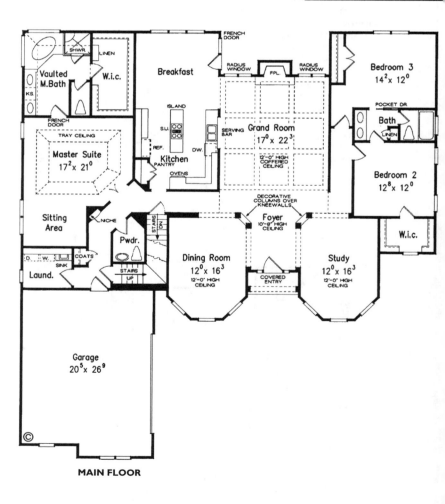

MAIN FLOOR

Units	Single
Price Code	F
Total Finished	2,645 sq. ft.
Main Finished	2,577 sq. ft.
Bonus Finished	68 sq. ft.
Bonus Unfinished	619 sq. ft.
Basement Unfinished	2,561 sq. ft.
Garage Unfinished	560 sq. ft.
Dimensions	74'x70'
Foundation	Basement
	Crawlspace
	Slab
Bedrooms	4
Full Baths	2
Half Baths	1
Main Ceiling	9'
Second Ceiling	8'
Max Ridge Height	23'
Roof Framing	Stick
Exterior Walls	2x4

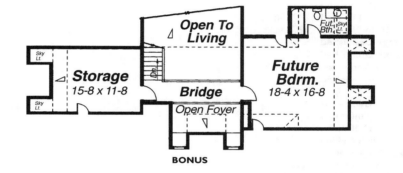

BONUS

Storage 15-8 x 11-8
Open To Living
Future Bdrm. 18-4 x 16-8
Bridge
Open Foyer
Fut. Bth.

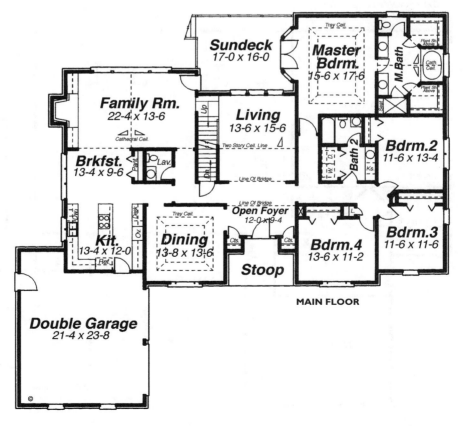

MAIN FLOOR

Sundeck 17-0 x 16-0
Master Bdrm. 15-6 x 17-6
M. Bath
Family Rm. 22-4 x 13-6
Living 13-6 x 15-6
Bdrm.2 11-6 x 13-4
Brkfst. 13-4 x 9-6
Bath 2
Kit. 13-4 x 12-0
Dining 13-8 x 13-6
Open Foyer 12-0 x 9-4
Bdrm.4 13-6 x 11-2
Bdrm.3 11-6 x 11-6
Stoop
Double Garage 21-4 x 23-8

Units	Single
Price Code	F
Total Finished	2,671 sq. ft.
Main Finished	2,671 sq. ft.
Garage Unfinished	528 sq. ft.
Porch Unfinished	298 sq. ft.
Dimensions	73'6"x58'8"
Foundation	Crawlspace Slab
Bedrooms	4
Full Baths	2
Half Baths	1
Main Ceiling	9'
Max Ridge Height	23'10"
Roof Framing	Stick
Exterior Walls	2x4, 2x6

MAIN FLOOR

Design 92275

Units	Single
Price Code	F
Total Finished	2,675 sq. ft.
Main Finished	2,675 sq. ft.
Garage Unfinished	638 sq. ft.
Dimensions	69'x59'10"
Foundation	Slab
Bedrooms	4
Full Baths	2
3/4 Baths	1
Max Ridge Height	28'
Roof Framing	Stick
Exterior Walls	2x4

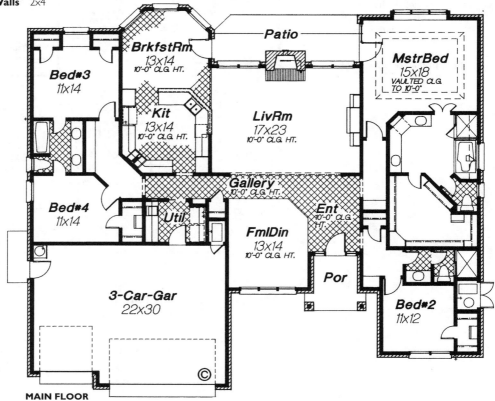

MAIN FLOOR

Design 96913

Units	Single
Price Code	F
Total Finished	2,677 sq. ft.
Main Finished	2,677 sq. ft.
Bonus Unfinished	319 sq. ft.
Garage Unfinished	543 sq. ft.
Deck Unfinished	676 sq. ft.
Porch Unfinished	43 sq. ft.
Dimensions	63'10"x80'4"
Foundation	Crawlspace
Bedrooms	3
Full Baths	1
3/4 Baths	2
Half Baths	1
Main Ceiling	8'-9'
Second Ceiling	8'
Vaulted Ceiling	15'
Max Ridge Height	28'6"
Roof Framing	Stick
Exterior Walls	2x4

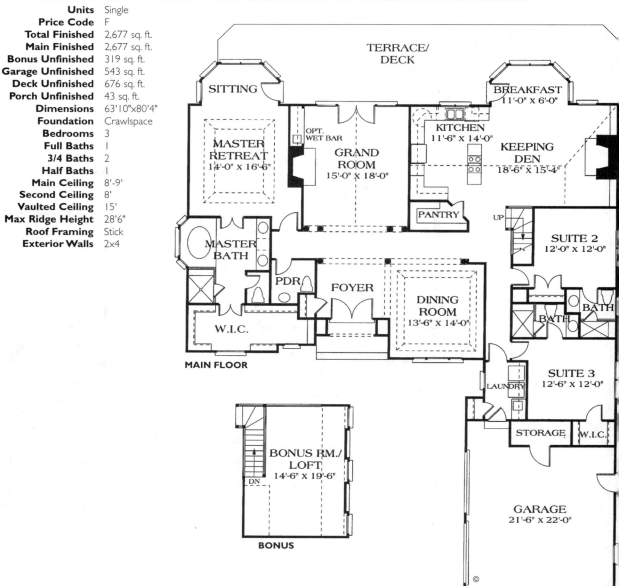

TERRACE/DECK

SITTING

MASTER RETREAT 14'-0" X 16'-6"

OPT. WET BAR

GRAND ROOM 15'-0" X 18'-0"

KITCHEN 11'-6" X 14'-0"

BREAKFAST 11'-0" X 6'-0"

KEEPING DEN 18'-6" X 15'-4"

MASTER BATH

PANTRY

UP

SUITE 2 12'-0" X 12'-0"

W.I.C.

PDR

FOYER

DINING ROOM 13'-6" X 14'-0"

BATH

BATH

MAIN FLOOR

LAUNDRY

SUITE 3 12'-6" X 12'-0"

STORAGE

W.I.C.

BONUS RM./ LOFT 14'-6" X 19'-6"

DN

GARAGE 21'-6" X 22'-0"

BONUS

Design 66098

Units	Single
Price Code	F
Total Finished	2,689 sq. ft.
Main Finished	2,689 sq. ft.
Garage Unfinished	638 sq. ft.
Dimensions	65'x68'4"
Foundation	Slab
Bedrooms	4
Full Baths	2
3/4 Baths	1
Main Ceiling	9'
Max Ridge Height	27'
Roof Framing	Stick
Exterior Walls	2x4

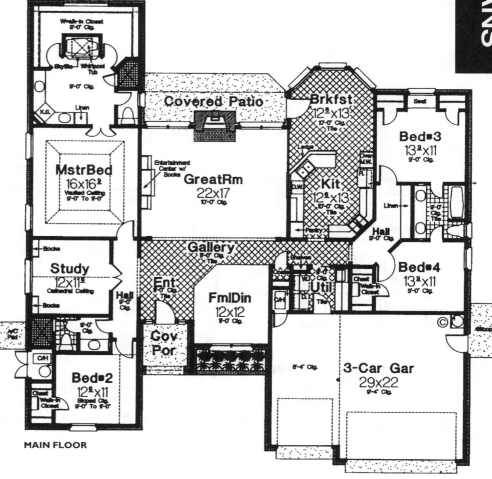

MAIN FLOOR

Units	Single
Price Code	F
Total Finished	2,690 sq. ft.
Main Finished	2,690 sq. ft.
Basement Unfinished	2,690 sq. ft.
Garage Unfinished	660 sq. ft.
Deck Unfinished	252 sq. ft.
Porch Unfinished	95 sq. ft.
Dimensions	87'6"x56'10"
Foundation	Basement
Bedrooms	4
Full Baths	3
Half Baths	1
Main Ceiling	9'
Vaulted Ceiling	14'
Tray Ceiling	11'
Max Ridge Height	25'4"
Roof Framing	Stick
Exterior Walls	2x4

OPTIONAL WHEELCHAIR BATH

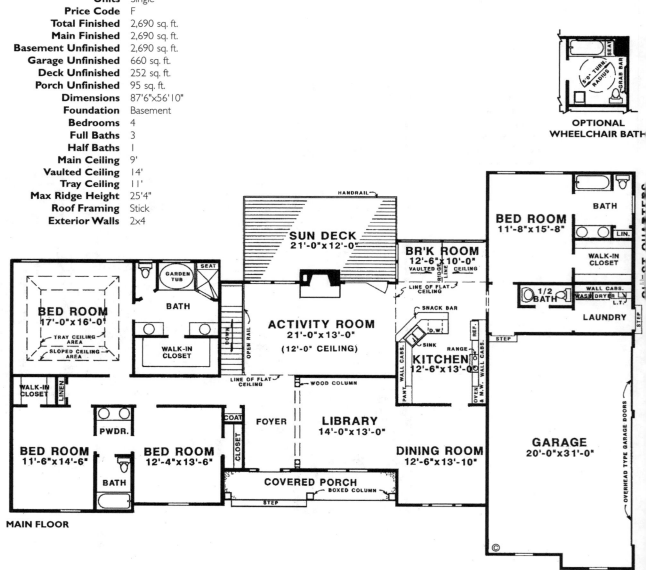

MAIN FLOOR

Design 92501

Units	Single
Price Code	F
Total Finished	2,727 sq. ft.
Main Finished	2,727 sq. ft.
Garage Unfinished	569 sq. ft.
Porch Unfinished	190 sq. ft.
Dimensions	70'10"×64'5"
Foundation	Crawlspace
	Slab
Bedrooms	4
Full Baths	3
Half Baths	1
Main Ceiling	9'
Vaulted Ceiling	11'
Tray Ceiling	10'
Max Ridge Height	24'
Roof Framing	Stick
Exterior Walls	2x4

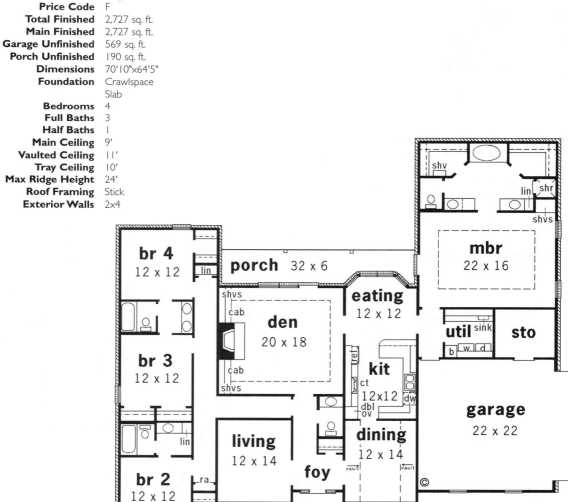

MAIN FLOOR

Units	Single
Price Code	F
Total Finished	2,742 sq. ft.
Main Finished	2,742 sq. ft.
Dimensions	84'6"x58'6"
Foundation	Slab
Bedrooms	4
Full Baths	2
Half Baths	1
Main Ceiling	9'

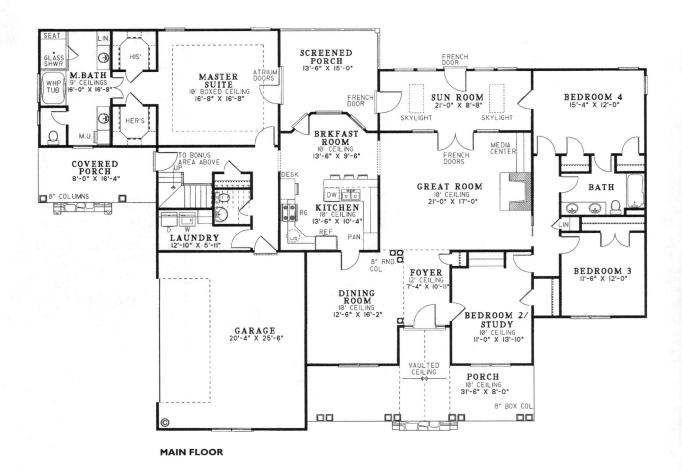

MAIN FLOOR

Design 66102

Units	Single
Price Code	F
Total Finished	2,744 sq. ft.
Main Finished	2,744 sq. ft.
Garage Unfinished	690 sq. ft.
Dimensions	66'6"x74'6"
Foundation	Slab
Bedrooms	4
Full Baths	2
3/4 Baths	1
Main Ceiling	9'-11'
Max Ridge Height	34'
Roof Framing	Stick
Exterior Walls	2x4

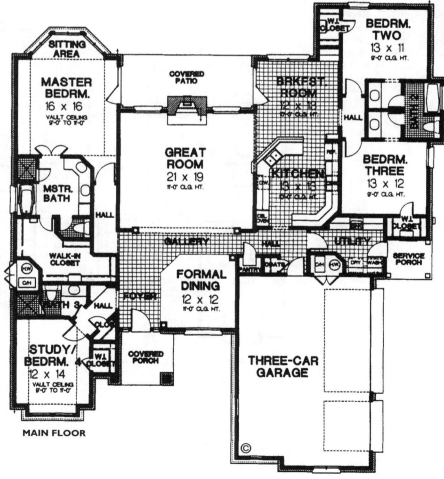

MAIN FLOOR

Units	Single
Price Code	G
Total Finished	2,755 sq. ft.
Main Finished	2,755 sq. ft.
Bonus Unfinished	440 sq. ft.
Garage Unfinished	724 sq. ft.
Porch Unfinished	419 sq. ft.
Dimensions	73'x82'8"
Foundation	Slab
Bedrooms	4
Full Baths	2
3/4 Baths	I
Max Ridge Height	22'
Roof Framing	Truss

Covered Porch

Family
20⁴ · 15⁵
10' Ceiling

Nook

Kitchen

Master
Bedroom
14⁴ · 21⁴
10' Ceiling

Bath

Living
13⁴ · 12⁴
10' Ceiling

Bedroom 4
13⁰ · 12⁰
10' Ceiling

Bath

W.I.C.   W.I.C.

Bedroom 2
11⁰ · 11⁰
10' Ceiling

Foyer

Dining
11⁰ · 14⁰
10' Ceiling

Utility

Bedroom 3
13⁰ · 12⁰
10' Ceiling

Master
Bath
10' Ceiling

Entry

MAIN FLOOR

3 Car Garage
22⁰ · 31⁴
8' Ceiling

Design 32145

PHOTOGRAPHY: RICHARD SEXTON

Units	Single
Price Code	G
Total Finished	2,780 sq. ft.
Main Finished	2,780 sq. ft.
Basement Unfinished	523 sq. ft.
Dimensions	67'x71'
Foundation	Slab
Bedrooms	3
Full Baths	2
Half Baths	1
Main Ceiling	10'
Vaulted Ceiling	18'6"
Max Ridge Height	21'6"
Roof Framing	Stick
Exterior Walls	2×4

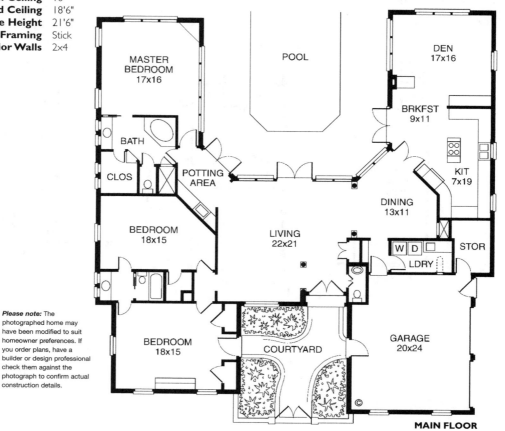

MAIN FLOOR

Please note: The photographed home may have been modified to suit homeowner preferences. If you order plans, have a builder or design professional check them against the photograph to confirm actual construction details.

Units	Single
Price Code	F
Total Finished	2,781 sq. ft.
Main Finished	2,781 sq. ft.
Bonus Unfinished	319 sq. ft.
Garage Unfinished	623 sq. ft.
Porch Unfinished	361 sq. ft.
Dimensions	64'10"x76'9"
Foundation	Slab
Bedrooms	4
Full Baths	3

Unfinished
Gameroom
11'4"x 26'

BONUS

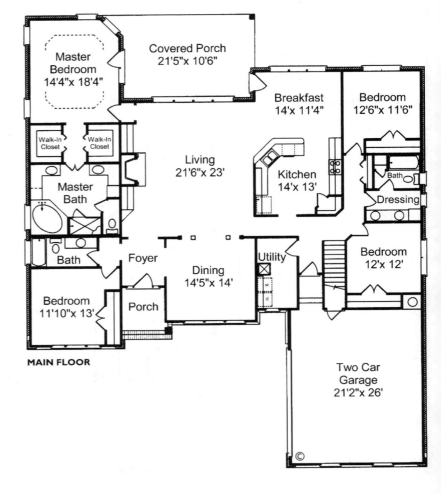

Master
Bedroom
14'4"x 18'4"

Covered Porch
21'5"x 10'6"

Walk-In Closet

Walk-In Closet

Breakfast
14'x 11'4"

Bedroom
12'6"x 11'6"

Master
Bath

Living
21'6"x 23'

Kitchen
14'x 13'

Bath

Dressing

Bath

Foyer

Dining
14'5"x 14'

Utility

Bedroom
12'x 12'

Bedroom
11'10"x 13'

Porch

Two Car
Garage
21'2"x 26'

MAIN FLOOR

Design 91476

Units	Single
Price Code	G
Total Finished	2,786 sq. ft.
Main Finished	2,786 sq. ft.
Garage Unfinished	445 sq. ft.
Dimensions	65'x75'
Foundation	Crawlspace
Bedrooms	3
Full Baths	2
Half Baths	1
Max Ridge Height	27'9"
Roof Framing	Truss
Exterior Walls	2x6

VAULTED
MBR
19/8 X 15/0

WI CLO   WI CLO

M BATH

DEN
12/6 X 11/0

UTIL

W/D

GARAGE
19/8 X 22/8

NOOK
12 X 10

KIT

PAN

GST

ST   PDR

COFFERED
DIN RM
13 X 14

FOYER

COVERED
PORCH

COFFERED
FAM RM
15/8 X 19/2

BI CABS

BI CABS

GALLERY HALL

COFFERED
LIV RM
12 X 14

COVERED
PORCH

COVERED
PORCH

BR
13 X 11

BATH

LIN

BR
11/6 X 12/0

MAIN FLOOR

Design 98927

Units	Single
Price Code	G
Total Finished	2,788 sq. ft.
Main Finished	2,788 sq. ft.
Basement Unfinished	805 sq. ft.
Garage Unfinished	506 sq. ft.
Deck Unfinished	275 sq. ft.
Porch Unfinished	314 sq. ft.
Dimensions	82'4"x60'5"
Foundation	Basement
Bedrooms	3
Full Baths	2
Half Baths	1
Max Ridge Height	31'
Roof Framing	Stick
Exterior Walls	2x4

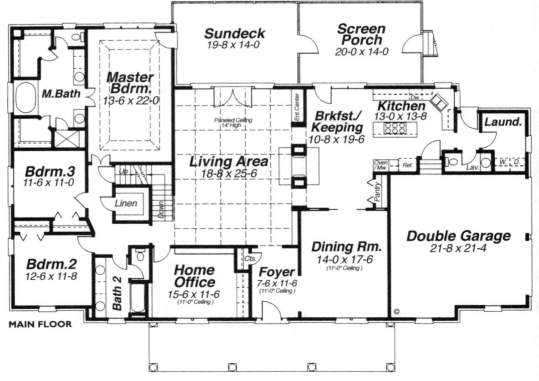

Design 63176

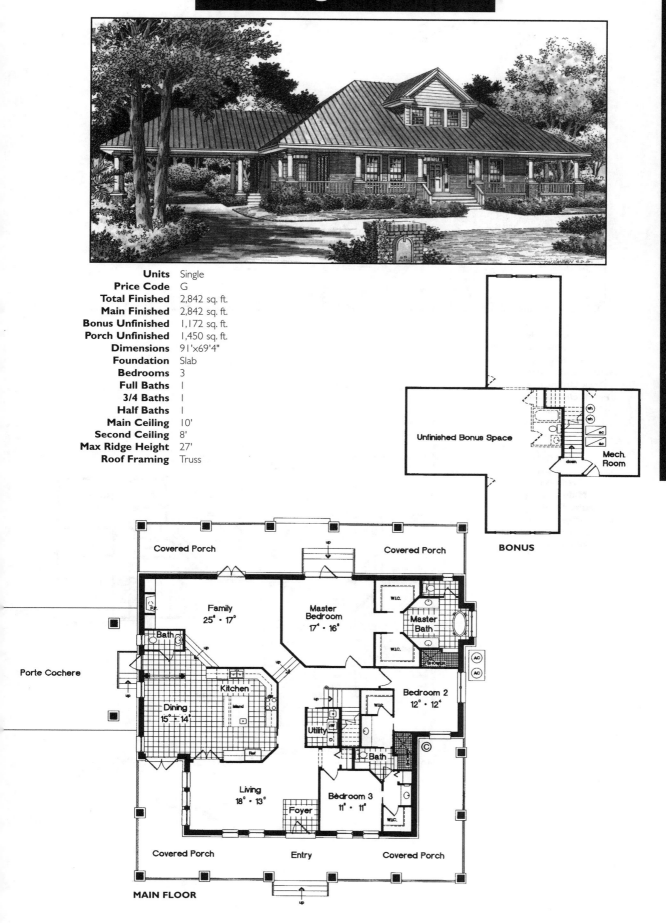

Units	Single
Price Code	G
Total Finished	2,842 sq. ft.
Main Finished	2,842 sq. ft.
Bonus Unfinished	1,172 sq. ft.
Porch Unfinished	1,450 sq. ft.
Dimensions	91'x69'4"
Foundation	Slab
Bedrooms	3
Full Baths	1
3/4 Baths	1
Half Baths	1
Main Ceiling	10'
Second Ceiling	8'
Max Ridge Height	27'
Roof Framing	Truss

Unfinished Bonus Space

Mech. Room

down

BONUS

Covered Porch

Covered Porch

up

Family
25⁰ · 17⁰

Master
Bedroom
17⁴ · 16⁰

W.I.C.

W.I.C.

Master
Bath

Bath

AC

AC

Porte Cochere

Kitchen

Island

W.I.C.

Bedroom 2
12⁰ · 12⁴

Dining
15⁰ · 14⁰

Utility

Ref

up

Bath

C

Living
18⁰ · 13⁰

Foyer

Bedroom 3
11⁰ · 11⁰

W.I.C.

Covered Porch

Entry

Covered Porch

up

MAIN FLOOR

Units	Single
Price Code	G
Total Finished	2,911 sq. ft.
Main Finished	2,911 sq. ft.
Garage Unfinished	720 sq. ft.
Deck Unfinished	220 sq. ft.
Porch Unfinished	48 sq. ft.
Dimensions	78'x79'9"
Foundation	Basement
	Slab
Bedrooms	4
Full Baths	2
3/4 Baths	1
Half Baths	1
Main Ceiling	9'
Vaulted Ceiling	9'-12'
Max Ridge Height	30'8"
Roof Framing	Stick
Exterior Walls	2x4

MAIN FLOOR

Design 94219

Units	Single
Price Code	H
Total Finished	2,986 sq. ft.
Main Finished	2,986 sq. ft.
Garage Unfinished	574 sq. ft.
Porch Unfinished	556 sq. ft.
Dimensions	82'8"×76'4"
Foundation	Slab
Bedrooms	4
Full Baths	2
3/4 Baths	1
Half Baths	1
Main Ceiling	10'
Max Ridge Height	28'6"
Roof Framing	Stick

* Alternate foundation options available at an additional charge.
Please call 1-800-235-5700 for more information.

private garden

guest/playroom
12'-0" x 13'-10"
10' clg.

verandah

© Sater Design Collection

leisure
17'-4" x 17'-0"
10' flat clg.

verandah
24'-0" x 12'-0" avg.

master suite
14'-0" x 16'-6"
11' stepped clg.

br. 2
13'-8" x 12'-4"
10' flat clg.

mitered glass

nook
9'-0" x 10'-0"

2 view fireplace

kitchen
14' x 13'

living
14'-0" x 14'-0"
14' stepped clg.

study
14'-2" x 12'-8"
14' stepped clg.

br. 3
11'-4" x 12'-10"
10' clg.

arch

books

gallery

books

arch

grand foyer

entry
arched clg.

utility

dining
12'-8" x 15'-0"
14' tray clg.

garage
21'-4" x 24'-8"

MAIN FLOOR

Units	Single
Price Code	G
Total Finished	2,987 sq. ft.
Main Finished	2,987 sq. ft.
Garage Unfinished	623 sq. ft.
Dimensions	80'4"×82'4"
Foundation	Slab
Bedrooms	3
Full Baths	2
3/4 Baths	I
Max Ridge Height	24'6"
Roof Framing	Truss

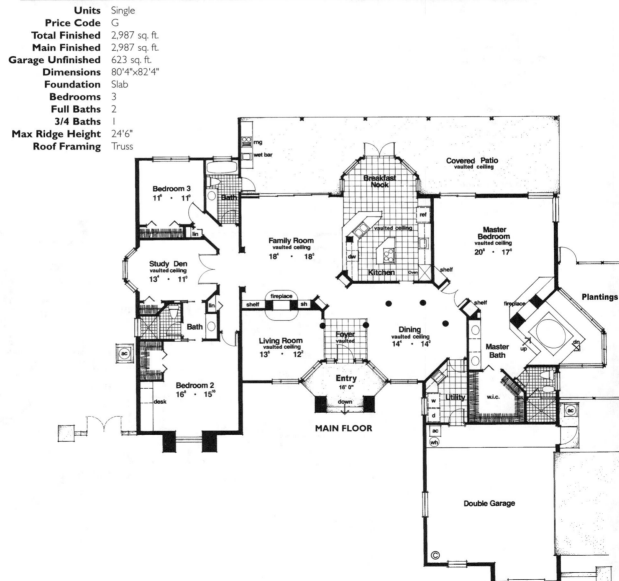

MAIN FLOOR

Design 63162

Units	Single
Price Code	I
Total Finished	2,816 sq. ft.
Main Finished	2,816 sq. ft.
Bonus Unfinished	290 sq. ft.
Basement Unfinished	286 sq. ft.
Garage Unfinished	463 sq. ft.
Porch Unfinished	716 sq. ft.
Guest House Unfinished	330 sq. ft.
Dimensions	94'x113'5"
Foundation	Slab
Bedrooms	4
Full Baths	2
3/4 Baths	1
Half Baths	2
First Ceiling	10'
Max Ridge Height	26'6"
Roof Framing	Truss

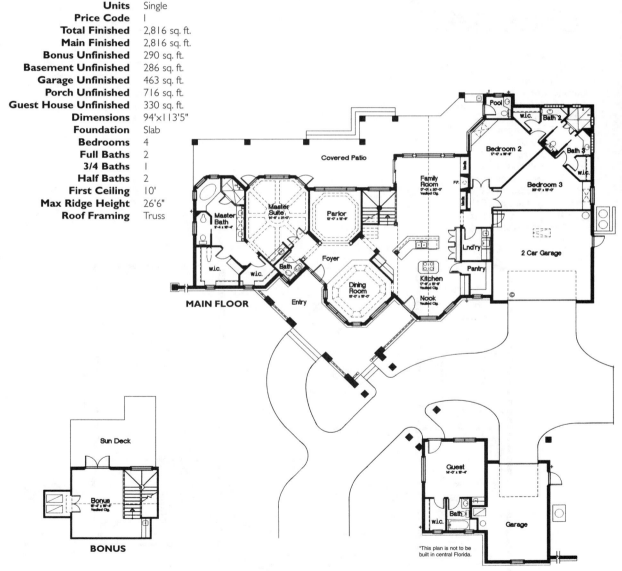

MAIN FLOOR

BONUS

*This plan is not to be built in central Florida.

Units	Single
Price Code	H
Total Finished	3,162 sq. ft.
Main Finished	3,162 sq. ft.
Garage Unfinished	662 sq. ft.
Deck Unfinished	240 sq. ft.
Porch Unfinished	62 sq. ft.
Dimensions	85'10"x66'3"
Foundation	Slab
Bedrooms	4
Full Baths	2
3/4 Baths	1
Half Baths	1
Max Ridge Height	31'
Roof Framing	Stick
Exterior Walls	2x4

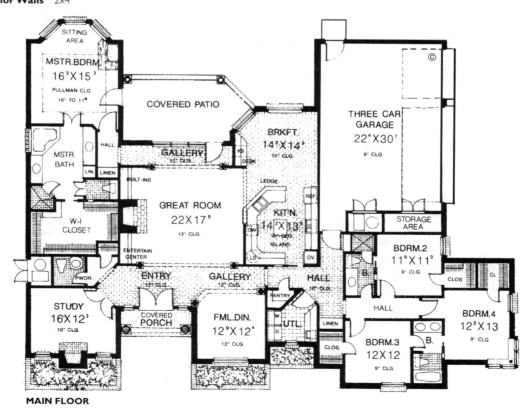

MAIN FLOOR

Design 52003

3,001-3,500 sq. ft. HOME PLANS

Units	Single
Price Code	H
Total Finished	3,190 sq. ft.
Main Finished	3,190 sq. ft.
Bonus Unfinished	305 sq. ft.
Basement Unfinished	3,190 sq. ft.
Garage Unfinished	696 sq. ft.
Dimensions	74'x84'6"
Foundation	Basement
	Crawlspace
Bedrooms	4
Full Baths	3
Half Baths	1
Main Ceiling	9'
Max Ridge Height	26'
Roof Framing	Stick
Exterior Walls	2x4

CAD FILES AVAILABLE
For more information call
800-235-5700

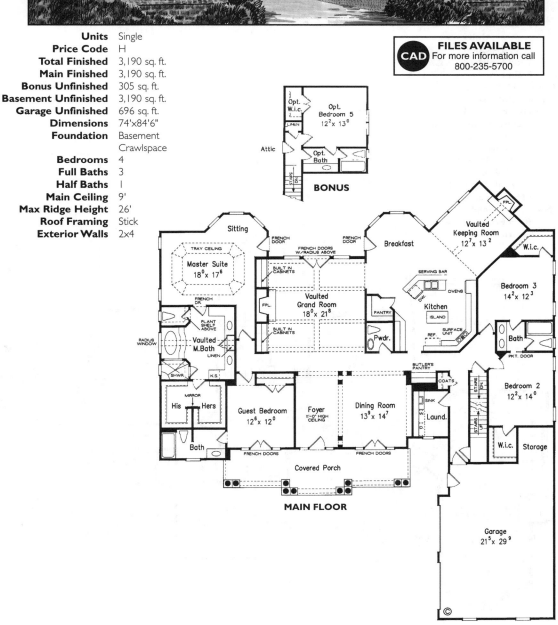

BONUS

MAIN FLOOR

Units	Single
Price Code	I
Total Finished	3,352 sq. ft.
Main Finished	3,352 sq. ft.
Garage Unfinished	672 sq. ft.
Deck Unfinished	462 sq. ft.
Porch Unfinished	60 sq. ft.
Dimensions	91'x71'9"
Foundation	Slab
Bedrooms	4
Full Baths	2
3/4 Baths	1
Half Baths	1
Main Ceiling	9'-11'
Max Ridge Height	28'2"
Roof Framing	Stick
Exterior Walls	2x4

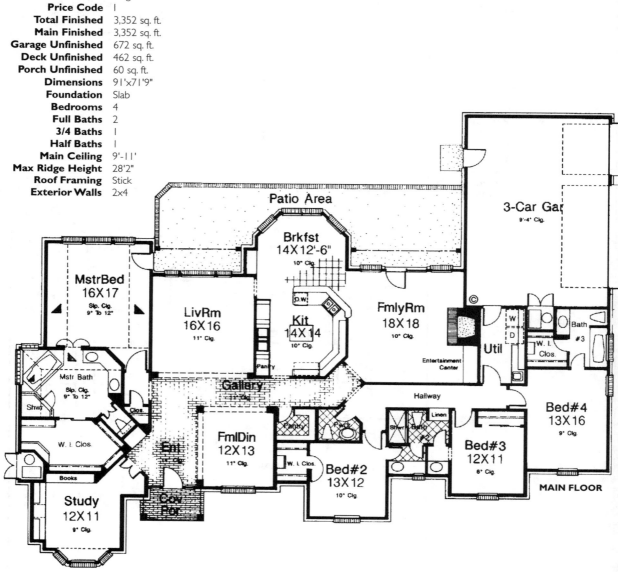

Design 63184

3,001-3,500 sq. ft. HOME PLANS

Units	Single
Price Code	I
Total Finished	3,386 sq. ft.
Main Finished	3,386 sq. ft.
Bonus Unfinished	444 sq. ft.
Garage Unfinished	765 sq. ft.
Porch Unfinished	602 sq. ft.
Dimensions	77'4"x99'
Foundation	Slab
Bedrooms	4
Full Baths	2
3/4 Baths	1
Half Baths	1
Main Ceiling	10'
Max Ridge Height	25'4"
Roof Framing	Truss
Exterior Walls	2x4

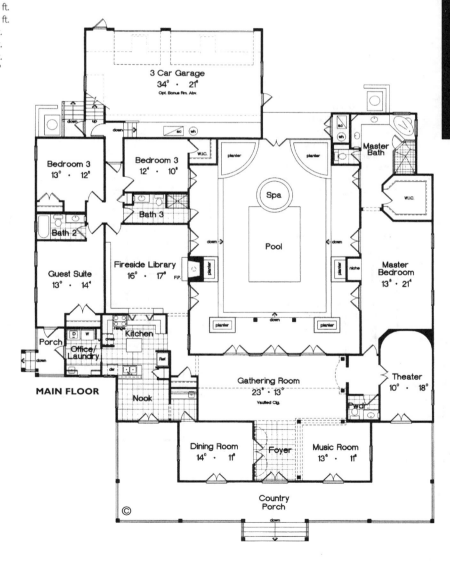

MAIN FLOOR

Units	Single
Price Code	I
Total Finished	3,418 sq. ft.
Main Finished	3,418 sq. ft.
Bonus Unfinished	388 sq. ft.
Basement Unfinished	3,418 sq. ft.
Garage Unfinished	577 sq. ft.
Dimensions	70'7"x81'10"
Foundation	Basement Crawlspace
Bedrooms	4
Full Baths	3
Half Baths	1
Main Ceiling	9'
Second Ceiling	8'
Max Ridge Height	30'6"
Roof Framing	Stick
Exterior Walls	2x4

CAD **FILES AVAILABLE**
For more information call
800-235-5700

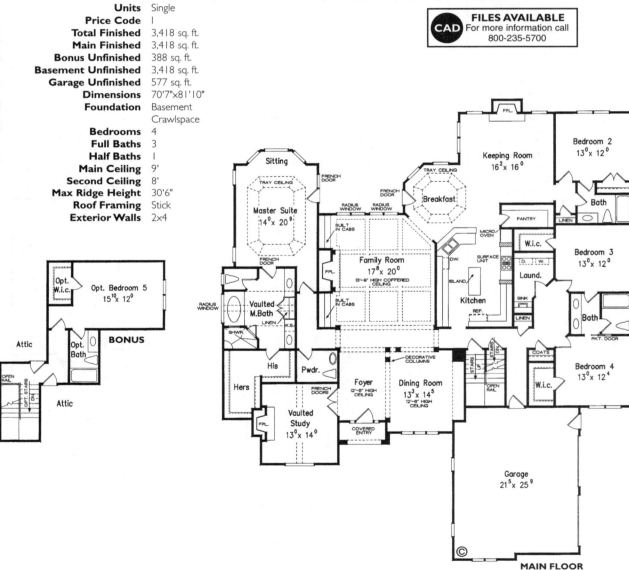

Design 63021

3,001-3,500 sq. ft. HOME PLANS

Units	Single
Price Code	I
Total Finished	3,434 sq. ft.
Main Finished	3,434 sq. ft.
Bonus Unfinished	512 sq. ft.
Garage Unfinished	814 sq. ft.
Dimensions	82'4"x83'8"
Foundation	Slab
Bedrooms	5
Full Baths	3
3/4 Baths	1
Main Ceiling	10'-12'
Max Ridge Height	23'5"
Roof Framing	Truss

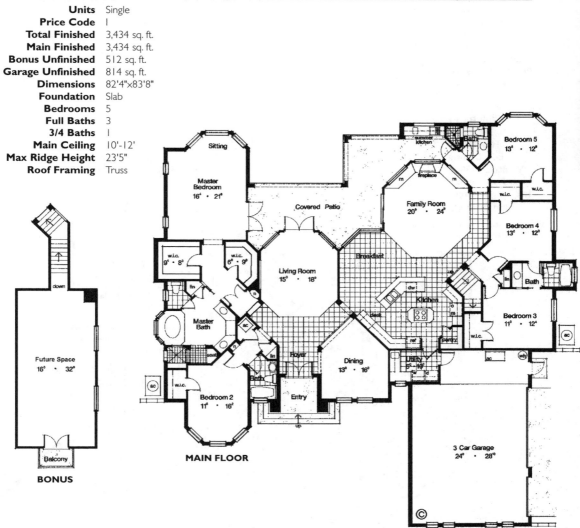

BONUS

MAIN FLOOR

Design 94220

Units	Single
Price Code	I
Total Finished	3,477 sq. ft.
Main Finished	3,477 sq. ft.
Garage Unfinished	771 sq. ft.
Porch Unfinished	512 sq. ft.
Dimensions	95'x88'8"
Foundation	Slab
Bedrooms	3
Full Baths	2
3/4 Baths	I
Half Baths	I
Main Ceiling	14'
Vaulted Ceiling	14'
Tray Ceiling	12'
Max Ridge Height	35'6"
Roof Framing	Stick

* Alternate foundation options available at an additional charge.
Please call 1-800-235-5700 for more information.

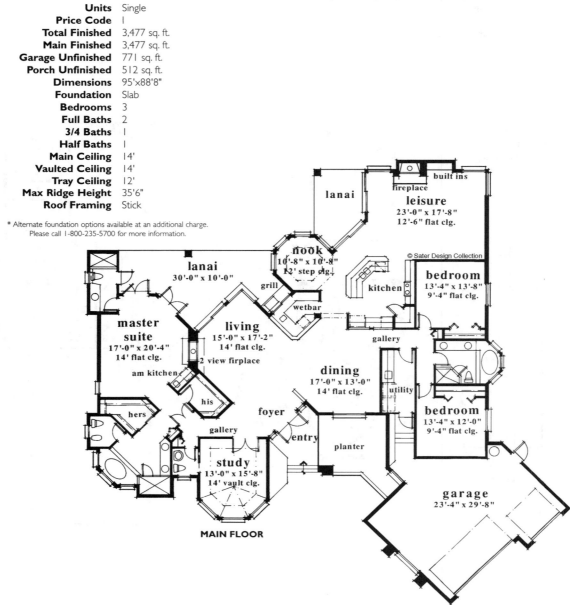

MAIN FLOOR

Design 92265

Units	Single
Price Code	K
Total Finished	3,818 sq. ft.
Main Finished	3,818 sq. ft.
Garage Unfinished	816 sq. ft.
Dimensions	107'4"×68'7"
Foundation	Basement
	Slab
Bedrooms	4
Full Baths	3
Half Baths	1
Main Ceiling	10'
Max Ridge Height	35'6"
Roof Framing	Stick
Exterior Walls	2×4

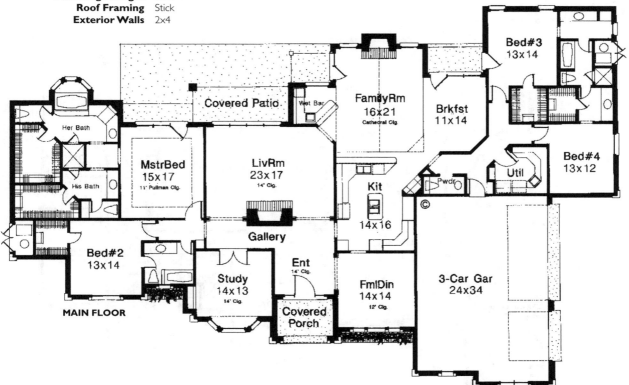

Her Bath

His Bath

Covered Patio

Wet Bar

FamilyRm
16x21
Cathedral Clg.

Brkfst
11x14

Bed#3
13x14

MstrBed
15x17
11' Pullman Clg.

LivRm
23x17
14' Clg.

Kit
14x16

Util

Bed#4
13x12

Gallery

Pwdr

Bed#2
13x14

Study
14x13
14' Clg.

Ent
14' Clg.

FmlDin
14x14
12' Clg.

3-Car Gar
24x34

Covered
Porch

MAIN FLOOR

Units	Single
Price Code	I
Total Finished	3,942 sq. ft.
Main Finished	3,942 sq. ft.
Garage Unfinished	920 sq. ft.
Dimensions	97'x82'
Foundation	Basement
	Slab
Bedrooms	4
Full Baths	3
Half Baths	I
Main Ceiling	9'-11'
Max Ridge Height	33'
Roof Framing	Stick
Exterior Walls	2x4

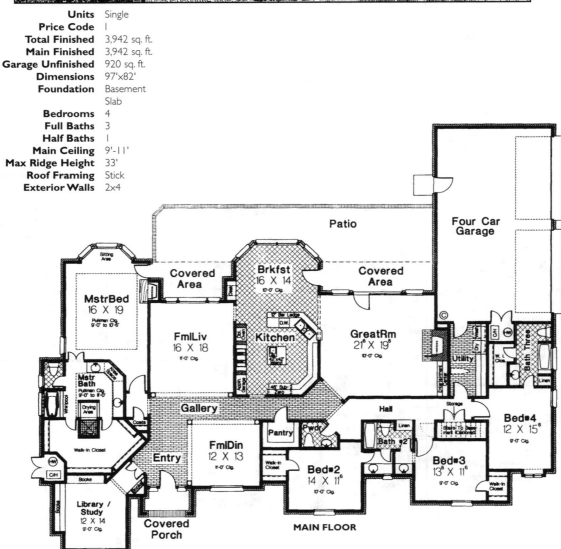

MAIN FLOOR

PHOTOGRAPHY: ROY INMAN

Units	Single
Price Code	L
Total Finished	5,212 sq. ft.
First Finished	2,453 sq. ft.
Second Finished	390 sq. ft.
Lower Finished	2,369 sq. ft.
Dimensions	78'10"x80'4"
Foundation	Basement
Bedrooms	4
Full Baths	4
Half Baths	I
Max Ridge Height	40'
Roof Framing	Stick
Exterior Walls	2x4

Please note: The photographed home may have been modified to suit homeowner preferences. If you order plans, have a builder or design professional check them against the photograph to confirm actual construction details.

SECOND FLOOR

DN

EXERCISE
11½x31

BRKFST
12x11

DECK

KIT
15½x14½

FAMILY
12x23½

D/W

UP

DECK

LIVING
19½x18½

DINING
13½x16½

GARAGE
22½x36½

ENTRY

MASTER
BEDRM
17½x21

DN

SUNRM.
7x11

DRESS

UP

BATH

BATH

DEN/GUEST
15½x14½

FIRST FLOOR

Exterior Elevations

These front, rear, and sides of the home include information pertaining to the exterior finish materials, roof pitches, and exterior height dimensions.

Cabinet Plans

These plans, or in some cases elevations, will detail the layout of the kitchen and bathroom cabinets at a larger scale. Available for most plans.

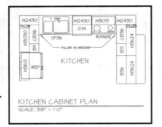

Typical Wall Section

This section will address insulation, roof components, and interior and exterior wall finishes. Your plans will be designed with either 2x4 or 2x6 exterior walls, but if you wish, most professional contractors can easily adapt the plans to the wall thickness you require.

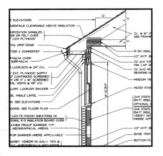

Fireplace Details

If the home you have chosen includes a fireplace, a fireplace detail will show typical methods of constructing the firebox, hearth, and flue chase for masonry units, or a wood frame chase for zero-clearance units. Available for most plans.

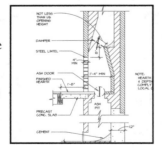

Foundation Plan

These plans will accurately show the dimensions of the footprint of your home, including load-bearing points and beam placement if applicable. The foundation style will vary from plan to plan.

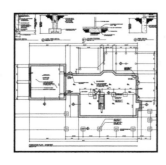

Roof Plan

The information necessary to construct the roof will be included with your home plans. Some plans will reference roof trusses, while many others contain schematic framing plans. These framing plans will indicate the lumber sizes necessary for the rafters and ridgeboards based on the designated roof loads.

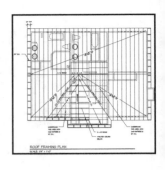

Typical Cross Section

A cut-away cross section through the entire home shows your building contractor the exact correlation of construction components at all levels of the house. It will help to clarify the load bearing points from the roof all the way down to the basement. Available for most plans.

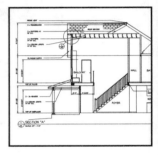

Detailed Floor Plans

The floor plans of your home accurately depict the dimensions of the positioning of all walls, doors, windows, stairs, and permanent fixtures. They will show you the relationship and dimensions of rooms, closets, and traffic patterns. The schematic of the electrical layout may be included in the plan.

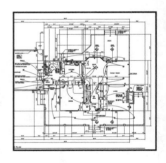

Stair Details

If the design you have chosen includes stairs, the plans will show the information that you need in order to build them—either through a stair cross section or on the floor plans.

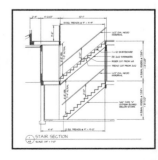

Garlinghouse Options & Extras

Reversed Plans can Make Your Dream Home Just Right!

You could have exactly the home you want by flipping it end-for-end. Simply order your plans "reversed." We'll send you one full set of mirror-image plans (with the writing backwards) as a master guide for you and your builder.

The remaining sets of your order will come as shown in this book so the dimensions and specifications are easily read on the job site. Most plans in our collection come stamped "reversed" so there is no construction confusion.

We can only send reversed plans with multiple-set orders. There is a $50 charge for this service.

Some plans in our collection are available in "Right Reading Reverse." Right Reading Reverse plans will show your home in reverse. This easy-to-read format will save you valuable time and money. Please contact our Sales Department at 800-235-5700 to check for Right Reading Reverse availability. There is a $135 charge for this service. **RRR**

Remember to Order Your Materials List

Available at a modest additional charge, the Materials List gives the quantity, dimensions, and specifications for the major materials needed to build your home. You will get faster, more accurate bids from your contractors and building suppliers—and avoid paying for unused materials and waste. Materials Lists are available for all home plans except as otherwise indicated, but can only be ordered with a set of home plans. Due to differences in regional requirements and homeowner or builder preferences, electrical, plumbing and heating/air conditioning equipment specifications are not designed specifically for each plan. **ML**

What Garlinghouse Offers

Home Plan Blueprint Package

By purchasing a multiple-set package of blueprints or a Vellum from Garlinghouse, you not only receive the physical blueprint documents necessary for construction, but you are also granted a license to build one (and only one) home. You can also make simple modifications, including minor non-structural changes and material substitutions, to our design as long as these changes are made directly on the blueprints purchased from Garlinghouse and no additional copies are made.

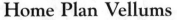

Home Plan Vellums

By purchasing Vellums for one of our home plans, you receive the same construction drawings found in the blueprints, but printed on vellum paper. Vellums can be erased and are perfect for making design changes. They are also semi-transparent, making them easy to duplicate. But most importantly, the purchase of home plan Vellums comes with a broader license that allows you to make changes to the design (i.e., create a hand drawn or CAD derivative work), to make copies of the plan, and to build one home from the plan.

License to Build Additional Homes

With the purchase of a blueprint package or Vellums, you automatically receive a license to build one home and only one home. If you want to build more homes than you are licensed to build through your purchase of a plan, then additional licenses must be purchased at reasonable costs from Garlinghouse. Inquire for more information.

Modifying Your Favorite Design Made Easy

MODIFICATION PRICING GUIDE

CATEGORIES	AVERAGE COST from... to
Adding or removing living space (square footage)	Quote required
Adding or removing a garage	$400-$680
Garage: Front entry to side load or vice versa	Starting at $300
Adding a screened porch	$280-$600
Adding a bonus room in the attic	$450-$780
Changing full basement to crawlspace or vice versa	Starting at $220
Changing full basement to slab or vice versa	Starting at $260
Changing exterior building material	Starting at $200
Changing roof lines	$360-$630
Adjusting ceiling heights	$280-$500
Adding, moving or removing an exterior opening	$55 per opening
Adding or removing a fireplace	$90-$200
Modifying a non-bearing wall or room	$55 per room
Changing exterior walls from 2"x4" to 2"x6"	Starting at $200
Redesigning a bathroom or a kitchen	$120-$280
Reverse plan right reading	Quote required
Adapting plans for local building code requirements	Quote required
Engineering stamp only	Quote required
Any other engineering services	Quote required
Adjust plan for handicapped accessibility	Quote required
Interactive Illustrations (choices of exterior materials)	Quote required
Metric conversion of home plan	$400

* Please remember that figures shown are average costs. Your quote may be higher or lower depending upon your specific requirements.

#1 Modifying Your Garlinghouse Home Plan

Simple modifications to your dream home, including minor non-structural changes and material substitutions, can be made by you and your builder by marking the changes directly on your blueprints. However, if you are considering making significant changes to your chosen design, we recommend that you use the services of The Garlinghouse Design Staff. We will help take your ideas and turn them into a reality, just the way you want. Here's our procedure:

When you place your Vellum order, you may also request a free Garlinghouse Modification Kit. In this kit, you will receive a red marking pencil, furniture cut-out sheet, ruler, a self-addressed mailing label, and a form for specifying any additional notes or drawings that will help us understand your design ideas. Mark your desired changes directly on the Vellum drawings. NOTE: Please use only a **red pencil** to mark your desired changes on the Vellum. Then, return the red-lined Vellum set in the original box to us.

Important: Please roll the Vellums for shipping—*do not fold*.

We also offer modification estimates. For a $50 fee, we will provide you with an estimate to draft your changes based on your specific modifications before you purchase the Vellums. After you receive your estimate, if you decide to have us do the changes, the $50 estimate fee will be deducted from the cost of your modifications. If, however, you choose to use a different service, the $50 estimate fee is non-refundable. (**Note**: Personal checks cannot be accepted for the estimate.)

Within five days of receipt of your plans, you will be contacted by a member of the design staff with an estimate for the design services to draw those changes. A 50% deposit is required before we begin making the actual modifications to your plans.

Once the design changes have been completed to your Vellum plan, a representative will call to inform you that your modified Vellum plan is complete and will be shipped as soon as the final payment has been made. For additional information, call us at 1-860-659-5667. Please refer to the Modification Pricing Guide for estimated modification costs.

#2 Reproducible Vellums for Local Modification Ease

If you decide not to use Garlinghouse for your modifications, we recommend that you follow our same procedure of purchasing Vellums. You then have the option of using the services of the original designer of the plan, a local professional designer, or an architect to make the modifications.

With a Vellum copy of our plans, a design professional can alter the drawings just the way you want, then you can print as many copies of the modified plans as you need to build your house. And, since you have already started with our complete detailed plans, the cost of those expensive professional services will be significantly less than starting from scratch. Refer to the price schedule for Vellum costs.

Questions? Call our Customer Service Department at 1-860-895-3715

Ignoring Copyright Laws Can Be A $100,000 MISTAKE

U.S. copyright laws allow for statutory penalties of up to $100,000 per incident for copyright infringement involving any of the copyrighted plans found in this publication. The law can be confusing. So, for your own protection, take the time to understand what you can and cannot do when it comes to home plans.

What You Can't Do

You Cannot Duplicate Home Plans
Purchasing a set of blueprints and making additional sets by reproducing the original is illegal. If you need more than one set of a particular home plan, you must purchase them.

You Cannot Copy Any Part of a Home Plan to Create Another
Creating your own plan by copying even part of a home design found in this publication without permission is called "creating a derivative work" and is illegal.

You Cannot Build a Home Without a License
You must have specific permission or a license to build a home from a copyrighted design, even if the finished home has been changed from the original plan. It is illegal to build one of the homes found in this publication without a license.

How to obtain a construction cost calculation based on labor rates and building material costs in your zip code area.

How does Zip Quote actually work? When you call to order, you must choose from the options available for your specific home in order for us to process your order. Once we receive your Zip Quote order, we process your specific home plan building materials list through our Home Cost Calculator which contains up-to-date rates for all residential labor trades and building material costs in your zip code area. The result? A calculated cost to build your dream home in your zip code area. This calculation will help you (as a consumer or a builder) evaluate your building budget.

All database information for our calculations is furnished by Marshall & Swift, L.P. For over 60 years, Marshall & Swift L.P. has been a leading provider of cost data to professionals in all aspects of the construction and remodeling industries.

Zip Quote can be purchased in two separate formats, either an itemized or a bottom-line format.

Option 1 The **Itemized Zip Quote** is a detailed building materials list. Each building materials list line item will separately state the labor cost, material cost, and equipment cost (if applicable) for the use of that building material in the construction process. This building materials list will be summarized by the individual building categories and will have additional columns where you can enter data from your contractor's estimates for a cost comparison between the different suppliers and contractors who will actually quote you their products and services.

Option 2 The **Bottom-Line Zip Quote** is a one line summarized total cost for the home plan of your choice. This cost calculation is also based on the labor cost, material cost, and equipment cost (if applicable) within your zip code area. Bottom-Line Zip Quote is available for most plans. Please call for availability.

Cost The price of your Itemized Zip Quote is based upon the pricing schedule of the plan you have selected, in addition to the price of the materials list. Please refer to the pricing schedule on our order form. The price of your initial Bottom-Line Zip Quote is $29.95. Each additional Bottom-Line Zip Quote ordered in conjunction with the initial order is only $14.95. A Bottom-Line Zip Quote may be purchased separately and does NOT have to be purchased in conjunction with a home plan order.

FYI An Itemized Zip Quote Home Cost Calculation can ONLY be purchased in conjunction with a Home Plan order. The Itemized Zip Quote can not be purchased separately. If you find within 60 days of your order date that you will be unable to build this home, then you may apply the price of the plans and the materials list towards the price of a new set of plans (see order info pages for plan exchange policy). The Itemized Zip Quote and the Bottom-Line Zip Quote are NOT returnable. The price of the initial Bottom-Line Zip Quote order can be credited toward the purchase of an Itemized Zip Quote order, only if available. Additional Bottom-Line Zip Quote orders, within the same order can not be credited. Please call our Sales Department for more information.

An Itemized Zip Quote is available for plans where you see this symbol. **ZIP**

A Bottom-Line Zip Quote is available for all plans under 4,000 sq. ft. or where you see this symbol. **BL** Please call for current availability.

Some More Information The Itemized and Bottom-Line Zip Quotes give you approximated costs for constructing the particular house in your area. These costs are not exact and are only intended to be used as a preliminary estimate to help determine the affordability of a new home and/or as a guide to evaluate the general competitiveness of actual price quotes obtained through local suppliers and contractors. **Land, landscaping, sewer systems, site work, contractor overhead and profit, and other expenses are not included in our building cost figures. Excluding land and landscaping, you may incur an additional 20% to 40% in costs from the original estimate.** Garlinghouse and Marshall & Swift L.P. cannot guarantee any level of data accuracy or correctness in a Zip Quote and disclaim all liability for loss with respect to the same, in excess of the original purchase price of the Zip Quote product. All Zip Quote calculations are based upon the actual blueprints and do not reflect any differences or options that may be shown on the published house renderings, floor plans, or photographs.

CAD Files Now Available

A CAD file is available for plans where you see this symbol.

Cad files are available in .dc5 or .dxf format or .dwg formats (R12, R13, R14, R2000). Please specify the file format at the time of your order. You will receive one bond set along with the CAD file when you place your order. NOTE: CAD files are NOT returnable and can not be exchanged.

The Garlinghouse Company

Order Form

BEST PLAN VALUE IN THE INDUSTRY!

Order Code No. H4OSH

_____ foundation

____ set(s) of blueprints for plan # _____ $____

____ Vellum & Modification Kit for plan # _____ $____

____ Additional set(s) @ $50 each for plan # _____ $____

____ Mirror Image Reverse @ $50 each $____

____ Right Reading Reverse @ $135 each $____

____ Materials list for plan # _____ $____

____ Detail Plans @ $19.95 each

     ❏ Construction ❏ Plumbing ❏ Electrical $____

____ Bottom-Line Zip Quote @ $29.95 for plan # _____ $____

____ Additional Bottom-Line Zip Quotes

     @ $14.95 for plan(s) # _____ $____

Zip code where building _____

____ Itemized Zip Quote for plan(s) # _____ $____

Shipping $____

Subtotal $____

Sales Tax (CT residents add 6% sales tax. Not required for other states) $____

TOTAL AMOUNT ENCLOSED $____

Send your check, money order, or credit card information to:
(No C.O.D.'s Please)

Please submit all United States & other nations orders to:
Garlinghouse Company
174 Oakwood Drive
Glastonbury, CT. 06033
CALL: (800) 235-5700   FAX: (860) 659-5692

VISA   **MasterCard**

Please Submit all Canadian plan orders to:
Garlinghouse Company
102 Ellis Street
Penticton, BC V2A 4L5
CALL: (800) 361-7526   FAX: (250) 493-7526

ADDRESS INFORMATION:

NAME: _____

STREET: _____

CITY: _____

STATE: _____ **ZIP:** _____

DAYTIME PHONE: _____

E-MAIL ADDRESS: _____

Credit Card Information

Charge To: ❏ Visa   ❏ Mastercard

Card # ⎵⎵⎵⎵⎵⎵⎵⎵⎵⎵⎵⎵⎵⎵⎵⎵⎵⎵⎵

Signature _____ Exp. ____/____

442

To order your plan on-line now
using our secure server, visit:
www.garlinghouse.com

CUSTOMER SERVICE
Questions on existing orders?
➡ **1-800-895-3715**

TO PLACE ORDERS
• To order your home plan
• Questions about a plan
➡ **1-800-235-5700**

Privacy Statement (please read)

Dear Valued Garlinghouse Customer,

Your privacy is extremely important to us. We'd like to take a little of your time to explain our privacy policy.

As a service to you, we would like to provide your name to companies such as the following:

- Building material manufacturers that we are affiliated with, who would like to keep you current with their product line and specials.
- Building material retailers that would like to offer you competitive prices to help you save money.
- Financing companies that would like to offer you competitive mortgage rates.

In addition, as our valued customer, we would like to send you newsletters to assist in your building experience. *We* would also appreciate *your* feedback by filling out a customer service survey aimed to improve our operations.

You have total control over the use of your contact information. You let us know exactly how you want to be contacted. Please check all boxes that apply. Thank you.

☐ Don't mail
☐ Don't call
☐ Don't E-mail
☐ Only send Garlinghouse newsletters and customer service surveys

In closing, we hope this shows Garlinghouse's firm commitment to providing superior customer service and protection of your privacy. We thank you for your time and consideration.

Sincerely,

The Garlinghouse Company

For Our USA Customers:
Order Toll Free: 1-800-235-5700
nday-Friday 8:00 a.m. to 8:00 p.m. Eastern Time
r FAX your Credit Card order to 1-860-659-5692
All foreign residents call 1-860-659-5667

CUSTOMER SERVICE	TO PLACE ORDERS
Questions on existing orders?	• To order your home plans • Questions about a plan
➡ 1-800-895-3715	➡ 1-800-235-5700

For Our Canadian Customers:
Order Toll Free: 1-800-361-7526
Monday-Friday 8:00 a.m. to 5:00 p.m. Pacific Time
or FAX your Credit Card order to 1-250-493-7526
Customer Service: 1-250-493-0942

Please have ready: 1. Your credit card number 2. The plan number 3. The order code number ➡ **H4OSH**

arlinghouse 2004 Blueprint Price Code Schedule
Prices subject to change without notice.

1 Set	4 Sets	8 Sets	Vellums	ML	Bottom-Line ZIP Quote	CADD Files
$395	$435	$485	$600	$60	$29.95	$1,250
$425	$465	$515	$630	$60	$29.95	$1,300
$450	$490	$540	$665	$60	$29.95	$1,350
$490	$530	$580	$705	$60	$29.95	$1,400
$530	$570	$620	$750	$70	$29.95	$1,450
$585	$625	$675	$800	$70	$29.95	$1,500
$630	$670	$720	$850	$70	$29.95	$1,550
$675	$715	$765	$895	$70	$29.95	$1,600
$700	$740	$790	$940	$80	$29.95	$1,650
$740	$780	$830	$980	$80	$29.95	$1,700
$805	$845	$895	$1,020	$80	$29.95	$1,750
$825	$856	$915	$1,055	$80	$29.95	$1,800

Shipping — (Plans 1-59999)	1-3 Sets	4-6 Sets	7+ & Vellums
Standard Delivery (UPS 2-Day)	$25.00	$30.00	$35.00
Overnight Delivery	$35.00	$40.00	$45.00

Shipping — (Plans 60000-99999)	1-3 Sets	4-6 Sets	7+ & Vellums
Ground Delivery (7-10 Days)	$15.00	$20.00	$25.00
Express Delivery (3-5 Days)	$20.00	$25.00	$30.00

International Shipping & Handling	1-3 Sets	4-6 Sets	7+ & Vellums
Regular Delivery Canada (10-14 Days)	$30.00	$35.00	$40.00
Express Delivery Canada (7-10 Days)	$60.00	$70.00	$80.00
Overseas Delivery Airmail (3-4 Weeks)	$50.00	$60.00	$65.00

Additional sets with original order $50

IMPORTANT INFORMATION TO READ BEFORE YOU PLACE YOUR ORDER

ow Many Sets of Plans Will You Need?

e Standard 8-Set Construction Package

Our experience shows that you'll speed up every step of construction and avoid costly building errors by ordering enough sets to go around. Each desperson wants a set—the general contractor and all subcontractors: foundation, electrical, plumbing, heating/air conditioning, and framers. Don't forget ur lending institution, building department, and, of course, a set for yourself. * Recommended For Construction *

e Minimum 4-Set Construction Package

If you're comfortable with arduous follow-up, this package can save you a few dollars by giving you the option of passing down plan sets as work ogresses. You might have enough copies to go around if work goes exactly as scheduled and no plans are lost or damaged by subcontractors. But for only 0 more, the 8-set package eliminates these worries. * Recommended For Bidding *

e Single Study Set

We offer this set so you can study the blueprints to plan your dream home in detail. They are stamped "study set only—not for construction" and you cannot ild a home from them. In pursuant to copyright laws, it is *illegal* to reproduce any blueprint.

Reorder, Call 800-235-5700

If you find after your initial purchase that you require additional sets of plans, you may purchase them from us at special reorder prices (please call for pricing details) ovided that you reorder within six months of your original order date. There is a $28 reorder processing fee that is charged on all reorders. For more information on rdering plans, please contact our Sales Department.

ustomer Service/Exchanges Call 800-895-3715

If for some reason you have a question about your existing order, please call 800-895-3715. Your plans are custom printed especially for you once you place your er. For that reason we cannot accept any returns. If for some reason you find that the plan you have purchased from us does not meet your needs, then you may change that plan for any other plan in our collection. We allow you 60 days from your original invoice date to make an exchange. At the time of the exchange, you will be arged a processing fee of 20% of the total amount of your original order, plus the difference in price between the plans (if applicable), plus the cost to ship the new plans you. Call our Customer Service Department for more information. Please Note: Reproducible Vellums can only be exchanged if they are unopened.

nportant Shipping Information

Please refer to the shipping charts on the order form for service availability for your specific plan number. Our delivery service must have a street address or ral Route Box number—never a post office box. (PLEASE NOTE: Supplying a P.O. Box number will *only* will delay the shipping of your order.) Use a work address if one is home during the day. Orders being shipped to APO or FPO must go via First Class Mail. Please include the proper postage.

For our International Customers, only Certified bank checks and money orders are accepted and must be payable in U.S. currency. For speed, we ship interna- nal orders Air Parcel Post. Please refer to the chart for the correct shipping cost.

nportant Canadian Shipping Information

To our friends in Canada, we have a plan design affiliate in Penticton, BC. This relationship will help you avoid the delays and charges associated with shipments m the United States. Moreover, our affiliate is familiar with the building requirements in your community and country. We prefer payments in U.S. currency. If you wever are sending Canadian funds, please add 45% to the prices of the plans and shipping fees.

n Important Note About Building Code Requirements

All plans are drawn to conform to one or more of the industry's major national building standards. However, due to the variety of local building regulations, your n may need to be modified to comply with local requirements—snow loads, energy loads, seismic zones, etc. Do check them fully and consult your local building icials.

A few states require that all building plans used be drawn by an architect registered in that state. While having your plans reviewed and stamped by such an chitect may be prudent, laws requiring non-conforming plans like ours to be completely redrawn forces you to unnecessarily pay very large fees. If your state has ch a law, we strongly recommend you contact your state representative to protest.

The rendering, floor plans, and technical information contained within this publication are not guaranteed to be totally accurate. Consequently, no information m this publication should be used either as a guide to constructing a home or for estimating the cost of building a home. Complete blueprints must be purchased r such purposes.

443

Index

Option Key

BL Bottom-Line Zip Quote   **ML** Materials List BL/ML   **ZIP** Itemized Zip Quote   **RRR** Right Reading Reverse   **DUP** Duplex

Index

Option Key

BL Bottom-Line Zip Quote **ML** Materials List BL/ML **ZIP** Itemized Zip Quote **RRR** Right Reading Reverse **DUP** Duplex

TOP SELLING
GARAGE PLANS

Save money by Doing-It-Yourself using our Easy-To-Follow plans. Whether you intend to build your own garage or contract it out to a building professional, the Garlinghouse garage plans provide you with everything you need to price out your project and get started. Put our 90+ years of experience to work for you. Order now!!

No. 06016C $24.95
Cape Cod Style Apartment Garage With One Bedroom

- 28' x 24' Overall Dimensions
- 544 Square Foot Apartment
- 12/12 Gable Roof with Dormers
- Slab or Stem Wall Foundation Options

No. 06015C $24.95
Apartment Garage With Two Bedrooms

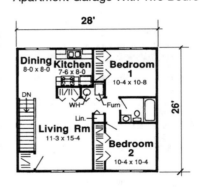

- 28' x 26' Overall Dimensions
- 728 Square Foot Apartment
- 4/12 Pitch Gable Roof
- Slab or Stem Wall Foundation Options

No. 06012C $16.95
30' Deep Gable &/or Eave Entry Jumbo Garages

- 4/12 Pitch Gable Roof
- Available Options for Extra Tall Walls, Garage & Personnel Doors, Foundation, Window, & Sidings
- Package contains 4 Different Sizes
- 30' x 28'   • 30' x 32'   • 30' x 36'   • 30' x 40'

No. 06013C $16.95
Two-Car Eave Entry Garage With Mudroom/Breezeway

- Attaches to Any House
- 36' x 24' Eave Entry
- Available Options for Utility Room with Bath, Mudroom, Screened-In Breezeway, Roof, Foundation, Garage & Personnel Doors, Window, & Sidings

No. 06001C   **$14.95**

12', 14' & 16' Wide-Gable Entry 1-Car Garages

- Available Options for Roof, Foundation, Window, Door, & Sidings
- Package contains 8 Different Sizes
- 12' x 20' Mini-Garage • 14' x 22' • 16' x 20' • 16' x 24'
- 14' x 20'   • 14' x 24' • 16' x 22' • 16' x 26'

No. 06003C   **$14.95**

24' Wide-Gable Entry 2-Car Garages

- Available Options for Side Shed, Roof, Foundation, Garage & Personnel Doors, Window, & Sidings
- Package contains 5 Different Sizes
- 24' x 22'   • 24' x 28'   • 24' x 36'
- 24' x 24'   • 24' x 32'

No. 06007C   **$16.95**

Gable 2-Car Gable Entry Gambrel Roof Garages

- Rear Stairs to Loft Workshop
- Front Loft Cargo Door With Pulley Lift
- Available Options for Foundation, Garage & Personnel Doors, Window, & Sidings
- Package contains 5 Different Sizes
- 22' x 26' • 22' x 28' • 24' x 28' • 24' x 30' • 24' x 32'

No. 06006C   **$16.95**

22' & 24' Deep Eave Entry 2 & 3-Car Garages

- Can Be Built Stand-Alone or Attached to House
- Available Options for Roof, Foundation, Garage & Personnel Doors, Window, & Sidings
- Package contains 6 Different Sizes
- 22' x 28'   • 22' x 32'   • 24' x 32'
- 22' x 30'   • 24' x 30'   • 24' x 36'

No. 06002C   **$14.95**

20' & 22' Wide-Gable Entry 2-Car Garages

- Available Options for Roof, Foundation, Garage & Personnel Doors, Window, & Sidings
- Package contains 7 Different Sizes
- 20' x 20'   • 20' x 24'   • 22' x 22'   • 22' x 28'
- 20' x 22'   • 20' x 28'   • 22' x 24'

No. 06008C   **$16.95**

Eave Entry 2 & 3-Car Clerestory Roof Garages

- Interior Side Stairs to Loft Workshop
- Available Options for Engine Lift, Foundation, Garage & Personnel Doors, Window, & Sidings
- Package contains 4 Different Sizes
- 24' x 26'   • 24' x 28'   • 24' x 32'   • 24' x 36'

Garage Order Form

Please send me 1 complete set of the following GARAGE PLAN BLUEPRINTS:

Item no. & description _____	Price
	$ _____
Additional Sets	
(@ $10.00 EACH)	$ _____
Garage Vellum	
(@ $200.00 EACH)	$ _____
Shipping Charges: **UPS Ground (3-7 days within the US)**	$ _____

1-3 plans $7.95
4-6 plans $9.95
7-10 plans $11.95
11 or more plans $17.95

Subtotal:	$ _____
Resident sales tax:	$ _____

(CT residents add 6% sales tax. Not required for other states)

Total Enclosed: $ _____

My Billing Address is:

Name: _____

Address: _____

City: _____

State: _____ Zip: _____

Daytime Phone No. (_____) _____

My Shipping Address is:

Name: _____

Address: _____
     (UPS will not ship to P.O. Boxes)

City: _____

State: _____ Zip: _____

For Faster Service...Charge It!
U.S. & Canada Call
1(800)235-5700

All foreign residents call 1(860)659-5667

MASTERCARD, VISA

Card # ⌷⌷⌷⌷⌷⌷⌷⌷⌷⌷⌷⌷⌷⌷⌷⌷

Signature _____ Exp. ___/___

If paying by credit card, to avoid delays:
billing address must be as it appears on credit card statement

or FAX us at (860) 659-5692

Here's What You Get

- One complete set of drawings for each plan ordered
- Detailed step-by-step instructions with easy-to-follow diagrams on how to build your garage (not available with apartment garages)
- For each garage style, a variety of size and garage door configuration options
- Variety of roof styles and/or pitch options for most garages
- Complete materials list
- Choice between three foundation options: Monolithic Slab, Concrete Stem Wall or Concrete Block Stem Wall
- Full framing plans, elevations and cross-sectionals for each garage size and configuration

Garage Plan Blueprints

All blueprint garage plan orders contain one complete set of drawings with instructions and are priced as listed next to the illustration. **These blueprint garage plans can not be modified.** Additional sets of plans may be obtained for $10.00 each with your original order. UPS shipping is used unless otherwise requested. Please include the proper amount for shipping.

Garage Plan Vellums

By purchasing vellums for one of our garage plans, you receive one vellum set of the same construction drawings found in the blueprints, but printed on vellum paper. Vellums can be erased and are perfect for making design changes. They are also semi-transparent making them easy to duplicate. But most importantly, the purchase of garage plan vellums comes with a broader license that allows you to make changes to the design (ie, create hand drawn or CAD derivative work), to make copies of the plan and to build one garage from the plan.

Send your order to:
(With check or money order payable in U.S. funds only)

The Garlinghouse Company
174 Oakwood Drive
Glastonbury, CT 06033

No C.O.D. orders accepted; U.S. funds only. UPS will not ship to Post Office boxes, FPO boxes, APO boxes, Alaska or Hawaii.

Canadian orders:

UPS Ground (5-10 days within Canada)
1-3 plans $15.95
4-6 plans $17.95
7-10 plans $19.95
11 or more plans $24.95
Prices subject to change without notice.